# ANTISEMITISM

# ANTISEMITISM

*Myth and Hate from Antiquity to the Present*

## MARVIN PERRY AND
## FREDERICK M. SCHWEITZER

First published 2002 by
PALGRAVE MACMILLAN™
175 Fifth Avenue, New York, N.Y. 10010 and
Houndmills, Basingstoke, Hampshire, England RG21 6XS.
Companies and representatives throughout the world.

PALGRAVE MACMILLAN is the global academic imprint of the Palgrave
Macmillan division of St. Martin's Press, LLC and of Palgrave Macmillan Ltd.
Macmillan® is a registered trademark in the United States, United Kingdom
and other countries. Palgrave is a registered trademark in the European Union
and other countries.

ISBN 0-312-16561-7 hardback

**Library of Congress Cataloging-in-Publication Data**
Perry, Marvin.
Antisemitism : myth and hate from antiquity to the present / Marvin Perry
and Frederick M. Schweitzer.
    p.   cm.
  Includes bibliographical references and index.
  ISBN 0-312-16561-7
  1. Anti-Jewish propaganda—History.   2. Antisemitism—History.   3.
Christianity and antisemitism.   4. Blood accusation.   5. Holocaust denial.
I. Schweitzer, Frederick M.   II. Title.

DS145.P415   2002
305.892'4—dc21
    2002022035

A catalogue record for this book is available from the British Library.

Design by Letra Libre, Inc.

First edition: December 2002
10  9  8  7  6  5  4  3  2  1

Printed in the United States of America.

# CONTENTS

# PREFACE

THIS BOOK HAS TAKEN MUCH LONGER TO WRITE than either of us anticipated when we embarked on it more than a few years ago, the principal reason being that there is no end to mythmaking about Jews. While we were in the last stages of revising our work, the events of September 2001 suddenly made the myths discussed in this book newly relevant and their irrational nature more glaring. Throughout the Islamic world the bizarre tale quickly spread that Jews had engineered the bombings of the World Trade Center and the Pentagon. As proof, its proponents, descending deeper into the world of delusion, maintained that four thousand Jews, warned by Israeli agents, did not report to their offices at the World Trade Center on September 11. This belief in an international Jewish conspiracy is only one of several classic myths about Jews that are widely believed in the Muslim world, all imported from the Christian West, copied in the most literal way from the enormous corpus, medieval and modern, of European antisemitism. The widespread propagation and acceptance in the contemporary Arab Islamic world of these discredited myths is another illustration, in a different time and place, of the historic antisemitism that scarred Christian Europe.

The vastness of the topic and space constraints have compelled us to be extremely selective. Thus even in our longest chapter, which discusses that common anti-Jewish delusion, the "rich Jews" and their putative economic wizardry, much material on Jewish economic history had to be deleted or drastically abbreviated. In writing the chapters, the memory of the Holocaust, which was the terrible fulfillment of mythical thinking, was ever present. Our research into the murky area of anti-Jewish myths, particularly those that demonize and dehumanize the Jewish people, reinforces our belief that historians need to explore more fully the power and significance of the nonrational in human affairs. Our experience also confirms the assertion that Jewish history is an integral part of general history, particularly in the generations after emancipation when Jewish genius contributed so much to Western thought, science, the arts, and economic life. Knowledge of Jewish history, literature, and institutions is required to explain this extraordinary burst of creativity. Nor can the rise of ultranationalist movements in the nineteenth century and their fascist heirs in the twentieth century, which saw Jews as an alien race and a threat to the nation, be understood without reference to the roles played by Jews in these nations and the negative images, inherited from the Christian past, that people had about Jews. The authors of this volume hope that an examination of the evolution, nature, and meaning of antisemitic myths will contribute, however modestly, to diminishing the power and appeal of what has been aptly called "the longest hatred."

In the process of writing this book, we have contracted many debts for guidance and assistance. Chapter 1 owes much to two recognized authorities in the field, Manhattan College colleagues Professors Donald Gray and Claudia Setzer. We wish to thank Manhattan colleagues Professor Robert Kramer for his translation of Hitler's 1920 speech, Dr. Eleanor T. Ostrau for her help with *Civiltà Cattolica* material, and Dr. Joseph Castora for his translation of Origen.

Librarians and libraries have greatly facilitated our researches. Most especially, Brother Thomas O'Connor, FSC, Ph.D. and the Hayes-O'Malley Library of Manhattan College; Eleanor Yadin and the Dorot Jewish Division of the New York Public Library; the Walsh Library of Fordham University and its Sidney Rosenblatt Holocaust Collection at Lincoln Center; the Research Department of the Anti-Defamation League in New York City; the Jacob H. Schiff Library of the Jewish Theological Seminary of America; Butler Library of Columbia University; the library of Union Theological Seminary; and the British Library in London.

For reviewing portions of the book, criticism, bibliographical suggestions, and various forms of assistance, we thank Manhattan colleagues Professors Joan Cammarata, Jeff Horn, Brother Patrick Horner, FSC, John Keber, Claire Nolte, Mark Taylor, and Nevart Wanger. On specific topics we have had the benefit of expert guidance from Professor Luc Dequeker of the University of Louvain, Belgium; Dr. Eugene Fisher, director of the Secretariat for Ecumenical and Interreligious Affairs of the National Conference of Catholic Bishops; Rabbi Steven Franklin of Riverdale Temple; Rabbi Leon Klenicki then of the Anti-Defamation League; Dr. John T. Pawlikowski, O.S.M., of the Catholic Theological Union of Chicago; Professor William D. Rubinstein of the University of Wales, Aberystwyth; Dr. John Weiss, Professor Emeritus of Lehman College, CUNY; and Mark Weitzman of the New York Wiesenthal Center. Special thanks to Mark Freiman and Caroline Zayid of McCarthy Tétrault LLP in Toronto. For some critical references, our thanks go to the renowned historian Bernard Lewis of Princeton and to Ms. Esther Webman of the Stephen Roth Institute at Tel Aviv University. For help with scanning, photocopying, proofreading, secretarial assistance, and general keeping track of things, our thanks go to Ms. Charlotte Schachter. Friends like Paul and Gerta Schuyler, and Sister Rose Thering, OP, have helped smooth the way. It is also a pleasure to acknowledge our indebtedness to the numerous scholars and writers whose works we have drawn on, those who are cited in the end-notes as well as the many not mentioned.

We gladly acknowledge the highly professional work performed in our behalf by our editors and the professional staff at Palgrave Macmillan, particularly our old (young) friend Michael J. Flamini, Vice-President and Editorial Director; Amanda Johnson, Assistant Editor; Donna Cherry, Production Manager; our copyeditor Debra Manette, whose scrupulous diligence and searching queries have greatly benefited our book. We would also like to thank AnnJeanette Kern for proofreading and Chris Cecot for indexing our book.

All these and others not named, we acknowledge with gratitude. Our book is certainly the better for their help. To be sure, whatever its faults might be, the responsibility is entirely ours. Our book is the result of a joint and fruitful collaboration in which we have worked closely for several years critiquing, editing, rewriting, and checking each other's work. If readers find our work helpful, it is due to the effectiveness of this collaboration. While preparing this volume we also worked on an anthology of historic and contemporary antisemitic myths, which we expect will be published in the near future.

Marvin Perry wishes to thank Phyllis Perry, his wife of more than forty-six years, for supporting unreservedly his commitment to this project, for providing the warm companionship that facilitated its completion, and for her computer expertise that saved him much time and frustration. He is grateful to Houghton Mifflin Company for permission to use some of his material from previously published works, particularly *An Intellectual History of Modern Europe* (1993) and *Western Civilization: A Brief History* (4th ed., 2001). His thanks also to Peter Lang for permission to use passages from his article in *Jewish-Christian Encounters over the Centuries* (1993), which he coedited with Frederick Schweitzer.

Frederick Schweitzer wants above all to avow his wife Jacqueline's tender loving care, sustained encouragement and great interest in this work, and her dauntlessly buoyant spirit despite the afflictions that the passing years mete out to us. A salute also to Manhattan College, his professional home for over

forty years, which has from the start been generous with summer grants, sab-
baticals, travel funds, and the like, but equally with the intangible support and
encouragement for his initially somewhat eccentric commitment to Jewish
history and Catholic-Jewish relations. It has been a remarkable venture for
him and Manhattan together in breaking free of inherited stereotype and the
bondage of age-old antipathy.

# INTRODUCTION

FROM 1941 TO 1945 THE NAZIS KILLED approximately 6 million Jews—
two-thirds of the Jewish population of Europe. Some 1.5 million of the murdered were children; almost 90 percent of Jewish children in
German-occupied lands perished. Written into the history of Western civilization was an episode that would forever cast doubt on the Enlightenment
conception of human goodness, rationality, and the progress of civilization.
Historians and moralists continue to ponder why Germans felt driven to murder every Jew in their grasp and, in the process, to deliberately humiliate and
abuse their defenseless victims. The Nazi leaders who ordered the Final Solution and many of their minions who sadistically clubbed, whipped, shot,
starved, and worked Jews to death and systematically gassed them did so because they were gripped by a demonological antisemitism that saw Jews everywhere as the source of all evil, dangerous criminals who plotted to rule
Germany and the world. Often their paranoia was expressed in pseudobiologi-
cal terms: The Jews were racial inferiors, subhumans who defiled Aryan blood
and corrupted European culture. Driven by this mythical image of the Jew, the
Nazis regarded themselves as noble idealists engaged in the biological and
spiritual purification of Europe.

Mythmaking was humanity's first way of thinking; it was the earliest attempt to explain the beginnings of the universe and human history, to make
life comprehensible. Originating in sacred rites, ritual dances, and ceremonies,
myths narrated the deeds of gods, who, in some remote past, had brought
forth the world and human beings. Holding that human destiny was determined by the gods, Mesopotamians and Egyptians, the founders of the first
civilizations, interpreted their experiences through myths. These myths gave
Near Eastern peoples a framework with which to pattern their experiences
into a meaningful order, make sense out of nature, justify inherited rules of
conduct, and try to overcome the uncertainty of existence. It was the great
achievement of the ancient Greeks to break with the mythopoeic outlook of

the Near East and to conceive a new way of viewing nature and human society, one that is the basis of the Western scientific and philosophical tradition. Rising above magic, miracles, mystery, authority, and custom, the Greeks discovered the procedures and invented the terminology that permit a rational understanding of the physical world and human experience. The Greeks forged the tools of rational thought, but mythical thinking has never been subdued. Myths, which appeal primarily to the emotions rather than to reason, have always exercised a powerful hold over human thought and behavior. The Nazi era demonstrated how quickly and completely people can surrender their capacity for logical and independent thinking and embrace mythical conceptions of history and race; it revealed that even in an age of sophisticated science, the human mind remains attracted to irrational beliefs and mythical imagery. On several levels September 11 demonstrated that fact anew.

In 1943 the Nazi researcher Helmut Schramm published *Jewish Ritual Murders: An Historical Inquiry*, which collected accounts of Christian children purported to be tortured and murdered by Jews as part of a religious ritual, a bizarre legend that had flourished in the Middle Ages and still endured into the twentieth century and helped make the Holocaust possible. Heinrich Himmler, Reichführer-SS and a principal organizer of the Final Solution, greeted the book enthusiastically. He ordered "a great many copies" to be distributed to fellow SS down to the rank of colonel and to *Einsatz-Kommandos* (company-sized murder-unit), above all those "busy with the Jewish question." To stir up local populations against Jews, he demanded immediate investigations of ritual murder in those areas that still had Jews and the initiation of legal proceedings. "Experts in Rumania, Hungary, and Bulgaria will take up the whole ritual murder question, and we shall sensationalize them in our press." So doing will "facilitate the evacuation [a euphemism for deportation and murder] of Jews from these countries." In cooperation with the German foreign office, Himmler proposed "pure antisemitic clandestine broadcasts" to England and the United States, which should be spiced up with lurid images of and tales about Jews such as those Julius Streicher, editor of the notorious weekly *Der Stürmer*, published. Himmler ordered investigation of English police reports and court records for instances of missing children, "so that we can report in our broadcasts to England that in locale X a child is missing and is probably another case of Jewish ritual murder." At the time Himmler's forces were murdering hundreds of thousands of Jewish children. Himmler was so convinced of the universal resonance of the ritual murder accusation that he was confident "we could give anti-Semitism an incredible virulence worldwide with the help of anti-Semitic propaganda in English and perhaps even in Russian by giving publicity to ritual murders."[1]

This canard of ritual murder, which true-believer Himmler circulated among his execution squads to strengthen morale, was one of several myths inherited from the Christian past that the Nazis employed to rouse hatred and mobilize public opinion against Jews. Over the centuries the cumulative effect of these myths was the dehumanization and demonization of the Jew. Thus in the Middle Ages Jews were seen as "children of the Devil," "servants of Satan" conspiring to destroy Christian society; in Nazi mythology, a product of a secular world, the servants of Satan were transmuted into worldwide racial degenerates plotting to destroy Germany and rule the planet.

This book treats several of the myths that have made antisemitism so lethal in various periods from the Middle Ages to World War II: the Jews as deicides; the Jews as ritual murderers; the Jews as agents of Satan and international conspirators; and the Jews as greedy, materialistic, conniving Shylocks and unscrupulous financial manipulators. In addition to these historic myths, we also treat the new, maliciously manufactured myth of Holocaust denial, another groundless belief that is used to stir up Jew-hatred. Finally, we examine the antisemitism of the Nation of Islam, which has recycled and adapted antique antisemitic myths for their own ends and also manufactured a new one— the Jews as the principal force behind the slave trade.

Antisemitism has very little to do with the actual behavior of Jews or the strictures of their highly ethical religion—indeed, antisemites usually are totally ignorant of the rich tradition of rabbinical writings that discuss, often wisely and insightfully, biblical themes and Jewish laws—but is rooted in delusionary perceptions that are accepted as authoritative and passed on and embellished from generation to generation. As such, antisemitism affords a striking example of the perennial appeal, power, and danger of mythical thinking—of elevating to the level of objective truth beliefs that have little or no basis in fact but provide all-encompassing, emotionally satisfying explanations of life and history. In the period from the late nineteenth century through World War II, the widespread belief in the myth of the world Jewish conspiracy demonstrates that even educated, intelligent people can be moved and unified by baseless myths that provide simple and gratifying explanations and resolutions for the complexities of the modern world. Democratic society is continually threatened by such an abandonment of reason and regression to mythical modes of thought and behavior.

It is a painful but inescapable truth that antisemitism, which seethes with hate, was spawned and nourished by Christianity, which reveres a Jewish

prophet who preached love and compassion. The New Testament and the
writings of the Church Fathers often refer to Jews and Judaism contemptu-
ously. Jews were depicted as an accursed people, children of the Devil collectively condemned by God to suffer for rejecting and killing Christ. This
degrading image of the Jew was propagated over the centuries in numerous
books, sermons, works of art, and folklore, and vestiges endure into the
twenty-first century. Two thousand years of Christian anti-Judaism, which
taught that Judaism was without value and that Jews were wicked, hardened
Christians' hearts against Jews. Why should Christians feel compassion for a
people cursed by God and fated to be victims for their unpardonable sin of rejecting Jesus? This mind-set, deeply embedded in the Christian outlook, helps
to explain why so many people were receptive to anti-Jewish propaganda, were
willing to participate in genocide, or were indifferent to Jewish suffering.

Typical of this uninterrupted flow of contempt for Jews is the Passion play
performed by the villagers of Oberammergau in Bavaria roughly every ten
years since 1634. In the Middle Ages and early modern times, after the performance of a Passion play, which was staged in many towns and villages, spec-
tators, inflamed by the depiction of a frenzied Jewish mob taunting Jesus,
often poured into the Jewish ghetto to kill, maim, and vandalize. For centuries
Holy Week, when Passion plays were performed, was a time of fear for Jews.
Since the Vatican's promulgation of *Nostra Aetate* (In Our Time) in 1965, the
Oberammergau text has been gradually revised to moderate the message traditionally conveyed to the audience: The treacherous and bloodthirsty Jewish
deicides are collectively and eternally guilty for the crucifixion. In 1860 a Scot-
tish writer, after seeing the play, thoughtfully commented on the hatred this
message fomented:

> With strange emotions you gazed upon the executioners as upon the wild
> beasts when they tore his mantle into shreds, and cast lots for his vesture; and
> the Jewish race appeared hateful in your eyes, as you watched them gathering
> around the cross, looking upon the man they had crucified and railing at him,
> and taunting him with his powerlessness and his pain. Then for the first time
> you seemed to understand the significance of those ungovernable explosions
> that in the history of the middle ages one reads of, when sudden outbursts of
> hatred against the Hebrew race have taken place, and have been followed by
> cruelties and barbarities unrivalled in history. Just such a feeling seemed ex-
> cited in this Oberammergau audience by this representation.[2]

Adolf Hitler, who saw a performance in 1934, told intimates during the
war that "to save future generations. . . . it is vital that the Passion Play be con-

tinued at Oberammergau; for never has the menace of Jewry been so convincingly portrayed as in this presentation of what happened in the times of the Romans."[3] And in the year 2000 a German author, after describing the Passion play as "the story of the man whose message set worlds in motion for two thousand years," added reflectively and solemnly: "But this is also the story of a man whose followers, the Christians, brought unbelievable suffering into the world. Their religious zeal recoiled from no act of violence and left a bloody trail through the centuries. Millions of Jews—the people who shared the faith of Jesus—died in the twentieth century. They had to die because the church, and yes, the Passion Play for centuries sowed the seeds of anti-Semitism, of Jew-hating. The Nazis harvested a well-fertilized field."[4]

To be sure, there is a crucial difference between Christian anti-Judaism, whose epicenter is the myth of deicide, and modern antisemitism, which is powered by nationalist and racist myths that castigate Jews as an alien and dangerous race threatening the survival of the nation.* During the nineteenth century, under the influence of the liberal ideas of the Enlightenment and the French Revolution, Jews in most European lands gained emancipation; that is, they could leave the ghettos, to which they had been legally confined, engage in trades and professions from which they had been barred, and vote and hold office like other citizens. The contributions of newly emancipated Jews to European intellectual, cultural, and commercial life was astonishing. But their very achievements often aroused resentment, and no matter how much Jews tried to assimilate, many of their countrymen, particularly those politically on the Right, continued to view Jews, even baptized ones who considered themselves Christians, as hateful people. And Christian clergy, as they had done for centuries, crudely denigrated and demeaned Jews to their parishioners in venomous language and images that perpetuated an ancient hatred. Walter Zwi Bacharach, who studied nineteenth-century German Catholic sermons, informs us:

> One need only examine a list of the terms and epithets used by the preachers to understand how their audiences perceived the Jews: murderers, criminals,

---

* The distinction between anti-Judaism and antisemitism is of fundamental importance to historical understanding, even though the boundary dividing them is vague and fluctuating. One must avoid any kind of apologetic in the use of the term anti-Judaism that would separate the two phenomena as unconnected. Historically, one is the seedbed of the other or, as Gavin Ian Langmuir argues in a seminal essay, it is necessary to approach "Anti-Judaism as the Necessary Preparation for Anti-Semitism," *Viator: Medieval and Renaissance Studies* 2 (1971): 385–89.

evil ones, sinners, enraged, inhuman, despicable, corrupt, desecrators, impudent, cunning serpents, poisonous, enemies of God. These words were not
directed at individual Jews, but at the entire Jewish people: "They, once the
preferred among all nations, have now become garbage, and in this miserable
conditions they live to this very day." "The sworn enemy of Christianity is the
*entire Jewish people* and the evidence of their rejection by God may be found in
the Scriptures."[5]

In the nineteenth century, the Catholic Church opposed the emancipation
of the Jews, insisting that they remain in ghettos, be prevented from interacting
with Christians, and be denied equal rights. In its view, which dated back to St.
Augustine in the fifth century, Jews should remain degraded until they renounced their anachronistic religion and embraced the saving truth of Christianity. The Jews immured since 1555 in the ghetto of Rome, which was ruled
by the popes until the completion—under liberal, anticlerical auspices—of Italian unification in 1870, suffered oppression, humiliation—including, as in the
Middle Ages, having to wear a yellow star of David on their clothing—and
poverty, consequences of long-standing papal policy. After 1870 and until the
Second Vatican Council of the 1960s, papal pronouncements regarding Jews
normally assumed that their proper status was ghetto subjugation and restrictions. In the 1840s Pope Pius IX had ended forced attendance at conversionist
sermons in the Papal States. But forced conversions—of which Edgardo Mortara* was a terrible example—ended only after 1870, when Italian unification
was completed and papal political power ended. To the eve of World War I,
Vatican-controlled publications crudely supported the accusation that Jews ritually murdered Christians for their blood; this accusation itself represented a
retreat from the condemnation of the ritual murder charge by several earlier
popes. Moreover, in their struggle against the forces of modernity—secularism,
liberalism, and socialism—which they identified with Jews, popes fostered antisemitic movements in Europe; from behind the scenes Pope Leo XIII
(1878–1903) supported the virulently antisemitic Catholic Social Party in Austria and smiled on its leader, Karl Lueger, as he smiled on the French antisemitic volcano Édouard Drumont, the publicist who utilized largely Catholic
sources and took pains to be sure that his work was free of theological errors.

---

* Edgardo Mortara was a Jewish child secretly baptized by a maid when he was ill and
kidnapped in 1858 by the papal guard from his parents in Bologna. The boy was taken
to a monastery and educated as a ward of Pius IX, then ordained a priest; all interces-
sions and protests by his family, Jewish organizations, and governments backed by
strong public opinion were in vain.

Moreover, Catholic writers like the journalist writing in the Vatican daily *L'Osservatore Romano* in 1892 gloried in antisemitism. He explained that there was true and good antisemitism, which is "nothing other than Christianity, completed and perfected in Catholicism." In contrast stood bad antisemitism, which, secular and political, is actually anti-Christian and nothing but a contrivance of the Jews to discredit good antisemitism. By such twists to blame the victim, the pogroms—widespread attacks on Jews that were organized, riotous, murderous, and sanctioned by the state—raging in Russia since 1880 were, according to the writer, designed to rouse public opinion in favor of the Jews, who were, in fact, "the true persecutors."[6]

It is true, of course, that Nazi racism, which reviled and condemned Jews because of their genes, was incompatible with Christianity, which welcomes all people who embrace Jesus, regardless of race or ethnic background. Traditional Christian anti-Judaism saw Jews as religiously, not racially, inferior. Nevertheless, long-standing negative Christian attitudes toward Jews, particularly when embedded in denigrating myths, prepared people, including many clergy, to believe and endorse the pagan Nazi mythology and to remain apathetic to Jewish suffering. The Nazis' definition of the Jew as an alien Other embodying pure evil predated Nazism; it was a core and broadly held view of Christianity for centuries. James Carroll, a Catholic writer and former priest, underscores this symbiotic relationship between Christian and Nazi antisemitism:

> Auschwitz is the climax of the story that begins at Golgotha [and] when seen in the links of causality, reveals that the hatred of Jews has been . . . a central action of Christian history, reaching to the core of Christian character. . . . Because the hatred of Jews had been made holy, it became lethal. . . . However modern Nazism was, it planted its roots in the soil of age-old Church attitudes and a nearly unbroken chain of Church-sponsored acts of Jew hatred. However pagan Nazism was, it drew its sustenance from groundwater poisoned by the Church's most solemnly held ideology—its *theology*.[7]

And David I. Kertzer, who examined Catholic publications from the early nineteenth to the mid-twentieth century, including some closely identified with the popes and upper echelons of the church hierarchy, assesses the close link between modern antisemitism and the church:

> As modern anti-Semitic movements took shape at the end of the nineteenth century, the Church was a major player in them, constantly warning people of the rising "Jewish peril." What, after all, were the major tenets of this modern anti-Semitic movement if not such warnings as these: Jews are trying to take

over the world; Jews have already spread their voracious tentacles around the nerve centers of Austria, Germany, France, Hungary, Poland, and Italy; Jews are rapacious and merciless, seeking at all costs to get their hands on all the world's gold, having no concern for the number of Christians they ruin in the process; Jews are unpatriotic, a foreign body ever threatening the well-being of the people among whom they live; special laws are needed to protect society, restricting the Jews' rights and isolating them. Every single one of these elements of modern anti-Semitism was not only embraced by the Church but also actively promulgated by official and unofficial Church organs.[8]

It is thus no exaggeration to say with the British historian Bernard Wasserstein that, once the Nazi regime was destroyed, "The most important antisemitic institution in Europe in 1945, one in which anti-Jewish doctrine was deeply embedded in profound historical foundations, was the Roman Catholic Church."[9] This rendition of the papal posture with regard to the Jews and Judaism suggests that the promulgation of *Nostra Aetate* in 1965 represents an extraordinary historical about-face.

For half a century after World War II, antisemitism was disreputable in many circles. In Western lands, academics, clergy, politicians, high government officials, business leaders, and other members of the elite, who had routinely voiced antisemitic sentiments prior to the Nazi era, no longer considered public expressions of Jew-hatred legitimate. Painfully aware of the threat antisemitism poses to democratic values, they were repulsed by classic antisemitic myths that the radical Right sought to perpetuate. They often spoke out forcefully against hate mongering and showed disdain for the extremists who maligned Jews and desecrated Jewish cemeteries and synagogues. Equally important, in recent decades, with the horror of the Holocaust searing Christian consciences, various churches have publicly condemned antisemitism as anti-Christian and eliminated denigrating references to Jews from their liturgies and religious education. Endorsing modern biblical scholarship, they have stressed Jesus' Jewishness and the spiritual heritage that Christians share with Jews—the Hebrew Bible, monotheism, and the prophetic teachings—the spiritual vitality of Judaism in the time of Jesus and after, and the decisive role of the Romans in Jesus' execution. Christian and Jewish groups work together on many levels to promote tolerance and interfaith understanding.*

---

* These are all hopeful signs, but antisemitism will not die easily. What labors under a strong taboo in public discourse may come forth in private conversation. Thus Billy Graham, the prominent evangelical Baptist minister who has been honored on numerous occasions by Jewish organizations for his defense of Jews and Judaism and the

In recent years, however, the exacerbation of the Arab-Israeli conflict has generated a resurgence of antisemitism in Europe, even among polite circles. The Israeli military campaign in the spring of 2002 in the West Bank in response to repeated suicide bombings that killed and mutilated hundreds of Israeli citizens resulted in a rash of antisemitic incidents in Europe. In several countries—Ukraine, Greece, Holland, Belgium, Germany, Britain, and France—cemeteries were vandalized, Holocaust memorials defaced, synagogues torched, buses transporting Jewish children stoned, and Jews beaten. Some 360 crimes against Jews and Jewish institutions were reported in France, where the violence was most extreme. It is likely that Muslim extremists were responsible for this violence, but antisemitic attitudes were not limited to people of Middle Eastern descent. In demonstrations held in many European cities in support of the Palestinians, Israelis were equated with Nazis, Prime Minister Ariel Sharon with Hitler, and the Israeli flag was burned. At times crowds shouted: "Death to the Jews!" In past decades the most virulent expressions of antisemitism were confined almost exclusively to the fringe groups of the extreme Right that idolized Hitler and revered the Nazi past. Now representatives of the Left—the Greens, trade unionists, socialists, and student organizations—actively participated in the demonstrations and denounced Israel in venomous language.

What is most distressing is the way the press and intellectuals, who previously glossed over the Israeli casualties of suicide bombers, were quick to condemn Israel, often sinking into the ordure of antisemitism. Thus a cartoon in the Italian newspaper *La Stampa* depicted a baby Jesus in the manger looking at an Israeli tank and saying, "Don't tell me they want to kill me again." The Vatican daily *L'Osservatore Romano* said that Israel was engaging in "aggression that turns into extermination." Accepting as true the grotesque Palestinian fabrication that a massacre had taken place at Jenin, the press in several countries accused the Israeli army of engaging in genocide. A number of prominent intellectuals sympathetic to the Palestinian cause revealed their true feelings about Jews: Several British authors rejected Israel's right to exist and José Saramago, a Nobel laureate in literature, felt it appropriate to "compare what is happening in the Palestinian territories with Auschwitz." Increasingly, as

---

religious advisor to several presidents, privately uttered a series of ugly stereotypes about Jews in White House discussions with President Nixon in 1972. All allegations and suspicions were dismissed until the Nixon tapes were made public in 2002. As reported in the *New York Times*, March 17, 2002, 29, Graham said Jews were responsible for "pornography," had a ruinous "stranglehold" on the United States, and that he hoped to "stand up" and "be able to do something" to correct things.

several commentators have observed, antisemitism is once more becoming intellectually and socially acceptable in Europe.[10]

In Muslim lands antisemitism is pervasive and vicious, routinely employing Christian and Nazi myths, which most westerners now regard as repulsive. It needs to be remembered that the Arabs imported German antisemitism in the 1930s and during World War II, a development that was extended when numerous Nazi war criminals and officials found refuge after 1945 in Arab states. Numbers of them were employed in information and propaganda offices and busily disseminated Nazi antisemitic materials, including the *Protocols of the Learned Elders of Zion,* a work forged by antisemites at the beginning of the twentieth century that purports to show that Jews conspire to dominate the globe. One predictable strand of Arab Islamic antisemitism is Holocaust denial, which "started in Arab writings much earlier than in Europe": "Did 6 million Jews die?" asked the Palestinian Authority's appointee, Sheik Ikrimeh Sabri, the mufti (a lay adviser on Muslim religious law) of Jerusalem; he answered in the accents of the neo-Nazi Holocaust denier Ernst Zündel: "Let's desist from this fairy tale exploited by Israel to buy international backing and solidarity."[11] Illogically, on the other hand, the same deniers can wax lyrical in praise of Hitler, lamenting that he did "not finish the job" and left the historic task to the Arabs.

The fountainhead of contemporary Jew-hatred in the Islamic world appears to be the Egyptian Sayyid Qutb (1906–1966), who wrote, while in jail in the 1950s, a seminal essay, "Our Struggle with the Jews." Those who murdered Egyptian president Anwar el-Sadat and those who brought the Ayatollah Khomeini to power in Iran are said to have been his disciples. According to Qutb, "The Jews have confronted Islam with enmity from the moment that the Islamic state was established in Medina [by Muhammad]," that in a "war of fourteen centuries" Islam suffered continuous "trials" and is now prey to "tribulations" and "machinations" by Jews as internal and external enemies. Jews seek the destruction of Islam, Qutb argues, both physically and "in creed." Thus Qutb makes Jews responsible for the assassination of the third caliph in 656 and the consequent division and permanent weakening of Islam. Thus, too, he explains the occupation of Egypt by the British from 1882 and the collapse of the Ottoman Empire in 1918. Moreover, in Qutb's view, Jews are the creators of modernity—equated with Karl Marx, Sigmund Freud, and other "Jews"—that is destroying Islam. Jewish/Zionist conspirators, by nature evil and malevolent, enlist "lackeys"—Western-educated and Westernizing Muslims, or "Jewish-manufactured Muslims"—who subvert Islam as well as the Muslims' fighting spirit. Muslims should always remember the teaching of the Koran that "the worst enemies of the Muslims are the Jews" and that "God has cursed them." Over the centuries God has sent "his servants" to punish the Jews, and thus he "brought Hitler to rule over them." Their plot to launch "a Crusader-Zionist war" will, likewise, cause Allah to punish them again by destroying Israel. The seeming continuity of contemporary Islamist conceptions of Jews with Muhammad's struggle against the Jews of Medina and with passages in the Koran, says Ronald Nettler, the editor and translator of Qutb's essay, renders those negative views "Islamically persuasive" in the Middle East and beyond, since they appear to be based on history and tradition.[12]

In the fall of 2001 a conference on racism sponsored by the United Nations in Durban, South Africa, was turned by Arab states into an antisemitic barrage. Among many other extreme antisemitic works, the *Protocols* was distributed wholesale at the conference, and anyone who raised objections on the grounds that the material was forged or fraudulent was shouted down. Elie Wiesel, the survivor of Auschwitz and Nobel peace laureate who was invited to participate in the conference, withdrew on the grounds that it had been turned into a "circus of calumny . . . a meeting of hatred characterized by wickedness" that would

> go down in history as a moral catastrophe. . . . The fact that militant Palestinians hate Jews—that is known already. One need only hear the various Islamic leaders and read the books printed by the Palestinian Authority: They preach hatred and violence, not against Zionists but against Jews. Their slogan, naked and brutal and identical everywhere, was keenly felt and even heard in Durban: "Kill the Jews." What is painful is not that the Palestinians and the Arabs voiced their hatred, but the fact that so few delegates had the courage to combat them [or walk out, as the U.S. delegation did]. It is as if in a strange and frightening moment of collective catharsis, everyone removed their masks and revealed their true faces.[13]

The events of September 11, 2001, showed how far antisemitic myths have penetrated the Arab Islamic world. In their response to Osama bin Laden's and Al-Qaeda's crimes, radical Islamists have dredged up long-discredited Christian and European antisemitic myths. In particular, they make wide use of the *Protocols*. And cartoons reincarnate the bloodcurdling originals of Nazi propaganda, including those that appeared in Streicher's *Der Stürmer*. An article of October 14 in *The Jihad Times*, entitled "Zionists could be behind Attack on World Trade Center and Pentagon," demonstrates, "on the basis of strong evidence," how the whole cycle of events follows from the *Protocols*. Thus, this "300-member apex Zionist body" of Elders launched the attacks in retaliation for the condemnation at the UN Conference in Durban of Israel's "religio-ethnic cleansing policy" against the Palestinians. Within two days of that conference the Elders of Zion ordered the Zionist-controlled Federal Bureau of Investigation and Israeli secret service to carry out the attacks. Meeting secretly in Europe, the organization of the Elders, "which has controlled world politics for long," sought to distract attention from the anti-Israel resolutions at Durban and launch massive propaganda attacks scapegoating Muslims and Islam. According to undisclosed "reliable sources," the Elders took several steps that reveal their secret hand: They prevented the prime minister of Israel from going on a scheduled visit to New York a day before the attacks, they issued a "secret directive" to four thousand Jews not to report for work on September 11 so that "not a single Israeli or American Jew working in the World Trade Center was reported killed or missing," and they directed the "Zionist-controlled" media so that "in no time Muslims were portrayed as the real culprits." September 11, "it is learnt," is another step by the Elders of Zion in their quest for world dominance: By igniting a great crusading war between Muslims and Christians, "a big chunk of world population were doomed to perish, giving way to the Jews, a tiny minority in the world, to emerge as a major power on the world scene." Also true to the *Protocols'* template, the Elders of Zion, their agents, proxies, and sympathizers, operate secretly in the shadows, have no known headquarters but, with tentacles encircling the globe, are constantly but untraceably in communication with each other although only the three hundred are known to each other, and so on.[14] In the same vein, Sheik Muhammad al-Gameia of Al-Azhar University in Cairo and, until he fled back to Egypt after September 11, *imam* (religious leader) of the Islamic Cultural Center of New York, argued that "only the Jews" could contrive and concert so far-flung and intricate a terrorist conspiracy.[15]

All the elements of the anti-Jewish myths dealt with in this book reappear in Muslim sources, some of them endorsed by mainstream journalists, academics, clerics, and even heads of state. The president of Syria, Bashar al-Assad, in May 2001 greeted Pope John Paul II at the airport in Damascus, using the historic occasion not to declare his own hopes for mutual understanding among the world's great faiths but to mount a vicious attack on the Jews. They have "tried," he inveighed in the presence of the pope, "to kill the principles of all religions with the same mentality with which they betrayed Jesus Christ," and in "the same way they tried to betray and kill the prophet

Muhammad."*[16] *Al-Ahram,* Egypt's leading government-sponsored daily, related in great detail how Jews use the blood of gentiles to make matzoh for
Passover. Not to be outdone, another columnist informed readers that, to understand the true intentions of the Jews, one must consult the *Protocols,* in
which the leaders of the international Jewish conspiracy acknowledge openly
their "limitless ambitions, inexhaustible greed, merciless vengeance, and hatred beyond imagination. . . . Cunning, [the "Elders" allegedly declare] is our
approach, mystery is our way." Still another article in *Al-Ahram* was dedicated
to the subject of Jewish control of the world, a composite of the work of four
investigative reporters. A great many Muslim newspapers took up the story
that Jews piloted the planes into the World Trade Center, reporting this delusional tale as fact.[17]

Islam has not been subject to anything comparable to the transformative
influence on the Western world of the Renaissance, Reformation, Scientific
Revolution, the Enlightenment, and the democratic revolutions that spread
from France and the United States at the end of the eighteenth century. Unlike the West, Islam has not embraced pluralism and toleration. Attempts at
democracy have largely failed; tyranny, authoritarianism, and theocracy characterize the political regimes in the Islamic world. The following excerpt from
"Islam and the 'Interfaith' Movement," an anonymous editorial on the website
sponsored by the Ministry of Awqaf and Islamic Affairs of the government of
Qatar, tells us much about Islamic fear of and hostility to modern democratic
ideas of equality and tolerance:

> One of the most dangerous ideological threats to Islam is the growing "Mus-
> lim-Christian-Jew" trialogue, or the "Interfaith" worship movement. . . .
> [T]he greatest danger of this movement is that it is part of a conscious strat-
> egy to erode the superiority of Islam as a religion, placing its followers on the
> same level as the Jews and Christians; leading the Muslims to accept the un-
> Islamic political concepts of equality, liberty, fraternity and secularism.
> Hence, the Muslim is led to support the ideological basis for the establish-
> ment of the secular nation-state. . . .
>
> We, as Muslims, should see an instructive lesson in the Jewish-Christian
> dialogue, which has been initiated by the Jews. . . . This movement has served
> only the interest of the Jews. First of all, they have gotten the Vatican to drop
> the Catholic belief that the Jews were the Christ's killers!

---

\* Unfortunately, the pope, who on previous occasions had condemned antisemitism,
did not, then or later, respond to this crude antisemitic jibe uttered in his presence.

Furthermore, they have been able to win the Christian world over to support the cause of Zionism, and to implicitly or explicitly recognize the creation of the Zionist state of Israel. These gains were made by the Jews because they have been able to determine the methodology and goals of this dialogue.[18]

No development comparable to the Second Vatican Council in the Roman Catholic Church or the deliberate efforts to break with an antisemitic past shown by some Protestant denominations, such as the Evangelical Lutheran Church in America, is in the offing in the Islamic world. A principal source of anti-Jewish prejudice and hatred in the Middle East is the Arab Christians, few of whom have renounced—as required by the Second Vatican Council and parallel Protestant guidelines—the inherited teaching of contempt in favor of the new teaching of respect. Virtually all Middle Eastern liberal, critical, independent scholars and thinkers have been either assassinated, jailed, or exiled, or have fled to Europe or North America, where they flourish quite outside the traditional parameters of Islam.[19]

Rejecting modern secular and liberal values, Islamists, the fundamentalists' own term for themselves, have sought to restore an idealized medieval past in which the teachings—purged of all accretions and foreign influences—of a pure and undefiled Islam will again hold sway, turning a face of stone to modernity. Fortified by a narrow fundamentalist outlook and rejecting non-Muslims as "infidels," Islamists are hostile to pluralist democracy and secularism; they have also demonstrated a fanatical mentality that sanctifies terrorism and demonizes the Jews. Islamism, according to the liberal Muslim scholar Khalid Durán, is a late-twentieth-century form of totalitarianism that follows in the wake of communism and fascism, and has been influenced by them in its methods of seeking domination; it is "a quest for power, an attempt to conquer the state."[20] In a region afflicted by poverty and ineffective tyrannical regimes, antisemitism provides governments and elites with a useful safety valve, as Bernard Lewis astutely observes: "[R]esentment of Israel is the only grievance that can be freely and safely expressed in those Muslim countries where the media are either wholly owned or strictly overseen by the government. Indeed, Israel serves as a useful stand-in for complaints about economic privation and political repression under which most Muslim people live, and as a way of deflecting the resulting anger."[21]

The perception of the Jews in the Islamic world is reminiscent of the days of Hitler and the Third Reich. Regrettably, leaders of European states, whose soil is drenched with innocent Jewish blood and whose culture is pervaded by

Judaeophobia, and the various churches, whose clergy for centuries had demonized the Jew, have remained silent. "Western elites," observes the British journalist Andrew Sullivan, "have voiced no protests against the Hitler-like demonization of the Jew that is rampant in the Middle East."*[22] It would be a worthy act of remembrance of the Jewish victims of the Holocaust and, in some instances, of repentance, if the European Union and the churches issued official statements to be read on al-Jazeera, the Arab news channel, simply declaring that Jews do not and never have used Muslim or Christian blood for Passover matzohs or Purim pastries; that Muslim Arabs, not Jews, were responsible for the terrorist attacks of September 11; that the *Protocols of the Elders of Zion* is a notorious forgery; that the Holocaust was a cosmic tragedy not a Jewish hoax; and that the propagation of these nefarious antisemitic myths, regardless of the feelings aroused by the Arab-Israeli conflict, is both morally abhorrent and a grotesque distortion of history.

Among other things, the events of September 11 have demonstrated that an irrational and lethal antisemitism is quite alive. The demonization of the Jews, which made the Holocaust possible, shapes the perception of millions of people in Islamic lands. We might all feel like the writer Jonathan Rosen in his response to Muslim antisemitism accentuated by September 11: "I felt kidnapped by history. The past had come calling."[23] This appropriation of European antisemitism by militant Muslims also poses a threat for Christians—that is, Americans and Europeans—the peoples purportedly linked with Jews in conspiratorial alliance and dedicated to Islam's destruction. Thus Jews/Zionists, who "control everything," are in league with the United States/Europe/"the West," according to Sheik Muhammad al-Gameia, and disseminate "corruption, heresy, homosexuality, alcoholism, and drugs" as well as pornography[24]; hence, as Osama bin Laden asserted in his recruiting videos, he is engaged in "the religious-cultural-historical struggle of Islam with the Judeo-Crusader conspiratorial alliance, which aims at defeating

---

* But there are hopeful signs. Catholic-Jewish relations have progressed sufficiently for the United States Conference of Catholic Bishops to state in 2001 that Christians have a special responsibility to denounce the conspiracy theories emanating from the Middle East, because they originated in antisemitic conceptions introduced by Christians. Its spokesman Eugene Fisher stated: "The *Protocols of the Elders of Zion* is a classic Christian antisemitic text, and it is disconcerting to see Muslims getting sucked into it. Since it is ours in origin we feel some responsibility to alert the Muslim community to its spurious nature." It is not known how this responsibility has been met. See Michael Paulson, "[American]Catholics See a Duty to Nip Attack Theories," *Boston Globe*, Oct. 27, 2001, B1.

Islam and conquering its sacred lands."[25] While Islamic spokesmen now propagate the myth of a world Jewish conspiracy, as invented by European antisemites, ironically it is the Muslim world that actually has spawned an international conspiracy, Al-Qaeda, a conspiracy that does indeed aspire to world domination. Nazi Germany and to some extent Stalinist Russia demonstrated the close link between demonological antisemitism and totalitarianism. The vicious Jew-hatred emanating openly and without challenge from within the Muslim world may portend a warning not only for Jews but also for Western civilization. It may be, as Professor Robert Wistrich argued in a lecture at Manhattan College on September 30, 2002, on "Muslim Antisemitism: A Clear and Present Danger," that the conflict inaugurated by the attack on the World Trade Center is "a war of civilizations, that Islamism is a fundamentally totalitarian mode of thought, and that it is the third great challenge in the last seventy years to Western democracy, the first being German Nazism, the second Soviet communism, and now Islamism, which in many ways is a form of fascism no less than the previous two."

## CHAPTER 1

# THE TRIAL AND DEATH OF JESUS:

## THE MYTH OF "CHRIST KILLERS" AND THE "CRIMINAL PEOPLE"

*Behold we journey a long way to seek the idolatrous shrine and to take vengeance upon the Muslims. But here are the Jews dwelling among us, whose ancestors killed him and crucified him groundlessly. Let us take vengeance first upon them. Let us wipe them out as a nation; Israel's name will be mentioned no more.*

—A chronicler of the first crusade, 1095–1099[1]

*It is true, as the laws declare, that in consequence of their sin [of rejecting and crucifying Jesus] the Jews were destined to perpetual servitude, so that sovereigns of states may treat Jewish goods as their own property.*

—St. Thomas Aquinas, 1274[2]

*As for the Jews, I am just carrying on with the same policy which the Catholic Church had adopted for 1500 years.*

—Chancellor Hitler to Bishop Berning, April 1933[3]

*It is not just a matter of deportation. You will not die there of hunger and disease. They will slaughter all of you there, old and young alike, women and children, at once—it is the punishment that you deserve for the death of our Lord and Redeemer, Jesus Christ—you have only one solution. Come over to our [Catholic] religion, and I will work to annul the decree.*

—Bishop Kmetko's reply to Rabbi Ungar, who asked him to intervene
with the head of state, Monsignor Tiso, to prevent the deportation
of Jews from Slovakia in 1943[4]

CHRISTIANITY'S UNDERSTANDING OF ITS ORIGINS centers on the New
Testament, particularly the poetic rendering in the gospels of the arrest, trial,
and crucifixion of Jesus, which is traditionally known as the Passion.[5] In the
gospels' rendition and as interpreted for centuries, the Jews are perceived as
"the Christ killers," a people condemned forever to suffer exile and degradation. This archcrime of "deicide," of murdering God, turned the Jews into the
embodiment of evil, a "criminal people" cursed by God and doomed to wander and suffer tribulation to the end of time. No other religious tradition has
condemned a people as the murderers of its god, a unique accusation that has
resulted in a unique history of hatred, fear, and persecution. When it came to
Jews, the central doctrine of Christianity, that Jesus was providentially sent
into the world to atone by his death for mankind's sins, was obscured.

Ultimately, all antisemitic accusations and justifications for persecution
and discrimination spring from that primal act of deicide. In the words of the
Catholic biblical exegete J. D. Crossan, "the passion-resurrection stories [are]
the matrix for Christian anti-Judaism and eventually for European anti-Semitism," that "without that Christian anti-Judaism, lethal and genocidal European anti-Semitism would have been either impossible or at least not widely
successful."[6] In the late second century, Bishop Melito of Sardis had already
converted the crucifixion into the archstereotype of the criminal Jews when he
proclaimed, "God has been murdered; the king of Israel has been slain by an
Israelite hand," preaching that provoked massive attacks on Jews. This
episode, comments the historian Robert M. Grant, shows what happens to
theology when it is divorced from history.[7] Almost every Christian writer in
the first five centuries of the church wrote an anti-Judaeos treatise or made
anti-Judaism a principal theme of other writings. Inferences drawn from the
Passion story by Christian theologians and apologists were developed into a
composite symbol of the Jew, one that combined the image of the Wandering
or Eternal Jew with that of the agent of Satan and the Antichrist. It is hard to
imagine a more destructive amalgam than this Christian myth of the Jew, rich
in its hydra capacity to be eternally transformed, secularized, adapted to
changing times and circumstances down to the present day, yet all the while
retaining its compelling religious appeal.

## "JESUS RESEARCH"

New Testament scholarship has gone far to emancipate itself from theological
suppositions; in the process it has established that no such sequence of events
regarding the trial and execution of Jesus as the gospels recount could have oc-

curred. The inquiry into the life and death of Jesus is a most difficult historical task because the early Christians were unconcerned with the biography of the human—as opposed to the divine—Jesus. The first Christian communities looked to the future and the second coming (parousia) of Jesus as the risen Christ, and they remembered of the historical Jesus little more than sayings, miracles, and the Passion story. It is impossible to write a biography of Jesus; the only thing not subject to doubt is that there was a historical Jesus.[8] The earliest sources, the gospels, date from a generation and more after Jesus' death (ca. 28–33 C.E.); Mark, the earliest, dates from around 70; Luke and Matthew from about 80–90; John from about 110–120, although his gospel may be as early as 85 or as late as 150. Moreover, by the second century there were many—estimates run from twenty to as high as eighty—"gospels" in existence, each of which reflected the beliefs and attitudes of the community for which it was written. Bishop Papias reported in about 140 a meeting of church authorities that was summoned to decide which gospels were accurate and to be followed. He says that the churchmen placed all the versions at the foot of the altar and prayed that the true ones would be lifted up so as to be placed on the altar. The bishop vouches that matters transpired as they hoped, although he fails to state which ones came out on top. The early church greatly edited and changed the sources: "[I]t deleted, added, altered and occasionally created Jesus-material," a process that went on with much contention until around 380 when the New Testament canon was widely accepted, although the end result is that "we have only transcripts of transcripts of transcripts."[9] One of the principal controversies and source of accusation in those centuries was the dejudaizing of these documents, the attempt to remove Jewish elements from Christian teaching and practice, to expunge any ritual or custom that betrayed any sort of Jewish affiliation or behavior, cutting Christianity off from its roots in Hebrew scripture. The most extreme example of this was Papias' contemporary Marcion (died ca. 160). His total rejection of the Old Testament and condemnation of the God of Israel as evil, as a mere "Demiurge" of nature, was condemned as heretical.[10] Dejudaization, nevertheless, persisted into the twentieth century as a recurring theme of Christian exegetical history; witness the "German Christians" of the Nazi period, Protestant pastors bent on "purifying" Christianity of its Jewish heritage and—to avert "racial fraud" and the "threat to our race of foreign blood"—expelling pastors of Jewish descent.

The gospels are *kerygma* (proclamation and exhortation, good news, homily, and so on), not history, and were not intended by the evangelists to serve as history. There is no evidence that the evangelists were eyewitnesses, although they probably made some use of eyewitness accounts. Their knowledge was based largely on oral tradition passed down by Jesus' followers; the earliest gospel, that of Mark, was written forty years or more after Jesus' death. Consequently, says the biblical scholar J. H. Charlesworth, in the generation between the crucifixion and Mark's gospel, "the Jesus of history has been lost."[11] In the view of many New Testament scholars, proof of the authenticity of Jesus' sayings and actions is very uncertain, if attainable at all. The gospels, then, are fundamentally theological and missionary in content and purpose. Their authors were not historians concerned with accuracy but evangelists seeking to strengthen belief and attract converts.

In a sense, however, Jesus' "biography" was written long before he was born: His life is presented in the New Testament as a midrash (interpretation) of the Old Testament, for the evangelists depict him as the fulfillment of the prophecies and divine promises of Hebrew scripture. In the words of Crossan, the evangelists' accounts often "come from searching the [Hebrew] Scriptures, not from remembering the history."[12] This complex development will become clear if we divide the evolution of Christianity into several stages:

1.  This stage consists of the messianic-eschatological community of Palestine in Jesus' lifetime, about 4 B.C.E. to about 33 C.E., whose central belief and hope are expressed in the message Jesus proclaimed: "Repent for the Kingdom of God is at hand" (Matthew 4:17) or simply that "The Kingdom of Heaven is at hand."[13]

2.  This is followed, around 50 to around 65, by the Pauline cult of Jesus the risen Christ and savior of all humanity; this represented a "spiritualization" of the Hebrew messianic hope of salvation in this world into the hope of eternal bliss in a heavenly afterlife. St. Paul preached "another Christ" and "a different gospel," for though "we once regarded Christ from a human point of view, we regard him thus no longer."[14]

3.  The next stage is that of the compilation of the gospels, about 70 to 120 or later, and was marked by the Roman destruction of the Jerusalem Temple in 70 and later Jewish revolts and their suppression, and also by the increasing gentilization of the nascent church that followed the refusal of the Jews to accept Jesus.

4.  The last stage came with the organization of the early Catholic church around its presbyters and bishops and the development of Christian doctrine by patristic theologians and churchmen (the Church Fathers from the second to the seventh century) when the church became a state power.

"Jesus research"—the term some New Testament scholars prefer to "the quest for the historical Jesus"—has been enormously enriched since the 1940s with new sources, most notably by the treasure trove of Dead Sea Scrolls and the Nag Hammadi documents discovered in Egypt; there are also the pseudepigrapha and apocrypha of the Old and New Testaments, many of them recent discoveries.[15] These hundreds of documents, together with archaeological finds, say nothing directly or new about the historical Jesus, but they have yielded a profound understanding of the Judaism of the time of Jesus and established in the fullest and most searching way his Jewishness. As Charlesworth enthusiastically describes the gains in understanding: The once "elusive background of Jesus' life is now much clearer than it was [up to 1965]. . . . The Judaism of Jesus' day was richer and more variegated than we had supposed."[16] One example of this enrichment that enhances our understanding of Jesus, although it does not bring us closer in any precise or factual way to the historical person, is the discovery that one of his titles, "Son of Man" (a son/descendant of Adam, ben-Adam), is not unique or original to Jesus or a Christian creation, as was long thought and argued, for it appears in documents that are definitely Jewish before Jesus' time.

Charlesworth claims that Jesus' followers and the evangelists were more historically conscious than has been traditionally acknowledged—that, therefore, the gospels have substantial reliability as sources; he concludes that "a feeling for history was one of the characteristics of [Jesus'] earliest followers," a necessity for them in their arguments and polemical encounters with opponents, but he also acknowledges that the sources for the life of Jesus are still "meager" and at best the historian can arrive at no more than "justifiable probabilities."[17] Despite these marvelous discoveries, the historian is still forced to conclude that somewhere in the generation between the crucifixion and Mark's gospel, "the Jesus of history has been lost."

The historical Jesus—the Jesus of a human nature in Christian teaching—was obviously a Jew. He lived, worshipped, and died as a Jew, a Jewish martyr it might be said. His name was Joshua or Yeshua. "Christ" is a Greek translation of the Hebrew *messiah* (meaning, as in 2 Samuel 22:51, an anointed one, a heaven-sent leader associated with the house of David from which the prophets sought a deliverer whose rule would bring universal peace, prosperity, piety, and justice as well as national freedom and independence from foreign rule and domination). Jesus spoke not New Testament Greek (although he probably knew some Greek) but Aramaic and Hebrew; this means that his sayings had to be remembered in Aramaic and Hebrew and translated into the Greek of the New Testament. Jesus was circumcised, his mother was purified

after his birth, and he attained his religious majority as a Jew at age thirteen—
all in accordance with Jewish law. In sum, Jesus was a faithful and observant
Jew who lived by the Torah (the Pentateuch or five books of Moses, literally
"teaching" or "instruction").

The gospels are, notoriously, full of attacks on the Pharisees, many of
them voiced by Jesus himself. Lay teachers of the Torah, the Pharisees challenged the Sadducees, the hereditary priests who controlled the Jerusalem
Temple. Whereas the conservative Sadducees insisted on a strict interpretation of Mosaic law, the more liberal Pharisees allowed discussion on varying
interpretations of the law and granted authority to oral tradition, the "oral
law" that was communicated from generation to generation, as well as to
scripture, the "written law." The historical Jesus shared much in common with
the Pharisees. "I am one of a growing number of scholars who doubts that
there were any substantial differences between Jesus and the Pharisees," writes
the distinguished New Testament authority E. P. Sanders, who concludes that
the gospel accounts of their conflicts "have more than a slight air of artificial-
ity," since sabbath observance and food matters were issues more likely at a
later date to engage gentile Christians than Jesus' Jewish followers.[18] Nevertheless, a reader of an unabridged dictionary or the *Oxford English Dictionary*
will find "Pharisee" defined pejoratively as "a self-righteous person," "a for-
malist," "a person observant of externals but indifferent to substance," "a hyp-
ocrite," "given to the letter of the law not the spirit," and the like.
Anti-Pharisaism predates Jesus and is not peculiar to Christianity. In the
Mishnah, which records the views and judgments of the rabbis before and
after the time of Jesus, there are passages as extravagantly critical of Pharisees
as anything that appears in the New Testament.

The Pharisees were not a monolithic party or doctrine. There were vari-
eties of Pharisees and Pharisaism, as there were of Essenes, Sadducees,
Zealots, Dead Sea Scrollers, and other Jewish groups,* in rivalry and jostling
one another in a Judaea that was remarkably pluralistic, notable more for reli-

---

* The Pharisees (from the Hebrew *perushim* for "separate") were the predecessors of
the talmudic rabbis; they became the dominant sect of Judaism following the revolt
against Rome, 66 to 73. The Essenes were an ascetic group described by some sources
as a major Jewish sect until the Roman destruction; many scholars equate them with the
Qumran or Dead Sea Scroll community, Qumran being the settlement near which are
the caves where the library collections of manuscripts of the sectarians (here called
Dead Sea Scrollers) dating from ca. 168 B.C.E. to ca. 68 C.E. were found from 1947 on.
The Zealots were described by the Jewish historian Josephus as one of the insurgent
parties in the revolt against Rome.

gious variety than for consensus.[19] That pluralism was obliterated, however, in the course of the Jewish revolt of 66 to 73, when the Roman conquerors suppressed all Jewish parties and factions except the Pharisees. In the aftermath of Roman suppression, when the gospels were being compiled, the only visible Jewish target for the evangelists to attack was "the Pharisees," all other groups having gone under.

St. Paul's epistles, which date from the 50s, are devoid of anti-Pharisaic vehemence—in fact he declares, "I belonged to the strictest group in our religion: I lived as a Pharisee"; he came from a long line of Pharisees and was a Pharisee among Pharisees (Acts 26:5; Philippians, 3:5–6). His letters are the oldest New Testament documents, but since he knew him not "in the flesh," he says little of the historical Jesus, instead preaching Christ crucified and risen for the salvation of humankind. Paul makes no reference to the Sanhedrin (the highest council and supreme court of the Jews until suppressed by Rome), high priest, hearings, trials, or executions at the Passover season. One is led to conclude that such criticisms as Jesus is reported as making are consistent with earlier and contemporaneous critics of Pharisaism; they are made within the fold and constitute a qualification, a criticism of some Pharisees and of some elements of Pharisaism, but not a rejection or rebuttal or abandonment of Pharisaism. Yet we know that the ensuing centuries are littered with the "Pharisaical" epithet. And since rabbinic Jews today define themselves as descendants of the Pharisees, anti-Pharisaism has been virtually synonymous with antisemitism and a source of inflamed hatred of Jews.

As terms of reproach, "Pharisaism" and "Pharisaical" have been decisive factors in thwarting cordial relations between Christians and Jews and have lent support to the notion of "supersession," namely that with the emergence of Christianity, Judaism has served its providential purpose, is obsolete, and is slated to disappear. "The cornerstone of Christian Antisemitism is the superceding or displacement myth, which already rings with the genocidal note," writes the Protestant student of religion and Holocaust scholar Franklin Littell.[20] That myth has long been the controlling assumption of Christian scholars and theologians, and over the centuries it has justified persecution of Jews by Christians who sought to implement heaven's supposed command. Various supersessionist theories flourished over the millennia, notably in the Catholic church down to Vatican II's *Nostra Aetate*, even though no pope or council ever sanctioned them as official church teaching. The destruction of the Temple and the Diaspora can no longer serve as "proof" of supersession: The 1985 Vatican "Notes on the Correct Presentation of Jews and Judaism," for example, states that "the history of Israel did not end in 70 C.E.

It continued, especially in a numerous diaspora which allowed Israel to carry to the whole world a witness—often heroic—of its fidelity to the one God . . . while preserving the memory of the land of their forefathers at the heart of their hope (Passover Seder)."[21] No Catholic *qua* Catholic can countenance supersessionism, anti-Pharisaism, and the like today. It remains a tragic irony that anti-Pharisaism has been so rife in Christianity, for without Pharisaism and its teaching of the afterlife, Christianity would never have developed.

Another of the besetting difficulties of New Testament interpretation is the "uniqueness" of Jesus, a claim that has had the effect of setting him off excessively from the Judaism(s) of his time: The more "unique" Jesus is depicted, the more "inferior" Judaism is rendered. No historical personage can be entirely "unique," and the scholarship of the last generation has insisted more clearly than previously that Jesus lived his life squarely *within* Judaism. That is an inescapable conclusion from the massive new documentary and archaeological material that has come into the scholarly domain since World War II.[22] "In fact," comments E. P. Sanders, "we cannot say that a single one of the things known about Jesus is unique"; he had much in common with John the Baptist, Judas the Galilean, Theudas the Egyptian, and other unnamed figures referred to by Josephus. John Meier, author of a 3-volume study of Jesus, remarks that New Testament scholars have associated Jesus with almost every one of the known parties in first-century Judaea, that undoubtedly "Jesus the Jew had points of contact with almost every branch of Judaism."[23] Helmut Thielicke, a German exegete who is consistently restrained in his judgments, nevertheless concludes that Jesus "hardly spoke a word that could not already be read, in [Jewish] literature before him, in substantially the same form."[24] As mentioned earlier, biblical scholars have long interpreted Jesus as a type of Pharisee; the new sources complicate but do not undermine this interpretation.

Recent scholarship also links Jesus to the Essenes. It is likely that Jesus knew of the Essenes and their ideas and practices. He may have known them personally and been influenced by them. His mentor John the Baptist fits the profile of an Essene perfectly. The archaeological discovery of the Essene gate and exploration of the sector of Jerusalem where Essenes lived raise the possibility that it was the site where Jesus lived with Mary and his brother, James, when they came up to the city. A negative instance of the Jesus-Essene connection might be found in Jesus' criticism of the too-stringent sabbath observance, which may be his censure of the Essene community at Qumran, whose members were very strict sabbatarians indeed. A positive instance of Essene influence might be the beatitudes in the Sermon on the Mount: Blessed are

the poor . . . , Blessed are the poor in spirit. . . . These terms are used in the
Dead Sea Scrolls to refer to the community; the Teacher of Righteousness
refers to himself as the Poor One and his followers are cited as the Poor in
grace or Poor in spirit.[25] Moreover, Jesus shared with the Qumranites the
practice of contemporizing exegesis, namely the conviction that all scriptural
prophecy pertained to the current moment. Building on this belief, Matthew
cites Isaiah's prophecy that a messiah will be born of a virgin in Bethlehem.

Most modern New Testament scholars interpret Jesus as an eschatological
prophet, that is, one who looked to the end time and the onset of the kingdom
of heaven, whether already being realized or to arrive soon. There is a straight
eschatological line from John the Baptist, to Jesus, to Paul, to the early church.
A dominant view has been that Jesus was an apocalyptist, holding that God
would intervene to bring history to a violent, cataclysmic end. And even
though the trend in recent, especially American, New Testament scholarship
is to conclude that Jesus was no fire-breathing apocalyptist, that, rather, he was
a prophet who "fits in the general framework of restoration eschatology," the
end result is the same because the gospels "apocalypticized" Jesus' teaching.[26]

First-century Jewish eschatological speculation was rich and varied. One
form of it was apocalyptic, what purported to be revelations from on high bestowed on a seer, typically in the form of visions for the benefit of the sect or
religious community; these works reveal heavenly mysteries and the nature of
the end time when the divine purpose is to be realized, often by means of a
climactic war between good and evil. Messianism often pervades these texts.
Some texts stressed ethical eschatology, when the lamb will lie down with the
lion. Still another strand of this eschatological speculation called for the destruction of the gentiles; no doubt this was a reaction to Roman occupation
and the earlier persecution inflicted on the Jews by Hellenistic rulers. Keyed
by "a light to the nations" of Isaiah 49:6, some religious thinkers believed the
gentiles would be gathered into the fold of the chosen. Jesus shared some features of first-century messianic apocalypticism: An identification with the
poor and downtrodden that is punctuated by warnings to the rich and com-
placent; the sharp split between the depraved present and a redeemed future,
a transformation that will be effected by divine intervention in human affairs;
and the vision that the present age and/or world will soon end. Such notions
were widespread and a common denominator to most groups in Jesus' time.
Thus Jesus was immersed in first-century Judaism: It was his "intellectual
homeland."

For centuries Christians have denigrated so-called late Judaism as mori-
bund, legalistic, ritualistic, trapped in externals, rigid, materialist, spurious,

and hypocritical. At long last, such stereotypes have been exploded as baseless calumnies.[27] Paul's and the nascent church's aspiration to win over the gentiles springs, like so much in the gospels, from Jewish ideas about the eschaton, the new age, the end of history.

## ANTI-JUDAISM IN THE GOSPELS

The most powerful warrant for persecution of Jews over the millennia has been the Christian indictment of "deicides" and "Christ killers." Unfortunately, the source has been the New Testament, which, taken at face value, is permeated by anti-Judaism and antisemitism, especially in connection with the Passion. According to New Testament scholars, the gospels "grew backwards"; that is, their inspiration was the Passion story, all the rest having been pieced in to explain and lead up to the culmination of the Passion and resurrection and the vindication of Jesus in the eyes of his followers. This mode of structuring went far to turn the whole gospel story into anti-Jewish polemic and reprobation.

Further explanation of the gospels' anti-Jewish sentiment is to be found in the fact that they date from the last third of the century, when the Jews and their Roman rulers were at daggers drawn, owing to the great revolt of 66 to 73, which saw the destruction of the Temple and the extinction of any remaining Jewish autonomy. To the Romans, certainly until the Antonine emperors after 138, the word *Jew* was synonymous with *traitor* and *rebel*.[28] The Christians, meanwhile, were perceived by Roman officials as another Jewish sect; sometimes they were tolerated as a *religio licita* (legal sect), but often they were persecuted for worshipping a "malefactor" whom Rome had executed and for refusing to adore the emperor, the imperial cult from which Jews remained exempt. The fact that the gospels do not report Christian persecution at the hands of Rome is part of their stance of loyalty to Rome, echoing Jesus' protestation to "Render unto Caesar. . . ." Similarly, by condemning the Jews, the evangelists probably were trying to appease Roman authorities, who still looked on Christians as just another Jewish sect, or possibly saw Christians as having it both ways, masquerading as Jews to retain the right of assembly and immunity from participating in emperor worship. At the time the gospels were being written, Christians, out of fear of Rome, sought to dissociate themselves from the Jews. And so the evangelists underplayed the Romans' role and blamed Jesus' death on the troublesome Jews by having Pontius Pilate, the Roman governor, recognize the innocence and legitimacy of Jesus' teaching and ministry. It is in this context that the English scholar S. G. F. Brandon commented that Mark (whose gospel is thought to be addressed to the Christian community at Rome itself) makes Jesus into a "pro-Roman pacifist."[29] The fourth gospel, John, is the most extreme in whitewashing the Romans and vilifying "the Jews."

In part, such antipathy for Jews and Judaism as appears in the gospels can be called—in Father Bruce Vawter's apt phrase—"Jewish anti-Jewishness" rather than antisemitism, and interpreted—as Paul Winter suggested—as a "defensive" rather than "aggressive" attitude born of fear of provoking Roman antagonism and suspicion.[30] It also reflects Jewish hostility toward the emerging Christian communities because they denied the law and thus ceased to be "Jewish."[31] Jewish persecution of Christians—which Paul engaged in and then was a target of—undoubtedly existed. One manifestation of it was the portion added, around 80, to the synagogal liturgy invoking divine wrath on the *minim* (meaning a miscellany of heretics, informers, apostates, but also Christians). However, by then, in the aftermath of the pitiless Roman suppression of the Jewish revolt, the capacity of Jewish authorities to interfere with or thwart Christian preaching was greatly diminished. With the second upheaval of 115 to 117 against Emperor Trajan and the third, the much more formidable Simon Bar Kochba revolt of 132 to 135 against Emperor Hadrian, the situation was tilted even more drastically against the Jews. There was great loss of life, enormous numbers enslaved, great devastation and destruction, and prolonged persecution. The Romans converted Jerusalem into a barracks town, erected a shrine to Jupiter, barred Jews from entering their holy city except once a year to mourn the destruction, and changed the name of the province from Judaea to Syria-Palestine.

Eager not to arouse Roman disfavor, the evangelists heaped guilt for the crucifixion on the Jews and not on the head of Pontius Pilate and the Roman majesty. What might have been tactical, apologetic, and cautionary initially, when the gospels took shape, was transposed into virulent antisemitism in later times and circumstances, when the church was established by law and exercised great power in contrast to Jews, who exercised none. "Defensive," in Winter's terms, then became "aggressive." As Crossan observes, Pilate's declaring his innocence and Jews' shouting for crucifixion was a "defensive strategy" on the part of the evangelists, but when we arrive three centuries later at the Christian Roman Empire, the narrative became "the longest lie" and was used by a now-powerful Christian world to persecute Jews.[32]

In the same period, moreover, the Christian mission to the Roman pagan world got under way, the hope to win over the mass of the Jewish people having failed and generated enormous animosity: The desire to convert the pagans was a prime motive inspiring the evangelists who, in their zeal, consciously and unconsciously excoriated the Jews by exempting the Romans from having any responsibility for Jesus' suffering, his arrest, indictment, trial, and crucifixion. To repeat, the gospels are *kerygma*, not history.

Thus the attitude in the gospels toward rabbis, scribes, priests, elders, Pharisees, and Jews (forgetting that the apostles and early Christians were themselves Jews) reflects Christian-Jewish strife and hostility from the last third of the first century on. The evangelists, anachronistically, read such antipathy and opposition to Jews and Judaism back into the time of Jesus, when they hardly existed.[33] This distinction is emphasized in the 1985 Vatican *Notes for the Correct Way to Present Jews and Judaism in Preaching and Catechesis of the Roman Catholic Church:* "The Gospels are the outcome of long and complicated editorial work. . . . Hence it cannot be ruled out that some references hostile to the Jews have their historical context in conflicts between the nascent Church and the Jewish community. Certain controversies reflect Christian-Jewish relations long after the time of Jesus. To establish this is of capital importance." Thus a cardinal principle of modern New Testament exegesis has become part of Catholic teaching and self-understanding.[34]

## THE TRIAL AND CRUCIFIXION

Let us turn the historian's searchlight on that most famous trial and execution in all history. Everything points to the conclusion that the trial and crucifixion were a strictly Roman affair, that Jesus was executed on a political charge as the would-be king of the Jews. To proclaim that the kingdom of God was at hand meant that God, not Rome, will rule. Moreover, as Stephen Patterson observed, "kingdom" is a translation of *basileia*, which is the same word that contemporaries used for the Roman "Empire"; Jesus' "daring" to speak in "the deeply political overtones of this terminology," *empire of God,* was an unmistakable challenge to Roman authority.[35] In the Roman view, Jesus appeared no different from the Zealots or *sicarii*, whom Rome had crucified in great numbers since the great anti-Roman ferment had begun after 6 C.E., when Roman governors displaced Jewish rule in Judaea. (Some scholars point to a link between Jesus and the *sicarii* in the person of the apostate Judas, suggested by the similarity of his name Iscariot to *sicarii*.)

According to Matthew 26:59 and Mark 14:53, on the night before he was tried by Pilate, Jesus was brought before the Sanhedrin, where he was tried, found guilty, and handed over to the procurator. The Sanhedrin probably still had the right down to 70 to impose capital punishment under Jewish law, although by the time of the proceedings against Jesus many of its legislative and judicial prerogatives had been shorn away by the Roman governors. Moreover, the priesthood and officials would have hesitated either to antagonize the Roman power or to bring down on their heads the clamors of the people, with whom Jesus was very popular, as his entry into Jerusalem applauded by "very great multitudes" would indicate. The Roman governors held the high priests on a very short political leash, appointing and dismissing them almost at will. Even the high priest's vestments were in custody of the governor, and without them he could not preside at the great festivals nor, in all probability, summon and preside over the Sanhedrin. Thus the high priests were Rome's political instruments and perforce had to collaborate, which did not endear them to the Jewish populace.

Yet Jesus may not have been tried before the Sanhedrin. In several ways the trial as depicted in the New Testament violated the prescriptions of the Mishnah collection of rabbinic law:

1. Capital cases had to be tried before the Sanhedrin during the day, not at night as reported in the gospels; there is no record that it ever met at night.

2. A trial and a verdict of guilty could not occur on the same day.

3. In the synoptics (the first three gospels, Matthew, Luke, and Mark, which are thought to be related in that much of their content derives from a common source) it was the eve of the sabbath or Passover (in John it was the eve of the Day of Preparation), when no courts were permitted to be in session.

4. The session was held in the high priest's palace, although the law prescribed that the Sanhedrin meet in the "hall of hewn stone" in the temple precincts.

5. Jesus was accused of blasphemy, but his actions did not constitute blasphemy under Jewish law, which defines it as cursing or reviling the name of God (Leviticus 24:10–16), something Jesus never did. Nor did the claim that he was the Son of Man or the Son of God expose him to the charge, since, as mentioned, such terms appear in Jewish texts of the period and do not signify blasphemy; the former could mean any ordinary Jew, as in Numbers 23:18, the latter one who stood in special relationship to God, as in Job 38:7. It may be that the accusation of "blasphemy" is an anachronism, a later Christian teaching about the divine Jesus read back into the gospels.[36] To Jewish judges, the term *messiah* would simply mean "an anointed

one," one anointed with sacred oils as in royal coronations, and was not an assertion of divinity or an expression of idolatry; in fact, there is no record of Jewish authorities ever prosecuting or attacking those proclaimed or self-proclaimed as messiahs.

6.  No one could be found guilty on his own confession alone; the testimony of two truthful witnesses is required, but the gospel authors dismiss the witnesses as untruthful.

7.  The mode of execution under Jewish law would have been stoning, not crucifixion.

8.  There is much confusion over the identity of the Jewish authority who arraigned Jesus and/or the high priest who presided over the Sanhedrin: He is named both Caiaphas and Annas or not named at all. Since there is unanimity that the Roman governor before whom Jesus was brought was Pontius Pilate, the identity of the high priest should also be known if a trial had indeed taken place.

9.  Had Jesus been tried and convicted by the Sanhedrin, there would have been no reason to turn him over for a second trial before Pilate; it is unlikely that the Sanhedrin sat as a grand jury, since neither Jewish nor Roman sources indicate such a practice, and it is dubious that any Roman court would receive or act on indictments of that origin.

10.  The Roman legionnaires dividing up Jesus' seamless robe confirm the view that the issues involved were political and Roman and did not involve the Sanhedrin: According to Roman law, in religious cases personal effects went to the family, while in political ones they were forfeited to the state. Also, Golgotha, the site of execution, was used to dispatch political prisoners. Moreover, Jesus' burial was the normal Jewish one, which, if he had been sentenced to death by the Sanhedrin or any Jewish court, would not have been permitted; burial then would have been in a cemetery reserved for those executed on capital charges and with no mourning allowed.

Two points must be made, if it is contended that Jesus would have been tried according to the older and strictly biblical Sadducean law, not these prescriptions of the Mishnah's Pharisaic law, because the Mishnah cannot be traced back earlier than 200 C.E., or more than a century and a half after Jesus' time. First, a Sadducean court would have followed the written law, that is to say, scripture, and at least three of the cited requirements stem directly from the Hebrew Bible: number 5 regarding blasphemy, from Leviticus 24:10–16; number 6 regarding guilt on one's confession, from Deuteronomy 17:6 and

19:15; and number 7 regarding the mode of execution, from Deuteronomy 17:2–5. Second, many of the Mishnah's stipulations were already in effect in Jesus' lifetime, dating from the period of the great sage Hillel (fl. 30 B.C.E. to 10 C.E.). Moreover, Josephus' father was a priest and thus a Sanhedrin member in Jesus' time; had there been so momentous a trial, he or other family members would have made it known to the historian, who, in fact, knew of Jesus and refers to him in a famous passage of his *Jewish Antiquities*, but is silent about any proceedings before the Sanhedrin.[37] While there is no mention of Josephus or his father in the New Testament, three who sat in the Sanhedrin and appear in the New Testament are Nicodemus and Joseph of Arimathaea (of whom practically nothing is known) and Gamaliel (who is cited in rabbinical literature). One would expect to have some word from them or other members of the Sanhedrin, which Josephus would have recorded, about so important an event, had it occurred.

What, then, the question becomes, were the nocturnal proceedings in the high priest's house all about? And what made it so urgent that it had to be resolved on the eve of Passover? "I submit that there can have been only one thing in which the Jewish leadership of the day was vitally interested," wrote the Israeli Supreme Court justice and scholar Haim Cohn, whose suggestive hypothesis shows that it is possible to have fresh thoughts on these issues even after two millennia.

> It was *to prevent* the execution by the Romans of a Jew . . . who happened to enjoy the affection and love of the people. Their motives were realistic and political. . . . While the Sanhedrin had . . . to be watchful not to alienate such good will of the Roman authorities as it still could enjoy, the first and foremost condition for its survival and effectiveness was to retain the confidence of the people. To do this it had to try to prevent the execution of Jesus and bring about his acquittal. . . . Jesus had to be persuaded not to plead guilty, and witnesses had to be found to prove his innocence. To secure at least a suspension of his sentence, Jesus had to be persuaded to promise that he would not, in the future, engage in [what the Romans regarded as] treasonable activities. . . . It is for this reason that the night meeting of the Sanhedrin took place.[38]

The famous scene of Caiaphas rending his garments (a gesture of mourning) conveys, according to this hypothesis, his grief at failing to persuade Jesus and the foregone conclusion of the proceedings before Pilate; the exclamations by the high priest's colleagues of "He must die" and the like, are expressions not of their verdict but of their frustration and distress at their failure to dissuade

Jesus. At most, that event is a hearing, not a trial, as indeed a long line of exegetes have averred.

Another historical problem is raised by the span of six or seven hours al-
lotted in the gospels for the cycle of events from Jesus' arrest to his death on
the cross; there could not have been enough time for the sequence of so many
legal proceedings (seven) and episodes of mockery and molestations of Jesus
(five) that the evangelists elaborate for dramatic effect and to vilify the Jews.
Paul Winter reduces the seven to one, namely the trial before Pilate, and the
five to one, namely the physical injury the Roman soldiers inflicted on Jesus.
One of these taunting incidents occurs in John 18:20–22, where Jesus is struck
in the face by a guard (Jewish, of course) for supposedly speaking ill to the
high priest: Such slapping incidents are the launching pad for one of the great
myths about Jews, that of the Wandering or Eternal Jew, doomed to the punishment of endless roaming and suffering, and fated never to die in an endless
agony of torment; St. Augustine stamped them with the stigmatic "mark of
Cain," so that in their "continued preservation" they will suffer the "subjec-
tion merited by those who . . . put the Lord to death."[39]

We come, then, to the trial before Pilate. How did Jesus come to the notice of Pilate? As stated, there probably was no trial or formal action by the
Sanhedrin. Josephus tells of Jewish leaders handing over Zealots to the Romans, but such were arbitrary, extralegal procedures, and Jesus was not, presumably, a Zealot and would not have been handled that way. On the other
hand, Jesus might have been so perceived and so handled, as a political trou-
blemaker preaching a new kingdom and recruiting followers, and at least one
of the Apostles was Simon the Zealot. We can conjecture only that some kind
of action initiated by Jews, probably the high priest and a few of his intimates,
was taken against Jesus and resulted in his transfer to Roman jurisdiction. According to Josephus, "Pilate, upon hearing him [Jesus] accused by men of the
highest standing among us [the Jews] . . . condemned him to be crucified."[40]

Over the centuries many explanations have been advanced as to what the
precise accusation against Jesus was. To many historians, it was his attack on
the Temple. He attacked it in word and deed: He upset the tables of the
money changers and the seats of the pigeon dealers and condemned the conversion of the Temple into a "robbers' cave,"* vowing that he would destroy

---

* As will be seen in chapter 4, prominent and primary to economic antisemitism, from
patristics to Hitler and beyond, is the New Testament story of Jesus' expulsion of the
moneylenders; it is invoked to show that Judaism is a materialist, amoral, profane religion, that the Jewish mentality is one of haggling and huckstering, and much else of the
same kind.

and in three days rebuild the Temple (Mark, 11:15–19, John, 2:14–21). Such action might be considered blasphemous. It was one thing to assail the priests, which was frequently done; it was quite another to attack the revered Temple (although that is precisely what the seceding Dead Sea Scrollers appear to have done). Taken together with his preaching the kingdom (i.e., "empire") and his triumphal entry into Jerusalem, Caiaphas and Pilate would have had more than enough to proceed against Jesus. His triumphal entry was a symbolic challenge to Roman authority: Hailed as king, he seemed like a political leader, the conquering hero, Judas Maccabaeus or King David himself.[41] His words and actions excited the people and gave him, or showed that he had, a large following, which of itself was sufficient to rouse the high priest's fears and Roman suspicions of tumult and disorder. It is notable that the triumphal entry and the Temple scene are the last public events of Jesus' life and that the sequel is his arrest and appearance before Pilate. Nevertheless, the gospels do not report his conviction before Pilate over the Temple incident. The witnesses who testify to it are dismissed as not agreeing, as being false witnesses (Mark 14:55–59; Matthew 26:59). In sum, Caiaphas and his colleagues certainly did not believe that Jesus and his followers were a physical threat to the Temple, nor that Jesus knew what God would do, whether destroy the Temple or another dire form of intervention. In that time of mass pilgrimage, with the people celebrating freedom from Egyptian bondage and the end of pharaoh's tyranny, the Jewish authorities "were probably anxious lest his prediction of coming upheaval and the intervention of God should touch off riots." Whatever the charges might have been, what made them fatal was the Roman determination to eliminate what the imperial government perceived as a growing challenge to its authority.[42]

Pontius Pilate, from what is known of him from independent sources like Philo* and Josephus, was a cynical, despotic, cruel, and rapacious Roman official—so much so that the emperor in 36 C.E. removed him. Philo reports him as crucifixion-crazy, responsible for "non-stop executions without verdicts, and endless and unbearable cruelties."[43] Pilate would be contemptuous of the Jews as "barbarians"—meaning they did not speak Latin or Greek—and of their religion as "superstition"; he would have them renounce their way of life and accept the superior Roman civilization. Under Roman law, he had no right of pardon in cases of treason, to which Jesus confessed when he replied "It is as you say" (or, in another translation, "The words are yours") to Pilate's question "Are you the king of the Jews?" In Roman law, in contrast to

---

* Philo Judaeus (ca. 20 B.C.E. to ca. 50 C.E.) Jewish philosopher of Alexandria, Egypt, who greatly influenced Jewish and Christian religious thought.

Jewish, confession by the accused was sufficient for conviction. Nor did Pilate have the prerogative to delegate his powers or functions in such a case to some other body, such as the Sanhedrin, still less to a crowd of people milling about. The picture in Matthew of Pilate "washing his hands of the blood of this innocent man" is entirely out of character for the imperious governor and quite un-Roman; it is a Jewish gesture and symbolic act, echoing Deuteronomy 21:1–9, and would have been lost on Pilate. It is hard to imagine a Roman official declaring his innocence before a crowd of subject peoples—as if they were the judges; moreover, since such trials were held behind closed doors, the Jews would not have been present to see him perform his ablutions, for they would have been kept at a distance in the courtyard or praetorium. Again, it is incongruous to picture a Roman governor, as does the gospel of John, who "would keep jumping up from his lordly seat of judgment at odd intervals and running out into the courtyard to talk with a mob of natives."[44] From what is known of Roman legal procedure, it is inconceivable that the Jews could have taken the active part that is ascribed to them in the gospels' account of the trial. The insistent cry of the crowd, "Crucify him! crucify him!" must be discounted for two reasons:

1. The crowd would not be in the courtroom to scream it out.
2. No high Roman official would tolerate such interference, certainly not the arrogant representative of that suspicious tyrant, Emperor Tiberius.

It seems obvious that the gospels transformed the historical Pilate to serve kerygmatic ends.[45] With the passage of time, Pilate's role was further reduced—by the patristic theologians—who idealized him as an admirer and friend of Jesus; in the Coptic church he was even honored as St. Pilate and celebrated on June 25. The Alpine peak Mt. Pilate also honors him and suggests how deeply rooted in Christian imagination is his favorable image and providential role. His wife (Matthew 27:19 reports her as sending a message to her husband that she was warned in a dream and that he should leave the "innocent" Jesus in peace) was honored as St. Claudia Procula in the Greek Orthodox church and is celebrated on October 27. One should note that it is a gentile who recognizes Jesus' innocence. Anatole France's short story, "The Procurator of Judaea," is an anti-Christian squib but offers a keen historical insight and corrective to the gospels. He depicts Pilate in retirement as host to his friend of long ago, Laelius Lamia, who has inquired about a young Galilean from Nazareth named Jesus, who was "crucified for some crime, I don't quite know what." Knitting his brow and searching his memory, "'Jesus?' [Pilate] murmured, 'Jesus—of Nazareth? I cannot call him to mind.'" In fact, there is no indication in historical sources of a popular or widely known religious figure being executed in Judaea about the year 30, suggesting that the crucifixion did not attract much attention at the time, that, as John Meier puts it, we are seeking "a marginal Jew leading a marginal movement in a marginal province of a vast Roman Empire" and that Pilate in old age would indeed have had to strain to recall the Nazarene.[46]

All the gospels explicitly say that it was Roman soldiers who executed Jesus and indulged in all kinds of brutal mockery. And there is no doubt that Pilate had Jesus scourged or flogged, as stated in the gospels, for it was a fixed part of the crucifixion procedure. That he thereupon turned Jesus over to the Jews is totally misleading. The implication of Pilate's words "My hands are clean of this man's blood; see to that yourselves" and the sequel that Pilate "handed him over to be crucified" (Matthew 27:24–25) is that the Jews did the killing. If the Jews had carried out the crucifixion after Jesus was "handed over" to them—as Pilate's words "see to that yourselves" insinuate—Joseph of Arimathaea would have had to gain permission of the high priest or Sanhedrin, not Pilate, to take the body for burial.[47] In the gospels it is notable also that as the procession makes its way to the place of execution at Golgotha and Jesus is nailed to the cross, it is Jews ("the passers-by" in Matthew 27:39) who torment and mock him. One of these incidents has Jesus being offered and refusing wine mixed with myrrh, which was a kind of anesthesia that diminished the pain and was a gesture of compassion, although in the gospels it has the opposite import.[48] The overall impression these scenes make on Christian imagination—especially when dramatized in Passion plays like that of Oberammergau (see page 4)—is one of the Jews dictating and controlling events, of Jewish malignancy and criminal intent. It is striking that this tendency to blame the Jews is even starker in the apocryphal gospel of Peter, discovered in the 1890s and a possible source for the canonical gospels: Pilate and the Romans have no role in the crucifixion whatsoever, for it is Herod, the Jewish ruler of Judaea when Jesus was born, and "the people" who are portrayed as totally responsible and totally evil.[49] So venomous is the deicide allegation.

It is also highly unlikely that it was "the chief priests" who induced the people to choose Barabbas rather than Jesus to be released. There is no record in either Roman or Jewish law of any custom by which a prisoner was released at the people's behest on Passover or any festival; the earliest mention of such a practice is the fourth century, and then it is the emperor alone who grants the pardon. The Barabbas episode may have some historical basis; he might have been wrongly arrested with a group of insurgents or rioters and subsequently released. Confusingly, the name *Barabbas* means "son of the father" or even "son of God." His full name was Jesus (a common name at the time) Barabba or bar Rabban or bar Abba, and it may be that the confusion of having two persons with the same name of Jesus before him prompted Pilate to inquire which was to be set free, because wrongly arrested, and which was to be tried for sedition. Whatever the historical background may or may not have been, the evangelists used the episode to exculpate Pilate and the Romans but to incriminate the Jews, who, in their evil, guilt, and criminality, chose to execute the innocent one and reprieve the murderer.[50] Whatever Matthew intended, the antisemitic use of such passages made by generations of Christian theologians and preachers is illustrated by Martin Luther's commentary in his translation of the New Testament: "Matthew means to say that Pilate wanted to propose Barabbas the most dreadful murderer so that the Jews could not ask for him. But they would have sooner pleaded for the Devil himself before they would have the Son of God released."[51]

In considering the Barabbas citation historically, one must ask why Jesus would be prosecuted if "there is no fault in this man." Simply acquit and release him. Why limit the choice to Jesus or Barabbas? If both were innocent, Pilate was empowered to free both. Why not also include the two "thieves" (the term for them, *lestes*, means "insurgents") with whom he was crucified? How could Barabbas' release be justified to the Emperor Tiberius? Why are the people so easily persuaded? The Jewish leaders and priests were unpopular with them, and one or two days before the people had "spread their garments in the way" by which Jesus made his triumphal entry into Jerusalem, hailed by "multitudes." Now suddenly the people hated him? Have the priests suddenly become popular and able to induce the people to choose Barabbas over Jesus to be released?[52] These queries remind one again that we are dealing with *kerygma*, not history.

The sources permit us to conclude that the high priest and his Sanhedrin colleagues played some part in Jesus' fate, but whether it was that of active initiators, bystanders, or intimidated agents is not possible to say, although the third choice is the one most consistent with the sources. It is inescapable, however, that Jesus suffered a Roman death in a Roman-occupied country at the hands of Roman soldiers carrying out a sentence for sedition against Roman authority imposed by a Roman judge sitting in a Roman court acting under Roman law. The historian must conclude that the Jews took no significant part in the trial of Jesus before Pilate, a strictly Roman matter. The Roman historian Tacitus says flat out in *Annals* XV:44 that Pilate executed Jesus: "Christus . . . suffered the extreme penalty during the reign of Tiberius at the hands of one of our procurators, Pontius Pilatus, and a most mischievous superstition, thus checked for the moment, again broke out not only in Judaea, the first source of the evil, but even in Rome, where all things hideous and shameful from every part of the world find their center and become popular."

The story of the faithless disciple Judas Iscariot is one of the most unfortunate portions of the gospels. He looms up as the eternal Jew, prototype of the betrayer. As Weddig Fricke quips, eleven apostles go into the church, one goes into the synagogue. According to John 6:70 and 13:27, Judas is a "devil" and Satan entered into him; thus Judas is demonized, as are all the Jews by John 8:43–47. The thirty pieces of silver, the notorious blood money, make Judas symbolic of greed and criminal machinations, of capitalist greed and "usury." (See chapter 4.) Jews and Judas—the names are similar sounding in every language—became synonymous. The historical Judas Iscariot (the name may mean dagger-man and he might have been an insurgent, perhaps a Zealot) was one of the disciples. Some scholars argue, perhaps apologetically, that there was a Judas who betrayed Jesus, but that he was not a disciple; to Crossan the Judas story is not "history remembered" but "prophecy historicized," namely Psalm 41:9: "Even the friend whom I trusted, who ate at my table/slanders me, exults over my misfortune."[53]

But the historicity of Judas is less important than the depictions of him down the centuries by Christian commentators, for whom the treasonous, treacherous, greedy, demonized Judas is synonymous with "the Jews." St. Jerome provides an example of the swath of vituperation that the image of Judas Iscariot cut in Christian theology and sermons: He reports Christ's lament that

> "Judas betrayed Me, the Jews persecuted and crucified Me." . . . In particular, this is the story of Judas; in general it is that of the Jews. . . . Judas, in particular, was torn asunder by demons—and the [Jewish] people as well. . . . Judas is cursed, so that in Judas the Jews may be accursed. [Even] the repentance of Judas became worse than his sins. [Just as] you see the Jew[s] praying; . . . nevertheless, their prayer turns into sin. . . . Whom do you suppose are the sons of Judas? The Jews. The Jews take their name . . . from the betrayer. . . . From this Iscariot, they are called Judaeans. . . . Iscariot means *money and price*. . . . [The] Synagogue was divorced by the Savior and became the wife of Judas the betrayer.[54]

Martin Luther gave Jerome's views a lease on Protestant life. He spoke of the Jews as "Judas' people" and as "the persecutors and enemies of Christ. For they are Judas' kin, who see nothing but God's anger in their misery. They remain in distress eternally; they descend into the abyss of hell." Citing John 19:11, Luther has it that Judas committed the greatest sin, for he was "the ringleader in guiding the mob against Christ" and delivering him up to the Romans.[55] Luther's conspiratorial motifs are reminiscent of the antichrist myth, to the creation of which the Judas image is central.[56] (See pages 77–78.) A striking counterpoint to Judas is Peter, one of the apostles who betrays Jesus thrice before the cock crows, but turns out to be the "rock," thoroughly dejudaized and canonized as St. Peter and the first pope, on whom the church is founded.

The antisemitic climax of the gospels' rendering of the Passion is Matthew's double condemnation. First, in 21:43 Jesus says, "I tell you, then, that the Kingdom of God will be taken from you and given to a people who will produce its fruit"—that is, the Jews will forfeit the kingdom to the gentiles and cease to be the chosen people—the renowned C. H. Dodd called that parable almost "a declaration of war."[57] Second, the most infamous passage in the New Testament is that verse of Matthew, 27:24–25, where the crowd accepts blame for Jesus' death: "Pilate could see that nothing was being gained, and a riot was starting; so he took water and washed his hands in full view of the people, saying, 'My hands are clean of this man's blood; see to that yourselves.' And with one voice all the people cried, 'His blood be upon us, and upon our children's.'" Together these two passages have been utilized innumerable times to provide a juridical basis to persecute Jews. Matthew 27:24–25 in particular is the passage most quoted by antisemites down the centuries and is "proof" of the "curse" or "malediction" that befell the Jews; it is the Jews' own self-indictment and self-arraignment, for they are made to acknowledge their malice aforethought in spilling his blood.

As with the washing, so with the blood: One is dealing with a matter that makes no sense in a Roman context and the phrase could have had no meaning to Pilate, even if one assumes—although one cannot—that the Jews said it and that the Jews were present and within earshot of Pilate to say it. In a Jewish context, such as Deuteronomy 21:1–9, the idea makes some sense: When a corpse is found, there is ritual washing of hands and proclamation of innocence, so that "guilt of innocent blood" shall not "rest upon thy people Israel," and so forth.

Historical analysis suggests that no such dialogue as Matthew fashions ever occurred in Pilate's court. But if it did take place, did all the Jews there say it, and did they do so in unison? By what warrant did they speak for "all" Jews? How can blame attach to Jews who said or did nothing whatsoever even if "the people" there blurted out some such remarks? Who bestowed on "the people" who pronounced that curse the power of attorney authorizing Christians to exact retribution on all Jews for all time?[58]

To put these questions is again to recall that one is dealing with *kerygma*, not history. The rub is, of course, that for centuries the gospels have been taken as impeccable history.[59] Indeed, reading the gospels as literal revelation and undiluted truth generates the conviction that Jews are "Christ killers," a deicide people who deserve to suffer, and Christians all too often have leaped at the chance to inflict due punishment on them. The image of the Jews that emerges from the New Testament became a perpetual incitement to attack them, in "revenge" for the death of the savior, as the crusaders were to put it a millennium later. Particularly in the fourth gospel, Jews are depicted as—by nature, inescapably, from the beginning, and for all time—enemies of Jesus; bound to Satan and dedicated to the lie, they conspire as a group—Jesus' enemies do not appear as individuals by name but always as an anonymous group—the destruction of Jesus and the ruin of mankind. This demonization of the Jews and predisposition to lie find their charter text in John 8:41–47. (See chapter 3.) While the fourth gospel is extreme in evoking a concerted Jewish plot in league with Satan to kill Jesus, it is only, says Paul Winter, "a bizarre exaggeration" of what already appears in the synoptic gospels, especially Mark.[60] One will concur heartily with Vawter's dictum that "the trial and death of Jesus have to be reconstructed rather than read from the Gospels"; thanks to the scholarship of the last two centuries and especially of the last fifty years, he was also sanguine that "if properly understood, the Gospels are not anti-Semitic."[61]

## THE BITTER LEGACY

The gospels attribute the Jews' indifference and hostility to Jesus to their "blindness." Several New Testament passages seem to point the way, notably the words from the cross, "Forgive them for they know not what they do," and Paul's much-used metaphor of the all-obscuring "veil": "Whenever Moses is read a veil lies over their minds" (2 Corinthians 3:15). Paul had explained in Romans 11:7–8 that God's grace had saved a remnant of the Jews but that on the rest God had laid "a numbness of spirit; he gave them blind eyes and deaf ears, and so it is still." There is no basis to be found in the New Testament for concluding that the evangelists or any of its other writers thought that the Jews knew Jesus to be the Christ but had killed him anyway, and several medieval exegetes argued forcefully that no one would knowingly kill God.

In the fifth century, St. Augustine argued, on the basis of these governing New Testament texts, that it was the Jews' ignorance and blindness that led them to reject Christ; they did not knowingly kill God. Augustine resolved the issue of why the Jews continued to exist. In the Augustinian tradition medieval theologians saw the Jews as bearing witness to the truth of Christianity by their holy scriptures—appropriated as the Old Testament and conferring a venerable antiquity on Christianity—and by their exile and degradation for spurning Jesus. Thus the Jews continued to serve a providential purpose in history and were therefore to be preserved and tolerated in Christendom; or, as this idea was expressed by a fifteenth-century writer, "To be a Jew is an offense, though one that is nonpunishable by the Christian."[62] And even though the Jews blindly and perversely adhered to it, Judaism was still recognized as biblical in origin and character, as was Jewish law, obsolete and nonsalvific though it was. At the end of time, Jews and Christians alike would be gathered together into the one fold, and, in the words of Paul, there would be neither Greek nor Jew, male nor female, slave nor free, and so forth.

In the centuries after Augustine, a corollary developed that the Jewish leaders recognized Jesus as the messiah promised to them in scripture but that they did not recognize his divinity. In this view, it was the ignorant masses who shouted for his crucifixion, because they rejected his messiahship and took his claim to divinity to be that of an imposter and blasphemer. In the eleventh and twelfth centuries, that line of theological reasoning weakened the Augustinian foundations that supported toleration of Judaism, but no clear inference of an extreme kind was drawn. By the thirteenth century, however, Franciscan and Dominican theologians provided a biblical basis for intolerance and forced conversions. They invoked other New Testament passages to conclude that the Jews knew the truth of Jesus' divinity but stubbornly refused to accept and act on it, and it was this deliberate and willful perfidiousness that inspired the knowing rejection of the divine messiah. The New Testament texts they singled out included the parable of the vineyard in the synoptic gospels; John 9:39–41, where Jesus tells Pharisees that they see and are not blind and are therefore "guilty"; and John 15:22–24, where Jesus says he has come and spoken, and Jews therefore have no excuse and are "guilty of sin." The Dominican St. Thomas Aquinas attributed more willfulness than ignorance to the Jews in committing deicide; they acted, he said, out of envy and hatred. More extreme were Duns Scotus and Nicholas of Lyra in stating that Jesus' divinity was manifest, that the Jews had the proof texts in their own scriptures, but that they acted willfully out of malice. Raymond Martini's *Dagger of Faith* (1278) concluded that the Jews were wicked and perverse in persisting knowingly in the error and lie of Judaism out of envy, depravity, and guile. He wanted to confront the Jews' "impiety and perfidy" to extinguish their "pertinacity and their impudent insanity"; driven "by the most impudent folly [they] go out of their minds" and persist in deliberate denial of the divine messiah, for "the devil undoubtedly . . . misled them and deprived them of a sense of understanding the truth."[63]

This paradigmatic shift in theology went far to nullify the Augustinian view that had prevailed for centuries, according to which it was providential for the messiah to suffer and that the Jews acted in ignorance. For the Dominican and Franciscan friars, and for some of the popes of the thirteenth and fourteenth centuries, the malignant Jews had not acted in ignorance but had willfully rejected and persecuted the savior; thus they forfeited the right of toleration. In the course of the twelfth century, Christian exegetes had discovered the Talmud and concluded, strangely, that that great work of biblical commentary and interpretation* had supplanted Hebrew scriptures in Jewish belief and behavior; thereupon they declared that Judaism was no longer biblical or holy but "of earth" and man-made, a heresy to be extirpated. The Talmud was, accordingly, repeatedly burned as heretical and anti-Christian, and forced baptisms and expulsions became the order of the day in waves of persecution and massacre that lasted to the end of the Middle Ages.[64] These developments flowed from the New Testament's accusation of deicide, the archcrime of a criminal people.

In all the centuries since, the image of the Jew as a deicide has continued to ignite base and cruel passions among Christians. The vile use that can always be made of the Passion narrative appeared in 1942 when the papal nuncio (it is not clear which or whether it was the nuncio or someone else) in Slovakia refused to intervene on behalf of Jewish children slated for deportation: "There is no innocent blood of Jewish children in the world. All Jewish blood is guilty. You have to die. This is the punishment that has been awaiting you because of that sin [of deicide]."[65] The nuncio's image of the Jews was not different from that of Hitler's propaganda minister, Joseph Goebbels, who specified in a 1944 press directive: "Stress: In the case of the Jews there are not merely a few criminals (as in every other people), but all of Jewry rose from criminal roots, and in its very nature it is criminal. The Jews are no people like

---

* There are two Talmuds, the Babylonian and Palestinian, containing the comments and discussions of the rabbis on the Mishnah from ca. 200 to ca. 500 C.E., the compilation of earlier Jewish legal tradition. Thus Talmudic or normative Judaism descends from the Mishnah, codified ca. 200 C.E, and the subsequent massive expositions.

other people, but a pseudo-people welded together by hereditary criminality. . . . The annihilation of Jewry is no loss to humanity, but just as useful as capital punishment or protective custody against other criminals."[66] Even after the Holocaust, in 1961, the Passion story could still impel an eminent Italian jurist to compare the trial in Jerusalem of the Nazi war criminal Adolf Eichmann to that of Jesus before the Sanhedrin. A Catholic magazine, also in Italy, condemned the proceedings against Eichmann, saying that "by not recognizing the divine innocence of Christ, [the Jews] must be considered as deicides even today. . . . [T]he unconscious and permanent authors of the crucifixion of Christ must be deprived of the possibility to judge those not belonging to their progeny. . . . Jews are totally lacking in morality"—a criminal people still, even after Auschwitz.[67] Kazimerz Switon, the self-appointed planter and protector of crosses at Auschwitz, is reported to have said when a law in May 1999 required their removal that "Our bishops [of Poland] have sold the cross to the sons of Satan, in other words, the Jews." Numerous such examples could be cited of how New Testament images of the Jew—the Jew as deicide, the Jew as satanic agent, the Jew as antichrist, the Jew as liar and deceiver, the Wandering Jew—persist down the centuries and resonate in contemporary antisemitism. It is all a reprise of the cycle of criminal guilt against the divine and of inevitable revenge and punishment for the perpetrators. The New Testament teaches a high morality and contains a message of salvation that continues to inspire. But judging from the role it has played in Jewish history, it needs also to be said, as the distinguished theologian and Holocaust survivor Eliezer Berkovits concluded, that "the New Testament is the most dangerous antisemitic tract in human history."[68]

## CHAPTER 2

# RITUAL MURDERERS

## CHRISTIAN BLOOD AND JEWISH MATZOHS

ON SEPTEMBER 22, 1928, IN THE SMALL upper New York state town of Massena, a four-year-old girl was reported missing by her parents. As neighbors and state troopers searched the woods, a rumor spread that Jews had murdered the child to drain her blood for a ritual related to the approaching Yom Kippur holiday, the most sacred of Jewish holy days. The accusation originated with one Albert Commas, a recent immigrant from Salonika, Greece, who operated a small café and ice cream parlor and had earlier voiced antisemitic feelings. Taking the accusation seriously, Mayor Hawes ordered trooper Mickey McCann to investigate. With the approval of Hawes and McCann, some zealous volunteer firemen, several with Ku Klux Klan affiliations, searched the basement of a Jewish-owned clothing store looking for incriminating evidence. The vigilantes then turned their lights on other stores owned by Jews that had closed for the night.

McCann called in Rabbi Berel Brennglass, the spiritual head of Massena's Jewish community, for questioning.

> McCann: "Can you give any information as to whether your people in the Old Country offer human sacrifices?"
>
> Rabbi Brennglass (indignant): "I am surprised that an officer of the United States, which is the most enlightened country in the world, should dare to ask such a foolish and ridiculous question."

McCann: "Was there ever a time when the Jewish people used human blood?"
Rabbi Brennglass: "No never, that is a slander against the entire Jewish people."
McCann: "Please don't think the idea originated with me; somebody else, a
     foreigner, impressed me with it."[1]

An enraged Brennglass demanded of McCann: "You will have to reveal
the name of the party who gave the information, that he should be taught he is
not in Poland or Rumania."[2] As the rabbi exited the station, his path was
blocked by a hostile crowd, which he addressed angrily: "What are you doing
here? Isn't it bad enough that a little girl has been lost? Why aren't you looking for her instead of standing around? You should be absolutely ashamed of
yourselves. By what nerve do you insinuate such things against your Jewish
neighbors? . . . Go home and pray to God that He'll forgive you for what you
are thinking."[3] The crowd drew back, allowing the rabbi to pass.

The child, who had lost her way in the woods and fallen asleep, was subsequently found. But, for some people, the Jews were still guilty. As the Jews
congregated on Yom Kippur eve, they were taunted by a mob that blocked
their path: "Scared you into returning the girl, didn't we." This time the blood
accusation did not escalate into wholesale arrests and massacre, as it had many
times in medieval Europe. After all, this was the United States and the twentieth century, not the "Dark Ages."*

Allegations of ritual murder, and the accompanying tortures, trials, burnings, massacres, expulsions, and pillaging of property, occurred frequently in
the Middle Ages. In modern times, enlightened people dismissed the charge of
Jewish ritual murder as so much nonsense, a lingering medieval fabrication
and superstition. Scholars conclusively refuted all the historical accusations. In
1912 a Catholic scholar, Abbé Elphège Vacandard, concluded that "not a single case [of ritual murder] has ever been historically established."[4] Nevertheless, as Hermann Strack, a German Christian theologian, wrote in 1892, "the
'blood-superstition' is even nowadays very wide-spread."[5] In a later edition of his
massive work on the blood libel, Strack noted that in March-April 1892, an

---

* Allegations of ritual murder were far fewer in the United States than in Europe and,
unlike in Europe, did not lead to violence against Jews. Nevertheless, there were incidents in Clayton, Pennsylvania (1913), Fall River and Pittsfield, Massachusetts (1919),
and Chicago (1919). In all four cases, the accusers were of Eastern European background; three were of Polish descent. In one instance, the hoax was staged by a priest.
See Abraham G. Duker, "Ritual Murder Accusations in the United States," *The Blood
Libel Legend: A Casebook in Anti-Semitic Folklore*, ed. Alan Dundes (Madison: University
of Wisconsin Press, 1991).

Italian newspaper, *Osservatore Cattolico*, published a series of forty-four articles entitled the "certainty of the ritual character of the murder practised by the Jews."[6] From 1881 to 1914 the Jesuit periodical *Civiltà Cattolica* printed numerous articles purporting to "prove" that Jews, in fulfillment of Talmudic law, murdered Christian children to obtain their blood for religious purposes. One article considered it "generally proved" that ritual murder "is a general law binding on the consciences of all Hebrews to make use of the blood of a Christian child . . . for the sanctification of their souls, and . . . to bring shame and disgrace to Christ and to Christianity." "It is in vain," said this extremely influential journal, "that the Jews seek to slough off the weight of the argument against them; the mystery has become known to all."[7] In 1896 Joseph Jacobs, an Anglo-Jewish folklorist, was "surprised to find in conversation with Christian friends, who have not the slightest taint of anti-Semitism, how general is the impression that there must be something at the bottom of all these charges [of ritual murder]."[8] Jacobs, a pioneer compiler of Jewish social statistics, established that Jewish children died, disappeared, and the like, at a much higher rate than gentile children, and he used his statistically supported insights to throw great doubt on the 1255 ritual murder of "Little St. Hugh of Lincoln" as well as the contemporary accusation in the Hungarian town of Tiszaezlar, 1882.[9] Thomas Masaryk (1850–1937), a distinguished Czech statesman related how his pious Catholic mother had solemnly warned her children that the Jews needed blood at Eastertime, a warning that was reinforced by the local priest. As a youngster, he avoided Jews lest he become a victim and furtively examined their hands for traces of blood. Later, contacts with Jews at secondary school and university led him to reject the libel and to come to the defense of a Czech Jew so accused.[10] Between 1887 and 1891 this deranged superstition produced twenty-two indictments of Jews in European lands. And in the early twentieth century, antisemitic agitators, particularly the Nazis, propagated and exploited the myth for political ends. Even after World War II, and the near annihilation of European Jewry, the libel did not die.

"Of all the accusations which fanaticism and ignorance have used as a weapon against Judaism, there is none which can be compared in terms of improbability and absurdity to that of ritual murder," wrote a Jewish scholar more than a hundred years ago.[11] The charge of ritual murder demonstrated the power and appeal of myths that disparaged and demonized the Jewish people. It showed the willingness, even eagerness, of Christians to believe any absurdity about Jews and to expect the worst of them. Belief in ritual sacrifice, an extreme form of Jew-hatred, exemplifies Gavin Langmuir's conception of "chimerical antisemitism." Rooted in feelings and sustained by deeply held convictions, this belief did not respond to logic or empirical evidence. Indeed, it distorted rational judgment and incited the basest feelings.

The Romans had persecuted and killed early Christians in the belief that they practiced ritual cannibalism, and in modern times Catholic missionaries in China, French officials in Madagascar, and Christian residents in Japan were also accused of murdering and devouring children. Christians, both ancient and modern, viewed these charges as horrendous lies. Yet to many medieval Christians—and even some modern ones—both simple folk and learned theologians, Jewish ritual murder was an unquestionable reality; having already convicted Jews of deicide and serving as Satan's agents, it seemed perfectly understandable that Jews would also thirst after the blood of pure Christian children. For Christians, ritual murder was another illustration that Jews, because of their grotesque religion, magical powers, and demonic ties, were driven to perform heinous acts. For these people, the will to believe evil of the Jews nullified the rules of evidence. At any rate, evidence could always be manufactured, twisted, or ignored, and confessions coerced through torture. Originating in the ancient world, the myth of ritual murder developed into a murderous force during the Middle Ages, despite the efforts of several popes and emperors to protect Jews from a grave injustice.

## THE MIDDLE AGES AND THE REFORMATION

The fable of Jewish ritual cannibalism originated during the reign of the Hellenistic king Antiochus IV Epiphanes, who ruled Syria from 175 to 163 B.C.E. Seeking to justify his desecration of the Jerusalem Temple in 168, Antiochus' Greek supporters vilified Jews. They fabricated a tale of Jews fattening up Greek captives and then killing and eating them, while swearing an oath of hostility to all Greeks. With some modifications, the story was repeated by Apion of Alexandria. But no Roman writer directed this charge against Jews, even though early Christians were frequently accused of ritual cannibalism.

During the Middle Ages, Christians leveled this accusation against Jews, a visibly alien group in a society dominated by the Christian worldview. In the popular mind, it was held that Jews, made bloodthirsty by the spilling of Christ's blood and abetted by demonic powers, kidnapped, tortured, and murdered Christians, particularly innocent children, to obtain blood needed for their religious rituals. Sometimes the Jews' detractors said that the child was sacrificed in a ceremony designed to replicate the crucifixion; other times they said that the Jews needed blood to heal the circumcision wound. Later, in the same irrational spirit, they asserted that Jews required Christian blood to make matzoh, the unleavened bread used during Passover.

These fables gained wide acceptance despite the facts that human sacrifice was unknown to the Jews and was considered a particularly abhorrent act, strictly prohibited by God. Demanding respect for all life, including that of animals, the Torah forbade the consuming of blood or meat with blood in it— "There I have said to the people of Israel, No person among you shall eat blood" (Leviticus 17:12)—a prohibition that was confirmed by rabbinical interpreters. To this day observant Jews eat only meat from which butchers have carefully drained the blood of the slaughtered animal; so abhorrent is blood to traditional Jews that they will not eat an egg with even a tiny speck of blood inside it. The defamed Jews would have identified with the cry of the Christian martyr Bibbas, who was tortured by the Romans for the same slander. "How would [Christians] eat children, when it is not even permitted them to eat the blood of . . . animals?"[12] Neither the Talmud nor any other authoritative work in the vast literature of Jewish law condones human sacrifice; no Christian theologian has ever cited such a passage, for none exists. And no trace of human sacrifices existed in Jewish rituals. (Ironically, while the consuming of blood is strictly forbidden to Jews, Christian tradition is very much concerned with the blood of Christ, and, in the Eucharist, Catholics ritually partake of his blood.) In the *Nizzahon Vetus* or *Old Book of Polemic*, written in the late thirteenth century, an anonymous Jewish scholar convincingly refuted the charge of ritual murder:

> The heretics [Christians] anger us by charging that we murder their children and consume the blood. Answer by telling them that no nation was as thoroughly warned against murder as we, and this warning includes the murder of Gentiles. . . . [The commandment] "Do not murder" refers to any man; thus we were warned against murdering Gentiles as well. . . . Moreover, we were also warned against blood more than any nation, for even when dealing with meat that has been slaughtered properly and is kosher, we salt it and rinse it and bother with it extensively in order to remove the blood. The fact is that you are concocting allegations against us in order to permit our murder.[13]

Although the charge is now seen as blatantly absurd (except in Muslim lands), it was readily believed because medieval Christians' perception of Jews as wicked deicides and black magicians who preyed on innocent Christians had become crucial to their outlook. Therefore, it seemed totally consistent with Jewish behavior that the people who had spilled Christ's blood would seek to reenact the crucifixion by torturing and draining the blood of an innocent child and that they would use that blood for some magical rite. Christians felt that by punishing these evil people in an appropriately cruel way, they were engaged in a salvific activity—avenging and honoring their Lord.

The first distinct case of ritual murder occurred in Norwich, England, in 1144, after William, a twelve-year-old apprentice boy, was found murdered. At the time, no one, including clergy, gave any special religious significance to William's death. Witnesses reported that somebody claiming to be the archdeacon's cook was the last person seen with the boy. Most likely this man, who was never seen again, was the murderer. Some four to six years after William's death, the monk Thomas of Monmouth went to Norwich. Reporting visions and attributing miracle-working powers to the deceased boy, Thomas claimed that the Jews had tortured William before Easter. The Jews, said Thomas, had stabbed William's head "with countless thorn-points and made the blood come horribly from the wounds they made. . . . And thus, . . . these enemies of the Christian name . . . fixed [him] to a cross in mocking of the Lord's passion. . . . [T]hey next laid their blood-stained hands upon the innocent victim, . . . fastened him upon the cross, [and] vied with one another in their efforts to make an end of him."[14] Thomas asserted further that the nature of William's wounds indicated a crucifixion, although no one had made the claim earlier.

Thomas' accusation rested largely on three sources. One was the deathbed confession of Aelward Ded, a prominent Christian, who claimed that four years earlier, he had stumbled on two Jews carrying William's body in a sack. Fearing discovery, the Jews bribed the sheriff, who then persuaded Aelward not to reveal what he had seen. A second source was the monk Theobold, who claimed that he had converted from Judaism in 1144 after hearing about the miracles worked through the martyred William. Theobold related to Thomas a fantastic tale. Every year in Narbonne, on the continent, Jewish leaders assembled to arrange the sacrifice of a Christian to show their contempt of Christ. It was decided by lot in which country the sacrifice would be carried out. The Jews in that land then selected, also by lot, the specific village or town where the victim would be apprehended. In 1144 they had chosen Norwich. Thomas also located a Christian woman who had worked in the house of Eleazar, a prosperous Jew who died in 1146, two years after William's murder. The servant told Thomas that through an opening in the door, she had seen William tied to a post. Fearing for her life, or at least her wages, she had told nobody at the time.

Initially, Thomas was not much believed, especially by a group of fellow monks and the prior who had been in Norwich at the time of the murder. Despite the lack of evidence or eyewitnesses, Thomas prevailed and Norwich became a famous shrine for pilgrims. An undistinguished monk with a rich fantasy life and intemperate religious zeal, Thomas had fabricated a myth that touched the raw nerves of his coreligionists, causing them to inflict terrible suffering on Jews for centuries.

After Norwich, allegations of sacrificial murder spread to several sites elsewhere in England. A contemporary account of a ritual murder allegation in Gloucester in 1168 illustrates the increasingly irrational and chimerical character of medieval antisemitism.

> The boy Harold, [found] dead in the Severn, is said to have been carried away secretly by Jews, in the opinion of many [they held him for three weeks until] the Jews of all England coming together . . . they tortured the lad placed before them with immense tortures. It is true that no Christian was present, or saw or heard the deed, nor have we found that anything was betrayed by any Jew [under interrogation. Nevertheless the boy's wounds having been examined] those tortures were believed or guessed to have been inflicted on him in that manner [of ritual crucifixion]. It was clear that they had made him a glorious martyr to Christ.[15]

Several other English communities replicated the charge against Jews: Bury St. Edmunds (1181), Bristol (1183), and Winchester (1192, 1225, 1235). In 1255 the Jews of Lincoln were accused of kidnapping "little Hugh" and carrying out a ritual crucifixion after first fattening him for ten days with white bread and milk. Threatened with death, a Jew named Copin confessed to the crime and declared that it was a Jewish practice to crucify a Christian child each year. Copin's "confession" did not save him from a cruel execution. Meanwhile, the pious and avaricious King Henry III saw an opportunity to revive a lucrative practice—plundering the property of Jews. Six months earlier Henry had sold his rights to fleece Jews to his brother, Richard of Cornwall; only by escheat from condemned criminals could Henry again appropriate Jewish wealth. For this reason—as well as a hatred for Jews—he gave his support to the incarceration of some ninety Jews in the Tower of London. In the subsequent trials, eighteen were condemned and hanged, and the king plundered their property. The others were pardoned, most likely after Henry was assured compensation in a deal made with his brother. "Little St. Hugh of Lincoln" is memorable as the first case of Jews being executed for ritual murder by a secular ruler.

The cathedral in Lincoln also benefited financially because miracles were attributed to Hugh's tomb, which, located in the cathedral, became a popular shrine for pilgrims. The shrine, Chaucer's "Prioress Tale," and popular folk ballads—one ballad still appeared in major folksong collections in the late nineteenth century—that described how Jews murdered "Little St. Hugh of Lincoln" and hid his body in a well perpetuated the myth. As late as the beginning of the twentieth century, a mock well was constructed in Jews' Court, Lincoln, to embellish the myth for tourists.* A popular school history textbook published in 1948 told students that there was evidence for Jewish ritual murder. In 1955 Anglican authorities dismantled the shrine at Lincoln Cathedral and incised a plaque with the confession that such "fictions cost many innocent Jews their lives."

Accusations of ritual murder also penetrated the continent with more terrible results for Jews than in England, for the massacre of Jews in the Rhineland in 1096, during the First Crusade, had established a murderous precedent. In 1171, at Blois in northern France, the local lord, prodded by a priest—very often in these cases the clergy would whip popular feeling into a frenzy—condemned more than thirty Jews to death by fire. In 1191, at Bray-sur-Seine, some hundred Jews perished. Following a blood accusation in Troyes in 1288, Franciscan and Dominican friars—who often were engaged in concerted attacks on Jews and Judaism—instigated the massacre of the town's Jews.

In Fulda, Germany, on Christmas 1235, the five sons of a miller died in a fire at home while the miller and his wife were at mass. The Jews of Fulda were accused of murdering the boys and siphoning off their blood into waxed bags for religious, magical, and medicinal purposes. An enraged mob murdered thirty-four Jews of the town. Not missing an opportunity, the bishop and provincial magnates robbed the Jews of their possessions. Emperor Frederick II intervened, appointing an international commission that included converted Jews; on the basis of its report, and probably also his own native skepticism, Frederick issued in 1236 a resounding condemnation of the myth of Jewish ritual cannibalism and prohibited clergy and laity from making such accusations. It reads pithily, and one would think unanswerably:

> Neither the Old nor the New Testament states that the Jews lust for human
> blood; on the contrary it is expressly stated in the Bible, in the law of

---

* In 1934, when Julius Streicher published a vicious account of the blood libel in Nazi Germany, the mayor of Lincoln and chancellor of the cathedral, after a meeting with the Jewish Historical Society of England, prepared a plaque and a new guidebook to the city that condemned the accusation.

Moses, and in . . . the Talmud, that they should not defile themselves with blood. Those to whom even the tasting of animal blood is prohibited surely cannot thirst for that of human beings, because of the horror of the thing; because it is forbidden by nature; because of the human tie that also binds the Jews to the Christians; because they would not willingly imperil their lives and property.[16]

In 1247 at Valréas, just across the German-French border, a two-year-old girl was found dead during Passion Week. Seeing an opportunity, the local lord despoiled Jews of their property and cast them into prison, where they were cruelly tortured—the genitals were torn off men and the breasts off women—into confessing that they had crucified the child to acquire its blood for ritual cannibalism. The unfortunate victims were then cut in two or burned alive. Several nobles in the same province (Vienne) and the bishop of Trois-Châteaux also imprisoned and robbed the Jews in their lands. The Jews of Vienne appealed to Pope Innocent IV, who denounced the condemnation and killing of Jews by those "covetous of their possessions or thirsting for their blood."[17] On July 5, 1247, at Lyons he addressed the bishops and archbishops of Germany: "Despite the fact that [Jewish law] prohibits the Jews, while solemnizing the Passover, to touch any dead body, nevertheless they are falsely accused that during this very festival they share the heart of a murdered child. . . . No matter where a dead body is found, their persecutors wickedly throw it up to them."[18] Four days later at Avignon, he enjoined all Christians not to accuse Jews "of using human blood in their religious rites, since in the Old Testament they are instructed not to use blood of any kind, let alone human blood."[19]

In 1272 Pope Gregory X elaborated on Innocent IV's pronouncement:

Since it happens occasionally that some Christians lose their Christian children, the Jews are accused by their enemies of secretly carrying off and killing these same Christian children and of making sacrifices of the heart and blood of these very children. It happens, too, that the parents of these children secretly hide these very children in order that they might be able to injure these Jews, and in order that they may be able to extort from them a certain amount of money by redeeming them from their straits.

And most falsely do these Christians claim that the Jews have secretly and furtively carried away their children and killed them, and that the Jews offer sacrifice from the heart and blood of these children, since their law in this matter precisely and expressly forbids Jews to sacrifice, eat, or drink the blood, or to eat the flesh of animals having claws. This has been demonstrated many times at our court by Jews converted to the Christian faith: nevertheless very many Jews are often seized and detained unjustly because of this.

We decree, therefore, that Christians need not be obeyed against Jews in a case or situation of this type, and we order that Jews seized under such a silly pretext be freed from imprisonment, and that they shall not be arrested henceforth on such a miserable pretext.[20]

But trapped by hate and seduced by myth, zealots ignored papal logic and appeals and continued with their bizarre accusations and murderous actions. Ritual murder had succeeded the Crusades as a pretext for the mass murder of Jews.

In the late thirteenth and early fourteenth centuries, a series of blood libels produced more horrors for the Jews of Germany. After enduring torture, Jews were broken on the wheel in Pforzheim and Weissenburg in 1270. In 1285 a mob burned down the synagogue together with one hundred eighty Jews who had sought refuge in it. In 1303 Jews were "slaughtered in heaps" in parts of Thuringia, and in 1305 they were put to death "in a horrible fashion" in Prague. In 1332 a house in Baden with some three hundred Jews crammed into it was set afire.

The case of "the good Werner" illustrates again the longevity of Christian bigotry and delusion. In 1286, at Oberwesel am Rhein, the body of fourteen-year-old Werner was found floating in the river. Christians believed that the corpse gave forth a halo and healed sick people; these "miracles," they concluded, were sufficient evidence that the boy had been slain by Jews. Between 1286 and 1289, persecuted Jews in Oberwesel and neighboring towns appealed to the emperor for help, which he provided. Nevertheless, in Catholic folklore "Saint Werner" was regarded as a victim of Jews; as late as 1889 a book for Catholic children described how the Jews hung Werner up by the legs and opened his veins to drain his blood.

It was common to view the Christian "victim" as a martyr and to enshrine the site of the martyrdom, which often brought considerable income to the nearby church. Two examples are illustrative. During Easter in 1475, in the northern Italian town of Trent, a two-and-a-half–year-old boy named Simon was reported missing by his parents. The boy's father, a tanner, accused the Jews of kidnapping his child. The authorities, with the support of the local bishop, rounded up the entire Jewish community.

Just prior to the incident, Bernardo da Feltre, a prominent Franciscan preacher, had gone to Trent and delivered sermons in which he vilified Jews and denounced Christians for having dealings with them. (It was a common occurrence for friars to preach Jew-hatred as they moved from town to town.) Friar Bernardo's sermons fanned the flames of Jew-hatred among the town's inhabitants, making them receptive to the accusation of ritual murder. Under brutal and repeated torture, several Jews "confessed," but when the torture subsided, some retracted their confessions. The enraged magistrates increased the torture's severity until the victims retracted their retractions. Fifteen Jews, including Samuel, the head of the community, were burned at the stake. "Blessed Simon of Trent" became the object of a pilgrimage cult, and by 1476, 129 "miracles" were attributed to the boy martyr.

Enthusiastically promoted by the Franciscans, the cult of "Little St. Simon" spread to many regions of northern Italy and southern Germany. The tale of bloodthirsty Jews torturing a nailed-down or tied-up Simon was widely transmitted through chronicles, pamphlets, poems, ballads, broadsheets, and woodcuts; by word of mouth in taverns; by priests from the pulpit; and by popular preachers who knew how to ignite the raw emotions of the common people. Taken as undisputed fact, the graphic description of Simon's suffering, reminiscent of Jesus' torment, fueled already deeply embedded anti-Jewish prejudices. Never doubting that Jews were lusting after Christian blood, medieval Christian persecutors of Jews saw themselves acting in self-defense against a satanic foe, an attitude shared by Nazi mass murderers.

In 1965, in the wake of the Second Vatican Council and after the trial records had been reexamined, the church abolished the cult by papal decree and the garish shrine to "Little Simon" was dismantled. The church declared the whole episode a lamentable fraud that had caused terrible suffering to many Jews.

In July 1462 three-year-old Andreas of Rinn, a village near Innsbruck, was found by his mother hanged on a tree after being sold by his uncle to traveling merchants. Years later it was claimed that the merchants were Jews. Andreas was declared a victim of ritual murder, and the church in which his bones were buried became a shrine and, with papal approval, a popular local cult in imitation of Simon of Trent developed. In 1961 Pope John XXIII ordered an end to Andreas' cult, but owing to local clerical reluctance and defiance by parishioners, the church could only erect, by "secret order," a plaque stating that the cycle of events centering on Andreas had "nothing to do with the Jewish people." Finally, in 1994, the bishop of Innsbruck, Reinhold Stecher, outlawed the cult and strongly condemned the blood-libel slander, declaring that there had never been a ritual murder martyrdom and that these false accusations have "caused innumerable Jews to lose their homes, possessions, freedom, health, and life."

Closely related to the libel of ritual murder was the accusation that Jews stole the communion wafer of the sacrament of the Eucharist and beat, stabbed, crucified, trampled underfoot, and cast into the fire this "body of Christ." Dating from the 1290s, this calumny followed from a long tradition that Jews, together with the Devil, defiled all the sacraments, holy water, blessed oils, crucifixes, biblical texts, indeed anything consecrated or sacred. Purloined and tortured hosts were said to cry out and to "bleed"; if, in truth, there was a discoloration, it was probably the result of a scarlet microbe that forms on stale bread kept in dark, damp places. Or, more likely, someone, often a priest, simply sprinkled blood on wafers to create a pretext for attacking Jews. By 1500 there had been over a hundred accusations of host desecration, with many shrines dedicated to such miracles, most in Germany and Austria where the charge flourished. The delusion produced massacres and expulsions. Over a period of six months in 1298, enraged Christians slaughtered between 20,000 and 100,000 Jews. From 1336 to 1338 the Armleder brothers led the ferocious *Judenschlachter* (Jew-slayers) band of pogromists across south Germany in a swath of murder and pillage, justifying it by invocations of mystical summonses to punish the Jews for deicide and host profanation. Because of these accusations of host desecration, the Bavarian village of Deggendorf became the scene of an annual antisemitic festival until 1992, when Bishop Manfred Muller of Regensburg corrected its history and erected a plaque acknowledging that the events of 1338 were simply the murder and robbery of Jews.

In 1370 clergy in Brussels accused local Jews of stealing and desecrating the Blessed Sacrament from St. Catherine's church. After some form of inquiry and with the sanction of Duke Wenceslas of Brabant, either six persons or six families were paraded in chains through the streets of Brussels and burned to ashes at the gates of the chapel of St. Catherine. Their property was confiscated by the duke and duchess of Brabant and the remaining Jews were banished. The townspeople believed that miracles had taken place—the mutilated wafers had bled—and a cult of the miraculous bleeding host speedily developed.

In 1402 Petrus de Alliaco, bishop of Cambrai and an eminent scholar, investigated the desecration and the miracle. He heard testimony from the local clergy, eager for the cult to flourish, that one Catherine, a Jewish convert, had discovered and reported the desecration. Rabbi Jonathan of Enghien, a wealthy financier and community leader, was said to have induced a Jewish convert to break into the chapel to steal hosts. Jonathan took the stolen hosts to the synagogue, where the congregants indulged in an orgy of stabbing and mutilation. Some time later Jonathan was killed—unexplained except as divine retribution—and his widow asked another female convert to get rid of the in-criminating hosts. The convert, however, decided to confess all to a local priest. The legend followed the typical pattern of these accusations modified somewhat by local conditions.

In 1435 the building that housed the synagogue where the desecration was presumed to have taken place was appropriated for a chapel dedicated to the Blessed Sacrament. A papal bull granted indulgences (spiritual gifts, such as remission of time to be spent in purgatory) for pilgrims to the sacred host. Shortly thereafter a second church claiming possession of the miraculous hosts constructed a chapel dedicated to the "Miraculous Sacrament"; again Pope Eugene IV granted indulgences. The papal bulls boosted the cult's popularity.

In 1451 and 1452 Cardinal Nicholas Cusanus, the prominent Renaissance scholar and legate of Pope Nicholas V, went to Brussels to investigate the cult. It is likely that he disproved the authenticity of the miraculous bleeding hosts (as he did in Germany), and he may even have nullified Eugene IV's bull. However, no stringent action could extinguish the cult or arrest the progress of the legend, so strong was the desire to confirm the belief that the commun-ion wafer was "the body of Christ."

Over the next two centuries chroniclers and poets embellished and styl-ized the tale in the telling and retelling. The cult's propagation was furthered in the sixteenth century by a series of stained glass windows in the chapel of the Blessed Sacrament in the church of St. Gudule, and by tapestries in the eighteenth century and stained glass windows in the nineteenth in the cathe-dral of St. Michael and St. Gudule that vividly depicted the whole story. In 1870 the quincentennial celebrations were drastically reduced, because by then the historicity of the desecration and the miracle was rejected by some scholars, notably Charles Poitvin. However, Catholic writers and clergy main-tained the authenticity of both, and the cult remained Brussels' most popular religious festival until World War II and the Holocaust.

As a consequence of the Second Vatican Council, in 1968 a bronze tablet was erected in the chapel of the Blessed Sacrament that sought to make histor-ical amends. It reads:

In 1370 the Jewish community of Brussels was accused of the profanation of the Holy Sacrament and punished for this act. On Good Friday 1370 Jews were supposed to have used daggers to stab communion wafers stolen from a chapel. These wafers were supposed to have bled.

In 1968, in the spirit of the Second Vatican Council, the authorities of the archdiocese of Mechelen-Brussels, in the light of historical research on this subject, drew attention to the tendentious character of these accusations and to the legendary nature of the "miracle."*

During the sixteenth century, two principal factors led to the suppression of ritual murder trials in German lands where accusations had been rife: intervention by Holy Roman emperors, who valued tax revenues and other financial assistance provided by Jews, and a general attack by theologians on the intrusion of magic and superstition—of which the Jew as a ritual murderer seemed an example—into Christian belief. Although charges continued to be made, beginning in the sixteenth century not a single Jew in German territory was executed for ritual murder. But in the popular mentality, the image of the Jew as a sinister child-murderer persisted, intensifying a deep, fanatical, chimerical hatred of Jews that would endure for centuries.

## SEVENTEENTH AND EIGHTEENTH CENTURIES: POLAND–LITHUANIA

In the seventeenth century, Poland-Lithuania became the nexus of blood-libel cases. "'Ritual Murder' did exist in reality," says the Polish folklorist Alina Cala, "but it was committed by Christians on Jews"; mobs did what they accused the Jews of.[21] In 1598, after a body of a Christian boy was discovered in a nearby swamp, the Tribunal of Lublin employed inquisitorial tortures on three Jews and then ordered their death by quartering. In that same year one Father Moyetzki wrote *Jewish Bestiality* in which he enumerated ritual murder trials that had taken place over the centuries, even inventing a few. In Lithuania a series of ritual murder trials fostered by fanatics led the king to issue decrees (1564 and 1566) prohibiting local authorities from instituting proceedings against Jews accused of ritual murder, because papal pronouncements had proven that these charges were without foundation.

The Polish clergy, particularly Jesuits, often inflamed antisemitic feeling, even to the point of manufacturing evidence. Thus in 1636 a Carmelite monk asserted that Jews had trapped him in a house and drained his blood while reciting weird incantations. On the basis of this fabrication, a Jew named Mordecai was systematically tortured and then executed. In the late 1630s two elderly Jews were executed for ritual murder and their mutilated corpses displayed on poles. Credulous Poles flocked to the local Bernardine church

---

* We are grateful to Professor Luc Dequeker of the University of Louvain for his assistance. His monograph on the subject appeared in 2000 in Dutch and French versions.

where the monks had placed the remains of the "martyr" and displayed pictures of his "terrible ordeal" at the hands of the Jews. Whatever the motives of the clergy, this was also criminal chicanery for the sake of "business" and inculcating prejudice.[22]

Increasingly, the Polish clergy took an active part not only in fomenting anti-Jewish hatred but also in engineering ritual murder cases. In Sandomierz a Jewish elder was found innocent of ritual murder—a Christian woman had hurled the corpse of her illegitimate child into his yard. But Father Stephen Zhukhovski pressed for a new trial, which employed inquisitorial tortures to wrest a confession, and the elderly Jew was executed. King Augustus II decreed the expulsion of all Jews from Sandomierz. Father Zhukhovski persuaded a converted Jew named Jan Sirafenovich to write a book proving that Jews use Christian blood for a variety of religious functions. The Jews challenged Sirafenovich to a public debate in Warsaw. He agreed but did not show up. Nevertheless, an antisemitic monk republished his work.

In the spring of 1747 a body was found in the melting snow in a rural village near Zaslav. At the same time a peasant reported that at a Jewish-owned inn, Jews were engaged in festivities. The conjunction of these two events led local Bernardine monks to conclude that the Jews were celebrating the ritual murder of the thawing body. In reality, the Jews were celebrating the circumcision of a new baby boy. S. M. Dubnow, the distinguished chronicler of Jewish history in Poland and Russia, spares us none of the Jews' anguish and the Christians' savagery: "The accused were all sentenced to a monstrous death, possible only among savages. Some of the accused were placed on an iron pole which slowly cut into their body and resulted in a slow tortuous death. The others were treated with equal cannibalism; their skin was taken off in strips, their hearts cut out, their hands and feet amputated and nailed to the gallows."[23]

A succession of ritual murder accusations produced more trials and executions in Poland. Terrorized Polish Jews dispatched a spokesman to Rome in 1758 to plead their case. Life had become intolerable for Polish Jews, their plea read, because "as soon as a dead body is found anywhere, at once the Jews of the neighboring localities are brought before the courts on these charges of murder."[24] The Jews' appeal was turned over to Cardinal Ganganelli, the future Pope Clement XIV. Ganganelli instructed the papal nuncio in Poland to submit detailed reports of ritual murder accusations and subsequent trials. After examining the evidence, the cardinal issued a report in 1759 declaring that "certain preconceptions, which are called prejudices by the enlightened people of the age,"[25] distort thinking. Not only is ritual murder contrary to

Jewish law, he declared, but why would Jews leave bodies exposed knowing full well that they would be blamed and persecuted? He pointed to another case where a child mutilated by her father was abandoned in a stable owned by Jews. Before the predictable ordeal for Jews took place, the little girl, who survived, implicated her father. Ganganelli then quoted a letter from Father Giovanni Battista de' Marini, a Franciscan: "[The Jews of Poland] are malignantly traduced with various calumnies . . . by the ignorant populace and by certain persons hostile to them through private malice; in particular on the charge that they are accustomed to use the blood of Christians in their rite of Unleavened Bread."[26] In 1763 the papal nuncio told the king's chief minister that "the Holy See, having investigated all the foundations of this aberration, according to which the Jews need human blood for the preparation of their unleavened bread . . . [concluded that] there is no evidence whatsoever testifying to the correctness of that prejudice." Yet Poland remained the land where "the Jewish *matza* [is believed to be] impossible without Christian blood."[27]

Ganganelli's condemnation of ritual murder accusations represented an enlightened viewpoint. Nevertheless, even the enlightened cardinal accepted the truth of two cases of child martyrdom—Andreas of Rinn and Simon of Trent—although he considered these to be isolated events. He thought they were not cases of ritual murder but simply crimes committed by Jews out of anger or hate, and did not constitute a Jewish practice.*

## THE NINETEENTH CENTURY

During the nineteenth century, ritual murder trials proliferated in Russia; the accusation had migrated eastward from Russia's Polish territories. In 1817 Count Gulitzin, minister of ecclesiastical affairs, unnerved by a recent series of blood libels that were exposed as lies and fearing religious fanaticism, warned governors not to tolerate blood accusations:

> In view of the fact that in several provinces acquired from Poland [in the partitions of 1772, 1793, and 1795], cases still occur in which the Jews are falsely accused of murdering Christian children for the alleged purpose of obtaining blood, his Imperial Majesty [Alexander I], taking into consideration that similar

---

* There were other exceptions to the general acceptance of the blood libel. In 1705 the municipal government in Venice ordered the removal of a painting exhibited on the famous Rialto bridge depicting Jews killing a child, and in England, in 1734, the *Rex v. Osborne* case made accusations of ritual murder punishable as "seditious libel."

accusations on previous numerous occasions have been refuted by impartial investigations, . . . has been graciously pleased to convey to those at the head of the governments his Sovereign will: that henceforward the Jews shall not be charged with murdering Christian children without any evidence and purely as a result of the superstitious belief that they are in need of Christian blood.[28]

For several years there was quiet, but in 1823, when the body of a three-year-old boy covered with stab wounds was found in a swamp outside the town of Velizh, two women, one a beggar and prostitute, the other mentally deficient, fabricated a tale of ritual murder. Responding to a petition by the prostitute, Terentyeva, Tsar Alexander ordered Khovanski, the governor-general of the region, to investigate. The antisemitic Khovanski, together with an aide, helped Terentyeva construct a fable that included the accusations that the blood of the tortured boy was collected for smearing the eyes of the newborn, since "the Jews are always born blind,"[29] and for preparing the unleavened bread for Passover. Forty-two Jews were arrested, chained, and tortured. When Khovanski reported to St. Petersburg that the boy was murdered for religious reasons, Tsar Nicholas I, who had recently ascended the throne, ordered the closing of Jewish synagogues in Velizh. But as the commission of inquiry continued to fabricate more bizarre tales of Jewish religious crimes, the tsar became suspicious. Finally, Mordvinov, a member of the Council of State, who was indignant over this abuse of justice, carefully examined the evidence and concluded that Khovanski and his aide had misled the government. The accused Jews, who had been sent to Siberia in 1831—several had already died—were released in 1835, and the synagogues, which had been sealed for nine years, were allowed to reopen. Terentyeva and two female cohorts were exiled to Siberia. Nicholas I now believed that although Jews in common did not engage in ritual murder, "there probably exist fanatics or sectarians who consider Christian blood necessary for their rites."[30]

In 1853 in the city of Saratov, Jews were again libeled, but a commission of inquiry, unable to find evidence, ordered the release of the incriminated Jews. However, the Council of State revived the charge and in 1860 three Jews were sentenced to penal servitude. Two committed suicide in prison and one was released in 1867 by order of Tsar Alexander II. In 1878, in the Caucasus, and in 1902, in Vilna, brilliant presentations by defense counsels produced not-guilty verdicts. In 1903, in Dubossary, the discovery of the mutilated body of a peasant boy—it was later learned that the crime was committed by his uncle—led the local newspaper to accuse the Jews of ritual murder and to call for their massacre. The pogrom was stifled by Jewish self-defense. In 1903, in

Ukraine, the suicide of a Christian servant girl on the eve of Easter was viewed as another case of ritual murder and helped to ignite the brutal Kishinev pogrom, which left hundreds of Jews dead or maimed. (The Beilis affair of 1911, the most famous case of ritual murder in Russia, is discussed below.)

A distressing feature of ritual murder cases in Russia and elsewhere was the willingness of scholars and clergy to provide the prosecution with "evidence" that religious murder was central to Jewish ritual. Often these authorities turned out to be frauds. Thus Hippolyte Lutostanski, a defrocked Roman Catholic priest (embezzlement, rape, and libel were among his crimes) who had joined the Greek Orthodox church, wrote *Concerning the Use of Christian Blood by the Jews* (1876). The book was presented to the tsar and was widely distributed by the secret police. In 1879 Lutostanski, who knew no Hebrew, produced another scurrilous work, *The Talmud and the Jews*. A Jewish scholar showed that Lutostanski had forged quotations and challenged him to a public disputation; the Jew-baiter declined.

Belief in Jewish ritual murder also penetrated the eastern Mediterranean: There were cases in Aleppo (1810), Beirut (1824), Antioch (1826), Hama (1829), Tripoli (1834), Jerusalem (1838), Rhodes (1840), Damascus (1840), Marmora (1843), Smyrna (1864), and Corfu (1894). The Damascus case had international repercussions.

The disappearance in Damascus of a Capuchin friar, Thomas, and his Muslim servant, prompted Syrian Capuchins to accuse the Jews of murdering Thomas to use his blood for Passover rituals. (Most likely Father Thomas, who was involved in shady dealings, was killed by a Muslim who, after a violent quarrel, was heard to have threatened the friar's life.) The Muslim authorities, with the support of the French consul—Syrian Catholics were under French protection—arrested several Jews. A young Jewish barber, after being tortured and threatened with death, told the authorities to investigate the city's leading Jews, several of whom were arrested. Another young Jew, who sold tobacco in a market far from the Jewish quarter where Father Thomas was purported to have been murdered, reported to the police that he had seen Thomas and his servant leaving the city on the date in question. Since this evidence contradicted the accusation that Thomas was seized and victimized in the Jewish quarter, the authorities tried to get the young man to confess that Jews involved in the crime had invented this story and coached him in how to tell it. He was flogged unmercifully—some five thousand lashes, said one usually reliable source—and soon died. As part of their investigation, the police incarcerated some sixty Jewish boys from five to twelve years of age and threatened to have them killed if their mothers did not reveal the details of Father Thomas' ritual sacrifice. For several weeks the children were held in two rooms and given a diet of bread and water.

After enduring extreme torture, three arrested Jews died without "confessing" anything. At least seven others, maddened by torture and fearful of death, agreed to testify that they had knowledge of the crime. One prisoner, after innumerable floggings and having the flesh torn off his feet, begged to become a Muslim and said that he had given the bottle containing Father Thomas' blood to the chief rabbi. When some bones turned up in the Jewish quarter, the Capuchins claimed they were Thomas' remains and buried them. The inscription on the tombstone described Thomas as a saint who was murdered by Jews.

The authorities declared that the case had been solved: Father Thomas was a victim of Jewish religious fanaticism, a blood ritual enjoined upon Jews by the Talmud. The accusation was widely believed by Christians and Muslims in Damascus and by foreign emissaries stationed in the region. Thus the American vice-consul in Beirut reported that "a most barbarous secret for a long time suspected in the Jewish nation . . . at last came to light in . . . Damascus, that of serving themselves of Christian blood in their unleavened bread at Easter, a secret which in these 1840 years must have made many unfortunate victims. . . . The French consul is seizing their religious books with the hope of clearing that abominable secret."[31] Leading Syrian bishops informed Pope Gregory XVI that "many Jews . . . cut his [Father Thomas'] throat in such a way as to be able to get all his blood. They bashed his head with hammers as one does to cattle . . . then cut him to pieces."[32] Pope Gregory actively supported the charges from behind the scenes—in his words, "with the least publicity and privately"—for now in the papal view ritual murder was enjoined upon Jews by the Talmud.[33] And, as in the Middle Ages, theologians argued learnedly but ignorantly that human sacrifice, supposedly practiced by the ancient Hebrews, still survived.

Newspapers often published uncritical accounts of the event, accepting at face value what were purported to be the facts of the case. Thus a German paper reported that Father Thomas had been "locked up in the cellar of a rich Jew . . . and there ceremoniously slaughtered by a Jewish butcher; his blood was secretly divided among the fanatical Jews."[34] The paper went on to praise the French consul and the local authorities for their zealous investigation. While liberal newspapers, particularly in Protestant lands, did not push the issue and even expressed doubts about the charges, ultra-Catholic papers presumed the worst of the Jews. They regarded the case to be of great importance, for, in their eyes, it was further evidence that the persecution suffered by the Jews during the Catholic Middle Ages was deserved; it was simply the result of their barbarous practices and fossil religion. Thus *Univers*, a French Catholic paper, declared: "The affair . . . is of incontestable importance. It has recalled the accusations so often repeated by our forefathers against the Jewish population dispersed among them, avid for their money . . . and at times stained with their blood. This is what explains those persecutions that some try to turn into a historical scandal, but which, in fact, only constituted legitimate self-defense."[35] In the decades after the Damascus case, the *Univers* continued to engage in vociferous attacks on the Jewish people.

In Britain the *Tablet*, a new Catholic weekly that dissented from prevailing Catholic opinion, attacked the *Univers* for lending "its countenance to those monstrous charges" and chided it for ignoring the fact that confessions had been exacted by torture. It drew a compelling comparison: "We confess that we feel warmly on this matter. We too know what it is to be a minority. . . . Men now alive can remember that, in the cities of this very empire, poor deluded Protestants believed that on Good Friday innocent children were murdered for the purpose of Catholic worship. . . . Is it for us to be the ready receivers, on no evidence at all, of wholesale calumnies against others?"[36]

Appeals from several Western governments and a delegation of Jews, headed by Adolphe Crémieux, a prominent French lawyer, and Sir Moses Montefiore, an English dignitary, which met with Muslim authorities in Cairo and Constantinople led to the release of the imprisoned Jews. The European Catholic press expressed outrage at the Jews' release, and for many decades the Catholics of Damascus told tourists the tale of "poor saint Thomas," a victim of Jewish inhumanity, and how the plotting of powerful foreign Jews enabled his murderers to escape justice.

In the nineteenth century the Habsburg Empire witnessed several accusations of ritual murder. Between 1829 and 1844, three separate instances of missing children produced blood libels. In two instances the children were murdered by their mothers; in the third, the young boy fled mistreatment. On April 1, 1882, a fourteen-year-old girl disappeared in the small Hungarian town of Tiszaeszlar. (It was later learned that she had committed suicide by drowning.) Rumors circulated that she was a victim of ritual murder. Among the accusers were town officials and the local priest; antisemitic deputies in the Hungarian parliament supported the charge. In the trial held the following year, the fifteen accused Jews were exonerated, but attacks on Jews that followed the acquittal compelled the government to proclaim a state of emergency.

Among those testifying for the prosecution was August Rohling, an unfrocked priest. In 1871 Rohling had published *Der Talmudjude* (The Talmud

Jew), an ignorant, vicious attack on the Talmud replete with forgeries. Most of Rohling's "evidence" was lifted from Andreas Eisenmenger's *Judaism Discovered*, a notorious antisemitic attack published in 1700 that had long been thoroughly discredited. In 1876, on the basis of *The Talmud Jew*, which had wide popular appeal, Rohling was appointed professor of Bible Studies and the Old Testament at the German University of Prague. Rohling, who continued to produce antisemitic writings, declared his willingness to testify at any ritual murder trials.

During the trial at Tiszaeszlar, Joseph Samuel Bloch, a young and learned rabbi, attacked Rohling in the press, exposing his ignorance of Jewish law and calling him both a liar and a perjurer. Bloch accused Rohling of fabricating evidence and questioned his competence in Hebrew, which Rohling claimed to possess but in truth did not have. With his reputation at stake, Rohling was compelled to sue Bloch for libel; he also declared that he could prove that ritual murder was prescribed by the Jewish religion. Bloch, who had enlisted the aid of prominent Christian scholars, was prepared to destroy Rohling's reputation. Shortly before the trial was to begin, Rohling withdrew his suit, exposing himself as a fraud. The ministry of education forced him to surrender his academic chair. Nevertheless, *Der Talmudjude*, translated into several languages and published in several editions, continued to provide ammunition for antisemites, including the Nazis and Islamists.

The 1890s saw a rash of ritual murder accusations, including ones in Hungary, the Rhineland, Prussia, Romania, Bohemia, Corfu, and France. After the discovery of a murdered child in the department of Vienne, a French clerical newspaper asserted confidently: "We find ourselves in the presence of a ritual murder achieved by the Jews; everything proves it."[37] It was later learned that the child was murdered by her unmarried mother.

A particularly significant case occurred in Bohemia, the Czech homeland; like the Dreyfus affair that was raging in France at the time, it pitted right-wing nationalists, clerics, and antisemites against liberal forces. On April 1, 1899, the body of nineteen-year-old Anezka Hruzova, a dressmaker, was found near the town of Polna. A rumor started and was quickly circulated by the antisemitic press that the girl was a victim of ritual murder. Leopold Hilsner, a twenty-two-year-old Jew, an idler of ill repute who sponged off his widowed mother, was arrested and put on trial. (The murder was never satisfactorily explained, but suspicion later fell on Hruzova's brother.)

The prosecution did not introduce the ritual murder charge; it was made at the trial by Dr. Karl Baxa, an extreme Czech nationalist who represented the victim's mother. In his summation, Baxa charged: "Disgusting people,

people of another race, people who acted like animals, have murdered a virtuous Christian girl so that they could use her blood."[38] Gripped by a persistent primitive superstition, the jury found Hilsner guilty and sentenced him to death. The liberal press condemned the verdict while Czech and Viennese antisemites applauded and anti-Jewish riots broke out in several Bohemian towns.

Enraged by Baxa's demagoguery and the jury's credulousness, Professor Thomas G. Masaryk, a staunch defender of Enlightenment ideals, denounced fellow Czechs for "blindly believ[ing] anything that incriminates the Jews."[39] He entered the case because he believed that "belief in ritual murder casts disgrace on the Czech people."[40] He did not want the clerical antisemitism that pervaded Vienna to distort the outlook of his own people. Such ignorance, he thought, would be a defeat for enlightenment and humanity, which he envisaged as the core ideals of the Czech nation. He denounced Baxa for relying on Rohling's lies, "which had been disproved ages ago," and for poisoning the Czech nation "with base, incongruent lies and ignorance. . . . Shame!"[41] Masaryk was joined by Social Democrats who shared his aversion to right-wing chauvinism and clericalism. After examining the evidence, Masaryk ruled out any draining of the murdered woman's blood—the whole purpose of ritual murder—a conclusion in which he was supported by the medical faculty of Prague's Czech University. Extreme nationalists attacked Masaryk for betraying the Czech people; heckled at the university by colleagues and students, including his own, he was placed on compulsory leave.

Pressure from Masaryk and Social Democrats compelled the Court of Appeals to order a retrial. In the second trial, Hilsner was also charged with murdering a woman who had been missing since July 1898, because the arrangement of the branches covering her recently discovered corpse was similar to the way Hruzova's body had been covered. Hilsner was again convicted and the verdict was again appealed. Although the appeals court ruled against Hilsner, it stated that the girl was murdered for sexual reasons, implying that no ritual murder had taken place. Hilsner remained in jail until Emperor Charles I, who succeeded to the throne in 1916, released him.

The Hilsner affair demonstrated in a frightening way the persistent appeal and power of the ritual murder myth. Of all central and eastern European peoples, the Czechs were most distinguished by a liberal and humanist tradition. Yet even these ideals could not dispel a primitive superstition fraught with hate. But the affair, like the Dreyfus case, also showed that there were Christians of conscience and reason ready to resist antisemitic calumnies.

The most famous ritual murder trial in modern times, one that attracted worldwide attention, took place in Ukraine in the autumn of 1913. Two and a half years earlier the beaten and mutilated body of thirteen-year-old Andrei Yuschinsky was found in a cave on the outskirts of Kiev. By mutilating the boy, his murderers hoped to make it appear he was a victim of ritual sacrifice. Reactionary and rabidly antisemitic forces, particularly the Union of the Russian People, immediately accused the Jews of killing the boy for his blood. At the funeral, the Union's shock troops, the Black Hundreds, distributed leaflets proclaiming "The Yids [a derogatory Russian term for Jews] have tortured Andryusha to death! Every year before their Passover, they torture to death several dozens of Christian children in order to get their blood to mix with their matzohs. They do this in commemoration of our Saviour, whom they tortured to death on the Cross. Russians! if your children are dear to you, beat up the Yids! Beat them up until there is not a single Yid left in Russia. . . . Avenge the . . . martyr! It is time! It is time!"[42] Similar leaflets had been circulated before the brutal Kishinev pogrom in 1903.

Evidence gathered by the police pointed to a gang of thieves associated with Vera Cheberyak, a known criminal, as the murderers. Apparently the boy had threatened to tell the police what he knew about the gang's criminal activities. Nevertheless, pressured by the radical Right and his own prejudices, the minister of justice urged local officials to treat the case as ritual murder and to incriminate a Jew. The authorities arrested Mendel Beilis, a dispatcher at a brick factory owned by a Jew.

Beilis was an unlikely choice to depict Jewish fiendishness. He was an ex-soldier who worked long hours to provide for his wife and five children, and was on excellent terms with the Russian employees at the factory and with the local priest, who was himself a member of the Union of the Russian People. During the pogroms of 1905 and 1906 in Kiev, members of the Union informed Beilis that no harm would come to him or his family. Although he came from a pious family and could recite traditional prayers, he had little Jewish learning and worked on the Sabbath and holy days, except for Rosh Hashanah and Yom Kippur. It would be no simple affair for the authorities to prove that this well-liked and only marginally observant Jew was driven by religious fanaticism to kill a Christian boy to drain his blood for the Passover matzoh.

High officials within the government, meeting no resistance from Tsar Nicholas II, who believed that Jews did indeed practice ritual murder, sought a trial to use the Jews, whom they hated anyway, as scapegoats for the tsarist regime's defeat in the Russo-Japanese War of 1904 to 1905 and the revolutionary upheaval that followed after it. These officials hoped that anti-Jewish agitation would deflect attention away from the misdeeds and failures of autocracy and gain support for the regime in its struggle against liberalism and revolutionary ferment. These conspirators had the support of reactionary monarchist, chauvinist, clerical, and antisemitic elements in Russian society, those elements that had promoted pogroms and had disseminated a wide range of antisemitic literature. Between 1905 and 1916 over fourteen million copies of some three thousand antisemitic works, including the infamous forgery, *Protocols of the Learned Elders of Zion* (see chapter 3), were printed and distributed in Russia. For their part, liberals, including many Jews both in Russia and abroad, sought to exploit the Beilis case to discredit tsarism.

The conspirators arranged to eliminate the intelligentsia from the jury and to stack it with members of the Union of the Russian People—seven known Union members sat on the jury. To provide scientific evidence that Andrei was murdered for a religious purpose, they bribed with four thousand rubles a professor of forensic medicine to attest that "The injuries were inflicted with the intention of obtaining as much blood as possible for some purpose."[43] Unable to find a Russian Orthodox theologian to confirm ritual murder practices among Jews, the conspirators produced an obscure Catholic priest, Justin Pranaitis, as a religious authority. In 1893 Pranaitis had published a pamphlet claiming to prove that ritual murder was an integral part of the Jewish faith. The prosecutors, all of whom had contempt for Jews, had absorbed and been influenced by the vast array of Russian antisemitic literature—one had himself written several antisemitic pamphlets. They tried to inflame the jury with Jew-hatred.

Beilis was ably defended by some of Russia's most outstanding jurists, both Jews and non-Jews, who volunteered their services. And prominent figures in the arts, sciences, politics, and religion in several lands, including Russia, signed protest manifestoes deploring the whole affair. Thus the British protest declared: "The question is one of humanity, civilisation, and truth. The 'Blood Accusation' is a relic of the days of Witchcraft and Black Magic, a cruel and utterly baseless libel on Judaism, an insult to Western culture and a dishonour to the Churches in whose name it has been falsely formulated by ignorant fanatics."[44]

The prosecution's case rested almost totally on the account of Vera Cheberyak's son, Zhenya, who had told the police that when he was playing with Andrei and other children near the factory, a black-bearded man seized Andrei. When questioned by the police, Kazimir Shachovsky, a lamplighter, declared that some three days after Andrei's disappearance, Zhenya had told him about the bearded man who had frightened his playmates and dragged Andrei toward the factory. Kazimir's wife, Yuliana, added that an acquaintance of hers had informed her that she had seen Andrei being grabbed by Mendel Beilis.

The prosecution's case, flimsy to begin with, collapsed at the trial. Young Zhenya, the key witness, died shortly after Andrei's murder—it was believed that his mother poisoned him, fearing that he would incriminate her in Andrei's death. Under cross-examination, the Shachovskys told a different story—they had been plied with vodka and coached by detectives to incriminate Beilis. Medical experts demolished the prosecution's charge that the boy had been murdered for his blood by someone trained in ritual slaughter. As V. A. Maklakov, the most outstanding member of the defense team, noted in his summation: "Members of the jury, if this was a ritual murder, witnessed by a *tzadik* [a holy man], with special containers on hand to accumulate the precious liquid, the boy would have been undressed and his hands tied prior to the assault. What actually happened was that the blood flowed freely, soaking up his shirt and jacket, the blows were administered indiscriminately with a dull instrument totally unsuitable for what was described as a premeditated, carefully planned religious exercise."[45]

Nor did Pranaitis help the prosecution. For two days he harangued the jury with an antisemitic diatribe. Judaism prescribed a "dogma of blood," he said. By perpetrating such a crime, Jews believe they are offering a sacrifice to God. The command to slay Christian children for their blood, declared Pranaitis, is known only to learned Jews who secretly pass it on to one of their sons. The victim's blood, he said, was mixed with flour to make matzohs that were consumed on Passover. The defense feared that the priest's imposing appearance, oratorical skill, and seeming knowledge of Jewish beliefs would sway the untutored peasants on the jury. Pranaitis asserted that his knowledge of Jewish wickedness stemmed from his deep study of the Talmud. But a skillful cross-examination destroyed his credibility. Pranaitis' replies to elementary questions showed utter ignorance of the Talmud. It was as if someone claiming to be an authority on American history had never heard of the Declaration of Independence and thought that Pearl Harbor was a woman. The priest was exposed as a fraud.

The jury of simple folk found Beilis not guilty of entering "into collusion with others who have not been discovered . . . in a premeditated plan, prompted by religious fanaticism, to murder the boy Andrei Yushchinsky."[46] The courtroom, which included many foreign observers, broke into applause; some wept. Jew and gentile openly embraced in the streets. Thousands of people, many of them gentiles, visited Beilis at home, and thousands more sent letters and telegrams. A Russian Orthodox priest, said Beilis, entered his house, "fell on his knees, made the sign of the cross, and wept like a child. 'Mr. Beilis,' he said after a while, 'you know that my action puts me in some danger. My conscience would not let me do otherwise. I came to ask forgiveness in the name of my people.' He kissed my hand."[47] Beilis received many letters of sympathy, but the radical Right persisted in maintaining his guilt, and their ominous threats to him and his family were one reason why he left the country. And antisemites in other lands remained unconvinced. In an article entitled "Ritual Murder among the Jews," published in the respectable *Catholic Bulletin and Book Review* (Dublin), the writer praised the "calm, deliberate, disinterested, and expert testimony [for the prosecution] of highly conscientious men" and attributed the verdict to "world-wide . . . powerful and unscrupulous intimidation" engaged in by Jewish communities.[48]

As a rule, the European Catholic press, including several publications with close ties to the Vatican, presented ritual murder as an uncontestable fact and a religious obligation required by the Jewish faith. In numerous articles that amounted to a campaign, they propagated, often in the crudest terms, this calumny that several medieval popes had condemned. Thus in 1895 the Jesuit journal *Civiltà Cattolica* published "Jewish Morality and the Mystery of Blood," by the Jesuit priest Saverio Rondina, who wrote: "All the veils have now been lifted, and the Judaic secret has been revealed in all its horrors. Up until now, we have known from centuries-long experience that the Jew sucked Christian blood, but for the most part people did not realize that this was something they did out of principle, in obedience to their law."[49] This revival and propagation of the blood libel met no resistance from popes and leading prelates, who generally believed in the truth of the accusation. At the end of the nineteenth century, three eminent English Catholics, led by the Cardinal-Archbishop of Westminster, petitioned Pope Leo XIII to condemn ritual murder as some of his medieval predecessors had done; the formal rejection explained that "ritual murder is a historical certainty," that the Vatican could not act in behalf of "a few dupes in England," to do so would cause "scandal."[50] Similar inaction on the part of the Vatican prevailed at the time of the Beilis case.

## POSTSCRIPT

After the Beilis case there were still outbreaks of the ancient calumny. In 1927 and 1928 ritual murder charges were leveled against Jews in Zaklikow, Poland; Petrovo Selo, Yugoslavia; Cologne, Germany; and Salonika, Greece. In its attempt to demonize the Jewish people, *Der Stürmer*, the Nazi weekly paper edited by Julius Streicher, repeated and embellished the legend—a good illustration of traditional Christian antisemitism merging with Nazi racial antisemitism. Between 1923 and 1933 nineteen issues of *Der Stürmer* featured articles on the subject. The paper often listed names of missing children and concluded that they were undoubtedly kidnapped by Jews, who kept them chained in dungeons while they sharpened their torture instruments in preparation for their Passover slaughter. A notorious special issue of May 1, 1934, was devoted entirely to the theme. Again we have hideous-looking Jews enticing, torturing, and butchering children and then draining their blood and mixing it with the matzohs and wine. As the Jews partake of this blood, they pray that all gentiles will speedily die. All of this is enjoined upon Jews by the Talmud. In protest, a Jewish leader wired Reich bishop Ludwig Müller (and Hitler): "Before God and humanity, we raise our voice in solemn protest against this unheard-of profanation of our faith. We are convinced that the deep outrage that we are feeling is shared by every Christian."[51] Bishop Müller did not reply.

Even Auschwitz did not bring an end to the libel. A particularly abhorrent incident occurred on July 4, 1946, just fourteen months after the end of World War II and the almost total extermination of Poland's Jews. In Kielce Poles, stirred by allegations that Jews were abducting Christian children for their blood, turned into a frenzied mob; they shot, axed, and clubbed to death forty-two Jews, including children, and wounded many more. Among the unidentified dead was a survivor of Auschwitz-Birkenau concentration camp, whose arm bore the number B 2969 tattooed by the Nazis.

In the Soviet Union a government-sponsored antisemitic and anti-Zionist campaign in the early 1960s led some official newspapers in remote regions of the country to reproduce the charge. With the liberation from communism and the reemergence of a neofascist and antisemitic nationalism, the allegation resurfaced in eastern Europe. In 1996 a Romanian weekly with national circulation accused Israelis of smuggling babies out of Romania for "organ transplants and blood. . . . As is well known, Jewish unleavened bread requires fresh, kosher Christian blood."[52] In Belarus the Orthodox Church recently resumed its commemoration of St. Gabriel, a child said to have been murdered by Jews to obtain blood for matzoh, and in 1997 a "documentary" on the subject broadcast on Belarus state television concluded that members of a fanatical Jewish sect murdered the child.

Arab states have employed the calumny as seemingly effective propaganda in their struggle against Israel. In 1972 King Faisal of Saudi Arabia asserted that "while I was in Paris on a visit, the police discovered five murdered children.

Their blood had been drained, and it turned out that some Jews had murdered them in order to take their blood and mix it with the bread they eat on that day."[53] In *The Matza of Zion* (1985), Mustafa Tlas, defense minister and deputy prime minister of Syria, who had been a doctoral candidate at the Sorbonne, propagated and embellished the legend. Referring to the Damascus incident of 1840, Tlas said: "The investigators uncovered not just the objective facts of the crime but also the religious motive behind it. . . . From that moment on every mother was warning her child: 'Do not stray far from home. The Jew may come by and put you in his sack to kill you and suck your blood for the matza of Zion.'"[54]

In the past few years, delegates from Arab countries have said at two UN forums that the recently published documents of the Damascus case prove that Jews engage in ritual murder. In November 1998, an Egyptian newspaper cited what it called "the important book," *The Jews in Egypt in the Modern Era* (1991), which describes how "the Jews carry out human sacrifices to please their blood-thirsty God," and claimed that the Talmud states: "We have . . . ways of satisfying our God . . . using matzoh mixed with human blood." The article, written by Dr. Fahmi Abd al-Salaam, describes in graphic ways how "rabbis slaughter a person prior to his being sacrificed to God" and mix the blood with flour when making matzoh, which is then devoured "with an appetite commensurate with their hatred for Jesus and Christians." The author then concludes: "I had thought that the matter of Jewish matzoh mixed with blood was a fabrication but the shocking thing is that it is a fact, a fact which has been proved in some 400 cases which have become known, while the number of cases that have not been revealed is far higher."[55] Reportedly an Egyptian producer is making a movie of the book. Not to be outdone, the Saudi government daily *Al-Riyadh* published an article by Dr. Umayma Ahmad Al-Jalahma of King Faysal University, on how "Jews Use Teenagers' Blood for 'Purim' Pastries." He describes "how the victims' blood is spilled. For this, a needle-studded barrel is used; this is a kind of barrel, about the size of the human body, with extremely sharp needles set in it on all sides, [which] pierce the victim's body. . . . [A]nd the victim's blood drips from him very slowly [and he] suffers dreadful torment—torment that affords the Jewish vampires great delight." This crude calumniation, plagiarized as so often from centuries-old European sources, caused an uproar abroad that induced the Saudi government to publish a retraction in English for foreign consumption, but none such in Arabic for the enlightenment of Muslims.[56] In 2001 the Arab gulf state Abu Dhabi featured a family-oriented television program that depicted Israeli prime minister Ariel Sharon as a vampire who craves the blood of Arab children. Sharon is made to reveal how he and the late prime minister Menachem Begin celebrated a birthday by drawing blood from twenty Arab youngsters and drinking it.

Undoubtedly the ritual murder myth in the West has lost much of its power and is no longer a major weapon in the arsenal of antisemites. Ritual murder trials belong to the past. Virtually all Christian theologians and historians would look askance at any of their colleagues trying to prove that Jews actually practice or practiced human sacrifice. Now the topic is confined largely to students of myth and popular folklore who examine manifold expressions of the irrational. Nevertheless, tapestries, frescoes, statues, inscriptions, and stained glass windows that adorn some Catholic churches still show the myths of Jews torturing an innocent Christian child or desecrating the host; monuments to alleged victims still stand in town squares; and, until a generation ago, organized festivals and pilgrimages, some of them centuries old, commemorated "martyred" youngsters. Even after World War II, these sites were visited by tourists, including busloads of schoolchildren, and featured souvenir postcards, pamphlets, and guided tours, all perpetuating old myths of Jewish villainy. It would be an interesting footnote to the history of the ritual murder libel to study these sites today. Do pilgrimages still take place? Do local church authorities inform parishioners and visitors about the true history of the events depicted in these centuries-old ornaments and monuments? Indeed, are the local clergy themselves aware of this history?

These questions are raised in the context of the papacy's repudiation of the blood libel after the Second Vatican Council of 1962 to 1965 and the removal of several shrines to "martyred" youngsters that had served as popular cults for hundreds of years. However, antique myths deeply embedded in popular folklore do not disappear by decree. Thus even after the Vatican enjoined the termination of the Andreas of Rinn cult in 1961, officially banned the pilgrimage in 1985, and both the Vatican and the bishop of Innsbruck decreed that there had never been a ritual murder martyrdom, some Austrians in the Tyrol continue to celebrate the cult of the boy "martyred by the Jews." In connection with this myth, in December 1997 a lecturer at an Austrian Catholic theological seminary published an article in a right-wing journal claiming that Jews had indeed killed Christians in the Middle Ages to use their blood for ritual purposes. He was soon removed from his post. Sodalizio Cattolico, a small and insignificant fundamentalist Catholic group in Italy that does not recognize the pope's authority or the decrees of the council, publishes a journal that contains articles accusing Jews of practicing ritual murder. In 1996 the group organized a sparsely attended demonstration in Trent and collected signatures on a petition calling for the restoration of the Blessed Simon of Trent cult, which the church had banned in 1965. In 1955 Anglican authorities had dismantled the shrine in Lincoln Cathedral of "Little St. Hugh" and declared that the fiction of ritual murder had cost the lives of many Jews. But as recently as a decade ago local clergy in the cathedral were reported to have retold the myth to tourists. In treating the revival of antisemitism in eastern Europe after the collapse of communism, *Newsweek* magazine reported in 1990 on one church in Poland:

> The Holy Mary basilica in Sandomierz, Poland, was built in the 17th century. Within the church there is a large painting entitled "Infanticida." It depicts a band of caricatured Jews kidnapping, stabbing, and dismembering Christian babies as part of a religious ritual. A plaque claims that "Faithless members of the Jewish community killed two Sandomierz babies in 1698 and 1710." A nun walks by. Did Jews really do these things? "Certainly," she says, "They once did, but no longer—there are no Jews left in Poland."[57]

## CHAPTER 3

# THE DIABOLIZATION OF JEWS[*]

## DEMONS, CONSPIRATORS, AND RACE DEFILERS

*The whole history of the world knows no other example of a homeless, definitively physically, and psychically degenerate people, simply through fraud and cunning, through usury and jobbing ruling over the orbit of the world.*

—Otto Glagau, 1876[1]

*Our war is not a Spanish civil war, it is a war of Western civilization against the Jews of the entire world.*

—General Queipo de Llano, October 6, 1936[2]

TWO RELATED FACTORS MAKE ANTISEMITISM A UNIQUE form of hatred. One is its seeming indestructibility. The Enlightenment's insistence that reason be applied to all inherited dogmas and its plea for toleration did not eradicate it. The late nineteenth century, which was the apogee of liberalism,

---

[*] Some of the material in this chapter first appeared in Marvin Perry, *An Intellectual History of Modern Europe*. © 1993 Houghton Mifflin Company. Reprinted with permission. Sections also appeared in Marvin Perry and Frederick M. Schweitzer, eds., *Jewish-Christian Encounters over the Centuries: Symbiosis, Prejudice, Holocaust, Dialogue*. © Peter Lang Publishing 1994. Reprinted with permission.

also saw the rise of organized antisemitic movements and the proliferation of the ritual murder libel; in the early twentieth century, Nazi antisemitism did not discourage Germans from electing Hitler to power and did not diminish his popularity after he had deprived Jews of their civil rights. The Holocaust silenced the antisemites only briefly; in recent years we have seen the reemergence of virulent Jew-hatred, particularly in eastern Europe and in Muslim lands. A second distinctive feature of historic antisemitism is its irrational nature—the willingness of people to believe incredible myths about Jews. And we are not talking only about illiterate and provincial-minded peasants. How is it that educated and seemingly rational people have diligently written books to "prove" that Jews kidnapped and murdered Christian children for their blood, conspired to dominate the planet, and manufactured a tale of extermination in order to extract money from Germany? Equally telling is the fact that adherents of such fables persist in their beliefs even when confronted with irrefutable evidence—so deep is their animus toward Jews.

It has been suggested that this unreasoning, or chimerical, hatred of Jews derives from centuries-old Christian perceptions of the Jews as an evil and conspiratorial people. Early and medieval Christians came to view Jews not simply as believers in an ancient faith that was the source of their own and as individuals struggling to cope with life's dilemmas, but as deicides abandoned by God and permanently stained with the mark of Cain and as Satan's henchmen who were avowed enemies of the true faith. Christian antisemitism, which saw Jews as vile and dangerous and Judaism as repulsive, fertilized the soil of modern antisemitism. In the nineteenth century this theological stain was transformed into a racial one—the wickedness of Jews stemmed from immutable genetic qualities. The demonization of the Jew by early and medieval Christians produced a mystical fear and hatred of the Jewish people that culminated in massacres and expulsions; channeled into modern nationalist and racist antisemitism, it ended in genocide. This diabolization of the Jewish people led their tormentors to believe that they were acting in self-defense and that these victims of humiliation, pillage, massacre, inquisitorial torture, burnings at the stake, expulsions, and systematic murder were getting what they deserved and what God had ordained. Such an accursed and evil people were undeserving of Christian compassion; humiliation and punishment were their just due.

## CHRISTIAN DEMONIZATION OF THE JEW

There is a crucial difference between ancient Greek and Roman attitudes toward Jews and that initiated by early Christians. Pagan authors were generally indifferent to Jews, viewing them simply as one of the many nations that comprised the Mediterranean world. Sometimes they showed respect for the Jews' monotheism, their long history, and their elevated ethical principles. At times Greeks and Romans criticized Jews, accusing them of disloyalty for refusing to worship the gods of the city or to accept the divinity of the Roman emperor. Also arousing pagan distaste were circumcision, which they viewed as a barbarous mutilation, and Jewish dietary laws, which they saw as primitive superstition. Moreover, armed resistance by the Jews to Hellenization (the revolt of Maccabees, ca.168 to 164 B.C.E.) and to Roman rule (the Jewish revolts of 66 to 70 and 132 to 135 C.E.) earned the Jews the reputation of being difficult to govern and a rebellious nation. But unlike their Christian successors, pagans rarely engaged in derisive polemics designed to set the Jews apart as an inherently wicked nation; there was no diabolization of the Jew. Unlike Christian anti-Judaism, which literally flowed with Christ's blood, pagan hostility to Jews did not derive from a theological worldview. For many Christians, love of the crucified redeemer required hatred for those "hard-hearted" and "evil" people—*and their descendants*—who, according to the New Testament, had willfully betrayed and murdered him. Passages like the one in Matthew stigmatized the Jews as a nation of deicides: "Let him be crucified. . . . His blood be on us and on our children" (26:25). For John, the Jews had descended from the Devil: "You are of your father the devil, and your will is to do your father's desires" (8:44). These venomous accusations were embellished by the Church Fathers. Thus Origen (ca. 185-ca. 251) maintained that "the blood of Jesus [falls] not only upon those who lived then but also upon all generations of the Jewish people following afterwards until the end of the world."[3] St. Gregory of Nyssa (died ca. 394) called the Jews "confederates of the devil, . . . Sanhedrin of demons, accursed, utterly vile, . . . enemies of all that is good."[4] In the late fourth century St. John Chrysostom described Jews as "inveterate murderers, destroyers, men possessed by the Devil." "[T]hey murder their offspring and immolate them to the devil." "They are impure and impious." The synagogue is "the domicile of the devil as is also the soul of the Jews." Their rites are "criminal and impure," their religion is "a disease." Because of their "odious assassination of Christ," the Jews have suffered and will continue to suffer degradation. For the crime of deicide, there is "no expiation possible, . . . no pardon." Jews will live "under the yoke of servitude without end." He concluded ominously that the Jews are like an old plow horse that is "marked for slaughter," that the resurrection makes Judaism obsolete, "ready for slaughter."[5]

Since the Devil was very real and very terrifying to early and medieval Christians, the Jews became identified with evil. Christians developed a mindset, concludes the Reverend Robert A. Everett, that was "unable to see anything positive in Judaism. . . . Judaism and the Jewish people came to have no real value for Christians except as a negative contrast to Christianity."[6] Because of the "teaching of contempt" and the "diabolization of the Jew," the Christian ethic of love did not extend to Jews. "[O]nce it is established that God has cursed the Jews, how can one argue that Christians should love them? If Jews have been fated by God to have . . . a long history of suffering, who are Christians to alter their history by doing anything to relieve Jewish suffering? The theology of victimization thus precludes Christian love as a basis of relating to Jews."[7]

What made Christian antisemitism particularly ominous was this effort of theologians to demonize the Jewish people. The myth emerged that the Jews, murderers of the incarnate God who embodied all that was good, were a cursed people, children of the Devil, who willfully and maliciously challenged God's design for humanity. A people who committed deicide was capable of any enormity. Because the Jews' refusal to embrace the true faith defied all that was sacred, God intended them to suffer. The diabolization of the Jew, which bore no relationship to the actual behavior of Jews or to their highly ethical religion, and the "theology of victimization," which held that the Jews were collectively and eternally cursed for denying Christ, became powerful myths. Reinforced during the Middle Ages, this distorted image of the Jew as a contemptible and demonic creature persists in the European mentality into the twenty-first century and accounts for the bizarre and hallucinatory charges hurled at them over the centuries.

During the Middle Ages, the myth of the Jew as "the seed of Satan" became a fully developed ideology that incited hatred and violence. Medieval art, poetry, drama, theological tracts, sermons, and religious instruction identified Jews with the Devil. Jews were given horns, tails, a goat's beard (a goat was seen as Satan's disguise), and a noxious odor, revealing their descent from the Devil. Satan was depicted in the likeness of a Jew and in the company of Jews, sometimes riding on a Jew's back. In a particularly degrading scene, Satan oversees a pig suckling Jewish babies. In Passion plays Jews were portrayed as evil demons with horns and tails gleefully and sadistically torturing Jesus as he carried the cross and then mutilating his crucified body; so diabolical were Jews that they did this even though they knew that Jesus was God's son. In other plays Jews were shown wearing grotesque costumes, stabbing the holy communion, desecrating holy images, conspiring with the Devil, and raving like mad dogs. To the medieval mind Jews were not just evil, they were also dangerous and fearful murderers and demons: They slew Christian children to obtain their blood for ancient rituals; armed by Satan with occult powers, they plotted to destroy Christendom and thwart the divine plan. Christendom had to be protected from these fiends.

The legend of the Antichrist, a wicked countermessiah, "the prince of evil," who incited people to vice, was another myth that demonized Jews. Lactantius, a fourth-century Christian scholar, and six centuries later, the monk Adso, described the Antichrist as the offspring of a Jewish prostitute sired by Satan, himself a Jew. "Fostered by the power of the Devil," said Adso, the Antichrist is the most evil and most powerful of all human opponents of God and moral good. The Jews, he continued, flock to the Antichrist in Jerusalem—the locus of the Antichrist's actions in almost every rendering of the tales—"in the belief that they are receiving God" and that the Antichrist will rebuild the Temple.[8]

Characteristically, the Antichrist was equated with the messiah whom Jews awaited. It was a Christian commonplace that the Antichrist will have a mighty army of Jewish soldiers who were also cannibals—a frequent link was forged between the Antichrist myth and the blood libel. (See chapter 2.) It was believed that the Antichrist would make the Jews powerful enough to destroy Christendom and "raise up Judaism again," as the refrain in one of the numerous medieval Antichrist plays put it. A fourteenth-century Viennese professor pronounced that the Antichrist, "with the help of Jewish money, would conquer the world in two and a half years."[9] In a reign of evil and tribulation, he would strengthen Judaism and crush Christianity. But the Antichrist would also usher in the end of days, for Christ shall descend, annihilate the godless, suppress evil, and reign with the righteous.

A striking example of the popular fear and hatred of the Antichrist and the Jews can be seen in the German Lenten play *The Duke of Burgundy* from around 1495, which depicts the Antichrist and the Jews as bent on destroying Christendom. The Antichrist admits to heinous crimes medieval Christians ascribed to Jews—poisoning, ritual murder, massacres, sorcery, and witchcraft. Foiled, the Antichrist confesses failure this time but announces that he will return again in later incarnations until ultimately he and the Jews achieve their horrifying aims. Thereupon, the duke's men torture and kill him and his followers, then dance in celebration over the mutilated bodies.

The medieval myth that the Antichrist was born a Jew and would preface the reign of heaven with a reign of terror survived into the twentieth century. Thus in the 1930s, when antisemitism was at its height in the United States, American hate merchant Gerald Winrod held that Franklin D. Roosevelt and the New Deal "seem to confirm what the prophecies indicate, namely, that prior to the Second Coming of Christ the Jewish nation will emerge holding the dominant power." He believed that "an international system of Jewish government, ... based upon Jewish money and power has already been created."[10] After World War II, another American, the antisemitic rabble-rouser

Gerald L. K. Smith touted his crusade as a "call and a challenge to all lovers of Jesus Christ to stand together against the onslaught of anti-Christs,"[11] by which he meant Jewish genes, Jewish communism, Jewish atheism. The Antichrist fantasy also served as the foundation for the *Protocols of the Learned Elders of Zion*. (See below.)

Still another Christian myth that fueled Jew-hatred was the legend of the Wandering Jew. The tale emerged that when Jesus, wearied from carrying the heavy cross to Calvary, rested briefly against a stranger's doorway, the man drove him away shouting: "Walk faster." Christ responded: "I go, but you will walk until I come again." Over the centuries it came to be believed that the Jew, Ahasuerus—a name commonly ascribed to Jews—was doomed to wander and suffer for the great crimes of insulting and blaspheming the Lord. Laboring under Christ's curse, he yearns for death, but this is not allowed him. The fate of the Wandering Jew was seen as evidence for the truth of Christianity and the abasement of Judaism. In some renditions, the wanderer was depicted as a soothsayer, a practitioner of black magic, or a necromancer, and the antisemitic tone and temper became more and more vicious. Ahasuerus became a stock figure in Passion plays and was equated with the Antichrist or appeared as his disciple. Called the Eternal Jew in German lands, it is not accidental that the vilest Nazi antisemitic film was entitled *The Eternal Jew*. Some two thousand writings and numerous works of art and music disseminated the image of the Jew as a cosmic fugitive who effects Christendom's destiny; these productions attest to the myth's hold on the Christian imagination.

The extraordinary feature of medieval Christian antisemitism is its delusional character. Medieval Christians transformed Jews—who, in reality, were a powerless and cowed minority—into mythical monsters. Consequently, medieval antisemitism reveals a great deal about the thought processes and attitudes of Christians, but it tells us virtually nothing about the behavior and beliefs of Jews. Indeed, medieval Christians knew very little about Jews. With some exceptions, they had very little real contact with them, for Jews, regarded as pariahs, were shunned and later forced by law to reside in ghettos. Christians' knowledge of postbiblical Jewish texts was minimal, selective, and distorted.

Historians regard the First Crusade as a turning point for medieval Jewry. Until then there were few instances of organized violence against Jewish communities. In 1096 bands of crusaders, consisting largely of commoners, marched through the Rhineland slaughtering Jews. Implicating contemporary Jews in the crucifixion that had occurred almost 1,100 years earlier, these crusaders, their vestments decorated with crosses, were bent on vengeance, as the following passage from a Jewish chronicle indicates: "Behold we journey a long way to seek the idolatrous shrine and to take vengeance upon the Muslims. But here are the Jews dwelling among us, whose ancestors killed him and crucified him groundlessly. Let us take vengeance first upon them. Let us wipe them out as a nation."[12] To these Christians, Jews were the historic and inexorable enemies of Christianity, even worse than the Muslims, a view that became increasingly commonplace. Thus Peter the Venerable, a leading twelfth-century theologian, referred to Jews as "wretched blasphemers far worse than the Saracens." Unlike the marauding crusaders, Peter did not urge killing Jews. God does not wish they be destroyed, he said, but "for the purpose of greater torment and ignominy they be preserved for a life worse than death. . . . Since they spilled the blood of Christ—their brother in the flesh—they are enslaved, afflicted, anxious, suffering, and wanderers on the earth until . . . the miserable remnants of this people . . . will be converted to God."[13]

The first specific allegation that Jews were conspiring to destroy Christendom was made in 1321 in Aquitaine, France. But this charge has to be understood in the context of two prior events: the terrible famine of 1315 to 1317 and the slaughter of Jews in Aquitaine by peasants who, still reeling from the famine, believed that they had a divine mission to fight "infidels." At one stronghold, besieged Jews fought desperately until, overcome by fire and smoke, they chose martyrdom, selecting one of their own to kill them rather than submit to their Christian oppressors. Some five hundred perished this way. The peasants baptized the few surviving children. Scores of Jewish communities were exterminated by these fanatics, who believed that in killing Jews they were serving Christ. The following year a rumor circulated in the same province that the Jews had conceived a plan to poison wells and springs in order to kill Christians and that they employed lepers to execute their fiendish plot. Léon Poliakov, the prominent French student of antisemitism, points out the significance of this conjunction between the initial act of the mass murder of Jews and then the charge of a Jewish conspiracy: "To massacre first, and then, from fear of revenge, to accuse afterward; to attribute to the victims one's own aggressive intentions; to impute to them one's own cruelty: from country to country and from century to century under various disguises, this is the device we find. (Thus Nazi killers, to justify themselves for having massacred Jewish children, were known to speak of 'potential avengers.')"[14]

The Black Death, or bubonic plague, which devastated Europe in 1348 and 1349, was seen either as God's punishment for sinful human behavior or as Satan's work, or both. Satan, it was believed, recruited lepers and Jews to carry out his sinister plan. The Jews, eager to extirpate the Christian faith and to make themselves lords of the world, relished the opportunity to serve Satan. The Jews were said to have hatched their fiendish conspiracy in Toledo, Spain. From Spain messengers armed with a deadly poison—a mixture of human blood, urine, powder from the "beaten" consecrated host, and secret herbs— were sent to various parts of Christendom. Working in collusion with local rabbis, they systematically poisoned wells.

Seeking to aid God in his struggle against Satan and hoping that he would end their suffering, roving hordes of flagellants,* joined by townsfolk, slaughtered Jews by the thousands, and municipal authorities ordered the mass execution of thousands more. In Basle, Switzerland, several hundred Jews were herded into a wooden house and burned to death; some two thousand Jews were burned at the stake in a huge pyre outside of Strasbourg, and their property distributed to the burghers; at Mainz, the flames consumed another six thousand. Whole Jewish communities in western and central Europe disappeared, victims of massacre, expulsion, and flight to the East. Pope Clement VI's reasoned appeal that Jews, too, were victims of the plague in great numbers and that it devastated regions uninhabited by Jews had no impact on the murderers whose reasoning capacities had been overwhelmed by fanaticism and myth. A contemporary Christian chronicler wryly noted: "Countless number of Jews were massacred in the Rhineland, in Franconia, and in all the other German countries. . . . [N]o German city had so many Jews as Vienna, and so many of them succumbed to the plague that they were obliged to enlarge their cemetery greatly. . . . They would have been very stupid to poison themselves."[15]

By the end of the Middle Ages, Jews had been dehumanized—they are "not humans, but dogs," declared the bishop of Speyer in April 1519; and demonized—they were seen as allies of Satan engaged in a diabolical plot against God and Christendom. Jew-hatred was regarded as a display of Christian virtue. Thus even the gentle Erasmus of Rotterdam, the great Renaissance humanist who spoke out passionately for toleration and peace, harbored a deep hatred for Jews: "If hate of the Jews is the proof of genuine Christians, then we are all excellent Christians."[16]

Martin Luther inherited medieval prejudices against Jews, but soon after initiating the Reformation, he called for a gentler attitude toward Jews in the hope that these kin of Jesus would convert to Christianity. In his pamphlet

---

* Panic-stricken people who marched from region to region beating themselves and each other with sticks and whips in a desperate effort to appease God, who, they believed, had cursed them with the plague.

"Jesus Christ Was Born a Jew" (1523), he expressed uncommon sympathy for Jews: "If the Apostles, who were also Jews, had dealt with us Gentiles as we Gentiles deal with Jews there would never have been a Christian among the Gentiles . . . we in turn ought to treat the Jews in a brotherly manner in order that we might convert some of them . . . we are but Gentiles, while the Jews are of the lineage of Christ. We are aliens and in-laws; they are blood relatives, cousins, and brothers of our Lord."[17] However, Luther was consistent in his theology of Judaism throughout his life—he was dismissive and contemptuous. Thus even in the 1523 treatise he asserts that: Jesus is the fulfillment of Hebrew scripture, the law of Moses is abrogated, the Romans' destruction of Jerusalem and the Temple was just punishment of deicide, and so on. For the moment it will suffice, Luther says, if the Jews "begin recognizing this man Jesus as the true Messiah"; he concludes with the vague threat that he will "let the matter rest for the present, until I see what I have accomplished." More and more frustrated in later years by his lack of success in winning Jews over to Protestant Christianity, Luther vented his wrath against them in letters and pamphlets, often in gutter language; he spewed forth the old calumnies—Jews engaged in ritual murder, poisoned wells, and served Satan.* In a treatise entitled *Concerning the Jews and Their Lies* (1543), he suggested his own "final solution" to the Jewish question:

> What shall we Christians do with this rejected and condemned people, the Jews? . . . I shall give you [the princes and civil powers] my sincere advice:
>
> First, to set fire to their synagogues or schools and to bury and cover with dirt whatever will not burn, so that no man will ever again see a stone or cinder of them. This is to be done in honor of our Lord and of Christendom. . . .
>
> Second, I advise that their houses also be razed and destroyed. For they pursue in them the same aims as in their synagogues. Instead they might be lodged under a roof or in a barn, like the gypsies. This will bring home to them the fact that they are not masters in our country, as they boast, but that they are living in exile and in captivity, as they incessantly wail and lament about us before God.
>
> Third, I advise that all their prayer books and Talmudic writings, in which such idolatry, lies, cursing, and blasphemy are taught, be taken from them.
>
> Fourth, I advise that their rabbis be forbidden to teach hence forth on pain of loss of life and limb. For they have justly forfeited the right to such an office. . . .

---

\* Other Protestant leaders, particularly the reformers John Calvin and Ulrich Zwingli, were not obsessed with validating Christianity by converting Jews or with blaming them for the crucifixion.

Fifth, I advise that safe conduct on the highways be abolished completely for the Jews. For they have no business in the countryside, since they are not lords, officials, tradesmen, or the like. Let them stay at home. . . . If you great lords and princes will not forbid such usurers the highway legally, some day a troop may gather [to lynch] them, having learned from this booklet the true nature of the Jews and how one should deal with them and not protect their activities. . . .

Sixth, I advise that usury be prohibited to them, and that all cash and treasure of silver and gold be taken from them and put aside for safekeeping. The reason for such a measure is that . . . they have no other means of earning a livelihood than usury,* and by it they have stolen and robbed from us all they possess. . . .

Seventh, I recommend putting a flail, an ax, a hoe, a spade, a distaff, or a spindle into the hands of young, strong Jews and Jewesses and letting them earn their bread in the sweat of their brow, as was imposed on the children of Adam. . . . In brief, dear princes and lords, those of you who have Jews under your rule—if my counsel does not please you, find better advice, so that you and we all can be rid of the unbearable, devilish burden of the Jews, lest we become guilty sharers before God in the lies, the blasphemy, the defamation, and the curses which the mad Jews indulge in so freely and wantonly against the person of our Lord Jesus Christ, his dear mother, all Christians, all authority, and ourselves. . . .

And you, my dear gentlemen and friends who are pastors and preachers, I wish to remind [you] very faithfully of your official duty, so that you too may warn your parishioners concerning their eternal harm, as you know how to do—namely, that they be on their guard against the Jews and avoid them so far as possible. . . .

Accordingly, it must and dare not be considered a trifling matter but a most serious one . . . to save our souls from the Jews, that is, from the devil and from eternal death. . . .

. . . [Rulers and clergy] must act like a good physician who, when gangrene has set in, proceeds without mercy to cut, saw, and burn flesh, veins, bone, and marrow. Such a procedure must also be followed in this instance. I have done my duty. Now let everyone see to his. I am exonerated.[18]

The authorities did not heed Luther's proposals to raze synagogues and homes—although some anti-Jewish measures were applied—and for several centuries Lutheran theologians gave little mind to Luther's antisemitism. In the late nineteenth century, however, German nationalists revived Luther's

---

* Luther's 1524 work *Trade and Usury* flays usurers and usury but amazingly does not mention Jews except to praise the Mosaic legislation and the jubilee year.

treatise and exploited his hostility to Jews, and the Nazis gleefully circulated his words as an authoritative endorsement of their antisemitic ideology. In 1938 the Lutheran bishop of Thuringia, Martin Sasse, celebrated the infamous Kristallnacht pogrom by issuing excerpts from Luther's diatribe and exulting in Germany's two greatest antisemites, Luther and Hitler. Hitler himself hailed the Luther who, "With one blow, heralded a new dawn. . . . He saw the Jew as we are only beginning to see him today."[19]

Anti-Judaism during the Middle Ages and the Reformation was essentially theological, not racial. Both Catholics and Protestants sought and welcomed the Jews' conversion to the true faith and believed that baptism would cleanse their evil character and terminate their special relationship with Satan. However, a new type of anti-Judaism had emerged in Spain, where it was claimed that Jews were made wicked not just by their religion but by their bad blood, a taint that baptism could not eradicate.

The centuries-old Spanish Jewish community had distinguished itself in commerce and intellectual pursuits, and Jews had served Spanish kings as ministers and physicians. However, the five-hundred-year struggle, seen as a crusade, to drive the Muslims out of Spain and the vitriolic preaching of clerics, particularly Dominican friars, exacerbated anti-Jewish feelings. In a three-month period in 1391, mobs slew some fifty thousand Jews and prompted many others to join the growing number of forced *conversos* (converts). But Old Christians disdained the conversos, or New Christians. They accused them of secretly practicing Judaism (many did) and resented their rise to positions of eminence in business, the professions, government service, and even the church. This hostility to conversos also contained a racial component as Old Christians insisted— even though it was heretical theology—that baptism could not cleanse the bad blood of Jews. Like the Nazis five hundred years later, Old Christians were obsessed with racial purity, refusing to intermarry with New Christians, even if the family had been faithful Catholics for generations, and barring their entry into certain military and religious orders. For social acceptance, one had to prove a lineage uncorrupted by Jewish blood. For centuries the Spanish Inquisition hounded the New Christians as crypto-Jews, torturing and burning them if they were suspected of observing any Jewish ritual or custom.

The chimerical image of the Jew as an evil demon and dangerous conspirator was deeply embedded in the medieval Christian psyche and did not perish with the weakening of Christianity in modern times. In modern secular society, hatred of the Jew found a new driving force in nationalism, which in the nineteenth century became the dominant spiritual force in European life. Late-nineteenth- and early-twentieth-century nationalists reformulated Christian myths to fit the outlook of a post-Christian secular

age. The children of Satan who conspired against Christendom were transmuted into capitalist plutocrats or red revolutionaries who aspired to world
domination. Sometimes, however, the very language of the Middle Ages
was preserved. For example, a popular Nazi poster read: "He who knows
the Jew knows the Devil."

In the Middle Ages Jews had faced brutal persecution, but they were not
threatened with extinction as a people. Christian culture had nurtured a cosmic hatred for Jews, but Christian morality imposed ethical barriers to systematic genocide and theology required the preservation of the Jews to the end of
time. Ironically, the weakening of Christianity, the Jews' tormentor for almost
two millennia, made possible the emergence of an antisemitic (and anti-
Christian) pagan ideology that had no qualms about total extermination.

## EXTREME NATIONALISM AND
## COUNTERREVOLUTIONARY CONSERVATISM:
## THE SETTING FOR MODERN ANTISEMITISM

In the nineteenth century, under the aegis of the liberal ideals of the Enlightenment and the French Revolution, Jews gained legal equality in most European lands. They could leave the ghettos and participate in many activities
that had been closed to them. Newly emancipated Jews generally aspired to
integrate into the majority while still retaining their Jewish identity. Many
gentiles, on the other hand, hoped that emancipation would lead Jews to abandon their faith. Seeking to take advantage of this new freedom and opportunity—and drawn by the anonymity and greater tolerance found in large urban
centers—large numbers of newly emancipated Jews migrated to the leading
cities of Europe, particularly Vienna and Berlin. Motivated by the fierce desire
of outsiders to prove their worth, aided by deeply embedded traditions that
valued learning and family life, and conditioned by many centuries of poverty
and surviving by their wits in a hostile environment, Jews were admirably prepared to compete in a society where effort and talent counted more than birth
or religion. Jews achieved striking success as entrepreneurs, bankers, lawyers,
journalists, doctors, scientists, scholars, and performers, particularly in Germany, where Jews fondly embraced German culture and many converted to
Christianity. By the early twentieth century no area of German life was un-
quickened by Jewish energy and creativity. By 1930 Jews, although less than 1
percent of the population, accounted for 30 percent of Nobel Prize winners in
Germany. Vienna affords much the same picture of Jewish achievement. In the
first decade of the twentieth century, Jews, who constituted less than 10 per-

cent of the city's population, made up 71 percent of its financiers, 63 percent of its industrialists, 65 percent of its lawyers, and 59 percent of its physicians. Vienna was home to Sigmund Freud and his circle, and Viennese cultural life before World War I was shaped to a large extent by Jewish writers, musicians, critics, and patrons.*

The meteoric rise of the Jews aroused resentment, particularly after the worldwide depression of 1873, among people who saw them as competitors in the professions, the arts, business, and finance. Antisemites called for reversing Jewish emancipation; they wanted to deprive Jews of their civil rights, bar them from professions, and even expel them from the country; some even proposed annihilation. Sometimes economic resentment fused with traditional Christian disdain for Jews. Thus in 1889 a French Catholic newspaper remarked with more venom than truth: "The Jews have a right to celebrate the anniversary of the [French] Revolution. They have been here only one hundred years** and already they own half the land; soon they will own it all. They control our land, our money, our government, and our press. Rothschild and his fellows are more the masters of France than the president and his ministers. They rule the stock exchange, and that is now the real center of action and power."[20]

In 1886 Édouard Drumont (1842–1917), a rabid conservative French journalist, published *La France Juive* (Jewish France), which argued that the Jews, racially inferior and believers in a primitive religion, had gained control of France and were plotting to dominate all of Europe. Reprinted many times, it sold over a million copies. Drumont blamed the Jews for undermining traditional French culture, including Catholicism, by promoting greedy capitalism and soul-destroying materialism. Seeking to win Catholic support, he propagated the deicide accusation and the ritual murder myth. (In rural France, the accusation of ritual murder still persisted, at times fomented by the clergy.) Adopting the new racial nationalist theories that were gaining appeal in conservative circles, he contrasted Jewish Semites with French Aryans, always

---

* But most European Jews—peddlers and laborers—were quite poor. Statistics for the Jews of Paris from 1800 to 1870 show that over 60 percent died paupers. Perhaps five to six thousand Jews of Galicia in Austria-Hungary died of starvation annually, and many Russian Jews fled to the United States to escape from desperate poverty. The antisemites, however, saw only "Jewish influence," "Jewish manipulation," "Jewish domination," "Rothschild power."

** Jews, of course, had lived in France since the Middle Ages and even centuries before in Roman times; they had been emancipated for a century.

viewing the former as morally and culturally inferior. His newspaper (founded with Jesuit funds) blamed all the ills of France on the Jews, called for their expulsion from the country, and predicted future massacres. Its sensational antisemitic polemics shaped public opinion for the conviction in 1894 of Captain Alfred Dreyfus, a Jewish officer appointed to the French General Staff, on faked evidence of high treason.

The Dreyfus affair led to an explosion of Jew-hatred in France. The church in France deliberately fueled the flames in the hopes that strategically employed antisemitism would reinvigorate Catholicism, which the church saw threatened by liberalism and secularism. Many churchmen blamed emancipated Jews for the spread of the hated liberal ideals of the Enlightenment and French Revolution. Numerous priests attended meetings of antisemitic organizations and denounced Jews from the pulpit in venomous language—as Christ killers, Satan's agents, ritual murderers, traitors, greedy capitalists, international conspirators—designed to inflame their flock. These vulgar attacks were repeatedly printed in *La Croix* (the cross), a daily newspaper published by the Assumptionists, an order of priests; the most widely read Catholic publication in the country—its readership included some 25,000 clergy—*La Croix* was influential in fomenting contempt for Jews. No doubt the thinking of French collaborators, who rounded up and deported Jews in France to Nazi death camps, had been shaped by the image of the Jew emblazoned in the pages of *La Croix* four decades earlier.

The success of the Jews—even though the majority, particularly in eastern and central Europe, remained poor, many desperately so—provided ammunition for extreme nationalists, who were the principal antagonists of Jews. Although fueled by such economic factors and a traditional Christian bias, modern antisemitism rested chiefly on national racial considerations. A xenophobic nationalism, which viewed the Jews as a conspiratorial race with limitless power for evil and an alien race that threatened the nation's very existence, had emerged in full force in several European countries in the decades before World War I. The extreme racial nationalism of this period was the seedbed of Hitler's ideology. Nationalism, whose emergence we shall examine briefly, provided the setting for modern antisemitism.

In the first half of the nineteenth century, nationalism and liberalism went hand in hand. Liberals sought both the rights of the individual and national independence and unification. Liberal nationalists believed that a unified state free of foreign subjugation was in harmony with the principle of natural rights, and they insisted that love of country led to love of humanity. As nationalism grew more extreme, however, its profound difference from liberalism became more apparent. Concerned exclusively with the greatness of the nation, extreme nationalists rejected the liberal emphasis on political liberty and civil rights. They regarded liberty as an obstacle to national power and maintained that authoritarian leadership was needed to fulfill the nation's mission. The needs of the nation, they said, transcended the rights of the individual. Placing the nation above everything, nationalists became increasingly intolerant of minorities within the nation's borders and hateful of other peoples. In the name of national unity, they persecuted minorities at home and stirred up hatred against other nations. In the pursuit of national power, they increasingly embraced imperialistic, racist, and militaristic doctrines, glorifying war as the expression of the nation's resolve and will.

Interpreting politics with the logic of emotions, extreme nationalists created a cult of ancestors and a mystique of blood, soil, and a sacred national past. In these ancestral traditions and attachments, nationalists found a higher reality akin to religious belief. Loyalty to the nation-state was elevated above all other allegiances. The nation-state became an object of religious reverence; the spiritual energies that formerly had been directed to Christianity were now channeled into the worship of the nation-state. In 1902 Friedrich Paulsen, a German philosopher, warned of nationalism's threat to reason and morality:

> A supersensitive nationalism has become a very serious danger for all the peoples of Europe; because of it, they are in danger of losing the feeling for human values. Nationalism, pushed to an extreme, just like sectarianism [religious conflicts], destroys moral and even logical consciousness. Just and unjust, good and bad, true and false, lose their meaning; what men condemn as disgraceful and inhuman when done by others, they recommend in the same breath to their own people as something to be done to a foreign country.[21]

In the late nineteenth century, conservatives in several European lands became the staunchest advocates of nationalism, and the reactionary nationalism preached by conservative extremists was stripped of liberal ideals of liberty, equality, and the fellowship of nations. Landholding aristocrats, generals, and clergy, often joined by business and industrial magnates, saw nationalism as a convenient way to gain a mass following in their struggle to keep democracy and socialism from penetrating political life. A radicalized Right championed popular nationalist myths and dreams and, particularly in Germany, employed Social Darwinist and racist doctrines in order to harness the instinctual energies of the masses.

Social Darwinists, who applied Darwin's biological theories to relations between nations, injected dangerous elements into nationalism. They maintained that nations and races were engaged in a struggle for survival in which only the fittest survive and deserve to survive. In their view, war was nature's stern way of eliminating the unfit. Darwinian biology was used to promote the belief in Anglo-Saxon and Teutonic racial superiority. Social Darwinists attributed the growth of the British Empire, the expansion of the United States to the Pacific, and the extension of German power to racial qualities. The domination of other peoples—American Indians, Africans, Asians, Poles—was regarded as the natural right of superior races. The Social Darwinist notion of the struggle of races for survival and domination became a core doctrine of Hitler's movement; it provided the "scientific" and "ethical" justification for genocide.

## VOLKISH THOUGHT

While extreme nationalism was a general European phenomenon, it proved particularly dangerous in Germany. The unification of Germany in 1870 and 1871 turned the new state into an international power of the first rank, upsetting the balance of power in Europe. To German nationalists, unification was both the fulfillment of a national dream and the starting point of an even more ambitious goal: the extension of German power in Europe and the world. Sometimes this goal was expressed in the language of Social Darwinism. The most ominous expression of German nationalism and a clear example of mythical thinking was Volkish thought.[22] (*Volk*, which originally simply meant "folk" or "people," became synonymous with "race.") Volkish thinkers romanticized and etherealized everything German and denounced as alien to the German soul everything non-German, particularly the liberal-humanist Enlightenment tradition that was identified with France and the West.*

To German Volkish thinkers, the Enlightenment and parliamentary democracy were foreign French and English ideas that corrupted the pure German spirit. These thinkers sought to bind the German people together through a deep love of their language, traditions, and fatherland. They felt that the Germans were animated by a higher spirit than that found in other peoples. With fanatical devotion, Volkish thinkers embraced all things German—the medieval

---

* While it is true that several *philosophes*, notably Voltaire and Diderot, despised Jews and Judaism, nevertheless, the Enlightenment provided the theoretical justification for Jewish emancipation, which the French Revolution enacted.

past, the German language, the German landscape, the simple peasant, the village. Volkish thought attracted Germans dismayed by all the complexities of the modern age, such as industrialization, urbanization, materialism, party politics, and class conflicts. They feared an impersonal and excessively rationalized capitalist system that destroyed ancient social forms, traditional virtues, communal ties, and alienated human beings from each other. Seeing their beloved Germany transformed by these forces of modernity—which they identified with the Jew—Volkish thinkers yearned to restore the sense of community that they attributed to the preindustrial age. Only by identifying with their sacred soil and sacred traditions would Germans escape from the rootlessness and alienation of modern industrial society. A return to roots would restore authenticity to life and stimulate genuine cultural creativity. Only then could the different classes band together in an organic unity.

Volkish thinkers glorified the ancient Germanic tribes that overran the Roman Empire, contrasting their courageous and vigorous German ancestors with the effete and degenerate Romans. They loved to cite the ancient Roman historian Tacitus' *Germania* as proof that they were an *Urvolk*, an original people not stained by race mixture, that they spoke an *Ursprache*, a pure and original language, and that they were morally superior to Latin peoples. A few Volkish writers tried to reconcile ancient heroic Germanic traditions with Christianity; this often meant expunging Jewish elements from Christianity. In this they made much of the quintessential German, Martin Luther, who had burst the bonds of a foreign, Latin Christianity to create a truly German faith. Luther's antisemitic tirades also served the cause of Volkish nationalists.

Volkish thinking led Germans to see themselves as a heroic people fundamentally different from and better than the English, French, Slavs, or any other people. It induced them to regard German culture as unique—intrinsically superior to and in opposition to the liberal humanist outlook of the Enlightenment. Volkish thinkers held that the German people and culture had a special destiny and a unique mission. They pitted the German soul against the Western intellect, setting off feeling, intuition, and spirit against a drab and dissecting rationalism. They accused liberalism and democracy of fostering a vulgar materialism, an anarchic individualism, and a soul-stifling rational-scientific outlook, all of which separated Germans from the true genius, the peculiar character, of the German nation. And behind the corrosive forces of modernity, said Volkish thinkers, was the Jew, the principal corrupter of the German soul, the principal underminer of traditional Germanic values.

The Jewish population of Germany was quite small: In 1900 it was only about 497,000, or 0.95 percent, of the total population of 50,626,000. Jews were proud of their many contributions to German economic and intellectual life and considered themselves patriotic Germans. They were bent on becoming "more German than the Germans," as Chaim Weizmann, the influential Zionist leader, said. In the nineteenth century, German Jews made a spectacular leap from "despised and rejected," in Arnold Zweig's phrase, to *Bildung* & *Besitz*, cultivation and wealth, so that by the early twentieth century, Jews had greatly enriched German commercial, artistic, and intellectual life.[23] Jews regarded Germany as an altogether desirable place to live—a place of refuge in comparison to Russia and Romania, where their kinsmen lived in terrible poverty and suffered violent attacks. Ironically, antisemitism seemed less extreme in Germany than in France, the land of the Enlightenment. German Jews, who felt that Germany was their homeland, had little enthusiasm for Zionism. Their love affair with German culture was evidenced by their disproportionate presence as publishers, cultural critics, editors, readers, and concert- and theatergoers. But the Jews' appreciation for things German was not welcomed by many fellow Germans, who continued to see Jews and Germans as fundamentally and unalterably different. To these Germans, the Jews, lacking in German consciousness, were a malevolent alien force corroding traditional German values and corrupting German culture.*

German (and other European) Jews who were members of the commercial and professional classes, like other bourgeois, gravitated toward liberalism. Moreover, as victims of persecution, they naturally favored governments that were committed to the liberal ideals of legal equality, toleration, the rule of law, and equality of opportunity. Their historical experience and the message of social justice preached by their ancient prophets also produced a social conscience that led them to empathize with the poor and oppressed. As strong supporters of parliamentary government, social reform, and the entire system of values associated with the rational humanist tradition of the Enlightenment, the Jews became targets of conservatives and Volkish thinkers who repudiated the humanist and cosmopolitan outlook of liberalism and professed a militant nationalism. These people castigated "Jewish liberalism," "Jewish capitalism," "Jewish socialism," and "Jewish materialism" as threats to traditional Christian Europe, and they denounced the "Jewish press" for fomenting social unrest.

---

* None of the following discussion is intended to imply that modern German culture was afflicted with a pathological antisemitism that made the Holocaust inevitable. Without the catastrophic effects of World War I, including the Bolshevik Revolution, there would have been no Hitler and no Holocaust, and in time the liberal, Social Democratic, and humanist elements in Germany might have reduced to insignificance the worst features of racial-nationalist antisemitism and created a more tolerant society.

Earlier many conservatives had opposed Jewish emancipation, interpreting it as a victory for the Enlightenment, the French Revolution, and liberalism, all of which they detested. And always, German conservative clerics, particularly in Catholic Austria, warned their parishioners that Jews, the ancient enemies of Christ, were now destroying Christian morals and the social order by promoting secularism, liberalism, capitalism, and socialism. Many ultraconservatives sought to reverse emancipation, that is, to bar Jews from government positions and many professions and to restore the ghetto.

Like conservatives in other lands, German conservatives deliberately and demagogically fanned the flames of antisemitism to win the masses over to conservative causes. The Christian Social Workers' party, founded in 1878 by Adolf Stoecker, a prominent Protestant preacher and court chaplain to Kaiser Wilhelm I, engaged in antisemitic agitation in order to recruit the lower bourgeoisie to the cause of the Protestant church and the monarchy. The party denounced Jews as capitalists and deicides and blamed them for all of Germany's problems. "Jewry is a drop of alien blood in our people's body," Stoecker declared[24] and he hoped that a future "liberator" would take up the fight against Jewry. He regretted the emancipation of German Jews but realized that it was too late to return them to the ghettos. He did, however, urge the government to continue its unwritten practice of barring unconverted Jews from civil service positions.

In German-speaking Austria, Karl Lueger was elected mayor of Vienna from 1897 to 1910. Lueger was a leader of the avowedly antisemitic Christian Social party, founded by conservative German nationalists, many of them prominent Catholic intellectuals and clergy. In no other Western nation had an openly antisemitic political party gained control over municipal government. Lueger realized that antisemitism would appeal to Viennese artisans and small tradesmen, who were losing out to the new and often Jewish-owned department stores and factories; for him playing the antisemitic card was an excellent way to succeed in politics. Lueger's ballot-box exploitation of antisemitism, which offered striking example of the ideology's mobilizing power, greatly impressed the young Hitler during his years in Vienna.

Also engaging in crude rhetoric designed to inflame Jew-hatred among the German masses in Austria was Georg von Schönerer, founder of the German National party. Schönerer viewed antisemitism as a great expression of popular consciousness and a great national accomplishment. He wanted to eliminate Jews from all areas of public life, and he specifically demanded the firing of all Jewish teachers.

Like their medieval forbears, modern antisemites abhorred and shunned Jews and protested against their social acceptance. German antisemites saw

Jews as interlopers, a foreign Asiatic tribe in their midst—even though the
Jewish presence in Germany went back to Roman times. In 1847 the play-
wright Heinrich Laube wrote: "In recent time a foreign element has penetrated everywhere in our midst, and into literature as well. This is the Jewish
element. I call it foreign with emphasis; for the Jews are an Oriental nation as
totally different from us today as they were two thousand years ago."[25] And a
half century later Austrian fraternities, echoing the same conviction, prohibited a German from dueling with a Jew because of the "deep moral and psy-
chic differences between Aryans and Jews."[26] Imbued with such sentiments,
antisemitic groups pressed for rescinding emancipation in part or whole.

The huge number of antisemitic publications and the numerous discussions of the "Jewish problem" in the press attest to the Germans' strange obsession with people who constituted a mere 1 percent of the population.
Antisemitic publications proliferated and some, like Wilhelm Marr's *Victory of
Judaism over Germanism* (1879), Theodor Fritsch's *Antisemitic Catechism* (1887),
and Julius Langbehn's *Rembrandt as Educator* (1890), went through numerous
printings and editions, reaching millions of readers. Antisemitism gained great
respectability in Germany and Austria in the late nineteenth century: Professional organizations, the churches, fraternal clubs, and schools perpetuated it as
a matter of course; and it was preached by leading university scholars, including
philologist Paul de Lagarde, economist Eugen Dühring, the greatly respected
historian Heinrich von Treitschke, the demagogic court chaplain Adolf
Stoecker, politicians, and the immensely popular composer Richard Wagner.

The synthesis of Volkish nationalism, antisemitism, "racial science," and
demagoguery was exemplified by Wagner. In *Judaism in Music*, first published in
1850 under a pseudonym and republished in 1869 under his own name, Wagner,
who resented the fame of the Jewish composers Felix Mendelssohn (who had
converted to Lutheranism) and Giacomo Meyerbeer, asserted that Jews debased
German music. They could not possess or express the feelings that animated the
German soul; they had their own folk soul, which had been shaped by a degenerate culture. Devoid of a creative imagination and concerned only with self-
centered materialist pursuits, said Wagner, Jews were the opposite of German
artists, who set aside personal gain in order to pursue the ideal. Wagner insisted
that Jews could have only a destructive influence on German culture. He expressed the view many of the German elite had toward the acceptance of Jews:
" . . . with all our speaking and writing in favor of Jewish emancipation, we always felt instinctively repelled by any real, active contact with Jews. [The German people have] the most profound repugnance for the Jewish nature."
Wagner protested that "the Jew has gone far beyond emancipation. He *rules* and
will continue to rule as long as money means power."[27] And in the concluding

passage of the essay, Wagner wrote: "There is only one possible way of redeeming the Jews from the terrible curse that hangs over them—annihilation." (No
doubt he meant the elimination of Judaism as a religion, not the physical extermination of the Jews as a people, although many readers took it literally.) In later
essays published in the Wagnerian journal, the *Bayreuther Blätter*, Wagner's antisemitism grew even more vitriolic and racist. Holding that artistic creativity was
a function of race, he saw Jews as the deadly opponent of the German spirit and
rejected their participation in the coming cultural regeneration of the Volk.

The thought processes of Volkish antisemites demonstrate the mind's
monumental capacity for irrational thinking. Antisemites invented a mythical
evil who could be blamed for all the social and economic ills caused by the
rapid growth of industries and cities and for all the new ideas that were undermining the old order. Their anxieties and fears concentrated on the Jews, to
whom they attributed everything they considered evil in the modern age, all
that threatened their traditional way of life and corrupted the German Volk.
They said that the Jews were responsible for the decay of a hitherto healthy
German body politic. To these people the great changes occurring in Germany did not stem from impersonal historical forces but were the work of
Jews who had uncanny powers.

In the mythical world of Volkish thinkers, Jews were regarded as evil entrepreneurs and international financiers who exploited hardworking and decent Germans, manipulated the stock exchange, and caused depressions; as
international socialists who were dragging Germany into class war; as democrats who were trying to impose an alien system of parliamentary democracy on
Germany; as cold and calculating intellectuals devoid of aesthetic sensibilities
who corrupted traditional German culture; as city people who had no ties or
love for the German soil; as materialists who were totally without German
spiritual qualities; as foreign intruders, "half Asiatics," who could never be
loyal to the German fatherland; as racial inferiors whose genes could infect
and weaken the German race; and as international conspirators who were
plotting to dominate Germany.

The last two accusations—the Jew as a racial inferior and the Jew as an international conspirator—were the most dangerous for the future of European
Jewry.

## RACE: THE KEY TO HISTORY

Volkish thinkers were especially attracted to racist doctrines. Racist thinkers
held that race was the decisive factor in history and that not only physical features but moral, esthetic, and intellectual qualities distinguished one race from

another. In their view, a race demonstrated its vigor and achieved greatness when it preserved its purity; intermarriage between races—"miscegenation"—contaminated the race, resulting in genetic, cultural, and military degeneration. Liberals, adherents of the universal principles of the Enlightenment and the French Revolution, held that anyone who accepted German law and was acculturated by German education was a member of the German nation; Volkish thinkers, on the other hand, interjected the notion that a person's nationality was a function of his or her "racial soul" or "blood." On the basis of this romantic-mystical conception of nationality, racists pitted Germans and Jews against each other; they argued that Jews, no matter how many centuries their ancestors had dwelled in Germany, could never think and feel like Germans and should be deprived of citizenship.

Like their Nazi successors, Volkish thinkers claimed that the German race was purer than, and therefore superior to, all other races; its superiority was revealed in such physical characteristics as blond hair, blue eyes, and fair skin—all signs of inner qualities lacking in other races. German racists claimed that the Germans were descendants of ancient Aryans. (The Aryans are thought to have emerged some four thousand years ago, probably between the Caspian Sea and the Hindu Kush. Intermingling with others, the Aryans lost whatever identity as a people they might have had, and so their very name and history are steeped in myth.) After discovering similarities among core European languages—Latin, Greek, Germanic, Celtic, Baltic, Slavic—and ancient Persian and Sanskrit (the language of the fair-skinned conquerors of India), nineteenth-century scholars contended that these languages all stemmed from a common tongue spoken by the Aryans. From there some leaped to the unwarranted conclusion that the Aryans constituted a distinct race endowed with superior racial qualities.

The Aryan myth enabled race-thinkers and antisemites to view the Jews as alien in race, language, religion, and civilization and therefore unbridgeably separate from Europeans. Here was philological and ethnographic "evidence"—scientific proof, as it were—that Jews must not be emancipated and integrated but ghettoized, expelled, or even annihilated. Some intellectuals drew a dichotomy between "Asiatic Judaism" and "Aryan Christianity" founded by the "Aryan Jesus" but vitiated by the "Jew Paul." Therefore, it was necessary to de-Judaize Christianity "in order that the spirit of the Indo-European race predominate in its bosom," as the famous French biblical scholar Ernest Renan declared.[28] Axiomatic was the racial superiority of Aryans and inferiority of Jews, who were seen as a danger to racial hygiene as well as to high culture.

German racist thinkers embraced the ideas of Houston Stewart Chamberlain (1855–1927), an Englishman whose boundless devotion to Germanism led him to adopt German citizenship and Volkish antisemitism. In 1888 Chamberlain wrote that the Germans "are menaced by a complete moral, intellectual, and material ruin if a strong reaction does not set in in time against the supremacy of the Jews, who feed upon [the Germans] and suck out—at every grade of society—their very life blood."[29] He came to see Jew and German as dialectical opposites, locked in a struggle of world historical significance, a theme that he developed in his major work, *Foundations of the Nineteenth Century* (1899).

In *Foundations*, Chamberlain asserted in pseudoscientific fashion that races differed not only physically but also morally, spiritually, and intellectually and that the struggle between races was the driving force of history. He held that the Germans, descendants of the ancient Aryans, were physically superior and bearers of a higher culture. He attributed Rome's decline to the dilution of its racial qualities through miscegenation. The blond, blue-eyed, long-skulled Germans, possessing the strongest strain of Aryan blood and distinguished by an inner spiritual depth, were the true ennoblers of humanity.

Demonstrating the typical irrationality of the antisemite, Chamberlain denied that Christ was a Jew, claiming that he was of Aryan stock, and held that the goal of the Jew was "to put his foot upon the neck of all the nations of the world and be Lord and possessor of the whole earth."[30] He pitted Aryan or Teuton and Jew against each other in a titanic struggle. As agents of a spiritually empty capitalism and divisive liberalism, the Jews, said Chamberlain, were undermining German society. Materialistic, cowardly, and devious, they were the antithesis of the idealistic, heroic, and faithful Germans. Bound to rigid laws and rituals, Jews lacked the spontaneous and dynamic creativity of Aryans. They mangled and destroyed Aryan cultural achievements.

Chamberlain's book was enormously popular in Germany with the nationalist and racist Right. Pan-German and other Volkish-nationalist organizations frequently hailed and cited it. Kaiser Wilhelm II called *Foundations* a "Hymn to Germanism" and read it to his children. What greater accolade could be bestowed on Volkish nationalism? "Next to the national liberal historians like Heinrich von Treitschke and Heinrich von Sybel," concludes German historian Fritz Fischer, "Houston Stewart Chamberlain had the greatest influence upon the spiritual life of Wilhelmine Germany."[31]

Chamberlain's loathing of liberalism, parliamentarism, Marxism, and materialism, his obsession with the Jews to whom he imputed a sinister influence, and his belief in Aryan/Teutonic superiority make him a spiritual forerunner of Nazism; and he was praised as such by Alfred Rosenberg, the leading Nazi racial theorist in the early days of Hitler's movement. Joseph Goebbels, the Nazi propagandist, hailed Chamberlain as a "pathbreaker" and "pioneer" after meeting him in 1926. In 1923 Chamberlain, then sixty-eight years old, met Hitler, whose movement was still in its foundation stage. Chamberlain subsequently praised the National Socialist movement as Wagnerism in politics and exulted "that Germany in its hour of need has given birth to a Hitler," that Hitler shares "our conviction about the pernicious, even murderous influence of Jewry on the German Volk."[32] Hitler visited Chamberlain on his deathbed and attended his funeral. The Third Reich placed Chamberlain in the Nazi pantheon and excerpted his writings in schoolbooks.

German racial nationalists and Volkish thinkers singled out Jews as the most wicked of races and a deadly enemy of the German people. To German doctors of race, for whom the fatherland was a mystical community nurtured and united by tribal blood ties, the Jews were both an unassailable alien people within the German nation and a *Gegenrasse*, an antirace that was contaminating Germany physically and spiritually.[33] German race mystics, employing the language of science, described Jews as a parasitical organism that had attached itself to the German body; the parasite had to be surgically removed before it spread further and irreparably damaged Germandom.

In the Middle Ages, Jews had been persecuted and humiliated primarily for religious reasons. In the nineteenth century, national-racial considerations supplemented the traditional biased Christian perception of Jews and Judaism. However, whereas Christian antisemites believed that through conversion Jews could escape the curse of their religion, racial antisemites said that Jews were indelibly stained and eternally condemned by their genes. Their evil and worthlessness derived from inherited racial characteristics, which could not be altered by conversion. In 1862 Moses Hess, a pioneer Zionist, noted insightfully: "The Germans hate the religion of the Jews less than they hate their race—they hate the peculiar faith of the Jews less than their peculiar noses. . . . Jewish noses cannot be reformed, and the black, wavy hair of the Jews will not be changed into blond by conversion or straightened out by constant combing."[34]

Hermann Ahlwardt, an antisemitic deputy in the Reichstag, the German parliament, who had written the *Desperate Struggle Between Aryan and Jew* (1890), confirmed Hess' insight in a speech before the German Reichstag in 1895: "If one designates the whole of Jewry, one does so in the knowledge that the racial qualities of this people are such that in the long run they cannot harmonize with the racial qualities of the Germanic peoples and that every Jew who at this moment has not done anything bad may nevertheless under the proper conditions do precisely that, because his racial qualities drive him to do it. . . . [T]he Jews . . . operate . . . like parasites. . . . You'd better exterminate these beasts of prey."[35]

Hitler, who lived in Vienna for six years prior to World War I, had familiarized himself with the racist pamphlets and tracts that circulated widely in the Austrian capital. These works employed many of the terms that became an essential part of Nazi ideology: Master race, inferior race, racial pollution, racial purity, and conflict between races. Thus there is striking continuity between Nazism and pre–World War I German racial nationalists who saw race as the key to world history, denounced Jews as an evil race, and insisted that as a superior race Germans had a national right to dominate other peoples, particularly the "racially inferior" Slavs of the East. Hitler, whose thought was an agglomeration of the nineteenth century's ideological detritus, declared in *Mein Kampf*: "All great cultures of the past perished only because the originally creative race died out from blood poisoning [racial mixture]. . . . All who are not of good race in this world are chaff. . . . A state which in this age of racial poisoning dedicates itself to the care of its best racial elements must some day become lord of the earth."[36] Aryanism was central to his worldview: "All the human culture, all the results of art, science, and technology that we can see before us today, are almost exclusively the creative product of the Aryan. . . . [h]e alone was the founder of all higher humanity. . . . He is the Prometheus of mankind from whose bright forehead the divine spark of genius has sprung at all times. . . . [t]he first cultures arose in places where the Aryan, in his encounters with lower peoples, subjugated them and bent them to his will."[37]

And the Jew was the Aryan's Manichean antithesis:

> The mightiest counterpart to the Aryan is represented by the Jew. . . . He is and remains the typical parasite, a sponger who like the noxious bacillus keeps spreading as soon as a favorable medium invites him. . . . wherever he appears, the host people dies out after a short or longer period. . . . He poisons the blood of others, but preserves his own. . . . the personification of the devil as the symbol of all evil assumes the living shape of the Jew. . . . With satanic joy in his face, the black-haired Jewish youth lurks in wait for the unsuspecting girl whom he defiles with his blood, thus stealing her from her people. With every means he tries to destroy the racial foundations of the people he has set out to subjugate.[38]

Rejecting the principle of equality, racial antisemites judged one not by one's accomplishments but by one's "blood," over which the individual had no control. Blood determined the way a person thinks, talks, behaves, and creates. While racist thinkers claimed that their ideas were rooted in science, ultimately their theories derived from primordial feelings; they rested on a mythical, not a rational, foundation.

## THE JEW AS INTERNATIONAL CONSPIRATOR

Racist thinking often was combined with the belief that Jews were conspiring to take over Germany and the world. This accusation was a secularized and updated version of the medieval demonological myth that Jews, in the service of Satan, were plotting to destroy Christendom. In an extraordinary display of irrationality, antisemites held that Jews throughout the world conspired to control the state, political parties, the press, and the economy in order to dominate the planet. According to Paul Johnson, prominent British historian and journalist, "antisemitism is the father of all conspiracy theory."[39]

The myth of a Jewish conspiracy found its culminating expression in the notorious forgery, the *Protocols of the Learned Elders of Zion*. The *Protocols* was written in France in the 1890s by an unknown author in the service of the Russian secret police, which sought to justify the tsarist regime's antisemitic policies. Drawing on earlier antisemitic conspiracy works—and one work that had nothing to do with Jews but satirized Napoleon III, attributing to him ambitions of world domination—the forger described an alleged meeting of Jewish elders in the ancient Jewish cemetery of Prague. In these eerie surroundings the elders plot to take over the world and to reduce non-Jews to slavery. To implement their plan for world domination, says the text, Jews employ every imaginable weapon: They undermine religion, assassinate monarchs, weaken the aristocracy, and hatch revolutions, including the French Revolution, which had advanced the dangerous ideas of liberty and equality. They manipulate the stock exchange, ignite class warfare, and cause economic crises. Proceeding by secret and invisible means, they strive to gain the commanding heights in the economy, judiciary, parliament, the press, education, and every other source of power. Their tentacles extend around the world. Their control of money, "over which we alone dispose," gives them power.[40] Through their control of the newspaper and periodical press, they manipulate intellectual life. They use socialism and trade unionism to dominate the workers, and promote alcoholism, prostitution, pornography, and humanism to befog the minds of non-Jews. After their successful revolution, continues the text, the Jews will eliminate all religions except Judaism and thus "we shall determine the destiny of the earth."[41] Antisemitism, confesses the *Protocols*, is merely a tool fabricated to hold Jews together until the grand plot is fulfilled.

The *Protocols* also sees Jews as armed with superhuman powers. Thus in many editions of the work the principal speech to the learned Jewish elders is delivered by the Devil himself. According to its early Russian translator, the book revealed the Jewish plot to establish the reign of the Antichrist, "who, springing from Jewish blood, will be tsar and master of the whole earth."[42] Linking the Jews to the Devil and the Antichrist is a legacy of medieval Christian diabolization of the Jews and serves to reinforce the belief that the evil and conspiratorial Jew wields immense power over national and international affairs. First published in Russia in 1903, the *Protocols* was widely distributed after World War I and widely believed.

## COMMUNISM AS A JEWISH CONSPIRACY

The *Protocols* probably was invoked more often to explain events in Russia than any other phenomenon of the age. In the communist government founded by Vladimir Lenin, Jews were perceived as disproportionately represented. A new myth quickly took form and became commonplace: "[A]lthough all communists are not Jews, still *all* Jews are communists."[43] For at least two generations before the Bolshevik Revolution of 1917, Russian Jewish intellectuals tended to be Marxist, revolutionary, and radical; from the Jewish masses in the last two decades of the nineteenth century there emerged a Marxist socialist workers' movement. The explanation is plain to see, except through antisemitic lenses that focus on Jews at all times and everywhere as conspiring to overthrow and destroy. Some foreign observers like the Englishman Harold Frederic thought that Russian Jews reacted as they did because they had been treated for so long largely as outlaws, and, indeed, that there would be something quite wrong with a people, whether Jews or not, who did not turn against oppressors who had persecuted them so mercilessly by discriminatory laws and repeated massacres. From the 1870s Russian Jews were increasingly marginalized, discriminated against, barred progressively (after a liberal period under Alexander II) from the universities, the liberal professions, and especially the professoriate, the civil service, and military careers except as conscripts. Murderous pogroms punctuated everyday life, once the government adopted in 1881 an official policy of antisemitism and the Black Hundreds (dressed in menacing black uniforms and dedicated to ravaging Jewish districts) of the Union of Russian People were organized in 1905. "Russia bathes in Jewish blood," commented a Jewish observer in 1914.[44] Goaded too by the extreme poverty and the squalid ghettos of the Pale (see page 134), itself one huge ghetto where, in 1897, a quarter of the population was *luftmenschen* (men of air) floating about like figures in a Chagall painting, Jewish intellectuals were drawn to extreme remedies. They became radicals of one militant stripe or another: Revolutionaries, Marxists, anarchists, socialists, or Zionists. In the revolution of 1905, over a third of those arrested as revolutionaries were Jews, although Jews accounted for only 4 percent of the population.

The Jewish proletariat evolved along a similar path: In addition to the scourge of institutionalized antisemitism and bloodthirsty pogroms, they were excluded from factory employment (except in a few Jewish-owned factories) and confined to small-scale handcrafts and petty trading to eke out a living. Jewish workers, like Jewish intellectuals, tended to join the Marxist Social Democratic party (which split into Bolsheviks and Mensheviks), the Zionist movement, or the Bund (the General Union of Jewish Workers in Lithuania, Poland, and Russia). Founded in 1897, the Bund's program was socialist and anti-Zionist, calling for Jewish national autonomy to be sustained by Yiddish culture rather than by Jewish religion. The Bund was remarkably successful in fusing the Jewish intelligentsia with the Jewish masses in quest of a Jewish future.*

In the actual revolution that brought the Bolsheviks to power in November 1917, Jews, aside from a few like Leon Trotsky, were not particularly numerous and those who did participate were, in an apt formulation, "non-

---

* The situation in Germany and Austria-Hungary, where there was mounting antisemitism but no pogroms, offers some parallels. Jewish socialists were numerous in Berlin, Vienna, and Budapest—about 10 percent in 1910—and a higher percentage among socialist leaders were Jews, and many of them were disaffected intellectuals. But there was no Jewish labor movement, no Bund in Germany or Austria. Jewish financial, commercial, and industrial success (see chapter 4) was not matched by access to the liberal professions (especially the professoriate), the civil service, the military officer corps, and so on. Discriminated against, subject to racist hatred, and uncertain how permanent or irreversible emancipation was, some Jews found careers in literature and the arts; others took to the theoretical barricades of socialism and revolution, but not in the numbers or radical extremism exemplified by their counterparts in the Russian Empire. In the West—France (despite the Dreyfus affair), England, and the United States—there was no *luftmensch* kind of poverty, careers were relatively open to talent and energy, emancipation was genuine, and antisemitism was little more than a nuisance. On the whole Jews were sedate citizens more dedicated to the status quo than to militant radicalism—Marxist or anarchist revolutionaries. All the while, however, influential people as well as vulgar antisemites were prating fantasies of the Bolshevik-Jewish menace and raising the bogey of a communist takeover, with Jews in the vanguard as the *Protocols* foretold.

Jewish Jews,"[45] atheistic, contemptuous of rabbinical obscurantism, thoroughly secularized, completely detached from the Jewish community, and dedicated to Karl Marx's solution of disappearance by assimilation. The Bund, at its December 1917 national conference, actually condemned the Bolshevik regime, and Jewish opposition and hostility to the Bolsheviks continued for a year or more. A British reporter noted in January 1918 that the Bolsheviks have "done much to estrange Jews from them" and "not a single thing to win Jews [over]."[46] In the course of the civil war of 1918 to 1921, however, Jewish acceptance and support for the Bolsheviks mounted decisively. The reasons are not far to seek.

Opponents of the Bolsheviks, the Whites, circulated the *Protocols* to inflame the antisemitic masses against the Reds. Counterrevolutionary propagandists described the Bolshevik Revolution as an attempt by Jews, agents of the Antichrist, to subjugate Christian Russia. It is likely that during the civil war the *Protocols* contributed to the brutal pogroms that took the lives of not less than one hundred thousand Russian Jews, principally in Ukraine where some seven thousand violent outbursts occurred between 1918 and 1921, although the traditionally antisemitic Ukrainians needed little provocation to undertake pogroms. General Simon Petlyura, a leader of the Ukrainian independence movement, gave his soldiers free rein to pillage and torture the defenseless Jews, explaining that this was the only way that he could maintain authority over his troops. By contrast, the Soviets defended Jews with force, punished militia units that engaged in pogroms, and outlawed antisemitism as criminal and counterrevolutionary: "There you must give the Bolsheviks credit. There are no pogroms," acknowledged one Jew who fled Soviet Russia.[47]

A 1919 summary to the American secretary of state reported soundly, "As far as could be learned, percentage of Jews among Bolsheviks [is] not very different from proportion of Jews in population but prominence [of] certain Jews in Bolshevik movement has aggravated feeling." However, many diplomats and journalists incompetently or willfully reported, as did the American ambassador to Poland in 1922, that "the Soviet regime is in the hands of the Jews and their oppression is Jewish oppression." The *Morning Post* of London alleged in 1920, it "is abundantly clear . . . that these men are overwhelmingly of Jewish origin, that their ideas are violently anti-Christian, and that their programme is to break down in its entirety the whole framework of modern civilization."[48]

The equation Jews = Bolsheviks has long joined the canard of the Jewish banker and usurer in the antisemites' arsenal; often, in the mode of the *Protocols*, antisemites imagined that international Jewish bankers and international

Bolsheviks colluded in global conspiracy, claiming that the Rothschilds, Schiffs, and Warburgs financed the Bolsheviks. In retrospect, the bogus Jewish-Bolshevik formulation is one of the great hoaxes of the age. It ignores the facts that at least as many Jews opposed the Bolsheviks as supported them and Jews were much more prominent in the Bund and in the Menshevik and Cadet parties. As one Briton remarked: The "Jews in Russia are the bourgeoisie not the Bolsheviki" and the proportion of Jews in the British government was greater than in the Soviet.[49] As so often in the annals of antisemitism, the Jews were depicted as indivisible and monolithic, an absurd assumption in light of the kaleidoscopic diversity that characterizes Jews, variegated and never of one mind. Such obvious points are nullified by a will to believe any evil of Jews.

The defeat of the Whites in the civil war and the securing of the Soviet regime provided opportunities for the Jewish intelligentsia. Persecuted and marginalized under the tsars, they now entered the civil service and government posts en masse, filling the vacuum left by defections or condemnations of the imperial bureaucracy. From pariah status into high public positions, the universities, and the liberal professions was one jump for the Jewish intelligentsia, and was, according to the historian Enzo Traverso, "a decisive element in inspiring the Jewish population in its entirety toward an attitude of support for the Soviet regime."[50] For a decade or so the promise of an antisemitism-free Soviet Russia and the prospects for an autonomous working men's Yiddish culture (the Bund's program) seemed bright, even though at the same time the atheistic regime was engaged in the repression of religion and Judaism in particular, condemned Hebrew as counterrevolutionary in a policy of "de-Hebrewizing," and expropriated the numerous Jewish tradesmen and petty bourgeois—so-called proletarianization—in the communist transformation of society and economy.

Because they were neither workers nor peasants, these "bourgeois" Jews fell into the category of *lishentsy*, those who were automatically deprived of all citizenship rights and means of livelihood; they also suffered refusal of medical care, exclusion of their children from school, expulsion from their homes, and denial of ration cards in a time of food shortages and famine. In the mid-1920s the American Jewish Joint Distribution Committee (a relief organization often considered to be an agent of the Jewish global conspiracy) endeavored to settle these desperate 800,000 displaced Jews in agricultural colonies in Ukraine and the Crimea.[51] From 1928, under Joseph Stalin, the Joint's much-heralded plan was abandoned, and antisemitism and murderous purges were the norm until Stalin's dying day in 1953. It was Stalin's boast at the time of the Hitler-Stalin Pact in 1939 that as soon as he had enough qualified non-Jews, he would oust the Jews from all the leading positions, as after the war it was his boast that there were no Jews on the Party's Central Committee. During the war Stalin sought to rally world Jewry and the Western powers to the cause of the Soviet Union through the Jewish Anti-Fascist Committee. But the Holocaust and the struggle of the Jewish community in Palestine to form the state of Israel stimulated a revival of national consciousness among Soviet Jewry, which greatly angered Stalin (although the USSR voted for the 1947 United Nations resolution creating Israel), who launched a murderous campaign against "cosmopolitans," those "people without origin or affiliation," and the like epithets for the ever-conspiring Jews. The Jewish Anti-Fascist Committee was disbanded, its members and many Jews (Yiddish writers especially) were killed or arrested. The official newspaper *Pravda* announced the so-called Doctors' Plot. Six of the nine physicians accused of trying to poison Stalin and the Kremlin leadership at the behest of the CIA and the Zionists were Jews. Pogrom-like attacks on Jews in the streets and schools occurred; they were dismissed from positions and jobs; a mass deportation of all Jews from European Russia to the Arctic or Siberia was underway. Thereupon Stalin died and *Pravda* announced that the Doctors' Plot was all a "base fabrication" by the KGB and the danger abated, but antisemitism did not ebb in the Soviet Union.

## THE *PROTOCOLS* IN GERMANY AND THE UNITED STATES

Germany's defeat in World War I and a revolution that replaced the kaiser's government with an unpopular democratic republic made many Germans receptive to the *Protocols'* message. In their twisted view, the *Protocols* provided convincing evidence that the Jews were responsible for starting the war—Jewish bankers saw an opportunity to enrich themselves; for American entry on the side of the Allies; for Germany's defeat—the "stab in the back"*; and for the revolution that toppled the monarchy. They saw further proof of Jewish power and machinations in the first meeting of the Zionist World Congress (1897); the Balfour Declaration (1917), which supported a Jewish homeland in Palestine; the Bolshevik Revolution (1917); the newly established but short-lived

---

* Some 100,000 German Jews had served in the war and 12,000 had died in battle. Medals for bravery had been awarded to 30,000 Jewish soldiers. But this meant nothing to the extreme Right or to antisemites who held the Jews responsible for fostering a defeatist attitude on the home front.

communist regime of Béla Kun in Hungary (1919); the Versailles Treaty (1919); and the League of Nations (1919). The radical Right, including the Nazis, embraced the *Protocols* as a simple and convincing explanation for every catastrophe that had befallen Germany. Catholic and Lutheran clergy urged their parishioners to read the work to protect Christian Germany from its insidious enemy. In 1924 a Jewish observer described the book's impact in postwar Germany:

> In Berlin I attended several meetings which were entirely devoted to the *Protocols*. The speaker was usually a professor, a teacher, an editor, a lawyer or someone of that kind. The audience consisted of members of the educated class, civil servants, tradesmen, former officers, ladies, above all students. . . . Passions were whipped up to a boiling point. . . . [The Jew] was the cause of all ills—those who had made the war and brought about the defeat and engineered the revolution, those who had conjured up all our suffering. This enemy . . . slunk about in the darkness, one shuddered to think what secret designs he was harboring . . . observed the students. . . . Now young blood was boiling, eyes flashed, fists clenched, hoarse voices roared applause or vengeance. . . . German scholarship allowed belief in the genuineness of the *Protocols* and in the existence of a Jewish world-conspiracy to penetrate ever more deeply into all the educated sections of the German population, so that now it is simply ineradicable.[52]

Next to the Bible, the *Protocols*, which was translated into all the European languages and published in many editions, was the most widely circulated book in the world in the two decades between the wars. Even intellectuals and statesmen endorsed it. As early as 1921 the *Protocols* was conclusively proven to be a forgery by the English journalist Philip Graves, in a series of articles in *The Times* of London, but the work continued to be translated and distributed.

The *Protocols* was challenged and rejected as false and fraudulent several times in courts of law since Graves' exposure. In 1934, in Berne, Switzerland, several people with Nazi sympathies who were connected with the editing, publication, and distribution of the *Protocols* were put on trial at the behest of the Swiss Jewish community. After hearing expert testimony and observing the total inability of the defense to either substantiate the authenticity of the *Protocols* or refute the testimony of the plaintiffs, the judge emphatically denounced the *Protocols* as "ridiculous nonsense" and "smut literature," a blatant forgery and species of plagiarism.[53] Nevertheless, the theme of an international Jewish conspiracy remained a core principle of Nazi propaganda until the very end of the war.

From the beginning of their movement to the end of the Third Reich, Nazi propagandists exploited the *Protocols* to justify their quest for power (to save Germany from the Jews); their fight against Bolshevism (the tool of the world Jewish conspiracy); World War II (started by the Jews); and extermination (ridding the world of evil). Thus at the end of December 1944, with Berlin in ruins, the war nearing its end, and the Jews of Europe only a bleeding remnant of a people, Goebbels' propaganda ministry continued to harp on the myth of the world Jewish conspiracy: "The central issue of this war is the breaking of Jewish world-domination. If it were possible to checkmate the 300 secret Jewish kings who rule the world, the peoples of this earth would at last find their peace."[54]

The *Protocols'* widespread acceptance in the United States, which Jews considered (and continue to consider) a "promised land," is a particularly distressing chapter in the work's history. In 1920 the automobile magnate Henry Ford published the *International Jew: The World's Foremost Problem*, a reprint of articles that had earlier treated the *Protocols* favorably in his weekly newspaper, *Dearborn Independent*. Quoting, paraphrasing, and plagiarizing the *Protocols*, the paper routinely accused Jews of undermining America through their control of the press, labor unions, and banks, and by promoting jazz, alcohol, and communism. They control the American theater and the motion picture industry; they secularize the schools and Judaize the universities; Jewish gamblers corrupt baseball and the Jewish liquor trust engages in bootlegging. Jews were blamed for World War I and the Bolshevik Revolution. Within a short period, 500,000 copies of the *International Jew* circulated in the United States, and it was eventually translated into sixteen languages. Confronted with a lawsuit, Ford stopped publication in 1927 and apologized for his "error" to the American Jewish community. Apparently his apology was not sincere, for he was later to blame Jewish bankers for starting World War II.

## FROM DEMONIZATION TO EXTERMINATION

The antisemites of the Wilhelmine era (from 1871 to 1918, when the German Empire was led by the Hohenzollern rulers Wilhelm I and Wilhelm II, until abolition of the monarchy in the aftermath of defeat in World War I) fought to revoke the civil rights of Jews, to bar them from influential positions, and to foster their emigration or expulsion. Some more radical antisemites even called for the physical annihilation of the Jews. German researcher Klemens Felder, who in the 1960s analyzed fifty-one leading German antisemitic writers and publications for the period 1861 to 1895, observed that of the twenty-eight that proposed concrete solutions to the "Jewish problem," nineteen called for the Jews' physical extermination. "In their eyes," Felder concluded, "the Jews were parasites and vermin that had to be exterminated. . . . Some advocated the simplest solution, to kill the Jews, since the duty to defend . . . 'morals, humanity and culture' demanded a pitiless struggle against evil. . . . The annihilation of the Jews meant for most anti-Semites the salvation of Germany."[55]

German antisemitic organizations and political parties failed to get the state to pass antisemitic laws, and by the early 1900s these groups had declined in political power and importance. But much mischief had been done. By joining a paranoid ultraconservative nationalism with a mystical belief in the sacredness of Aryan blood, late-nineteenth-century antisemites had constructed an ideological foundation on which Hitler would later build his movement. Their convictions that the Jews were defiling the German bloodstream, corrupting German culture, destroying ancient social bonds, and conspiring to dominate Germany and the Christian world all preceded Hitler. Also prior to Hitler, extremists and intellectuals—many of them second-rate alienated thinkers—disseminated the beliefs that Germans and Jews were engaged in an apocalyptic struggle to the death and that the degeneration of Germany would continue until the Jews were eliminated from German life. In words that foreshadowed Hitler, the ferociously antisemitic biblical scholar and philologist Paul de Lagarde (1821–1891) said of the Jews: "One does not have dealings with pests and parasites: one does not rear them and cherish them; one destroys them as speedily as possible."[56] The theory, language, and justification of extermination were in place.

Racist and antisemitic ideas had become a mobilizing ideology; in varying forms and intensity, antisemitic assumptions and vocabulary characterized the political and cultural views of many Germans before 1914, and they were not contested in any systematic way. In the minds of many Germans, even in respectable circles, the image of the Jew as an evil and dangerous creature had been firmly established. It was perpetuated by the schools, youth groups, the Pan-German League, and an array of incendiary racist pamphlets and books. In 1892 the Conservative party, which attracted many aristocrats, clerics, military leaders, and others from the educated and socioeconomic elites, and had the support of the kaiser, borrowed from the fringe Jew-hating parties, and adopted antisemitism as a plank in its national platform: "We combat the manifold upsurging and decomposing Jewish influence on our national life."[57] Seeking to deprive Jews of the civil rights granted to them in previous decades, the plank called for barring Jews from judgeships and the civil service. Thus many German dignitaries shared with simple country folk, struggling artisans, and small businessmen the belief that Jews could not be true Germans and that patriotic Germans had a duty to fight these aliens. Like medieval Christians who believed that hating and harming Jews validated Christianity, German nationalists of all classes believed that Jew-hatred was a necessary and legitimate way of expressing love for Germany.

It is indeed astonishing that Germans, many of whom had virtually no contact with Jews, were so obsessed with them and that they believed that a nation of fifty million was mortally threatened by a half-million citizens of Jewish birth, or that the eleven million Jews of the world (by 1900) had organized to rule the planet. The Jewish birth rate in Germany was low, the rate of intermarriage high, and the desire for complete assimilation into German life great; assimilated German and Austrian Jews identified completely with German culture. Within a few generations the Jewish community in Germany might well have disappeared. Moreover, despite the paranoia of the antisemite, the German Jews and the Jews in the rest of Europe were quite powerless. There were scarcely any Jews in the ruling circles of governments, armies, civil services, or heavy industries. As events were to prove, the Jews, with no army or state and dwelling among people many of whom despised them, were the weakest of peoples. But the race mystics, convinced that they were waging a war of self-defense against a satanic foe, were impervious to rational argument. Antisemites, said Theodor Mommsen, the great nineteenth-century German historian, would not listen to "logical and ethical arguments. . . . They listen only to their own envy and hatred, to the meanest instincts. Nothing else counts for them. They are deaf to reason, right, morals. One cannot influence them. . . . [Antisemitism] is a horrible epidemic, like cholera—one can neither explain nor cure it."[58]

A deeply illiberal Volkish nationalism and antisemitism fertilized right-wing politics in Germany, demonstrating that segments of the population could be aroused by irrational ideas and demagogic appeals and that idealism could be debased and science misused. This witches' brew, heated to the boiling point by the humiliation of defeat in World War I, an unpopular revolution in the last days of the war that overthrew the kaiser and led to the establishment of the Weimar Republic, and the hard times in the immediate aftermath of the war, was the larva from which Nazism sprang.

The racial nationalists' denigration of Jews and glorification of Aryanism, their popularization of irrational but emotionally satisfying racial myths that purported to explain history and life, and their linking of a crude racial ideology with noble idealism inspired a large number of racial activists and helped to account for the capitulation to National Socialism in a later generation by

even the high-minded and the respectable. The Nazis employed the antisemitic myths and stereotypes propagated by their Volkish predecessors. After
World War I racists were more radical in thought and deed than their Wilhelmine mentors. They eagerly responded to Hitler's racial nationalism and
did not shrink from translating their hatred into state persecution and ultimately mass murder.

Nazi racial antisemitism should have been sufficient indication to decent
Germans of the kind of man Hitler was and of the moral barbarism of his
movement. But antisemitism was not only commonplace in Germany, it was
also *respectable*. In the closing decades of the nineteenth century, had not the
Conservative party and numerous influential Germans, including Adolf
Stoecker, Richard Wagner, and Heinrich von Treitschke, openly embraced it?
Had not blatantly antisemitic books, such as Julius Langbehn's *Rembrandt as
Educator*, become national bestsellers, bringing their authors effusive praise by
conservative elites? By 1914 had not conservatives effectively barred Jews from
most civil service positions, judgeships, and full professorships? Had not the
army, the symbol of Germandom, barred Jews from becoming reserve officers,
let alone members of the general staff? Had not Kaiser William II rejoiced at
news of the brutal Kishinev pogrom in Ukraine and urged the authorities to
"throw the pigs out" when informed that fleeing Russian Jews were seeking
refuge in Germany? And like other ultraconservatives, had he not wanted to
reverse civil rights for Jews? Did he not repeat the lie that Jews controlled the
economy and the government and were conspiring with Masons and Jesuits[!]
to dominate the world? In referring to Jews, did he not employ the vilest antisemitic slurs, saying they were parasites, deicides, polluters of the race, Satan,
and the Antichrist?* Even if Nazi antisemitism did not attract many voters to
Hitler—as recent research seems to indicate—neither did it repel Germans.
Decades of national racial antisemitism layered on the granite foundation of
centuries-old Christian antisemitism still perpetuated by many clergy had poisoned the German (and European) mind, blinding both elites and commoners
to the dangerous implications of Jew-hatred when Hitler was building his
movement and making them insensitive to the persecution of Jews after he had
gained power.

Members of the economic and cultural elites, with all their education and
civilized values, were no less insensitive, no less imbued with antisemitic
stereotypes that reduced flesh-and-blood men and women to abstractions. Ul-

---

* In 1927 ex-Kaiser Wilhelm said that "Jews and mosquitoes [constitute] a nuisance
that humanity must get rid of in some way or another. I believe the best would be gas."

timately, they were no less indifferent to the Jews' humiliation, despoliation, and massacre than their less advantaged compatriots. When it came to anti-semitism, the German elite, with some exceptions, set no moral example, as Fritz Stern, who has written extensively on Volkish thought and modern Germany, reminds us: "The antisemitism of the upper classes was part of a good form, part of what I have called vulgar idealism, and for many it paved the way either for accepting the radical antisemitism of the [Nazi] regime or for shutting one's eyes to the ever-worsening persecutions."[59] No doubt the reflection of Albert Speer, the gifted architect and Hitler's minister of armaments and war production, applied to many of the elite for whom Jew-hatred was either acceptable or a matter of indifference: "Hitler's hatred for the Jews seemed to me so much a matter of course that I gave it no serious thought."[60]

In 1933, when the Nazis were still uncertain about public support for an anti-Jewish campaign, the German academic and cultural elite and church authorities—with rare exceptions—did not publicly protest against the boy-cotting of Jewish businesses, the driving out of some twelve hundred Jewish faculty, including prominent Nobel laureates, and the expulsion of Jews, in-cluding some of the country's most prominent musicians, artists, and writers, from the arts. Indeed, many of the conservative cultural elite endorsed these measures, which coincided with their traditional position that German public and cultural life should be free of a contaminating Jewish spirit. Thus, in 1936 Carl Schmitt, perhaps Germany's most prominent legal thinker, called for the "cleansing" of Jewish authors from the libraries and the compilation of a legal bibliography that noted if the writer were Jewish; and if a Jewish au-thor were quoted, he had to be identified as such. Johannes Stark, a Nobel Prize winner in physics, maintained that scientific thought is a function of race: "[N]atural science is overwhelmingly a creation of the Nordic-Germanic blood component of the Aryan peoples. . . . The Jewish spirit is wholly different in its orientation. . . . True Heinrich Hertz made the great discovery of electromagnetic waves, but he was not a full-blooded Jew. He had a German mother, from whose side his spiritual endowment may well have been conditioned."[61]

Hoping to establish biological criteria for identifying Jews, anthropolo-gists and biologists made comparative studies of craniums and blood types—to no avail, of course. And the Nazis could always rely on academics to write "learned" treatises, as they had done in the Wihelmine era, attesting to Jewish inferiority and wickedness. Thus Eugen Fisher, professor of anthropology at the University of Berlin, told an audience of French intellectuals in Paris in 1941, shortly after the Nazi invasion of Russia, that the "morals and actions of the Bolshevist Jews bear witness to such a monstrous mentality that we can only speak of inferiority and of beings of another species."[62] More chilling is the fact that many of the officers of the Einsatzgruppen—the murder squads that slaughtered more than a million Russian Jews, including little children— had university degrees, including doctorates.

Antisemitism provides a striking example of the perennial appeal, power, and danger of mythical thinking. Ancient Christian myths that had demonized the Jews—myths that liberals thought would disappear in a world pervaded by the Enlightenment's legacy—were secularized by radical nationalists who held the Jews responsible for all the ills afflicting the nation. Nationalist and racist myths and stereotypes provided true believers with a comprehensive world-view, an interpretation of life and history that fulfilled the mind's yearning for coherence and meaning. By defining themselves as the racial and spiritual op-posites of the "vile Jew," true believers of all classes derived a feeling of worth and felt joined together in a mystical Volkish union. True believers also felt that they were engaged in a struggle of universal significance—defending the Aryan race and a higher civilization from a deadly enemy. "There cannot be two Chosen People," Hitler reportedly said. "We are God's people. . . . Two worlds face one another—the men of God and the men of Satan."[63]

By cloaking their hatred under the mantle of idealism and spiritual ab-solutes—Germany's welfare demands the destruction of the wicked race— racists could view persecution and even liquidation coldly, matter-of-factly, undeterred by human values. Many of the SS, who carried out mass murder with fanatical zeal and bureaucratic efficiency, were motivated by just such an outlook. In exterminating the Jewish people they believed that they were noble souls defending the sacred Volk and civilization itself from fiendish foes, "an all-embracing world power" as Hitler defined the Jews. They saw them-selves as idealists charged with a noble mission to rid the world of life that was both worthless and wicked—human devils, poisonous bacteria that were in-fecting the sacred Volk, "life unworthy of life." They accepted unquestion-ingly Goebbels' description of the Jew as "the enemy of the world, the destroyer of cultures, the parasite among the nations, the son of chaos, the in-carnation of evil, the ferment of decomposition, the visible demon of the decay of humanity."[64] These race mystics believed that they were engaged in a life-and-death struggle with evil itself, as the following tract issued by SS headquarters during World War II indicates:

> Just as night rises up against the day, just as light and darkness are eternal en-
> emies, so the greatest enemy of world-dominating man is man himself. The

sub-man—that creature which looks as though biologically it were of absolutely the same kind, endowed by Nature with hands, feet and a sort of brain, with eyes and mouth—is nevertheless a totally different, a fearful creature, is only an attempt at a human being with a quasi-human face, yet in mind and spirit lower than any animal. Inside this being a cruel chaos of wild, unchecked passions: a nameless will to destruction, the most primitive lusts, the most undisguised vileness. A sub-man—nothing else! . . . Never has the sub-man granted peace, never has he permitted rest. . . . To preserve himself he needed mud, he needed hell, but not the sun. And this underworld of sub-men found its leader: the eternal Jew![65]

Many of the SS were ideologues committed to racist doctrines that they believed were supported by the laws of biology; they were true believers driven by a utopian vision of a new world founded on a Social Darwinian fantasy of racial hierarchy and delusional images of the Jew. Awaiting execution in 1947 for war crimes, SS Captain Dieter Wisliceny perceptively analyzed the mythical component of Nazi antisemitism. He described it

as a mystical and religious view which sees the world as ruled by good and evil powers. According to this view the Jews represented the evil principle. . . . It is absolutely impossible to make any impression on this outlook by means of logical or rational argument. It is a sort of religiosity. . . . Against this world of evil the race mystics set the world of good, of light, incarnated in blond, blue-eyed people who were supposed to be the sources of all capacity for creating civilization. . . . Now these two worlds were alleged to be locked in a perpetual struggle. . . . The usual view of [Reichführer SS] Himmler is that he was an ice-cold cynical politician. . . . [In reality] Himmler was a mystic who embraced this world-view with religious fanaticism.[66]

Racial nationalism, a major element in nineteenth-century intellectual life, attacked and undermined the rational tradition of the Enlightenment. Racial nationalists denied equality, scorned toleration, and dismissed the idea of the oneness of humanity. They employed reason and science to demonize and condemn an entire people and to justify humiliation and persecution. They succeeded in presenting a racial ideology fraught with unreason and hate as something virtuous and idealistic, and made anti-Jewish myths a vital force in political life. In 1933, the year Hitler came to power, Felix Goldmann, a German Jewish writer, commented astutely on the irrational quality of racial antisemitism: "The present-day politicized racial antisemitism is the embodiment of myth, . . . nothing is discussed . . . only felt, . . . nothing is pondered

critically, logically or reasonably, . . . only inwardly perceived, surmised. . . .
We are apparently the last . . . of the age of the Enlightenment."[67] That many
people, including intellectuals and members of the elites, believed these racial
theories—indeed, for some it was a passion, an obsession—was an ominous
sign for Western civilization. It showed how tenuous the rational tradition of
the Enlightenment is, how receptive the mind is to dangerous myths, and how
speedily human behavior can degenerate into inhumanity. Ending in the
Holocaust, racist thinking constitutes a radical counterideology to the highest
Western values, both Christian and humanist. For this reason, the Holocaust
is the central event of the twentieth century or, as a Jewish prayer expresses it:
"Auschwitz is the fact and symbol of our era."

## EPILOGUE

In the Western world, there is a crucial difference between antisemitism before
and after the Holocaust. Today overt expressions of Jew hatred are no longer respectable. People aspiring to careers in government, business, and the arts rarely
avow antisemitism openly—it has become detrimental on a professional level to
do so—and many organizations, including established churches, publicly deplore revivals of the old calumnies directed against Jews. Indeed prominent
Catholic and Protestant clergy have voiced regret for the anti-Judaism/anti-
semitism propagated by their churches that had poisoned people's hearts against
the Jewish people with disastrous consequences. One cannot but wonder, however, whether the blatant antisemitism recently directed at Israelis by Europeans
who are not identified with the far Right will compel a modification of this sanguine view. Today virulent antisemitism is confined largely to fringe groups,
many of them openly sympathetic to Nazism. These extremists deliberately perpetuate antisemitic myths, particularly that of an international Jewish conspiracy. They publish and circulate the *Protocols* and, in an act of calculated cruelty,
claim that the Jews, in still another expression of their collective wickedness,
made up a story of Nazi genocide. (See chapter 5.) Hate and conspiratorial delusions about Jews still persist, as the following passage from an antisemitic periodical illustrates: "Talmudic Jewry is at war with humanity. Revolutionary
communism and International Zionism are twin forces working toward the
same goal: a despotic world government with the capital in Jerusalem."[68]

And on the Internet, the same rubbish is found: "[W]e must first realize
that Satan is real and that he is at war with God. This being the case, it would
be strange indeed if there were no conspiracy dreamed up by him to rule the
world, using agents . . . [and] the Talmudic system of Jewry plays a prominent
role in this plan."[69]

Since 1945 the *Protocols* has been printed and distributed, generally by neo-Nazi organizations in many Western countries, and now it can be downloaded on the Internet. To be sure, in Western lands intellectual and public figures, if they give the work any thought at all, view it as a hate-filled canard from a hate-filled past. Its appeal now, unlike in the interwar years, is almost exclusively with professional antisemites and the marginal figures who constitute their audience. Objectivity has little influence on the mind-set of these antisemites, for whom a Jewish world conspiracy has become an integrating principle that provides emotionally satisfying answers to the crucial questions of existence. For purveyors of hate, the sinister hand of the Jew lies behind all the problems of the modern world; the Jews' victims must unite in self-defense against their evil enemy.

At times governments have responded to the book's circulation. In 1965 the United States government issued a report entitled "Protocols of the Elders of Zion: A Fabricated 'Historic' Document." The Senate committee concluded: "It is impossible for a fair-minded person of any common sense not to see that the 'Protocols' are the fictional product of a warped mind and that for years they have been and still are the chief staple of the anti-Jewish pamphleteer. . . . [T]he peddlers of the 'Protocols' are peddlers of un-American prejudice who spread hate and dissension among the American people."[70] In 1991 a South African court declared the *Protocols* to be fraudulent.

Curiously, the Nation of Islam displays the *Protocols* at college conferences and in its bookstores; it also endorses speakers who claim that Jews are engaged in still another conspiracy—this time Jewish doctors are deliberately injecting black babies with the AIDS virus as part of a genocidal plot. (See chapter 6.) And periodically American populists conjure up "international Jewish bankers" to explain the economic woes of the "little man." But, to repeat, attempts to demonize the Jew in Western lands do not receive public support from established political, financial, and intellectual elites.

In eastern Europe, where antisemitic feelings have always been vicious and vile, conspiracy theories directed at Jews have had a resurgence. After the Six Day War (1967), in which Israel trounced several Arab states that had both military and political support of the Soviet Union, the USSR unleashed an "anti-Zionist" campaign that branded Judaism as a criminal, bloodthirsty, and racist religion. Soviet propaganda asserted that Jewish bankers and Zionists had collaborated with Hitler and, in the spirit of the *Protocols*, insisted that Jewish capitalists were using Zionism as a front to fulfill their goal of world domination. The dissolution of the Soviet Union has been accompanied by a revival of conservative nationalist organizations; employing the same logic and rhetoric as their pre-Bolshevik ancestors (and German Volkish thinkers), these xenophobic Russian nationalists accuse the Jews of being a rootless people, foreigners fundamentally hostile to traditional Russian culture, and exploiters who suck the blood of decent Russians. In the tradition of the *Protocols*, conservative nationalists view the Russian Revolution and Stalin's terror as part of a world Jewish conspiracy. In 1992 Pamyat, the most extreme of these groups, published the *Protocols;* the following year a Russian district court ruled it a forgery and fined Pamyat for libel. In addition to promulgating the myth of Judeo-Marxism, the Russian radical Right has disseminated the myth of Zionist-Nazi cooperation manufactured decades earlier by Soviet propagandists. Ukrainian antisemitic publications routinely quote the *Protocols*. One paper, in an edition devoted to the fiftieth anniversary of the end of World War II, claimed that Jewish capital created both the Nazi and Bolshevik regimes to facilitate the creation of Israel by weakening Germany and Slavic lands.

Nationalists in lands formerly dominated by the Soviet Union also employ conspiracy theories, accusing Jews of imposing communism on their countries and stressing the need to defend them against international Jewish influence and machinations. With today's greater freedom in the former Soviet bloc, the *Protocols* has been published in virtually all the states, most recently in April 1996, on the first day of Passover, when excerpts were published in Estonia's third largest newspaper.

The *Protocols* is also published in several Latin American countries. During the 1970s the press in Argentina carried stories—billed as a contemporary illustration of the *Protocols*—about a Rabbi Gordon (there was no such person) of New York City, who with the help of an international Zionist organization was plotting to create a Jewish republic in the Argentinean state of Patagonia (why Patagonia of all places?). A dozen books containing excerpts from the *Protocols* appeared immediately, purporting to prove the existence of the conspiracy.

Muslim lands, where antisemitism has been at a fever pitch in recent decades, are rife with Jewish conspiracy theories. In a manner reminiscent of *Der Stürmer,* Arab and Iranian newspapers employ ugly caricatures of Jews— hooked noses, hunchbacks, scraggly beards—to dehumanize them. When the peace process was operative, Egypt attempted to remove antisemitic references from school textbooks. However, the Egyptian media never ceased depicting the Jewish people as satanic conspirators responsible for imperialism, communism, the world wars, and economic misery; for spreading pornography, drugs, AIDS, and homosexuality; and for destroying religion and family life by promoting secularism and female equality. In April 1996 a

Syrian paper argued that the Jews believe in a warrior God who has ordered them to destroy other civilizations and kill all non-Jews; in September the same paper claimed that the Israeli rabbinate teaches that it is a sacred duty to kill Arabs.

To demonstrate that the Jews are an evil force in international affairs, Islamic propagandists make considerable use of the *Protocols*, which circulates widely in the Middle East—for example, in 1994 two leading Iranian dailies published the *Protocols* in numerous installments. Muslim scholars, either in the Middle East or living abroad, have not seen fit to inform their coreligionists that the *Protocols* is a lie and a libel. In 1986 Bernard Lewis, the distinguished student of Near Eastern history, described the popularity and pernicious influence the *Protocols* and other standard antisemitic works, such as Rohling's *Talmudic Jew*, have had in several Muslim lands

> . . . these two books are the most frequently cited authorities on Jewish matters—not only on Israel and Zionism, but on Jews and Judaism in general. . . . Nor are these publications confined, as in the West, to the lunatic fringe. They are published by major, sometimes government, publishing houses; they are endorsed and sometimes introduced by prominent political, religious, and intellectual figures; they are quoted on national television and radio programs and in some of the most respected newspapers and magazines; they form the basis of discussions of Jews and Judaism in many schools, colleges, and teacher-seminary textbooks. . . . There are at least nine different Arabic translations of the *Protocols*, and innumerable editions, more than in any other language including German. Until a few years ago, the reader with access only to Arabic would not have known that the authenticity of the *Protocols* had ever been called into question. . . .
>
> The *Protocols* have at different times been publicly recommended or cited by . . . numerous . . . kings, presidents, prime ministers, and political and intellectual leaders. In addition to local use and distribution, agencies in several Arab countries, and lately in revolutionary Iran, have undertaken the distribution of the *Protocols* and related literature all over the world.[71]

The extent to which Muslims have absorbed the most vicious and dangerous form of Western antisemitic myths is seen in the following extract from a book written in 1974 by the former rector of Cairo's al-Azhar University, the most prestigious seat of learning in the Muslim world: "Among Satan's friends—indeed his best friends in our age—are the Jews. They have laid down a plan for undermining humanity, religiously and ethically. They have begun to work to implement this plan with their money and their propaganda.

They have falsified knowledge, exploited the pens of writers and bought minds in their quest for the ruination of humanity. Thus they proceed from this to seizing power . . . domination, mastery, and gaining full control."[72]

In the aftermath of the Al-Qaeda terrorist attacks on the United States on September 11, 2001, the Palestinian Authority newspaper *Al-Hayat Al-Jadeeda* proclaimed that "the Muslim-Jewish conflict resembles the conflict between man and Satan, [that] this is the fate of the Muslim nation, and beyond that [it is] the fate of all the nations of the world, to be tormented by [the Jews]."[73] In calling for holy war against Israel, the covenant of Hamas, drawn up in 1998, also employs the language of the *Protocols:*

> Our enemies have planned from time immemorial in order to reach the position they've obtained now. They strive to collect enormous material riches to be used in the realization of their dream. With money, they've gained control of the international media beginning with news agencies, newspapers and publishing houses, broadcasting stations. . . . [W]ith their money, they have detonated revolutions in different parts of the world to obtain their interests and reap their fruits. They were behind the French Revolution and the Communist Revolution and were also responsible for most of the revolutions we've heard about elsewhere. With their money, they have created secret organizations which spread throughout the world in order to destroy societies, and to achieve the Zionist interest such as the Free Masons, the Rotary and the Lions Club. All these are destructive espionage organizations. With their money, they've been able to take control over the imperialist countries and push them to occupy many states in order to suck the riches of these countries and spread corruption there. The same goes for international and local wars. They were behind World War I. . . . [T]hey established the League of Nations in order to rule the world. They were also behind World War II where they made enormous profits from speculation in war material. . . . [They promoted] the establishment of the United Nations and Security Council . . . in order to rule the world through them. . . . After Palestine, they . . . will still aspire to further expansion. Their plan is the *Protocols of the Elders of Zion.*[74]

In April 1998 *El-Telegraph*, Australia's leading Arabic newspaper, quoted the *Protocols* to substantiate the view that Jews seek world domination. It was forced to make a public apology for what it called "an innocent mistake." Also in 1998, in a bizarre but classic illustration of the conspiracy myth, Prime Minister Mahathir Mohammad of Malaysia blamed the precipitous decline in the value of the country's currency on a Jewish "agenda." "We are Muslims," he told the audience, "and the Jews are not happy to see the Muslims progress.

The Jews robbed the Palestinians of everything, but in Malaysia they could not do so, hence they do this, depress the ringitt."*[75]

Japan is another place that abounds in Jewish conspiracy theories and antisemitic publications based on the *Protocols*. Bookstores prominently display such titles as *The Jewish Plot to Control the World* (written by a Shinto priest); *The Expert Way of Reading the Jewish Protocols* (written by a university professor); and *The Secret of Jewish Power* (written by a senior member of parliament). Japanese newspapers routinely print antisemitic ads. For example, on July 27, 1993, a leading business paper printed an ad for a three-volume work entitled *Get Japan, The Last Enemy: The Jewish Protocols for World Domination*. The ad contained stars of David and an image of Satan and claimed that "Jewish cartels surrounding the Rothschilds control Europe, America, and Russia and have now set out to conquer Japan."[76]

The most popular Japanese writer of antisemitic diatribes is Uno Masami, a Christian fundamentalist preacher with ties to the Liberty Lobby, probably the most active antisemitic organization in the United States. (See page 182.) In 1986 he published *If You Understand the Jews, You Will Understand the World* and *If You Understand the Jews You Will Understand Japan*, which became sensational bestsellers—a combined total of more than a million copies sold in just six months. Interpreting contemporary events according to the guidelines found in the *Protocols*, Uno claimed that the Jews rule the United States; control IBM, Ford, Standard Oil, AT&T, and other leading corporations; fabricated the Holocaust; manipulate the world economy; and were plotting to destroy Japan. He became a frequent guest on television and responsible circles cited him as an authority.

That antisemitic literature flourishes in a country that has had the most limited historical experience with Jews** and where the Jewish population, both foreign residents and converts, is minuscule—2,000 out of a population of some 125 million—demonstrates the strength and protean character of an antique Christian demonological myth, and its extraordinary capacity to survive and adapt itself to different times, places, and cultures.

---

* Some Arab commentators do examine Jewish history with a more critical historical eye. In an extraordinary three-part article published in *al-Hayat* (November 12–14, 1997), a Lebanese newspaper, Abu Fakhr criticized Arabs for embracing classical European antisemitic myths. He systematically refuted the myth that Jews practice ritual murder, showed that the *Protocols* was a forgery, and rejected the legend that Jews were conspirators with hidden powers.

** It should be noted that during World War II, despite its alliance with Nazi Germany, Japan offered havens to European Jews—approximately sixty thousand found refuge in domains it ruled, including almost twenty thousand in Shanghai. The two thousand Jews living in Japan today, most of them in Tokyo, have been consistently well treated.

## CHAPTER 4

# HOMO JUDAICUS ECONOMICUS

## THE JEW AS SHYLOCK, PARASITE, AND PLUTOCRAT

*... wherever Jewish businessmen were* permitted *to be successful, many of them have been successful.*

—James Yaffee, 1968[1]

*I am persuaded that in Russia, Austria, and Germany nine-tenths of the hostility to the Jew comes from the average Christian's inability to compete successfully with the average Jew in business.*

—Mark Twain, 1899[2]

*It was the Jews, of course, who invented the economic system of constant fluctuation and expansion that we call Capitalism. ... Let us make no mistake about it—it is an invention of genius, the Devil's own ingenuity.*

—Adolf Hitler, 1934[3]

BEGINNING IN THE MIDDLE AGES, Jews became important actors in European economic life. Over the centuries Jewish economic activity gave rise to myriad myths and fantasies: The Jew as Shylock or capitalist exploiter, on one hand, and the Jew as Marxist predator or socialist agitator, on the other, the twain meeting as international Jewish bankers conspiring with the international Jewish Bolsheviks to destroy, enslave, and dominate by the techniques of the *Protocols of the Learned Elders of Zion*. The peculiar role of Jews in the European economy and the historic myths that evolved regarding this role ultimately sprang from the theological anti-Judaism promulgated by Christian thinkers; these myths contributed decisively to the virulence of modern anti-semitism, which remains rooted in theology. Over the centuries since the earliest Christian commentators, the image of Jesus' "cleansing of the Temple" and the expulsion of the money changers (Mark 11:15–19) have been used to condemn Jewish business activity, contrasting the crass materialist mentality of Judaism to the spirituality of Jesus and Christianity. The belief that the Temple worship was desecrated by sordid trade and profiteering and that *purity* was restored by the ex-pulsion of the money changers became a leitmotif of our culture.[4]

Without the theological reprobation, the Jew would have been a merchant, banker, or property owner, normal and respectable, rather than wicked money-grubber, usurer, bloodsucker, and the like. "Historically," wrote the French his-torian of antisemitism Léon Poliakov, "the Jew's theological function [as deicide, and the like] preceded and determined his economic specialization."[5] Condemnation of the Jews as economic exploiters followed from their theolog-ical condemnation as a criminal people. Excluded from owning land and barred from the crafts, medieval Jews first entered trade and then finance, economic callings then considered repugnant. Reflecting on these developments, Hein-rich Heine, the nineteenth-century German Jewish poet, wrote: "In this way the Jews were legally condemned to be rich, hated, and murdered."[6]

It has to be understood, however, as the great scholar of Jewish antiquity Jacob Neusner has argued, that there is no such thing as the economic history of the Jews, since Jews never constituted a single society and distinct economy. Jewish history is too disjunctive to present it as having anything even resem-bling unified, continuous developments that could possibly be presented as economic history.[7] There are, however, what Neusner calls "the economics of Judaism," ideas about how economic activities should be conducted, techni-cally as well as morally, and these have great importance in general economic history; of even greater significance is the role that has fallen to Jews as eco-nomic factors, agents, and middlemen. Both categories—Jewish conceptions of economic theory and practice and the Jews as economic actors—have given rise to a plethora of myths and fantasies that are the subject of this chapter.

## THE MIDDLE AGES

Jewish prominence or dominance in certain economic callings, at certain times and places, has its origin in the Christian Middle Ages, when, as the great nineteenth-century German Jewish historian Heinrich Graetz piquantly put it, "Christianity . . . confiscated the heavens, and feudalism . . . confiscated the earth [and] both deprived Jews of the right to own land."[8] Two factors operated to raise Jews to positions of economic importance during the Middle Ages, and once those two factors are understood, the rest is footnotes of detail and qualification. First, early medieval Europe (500–1050) was economically backward in comparison to the Byzantine and Islamic civilizations and ancient Rome. The characteristic unit of production was the agricultural manor: It was remote and isolated, essentially self-sufficient, its local economy largely barter, and it was dependent on the outside world only for such items as fish, plowshares, salt, and wine. The merchant who supplied these needs was regarded as more a vagabond than member of a professional class: He was a peddler with his pack wandering about the countryside. Business and financial operations were primitive and existed only on the smallest scale. The economic map of Europe and the Mediterranean basin was the reverse of what it is now: Europe stood in thrall to the Byzantine East and particularly to the Muslim world. The situation is nicely caught by the boast—excessive we now know—of Ibn Khaldun, a later Muslim historian, that the Christians "can no longer float a plank" without the caliph's permission. So it remained until the twelfth century, when the Italian city-states began to clear the Mediterranean of Muslim shipping.[9] Until then the Jews, a protected minority on all shores of the Mediterranean, could, as it were, float a plank and have "a large share of the meager trade of the early Middle Ages." In the eighth and ninth centuries the Jewish guild of merchants known as the Radhanites, based in southern France and Mediterranean-centered, forged as far afield as the Black Sea and Khazaria (a state in southern Ukraine whose dominant group had converted to Judaism).[10]

The second factor contributing to Jewish economic prominence was the prevalence in the Latin Christian world of a strongly ascetic, anticommercial ethic that derived from Jesus' teaching in the Sermon on the Mount. Jesus' central teaching is an apocalyptic eschatology: "Repent for the Kingdom of Heaven is at hand." He therefore urges his followers to throw over worldly possessions and all considerations of getting and spending, family, position, and status. On the brink of the eschaton (the dawning era of the reign of heaven), prepare first for the Kingdom, all else is irrelevant or a dangerous distraction. This ascetic unworldliness was embodied in the medieval monastic ideal of poverty and had the force of a cultural imperative. The merchant's trafficking entailed the taint of this world and was a dangerous distraction from the real business of life: piling up heavenly treasure through prayer and contemplation.

In the earlier medieval agrarian world, economic fact corresponded closely with Christian theory. The merchant's function, considered economically unimportant and morally suspect, was uncoveted, indeed frowned on by Christians and thus left open to Jews among other outsiders, such as Byzantines and Muslims. Coming from the economically advanced Islamic world where commerce labored under no religious prohibition or taboo, enjoying far-flung contacts and access to credit, and having a single commercial code enforceable equally in Paris or Baghdad, Kairuwan or Khorosan, Constantinople or Toledo, Jews were able to fill the vacuum left by Christian aversion and European backwardness. Jews were barred from the lucrative and honorable professions and sources of livelihood. Obviously they could not be priests or monks, but equally they were prevented from being barons or knights; all these callings were endowed with landed estates, the holding of which required Christian oaths and contracts. During the Roman period Jews had owned land extensively; eventually they were displaced from the land by their inability to take the oath of a Christian, the danger of residing exposed in the countryside in an increasingly hostile Christian world, discriminatory taxation, and, finally, outright prohibition by law of Jewish land ownership. "Land has only been given to strong-armed men" says the Talmud sardonically.[11] Nevertheless, we now know that more Jewish landholding, notably in Spain and southern France, persisted than had been usually thought.

By 1100 commerce had grown in importance and begun to be respectable. It began to be an enterprise coveted by Christians, who displaced Jews, often, as during the Crusades, by sack and massacre. Jews also were eliminated by monopolistic Christian merchant guilds that enjoyed many advantages over Jewish rivals, such as the patronage and protection of monarchs, princes, town governments, and ecclesiastics. In many parts of Europe, Jews, forced out of trade, turned to an area still open to them by the church's war on clerical usury as well as by European backwardness in that sphere: banking and finance.

Jesus' asceticism generated an even more tenacious taboo in the area of banking and finance than in commerce, crippling Christians' enterprise under the prohibition on "usury," or interest taking.* Here the New Testament precept sprang from the Old without modification, as so often was the

---

* These two terms were long interchangeable and the practice by either name was equally condemned; only with the emergence of free enterprise and commercial societies did the distinction arise between interest as a legitimate rate and usury as exorbitant and illegal. Christianity and Islam followed Judaism in forbidding and eventually condoning interest; in some parts of the world the prohibition on "usury" still operates, as among fundamentalist Muslims in Saudi Arabia.

case. In the Torah, the main texts are Exodus 22:25: "If you advance money to any poor man amongst my people, you shall not act like a money-lender: you must not exact interest in advance from him"; Leviticus 25:35–37: "When your brother-Israelite is reduced to poverty and cannot support himself in the community, you shall assist him. . . . You shall not deduct interest when advancing him money nor add interest to the payment due for food supplied on credit"; Deuteronomy 23:19–20: "You shall not charge interest on anything you lend to a fellow-countryman, money or food or anything else on which interest can be charged. You may charge interest on a loan to a foreigner but not on a loan to a fellow-countryman." In Proverbs 28:8, we learn that "He who grows rich by lending at discount or interest is saving for another who will be generous to the poor," a verse invoked by medieval Christian anti-usury warriors in compelling moneylenders to make restitution to the "victims," their descendants, or "the poor." Psalm 15:5 defines one of the characteristics of the righteous man as he "who does not put his money out to usury." There is ample warrant for the condemnation by the Council of Poitiers, 1280, of that "usury which both Testaments detest,"[12] and one can readily see that the religious prohibition on usury-interest constituted a grave problem, a brake on economic activities for both Christians and Jews in what remained essentially an agrarian society.

The church declared war on usury as of the mid-twelfth century, especially under the goad of Pope Alexander III (1159–1181). The church prosecuted usury rigorously until the mid-fourteenth century and was still at it in the sixteenth, in the heyday of Renaissance capitalism, compelling "manifest, public, notorious usurers" to make restitution.[13] Every kind of usurer—clerical, lay, noble, Jewish, foreign—was condemned by the church. In the numerous synods and councils that took up the subject (beginning with the Second Lateran Council of 1139), the war went on. Usurers were equated with arsonists, adulterers, witches, highwaymen, and, finally, at the Council of Vienne (1311–1312), heretics, thus placing them within the jurisdiction of the Inquisition. As a sin usury was put in the same category as homicide, parricide, sacrilege, and incest. Churchmen had their hands full, however, in prosecuting clerical violators, who were, especially the monasteries, among the chief suppliers of credit as late as the twelfth century. By the early fourteenth century, clerical usury was virtually eradicated. Churchmen were less effective against nonclerical offenders, owing partly to the intervention of kings and lay authorities and partly to the sheer need for capital. In the mid-thirteenth century King St. Louis IX of France, who was more papalist than the popes in stamping out usury, was quite exceptional. His campaign to liquidate Jewish usury was opposed by his advisors who argued, according to the chronicler William of Chartres, that society needed moneylending, that it might just as well be carried on by the Jews who were "damned anyway," and that the outcry was greatest against the excesses of Christian usurers.[14] Although there is ample record of ecclesiastical efforts to enforce the prohibition of usury law on Jews, including cutting off whole communities from contact with Christians and interdicting their food supply, in general the church granted de facto toleration to Jewish moneylending.

Medieval Christian writers, most of them churchmen, were unanimous in condemning usury and almost equally so in attacking Christian usurers as far worse than Jewish ones. Once the Jews were expelled from a town or country, there was a characteristic demand by the poor and others who depended on loans that they be restored as the lesser of two evils. Thus Sebastian Brant's poem "Ship of Fools" (1493) inveighed against the "Christian Jews," that is, usurers, who "drove out" the Jews and attained a monopoly on moneylending.[15]

Jews also had to comply, as a religious obligation, with the prohibition of "usury" in the Torah, and for them, too, Deuteronomy 23:19–20 long remained a critical text. The Talmud, which is based on and adhered closely to the precepts of the Mishnah (a body of Jewish commentary and legal interpretation of the Bible, dating from 200 B.C.E. to 200 C.E.) ruled out "usury" for Jews as completely as did canon law for Christians. The authors and compilers of the Mishnah condemned interest taking as usury, as something unnatural—lending should be a form of charity. In both the Mishnah and the Talmud, according to Neusner, "all forms of profit—all forms!—constitute nothing other than 'usury' that Scripture condemned."[16] The Baba Mesia 5 portion of the Mishnah deals specifically with "usury" and expands and extends the biblical strictures and prohibitions. But, following Deuteronomy 23:19–20, it makes an exception that was to be crucial for the Jews of the Middle Ages: "Israelites may pay [to] or exact interest from gentiles."[17]

Theoretically at least, the rabbis, like the canonists (and like Muslim religious thinkers who had to wrestle with the same issue) adhered to the ancient prohibitions against usury, but the sheer necessity for Jewish survival compelled them to suspend the legal requirement. The suspension could be enacted on the grounds that the law was a reflection of the simple agrarian society of biblical times, when the function of credit was essentially to help a relative or neighbor temporarily in need: "If you take another's cloak in pledge, you must give it back to him before sunset. It is all the covering he has; it is the cloak he wraps his body in; what else would he sleep in?" (Exodus

22:25–27). But those conditions had long ceased. For Jews living in that succession of commercial, urban empires under Babylonian, Persian, Greek, Roman, and Muslim rule, an adjustment had to be and was made by the rabbis, so that their kinsmen could support themselves in what was often an alien and threatening world. Until well into the later Middle Ages, however, some talmudists sought to block loans by Jews to Christians, less perhaps on the grounds of biblical proscriptions than for the entanglements and dangers such dealings with Christians often entailed. Most, however reluctantly, modified theology to fit a stubborn reality, as did Rabbi Eliezer ben Nathan of Mainz (died ca. 1170), arguing that moneylending had to be tolerated, because "in the present time, where Jews own no fields or vineyards whereby they could live, lending money to non-Jews is necessary and therefore permitted."[18]

By the thirteenth century Jews had long been displaced from agriculture and were increasingly so from trade and from crafts and industry, where they had been strong, especially in southern Europe, having had their own craft guilds; here too they had been pioneers in transmitting from the Islamic world techniques for the production of items like silk, glass, paper, and dyes. The same pattern we have seen in commerce repeated itself in finance: From being an indispensable pioneer, the Jewish moneylender was transformed into an expendable competitor who was expelled by force and by his inability to match rival financial organizations, like those of the Lombards, "the Pope's usurers."[19] Christian bankers were among the most vociferous in demanding expulsion of the Jews so that they would have less competition and raise their rates.

In medieval Jewish economic history, kings loomed as large as the popes and canonists. Insofar as the Jews were concerned, the monarchs combated the church's war on usury, seeing in it an infringement of royal claims to sole jurisdiction over the Jews and their property. In England particularly, the Jews were among the most lucrative of several royal "monopolies." King John, for example, protected Jews against everyone else the better to exploit them himself.[20] Ferdinand IV of Aragon refused the papal demand, in the early fourteenth century, that certain Jews make restitution of usuries to their Christian debtors: "You well know that all Jews and whatever they own are Mine. Should such an action against them be allowed to pass, they would be ruined and be unable to pay My taxes. For this reason I firmly order that none of you should dare to [interfere]."[21] "One may almost refer to Jewish moneylenders as 'officials' of the Christian rulers," is Israeli historian H. H. Ben-Sasson's insightful suggestion.[22] If interest rates were high, it was because capital was acutely scarce, the difficulties and uncertainties of repayment great, and the moneylender's overhead in the form of payments he had to make to the king exorbitant.* Indeed the king, who made himself the Jew's silent partner, was the chief maker of the Shylock image.

For a Jew to function as a banker, he had to have royal permission in the form of a charter, which was costly to purchase and to renew annually. There was little chance for him to collect debts without the king's assistance, for which the royal fee was about 10 percent, although often it was much more; debts outstanding were subject to a hefty tax on the creditor, which was a chief source of royal revenue in twelfth- and thirteenth-century England. If a Jew died without heirs, all his property and the debts payable to him went to the king; surviving heirs had to pay any sum the king demanded, usually about a third, as an inheritance tax. Kings ordinarily did not borrow from the Jews but periodically simply bilked these "serfs of the royal chamber" of any amount according to the needs of the treasury or the whims of the monarch. The doctrine of the "eternal serfdom of the Jews," which had originated with the Church Fathers, was very serviceable in providing a legal basis for such royal expropriations. By the same warrant—when it suited their purposes, fiscal and political in the case of John of England, moralistic in the case of St. Louis IX of France—kings reduced or canceled the interest or principal of anyone's debts owed to Jews; sometimes they made such debts payable to the crown. The pound of flesh extracted by the king from the Jewish moneylender, the Jewish moneylender had, perforce, to extract from his clients. "The Jews," wrote Montesquieu, "enriched by their exactions, were pillaged by the tyranny of the princes."[23] It was a vicious cycle that ended when the Jewish community was, as a result of royal exactions, bankrupted and then, of no further utility, expelled, as in England in 1290 and France in 1306 and 1394. Thus was the golden goose killed.

Jewish wealth and royal toleration were directly proportionate to each other, so much so that Jewish communities frequently concealed their poor members and paid their taxes. Taxpaying was the Jews' one shield: "Taxes are our saviors," said the talmudist Asher ben Yehiel (ca. 1250-1327).[24] "All kinds of taxes are in the category of defense, for they guard us among the nations. What other benefit do the nations derive from defending us and allowing us to live among them, unless it be to their advantage to collect from us taxes and

---

* The rates charged by Christian bankers were generally not lower than those charged by Jews. In the twelfth century St. Bernard of Clairvaux admitted, "Where there are no Jews, Christians judaize far worse" (quoted by Poliakov, 3:397); and the Emperor Charles V lamented in 1520 that religious scruple did not restrain Christian bankers who "sucked the blood" of his fellow Christians (quoted by Baron, 12:161); like sentiments were expressed in every age.

imposts?" Another concluded that siphoning off Jewish wealth was the motive "in every grant [of privileges] the Jew had ever obtained from the royal power."[25] Other forms of "insurance" proved to be necessary.[26] Not surprisingly, what was a kind of annex to their taxes, Jewish communities maintained, formally or not, "the bribery fund" to which all had to contribute, "wherewith they bribed [royal officials] to forestall forcible abuses," since normally it was bribery to insure compliance with the law rather than the more familiar form of making exceptions or seeking special favors that violate the law.[27] The great Christian scholar James Parkes called this whole system of royal dependence "Life by Bribery," and he deplored how much Jews "lived between the devil of royal extortion and the deep sea of ecclesiastical repression."[28] A much-used metaphor had it that Jews were the "sponge" that soaked up much of the money in the country; the king wrung out the sponge to the benefit of his treasury. This situation is captured in the pathetic words that Peter Abelard (1079–1142) had the Jew speak in his *Dialogue between a Philosopher, a Jew, and a Christian:*

> Dispersed among all nations, without king or secular ruler, we Jews are oppressed with heavy taxes, as we had to repurchase our very lives every day. . . . If we want to travel to the nearest town, we have to buy protection with the high sums of money from Christian rulers who actually wish for our death so that they can confiscate our possessions. Even when allowed to exist, we are not permitted to own fields, vineyards, not even a patch of ground—and there is no one to defend us against open or concealed attacks. Thus filthy lucre is all that is left us. To keep our miserable lives going, we must charge exorbitant interest, which in turn makes us hated by those who think we oppress them.[29]

Subject to such capricious and contemptuous treatment and always on the threshold of expulsion, it is not surprising that the Jewish moneylender often tried to disguise his wealth; was secretive, deceptive, and suspicious; and resorted to subterfuges in his loans and business transactions. It is in the peculiar circumstances of the later Middle Ages that the Shylock myth took shape, Shakespeare's character being a coarsely exaggerated and stereotypic representative of a reality generated by royal policy. Shakespeare's "devil incarnal" and "fiend" clearly reflect the polemics of the church's war on usury and the Jews in the age of the Crusades and after. Until Parliament's 1624 act legalizing "interest" at 6 percent, a spirited debate persisted in England. As elsewhere, Judas was cited as the quintessential Jewish usurer, he who sells his soul for "blood money," and all usurers were damned as "children of the devil." Although there had been no Jews in England since 1290, the debate, like stage plays, was haunted by the image of scheming Jews, with much fulmination that interest taking is "judaisme" and usurers are "mercatore Judaizantes" (judaizing merchants). With the 1624 act, "as far as usury is concerned, the Middle Ages had ended," but the Shylock image of the Jew remained.*[30]

## EARLY MODERN EUROPE

In the early modern period, 1500 to 1789, there emerged a far-flung network of Jewish communities that centered in the Netherlands. This international network linked the Jews expelled from Spain in 1492** and Spanish and Portuguese Marranos (forced converts to Catholicism); the *arendars*, agents of Polish kings and nobles, and merchants of Poland-Lithuania-Ukraine; and the court Jews who served the rulers of central Europe.

Fourteenth-century Spain saw the emergence of the Marranos (Castilian for "pig"), known variously as New Christians, crypto-Jews, or *conversos*. By 1450 the converts or their descendants were "overwhelmingly Christianized" but were nevertheless exposed to an antisemitism that was "basically an extension of Christian hatred of the Jews." That hatred was of a *"non*-religious Jewishness," for their "impure blood" made Marranos the object of fear and loathing—the vocabulary and thought idiom of racism originated in Spain. Their economic achievements arousing "both ferocity and vengefulness," the Marranos were pursued relentlessly by the Inquisition, which profited enormously in the prosecution and confiscation of the property of "heretics" and

---

* If space permitted, a substantial portion of this chapter would deal with Jewish economic activity in Islamic societies and the Jews' status as *dhimmis* (people of the covenant); for a brief analysis of this subject, see appendix I.

** In 1391 an orgy of bloodletting and destruction spread over Spain, presenting Jews with the choice of baptism or death. Before the wave spent itself as many as 50,000 were dead. The 200,000 converted Jews of 1391 were augmented in subsequent decades by numerous sword-point conversions. Unconverted Jews could practice Judaism openly, technically still enjoying the old freedom and autonomy but increasingly exposed to raging mobs and inflammatory preachers. To deal with the Marranos, who were suspected of crypto-Judaism, the Spanish Inquisition was established in 1478. But the Inquisition—despite its ruthlessness, persistence, and slaughterhouse efficiency—made little headway against the Marranos. Nor did the policy suffice of decimating Jews by massacre and forced conversion, or reducing them to beggary and degradation by steady erosion of their legal rights. The only solution was baptism or expulsion. It is not known how many Jews fled in 1492 (perhaps 150,000 to 200,000), or how many remained and converted.

"judaizers"; it enforced the *limpieza de sangre* (purity of blood) racial laws, by which Marranos were excluded from the professions, guilds, public office, and the like—a severe blow to the Spanish and Portuguese economies that compounded itself generation by generation.[31] The Spanish Jews who had been expelled but remained Jewish and the Marranos wrote one of the most remarkable chapters in economic history. Initially they fled mostly to the Ottoman Empire, moving all over the eastern Mediterranean, to Istanbul, Salonika and the Balkans, the Levant, and North Africa. With the establishment of the Marranos in Amsterdam, the Dutch Republic became the center of an interdependent commercial and industrial web meshing together those areas, Poland, northern Germany and in particular Hamburg, England, and such ports as Bayonne and Bordeaux in France, Italy and especially Venice and Leghorn, the Spanish and Portuguese colonial empires, India and the Far East, and, not least, the Dutch colonial empire. Almost everywhere they went the Marranos and Spanish expellees rose to prominence in foreign trade, manufacturing, and finance. Their geographical dispersion, common culture, and ties of kinship enabled them to build up an efficient, close-knit, cosmopolitan trading network, a kind of common market that afforded them credit, protection, hospitality, local political news and market information, and the like. Without fear of the Inquisition in tolerant Amsterdam, some of the Marranos, who had been living secretly as Jews, shed their Catholic disguise and returned to the Jewish fold. However, most Marrano families, particularly those living in Catholic lands with the ominous presence of the Inquisition, lost all contact with their Jewish heritage. Nevertheless, for many generations Marranos were detested as crypto-Jews masquerading as Christians. Moreover, merchants and craftsmen, resenting them as enterprising competitors, often castigated them with antisemitic aspersions. The commercial success of former Iberian Jews contributed to the myth, born in the Middle Ages, that Jews operated by deceit and were taught to swindle Christians.

As of the thirteenth century Polish kings invited Jews to settle as an urban, commercial middle class in a Poland that was and long remained an agrarian society of nobles and peasants. The *arenda* (from medieval Latin, meaning "to rent") system enabled Jews to diversify beyond moneylending (initially their main function and the primary motive of the kings in inviting them) to leasing real estate. The Jewish *arendar* (lessee) had made his debut in the service of the kings as collectors of revenues, taxes, tolls, customs duties, operating mines, the mint, and other royal monopolies leased out to him. The agricultural arendar managed land, forests, tolls, inns and taverns, breweries, distilleries, tanneries, and the like for the king, municipalities, ecclesiastics, but especially the nobles; as agent of the estate, he wrested taxes and labor services from an army of serfs, over whom the arendar had real power, thus violating a fundamental principle of Catholic teaching. Arendas were fraught with danger, mostly from the noble owner, periodically from the peasantry who hated both noble and Jew, but it was the Jewish arendar whom the serf saw directly and continuously and felt to be his cruel, exploitative master. The system was most fully developed in Ukraine, an underpopulated region of frontier settlements, whose colonization under the auspices of Polish and Lithuanian nobles went on apace in this period. A commercial agriculture developed in this vast area and a class of Jewish merchants arose by whom the goods produced by the arenda system were conveyed far and wide, especially to central Europe, where much of their dealings were with court Jews, who were able to fulfill their obligations as army contractors to the Austrian Habsburgs and many German princes by drawing on the goods supplied by the arendar system. These same merchants and arendars were instrumental in stimulating craft industries—producing clothing, leather and shoes, furniture, metalwork, and much else; they built up extensive networks of craftsmen, subcontractors, lessees, petty merchants, and peddlers, most of whom were their coreligionists. Until the Holocaust, Polish Jews were concentrated in crafts.

A chief item in Poland-Lithuania's domestic commerce was the sale of liquor, produced under the arenda system on the noble estates and marketed in villages and towns across the commonwealth. Fundamentally, the economic transformation by which much of the grain grown on the estates was processed into liquor rather than exported was the nobility's response to the decline in world grain prices. Liquor was a more valuable product and more easily transported. From the sixteenth to the nineteenth century the *propinacja*—the production, distribution, and sale of alcoholic beverages, a specialized form of arenda—was a major industry, not only in Poland-Lithuania-Ukraine but also in Bohemia, Silesia, Hungary, and Romania. The Jewish village tavern keeper dealt directly with the peasantry, plying them with liquor, purchasing their agricultural surplus, extending them credit until the harvest, and so on. Perhaps inevitably, the Jewish taverner was blamed for peasant drunkenness and indebtedness, and he became a fixed feature in Polish (and Russian) antisemitism. This was hardly just or accurate, for as the Polish historian Wladyslav Smolenski wrote, "Although the peasant's drink was sold to him by the Jew, the liquor in his glass belonged to the owner of the estate; it was in the latter's tavern that the [Jewish arendar] lived and filled the nobleman's coffers with coins of the realm."[32] Thus Jewish tavern keeping, as the economic historian Hillel Levine has said, was "a masking device," concealing the nobles' domination and economic exploitation of the peasantry and the damage done to the kingdom's economy, but exposing the Jews to blame and vilification.[33]

The stereotype of the Jewish innkeeper is very prominent in Polish folk-lore, popular mythology, and literature. He is the middleman, depicted as alien and dangerous; from the netherworld, he is provided with the demonic features that popular culture and Christian iconography attributed to the devil. Thus in a tale of 1856 the reader is told, "This tavern was truly one of those Jewish pits where they lie in wait for the poor peasant's soul—Icek, the local innkeeper, was the humblest sort of Jew, red-haired, lame, [cannily] stupid and evil in the most wretched way."[34] He is the embodiment of village capitalism: He lends money to peasant and nobleman at "usury" and runs a kind of country general store, bank, post office, and news agency, and he is the peasant's link to the market, local and distant. Folklore and literature portray the Jewish taverner as acting under the prompting of his religion, which guides all his business dealings and inspires all his tricks and moneymaking schemes—the capitalism of the taverner is the product of Jewish teaching, according to these village economic theorists in the spirit of the latterday Werner Sombart. (See page 158.) Thus the stereotype of the Jewish village innkeeper was elaborated to express in miniature the economic myth of the Jew as, by nature, the predatory capitalist, enveloping parasite, and demonic conspirator in the image of the *Protocols*. Polish *philosophes* and reformers castigated Jews as economically corrupting—as the conspiratorial source of Poland's manifold ills and the tragedy of its dissolution in the Partitions. The country's anarchical but tightly controlled rural economy under the nobles remained in the rut of the arenda system, precluding economic modernization by the Jews working in tandem with other urbanites, as was to be the case in modern Germany.

The court Jews were astute businessmen and administrators whose services to the rulers gained them privileges. They tended to be concentrated in Austria, Germany, and Holland but were a significant element in the financial and administrative evolution of Denmark, England, Hungary, Italy, Poland-Lithuania, Portugal, Spain, and elsewhere, functioning variously as ministers of finance, army contractors, court purveyors, mint masters, and many other specializations. One of their fortes was as army contractors. As private individuals or companies, they made their resources and credit available to the state. Their secret weapon was the unmatched speed, reliability, and secrecy with which they could mobilize their own resources and those of that skein of far-flung but close-knit Jewish communities to which they had access. Court Jews were thus "able to transmit information, credit, and bullion from one part of the western hemisphere to another. . . . No other grouping could match the Jews in the vast scope and range of their operations. . . . [b]ecause they could draw on the assistance and resources of a host of money-changers, metal-dealers, colonial wholesale merchants, and brokers, who then, in turn, depended on . . . Jewish pedlars and hawkers."[35] Court Jews also supplied the art and luxury goods craved by princes eager to emulate Louis XIV's court at Versailles. So the Rothschilds began. Court Jews also operated as entrepreneurs in trade and industry in partnership with the ruler, often as pioneers in establishing new ones as well as in expanding traditional ones, engaging in such trades as lace and silk, cotton goods and canvas, and leather goods.

The court Jew was the ally of the ambitious ruler seeking to expand his political power. By assisting in modernizing the prince's finances and the reorganization of his government in the direction of bureaucratic, centralized absolutism, court Jews helped build the absolute state. The most notable example was "Jud Süss" (Joseph Süsskind Oppenheimer), "Cabinet Factor" to Duke Karl Alexander of Württemberg. Jud Süss died on the gallows—not a unique fate for court Jews.[36] The death of their protector and resentment of nobles, whose power was weakened by the centralizing efforts of these servants of the ruler, placed court Jews in a precarious position. Their activities contributed to the image of the Jew as a powerful, devious, and traitorous conspirator, as in the 1940 Nazi film *Jud Süss*. The court Jews certainly lived on in myth and stereotype, their notoriety having made them subjects of a bizarre medley of conspiratorial accusations. As mint masters they were blamed for the severe hardships that came in the wake of debasing the currency and the inflationary cycles. Coin clipping and debasement were, however, the policy, and the profit, of the king or noble and were much-used expedients throughout the age. It was the Jews, however, who were singled out, as in a woodcut of the 1620s showing them busy clipping coins: They work under the gaze of the Devil, who is dressed unmistakably in Jewish garb—the familiar and fatal motif of the Jew as Satan's agent. In addition, putatively, the few wealthy court Jews conspired with the numerous pauper Jews (the *Betteljuden*, or vagrant Jews, who increased greatly owing to wars' dislocations, expulsions, denial of residence rights, and so on, and accounted for half or more of the Jewish population). Feared as "savage" highwaymen, pauper Jews and court Jews alike were labeled "parasites" and believed to operate in collusion, the "criminal" ones wreaking damage from below, the "powerful" ones from above. "For the thief and the [court] purveyor, the beggar and the banker form two sides of the same coin, the common currency of modern economic antisemitism," writes Derek Penslar.[37]

Although court Jews were resented and resisted by a country's merchants, the rulers competed for Jews—who were readmitted to many countries: They were the great economic secret weapon of the age. The Jews "are like the pegs and nails in a great building," the English essayist Joseph Addison wrote of these catalysts in 1712, "which, though they are little valued in themselves, are absolutely necessary to keep the whole frame together."[38] The great mercantilist minister Jean Baptiste Colbert understood their value: He ordered his officials to be aware that "commercial jealousies will always induce merchants to favor the banishment of the Jews. But you ought to rise above such agitation by special interests, and calmly judge whether the commerce which they conduct through their relations with members of their own sect in all parts of the world is likely to accrue to the state's advantage."[39] Historian Jonathan Israel aptly designates this widespread employment of Jews "to the state's advantage" "philosemitic mercantilism."[40] As the pioneer economist Sir Josiah Childs said speaking in their behalf: If readmitted to England, the Jews would likely increase trade "and the more they do that, the better it is for the Kingdom in general, though the worse for the English merchant,"[41] who deployed the antisemitic arsenal to bar or expel them.

In the early modern period, Jewish economic endeavors labored under the stigma, variously, of being "unproductive," sterile, parasitic, usurious, dangerous, dishonest, criminal, abnormal, and the like. "Usury" was reportedly one form of "Jewish revenge."[42] In this view, as venerable as Plato and Aristotle, only agriculture and handicrafts were "productive" and creative, while commerce and finance, purportedly not involving physical labor, were dismissed as corrupting. Beginning in the Enlightenment—an age of "decline"[43] and growing impoverishment for European Jewry until the 1790s, when the revolutionary period brought new economic opportunities—there were repeated calls for the "productivization" and the "regeneration" of the Jews. This was to be accomplished by a systematic *Berufsumschichtung*, a reordering of the occupational profile of Jews by which they renounced trade and industry to become farmers and artisans. "Everyone advised the Jews to take up agriculture."[44] So compelling seemed the argument that the Jewish vocational distribution was abnormal and pathological that many Jews accepted the indictment. And, predictably, it was widely asserted that Judaism was the source of this aberration. Efforts to place Jews on the soil and engage them in agriculture were numerous and persistent over many generations but failed almost completely, not least because peasants already on the land did not want Jewish competitors. Some vocational schools trained Jews for crafts, but with little result. Jealous artisans in their monopolistic and exclusive guilds, finding themselves more and more at a loss in competing with factory production, resented Jewish intruders and rivals. Both agriculture and crafts were contracting, not expanding, fields. And ironically, opportunities in the traditional Jewish callings of commerce and finance were, thanks to industrialization and rail transportation, expanding rapidly. Curiously, the aspersions cast on "sterile" or "abnormal" economic activities of Jews found no corresponding strictures on non-Jews in the same occupations. Given how much agriculture and handicrafts have shrunk on the modern economic spectrum, dwarfed by commerce, finance, and all the "Jewish" callings, an obvious conclusion is that the "abnormal" Jewish economic structure has become the "normal" one in the West and worldwide. Jewish economic activity was "distinctive" rather than "abnormal." To antisemites this phenomenon was another form of "Jewification," for the anticapitalist opprobrium attached to trade and finance persisted in antisemitic stereotype, partly because it was a controlling assumption of Karl Marx. (See page 153.) Antisemites of the day saw only rich and powerful Jews everywhere engaged in "parasitic" dealings.

## MODERN EUROPE

Jews were major participants in the economic life of Europe in the nineteenth and early twentieth centuries. In France, for example, the Péreire brothers and the Rothschilds were prominent railroad builders and financial organizers. In 1852 the Péreire brothers established the Crédit Mobilier, a joint-stock bank, in contrast to the Rothschilds' family-owned banks. In the fifteen years until its demise in 1867, the Crédit Mobilier is said to have accounted for a quarter of France's industrial development, and it forged ahead in foreign investments in the same fields. In Germany and Austria, we shall see that Jewish economic achievement was particularly impressive.

By 1900 many Jews had achieved middle- and even upper-class status. But in regions of eastern Europe where Jews were heavily concentrated, notably in Russia and Galicia—the territory acquired by Austria in the partitions of Poland in 1772 and afterward—Jews were abysmally poor and generally lacked access to modern education. Their lives remained largely untouched by those cultural forces that had transformed Jewish communities farther to the west. Even in Vienna, where Jews were a major force in the city's economic and cultural life, in 1880 two-thirds of its 95,000 Jews were classified as destitute.

And in Russia nearly 5 million Jews were ensnared in the Pale of Settlement, the region of varying boundaries from the Baltic to the Black Sea where Jews were confined and restricted in countless ways from 1791 to 1917: Their story is one of poverty, famine, and pogroms; the tsars' government, with its official policy of antisemitism and economic discrimination, was a mortal enemy bent, at its most benign, on the conversion of the Jews, whose only real recourse was massive emigration, especially to the United States.* Typifying the Russian situation, a "moderate" government commission reported in 1888 that Jews "shirk state obligations" and dodge "physical manual labor"; "[t]he passion for acquisition and money-grubbing is inherent in the Jew from the day of his birth; it is characteristic of the Semitic race, manifest from almost the first pages of the Bible."[45] Some 650 laws, repealed in 1917 when the provisional government emancipated the Jews, hampered their civic rights in the Russia of the tsars.

Space limitations preclude an extensive account of Jewish economic activities in the several countries of modern Europe. We focus on Austria-Hungary and Germany, because it was in those countries that Jewish entrepreneurial dynamism and creativity most distinguished themselves; and in those countries also Jewish economic success was most thoroughly vitiated by antisemitic myths and chimeras.

## AUSTRIA-HUNGARY

Jews thrived in major cities of the Habsburg Empire, Vienna, Prague, and Budapest. By 1850 they were preeminent in much of Vienna's commercial and financial life, including banking, railroad promotion and management, and stock market brokerage. In 1859 the guilds were abolished, which, by extinguishing

---

* Jews fleeing the Russian pogroms 1880 to 1914 made their way far and wide and often afford the historian striking examples of economic pioneering. One remarkable group from *shtetls* (hamlets) in Lithuania escaped to British South Africa, where they settled in Oudtshoorn, the center of the ostrich feather trade. Jewish enterprise began in the familiar way as peddlers, "feather buyers," trudging from farm to farm selling the usual list of items in exchange for ostrich feathers. If fortunate, the peddler soon acquired a donkey or a bicycle to carry the load, then a one-horse cart, a two-horse cart, an automobile, then renting and finally buying his own ostrich ranch, then additional ranches. Such was the story of "the ostrich king," Max Rose, who arrived as a teenager in 1890 and, having improved productivity by irrigation and growing alfalfa, in a dozen years or so became Rothschild-rich and built one of the huge, extravagant "feather palaces" in Oudtshoorn, the "Jerusalem of Africa." But with World War I, Ford's Model T, and the debut of the flapper, women's styles and high fashion had no use for the flouncy "boas" and extravagant hats decorated with the resplendent plumes. The ostrich ranches went bankrupt, the "feather palaces" were abandoned, and most of these "Litvaks" (Lithuanian Jews), by the third or fourth generation, migrated away, perhaps to pioneer other ways of earning a living. See Rob Nixon, *Dreambirds* (1999).

monopolies in the name of free trade, was a great fillip to Jews, who were no longer excluded; but this caused the Christian lower middle class and artisan/crafts segment of the economy to decline all the more sharply, owing to their inability to compete with factory production and large-scale distribution, much of which was in Jewish hands, as well as with peddlers, who were also largely Jewish, many of them those medieval apparitions, *Ostjuden* (eastern Jews) recently come from Galicia. The enraged artisans, in their "artisan anti-semitism," organized themselves, trumpeting that "all Jews are capitalists."[46] Such displacements fueled the antisemitism that intensified as the century wore on; Karl Lueger capitalized on artisan phobias in founding the antisemitic Christian Social party in 1891.

Partly in response to these developments, Jews began entering the liberal professions in great numbers. From midcentury and particularly in the aftermath of the great financial crash of 1873, business offered less opportunity for Jews. Gentiles were entering the field in much greater numbers, the old-fashioned Jewish family firm ran into the more intense competition of joint-stock companies,* antisemitism was mounting, and the liberal professions, enjoying great prestige, proved more and more attractive. The traditional high valuation Jews placed on education and intellectual attainment paved the way for their entrance into the professions. Statistics regarding Jewish attendance at school and university tell much of the story: Jewish students in nine of Vienna's *Gymnasien* (elite schools with a classical humanist curriculum) averaged over 30 percent of the student body from 1870 to 1910 when Jews accounted for 6.6 to 8.6 percent of the capital's population; such overrepresentation prevailed throughout the empire. Vienna University presents much the same picture: The proportion of Jewish students ranged from 33 percent in 1881 to 24 percent in 1904 (the decline reflecting in part the antisemitism that was rife in the university). From the 1880s to 1938 some 50 percent of Vienna's lawyers and physicians and well over half its journalists were Jews.**[47] In 1936, 62 percent of Vienna's lawyers were Jews, 47 percent of its physicians, and 29 percent of it ac-

---

* As in Germany, there was a decided shift from Jewish business ownership and company promotion to managerial positions in joint-stock firms.

** Unless they were converts, Jews were passed over for the higher civil service and the judicial bench, which limited Jewish lawyers essentially to private practice; medicine had for centuries been the only profession open to Jews, and they, too, tended to be in private practice since hospitals normally did not hire them; journalism was the Jewish profession, a new field in which Jews were once again pioneers and in which they dominated as journalists and owners and editors of newspapers and magazines.

ademics; 45 percent of Vienna's Jews were self-employed in small businesses, which accounted for three-quarters to one-quarter of its bookstores, wine stores, textile merchants, movie houses, shoe stores, jewelers, photographers, pharmacies, and department stores.[48] Moreover, the Jews were "the most culturally creative of the Danube minorities." Most of the creators of modern culture in turn-of-the-century Vienna were either Jewish or of Jewish origin: In literature and thought Arthur Schnitzler and Ludwig Wittgenstein; in music Gustav Mahler and Arnold Schönberg; in psychoanalysis Sigmund Freud.* In backward eastern Galicia, Jews accounted for nearly half of those engaged in the professions although they comprised only 13 percent of the population; in Galicia as a whole around 1900 some 82 percent of the traders were Jews, most of them poverty-stricken petty shopkeepers and peddlers who were, nevertheless, a grade above the even poorer *Lumpenproletariat* of artisans, all of whom tended to blend into the mass of *Luftmenschen* (literally, those who lived on air).

In the nineteenth century Hungary experienced a tremendous increase in its Jewish population, mostly poor Jews flooding in from Galicia. With good secular schools, efficient railways financed largely by the Péreires and the Rothschilds, and efficiently managed great estates producing food for Vienna and other Austrian towns, Hungary offered many opportunities for enterprising individuals, including Jews. In independent Hungary in 1930, a Jewish population of 5.1 percent accounted for 34.4 percent of doctors, 49.1 percent of lawyers, 45.1 percent of pharmacists, 31.7 percent of journalists, 28.9 percent of musicians, 24.1 percent of actors, and stood at the "commanding heights" of banking, trade, and industry, so that a fifth to a quarter of the national wealth was "Jewish."[49]

## GERMANY

Germany's economic transformation from 1850 to 1914 has been called "one of the most amazing chapters in the entire history of modern times."[50] From a backward, precapitalist, essentially agricultural society, it became a capitalist, highly efficient industrial, technological economy. Its technology and industrial

---

* Hugo Bettauer's satirical novel *Die Stadt ohne Juden* (City without Jews) appeared in 1922. It featured an antisemitic government that expelled all Jews (including half Jews and converts but, like the Nazi race laws, permitted quarter Jews to stay). Vienna forfeited all its vitality culturally, socially, and economically, and the Jews had to be invited to return. A Nazi assassinated Bettauer in 1925.

and financial organization owed much to British, American, and especially French capital, ideas and techniques, and institutions. Within the epic story of nineteenth-century German economic development, one of the most remarkable chapters—although it is relatively untold and certainly unsung—concerns the German Jews over four or five generations from around 1800 to around 1930. In the words of Fritz Stern, "Perhaps never before in Europe had a minority risen as fast or gone as far as did German Jews."[51] The German Jewish economic elite contributed decisively to the country's economic development, its financial institutions, its industrialization, and its entry into the world market as a great economic power by 1890. That elite also played a significant role in underwriting the costs of Germany's wars of unification (1864–1871).

Over the period from the mid-nineteenth century on, statistics showed Jews, who constituted only 1 percent of the population, consistently accounted for nearly one-fifth of German economic activity and development. For decades there were very few gentile banks in Prussia, the largest German state: In 1860 there were 51 gentile as opposed to 106 Jewish banks in Berlin; in 1871, of 580 banking houses, 40 percent were gentile, 23 percent Jewish, and 37 percent "mixed." In 1881, when Jews accounted for 4.8 percent of Berlin's population, only 0.4 percent were civil servants, but 8.6 percent were writers and journalists, 25.8 percent financiers, and 46 percent retailers, wholesalers, and shippers; by then Jews were verging on 10 percent of the students in Prussia's universities. Another indication of their economic success is the number of Jewish millionaires. In 1908, in Prussia, there were 162 Jews among 747 millionaires (possessing five million or more marks), which is about one-fifth. Of the 25 wealthiest Germans, 11 (44 percent) were Jews; of the 100 wealthiest, 29 (29 percent); of the 200 wealthiest, 55 (27.5 percent); and of the 800 wealthiest, 190 (23.7 percent); the percentages for Germany at large are roughly the same as in Prussia. In an oft-cited statement of 1912, Walter Rathenau, son of a famous Jewish entrepreneur and future cabinet minister, asserted that 300 men, all of whom knew each other, controlled Europe's economic destinies; the historian Werner Mosse estimates that 125 were Germans and of those 40 to 50 were Jews or of Jewish descent.[52] A Nazi document from 1933, statistically reliable, reported that of 147 members of the stock, produce, and metal exchanges, 116 were Jews, and 17 of the 47 officers of the exchanges were Jews. Of the honorary commercial titles (*Geheimrat* or *Kommerzienrat*, etc.) awarded annually by the state—before the Third Reich—in recognition of public service, an average of 15 to 18 percent went to Jews. These are the years, 1850 to 1933, of the German-Jewish symbiosis: "The time seemed near when [Jews] might fully enter the German economy, German civil service, and German high culture"; Germany's Jews were *Kaiser-*

*treu* (patriotic and loyal) and gloried in their German fatherland and were, as the proverbial expression had it, more German than the Germans themselves.[53]

The first stage in the upward sweep of German Jewry (to 1850) came with the revolutionary and Napoleonic wars and the beginnings of German industrialization in the early nineteenth century. Until about 1820, almost all of German Jewry made its living as peddlers or petty shopkeepers—in Bavaria 96 percent were so employed. It was principally from this reservoir that the economic elite was to be drawn. In an age of freer trade, the end of guild monopolies, freer choice of occupation, and greater geographical mobility, these semiemancipated Jews began to make their way. Some of the emerging economic elite descended from the eighteenth-century court Jews, although most of those families had disappeared from view. The most famous example, of course, was the Rothschilds, with their headquarters in Frankfurt am Main and branches in London, Paris, Vienna, and Naples. Of the forty to fifty prominent Jewish families that emerged as bankers and entrepreneurs in this period, however, most were new men, by-products of the manifold commercial and banking operations of that turbulent era when Jews functioned, as in the past, thanks to their networks of contacts near and far, as military contractors and financial agents moving money and extending credit across international boundaries and military conflicts.

The railway age followed for the next quarter century to about 1875. The demand for capital investment in railways and allied fields like coal and steel was, as elsewhere, virtually insatiable, and "it was met in no small degree by Jewish financiers."[54] More new family banking houses rose from the petty traders, such as the Mendelssohn-Bartholdy, Bischoffscheim, Goldschmidt, Abraham Oppenheimer of Mannheim, and many others. It was the great age of the Jewish private bank, which flourished, often under the aegis of the Rothschilds. The Bleichröder bank in Berlin rose from obscurity once it was taken on as one of the Rothschilds' agents in the Prussian capital. When, in 1858, the maker of modern Germany, Otto von Bismarck, sought a personal banker who had to be a Jew because he regarded Jews as perspicacious and honest, on the recommendation of Rothschilds he chose Gerson Bleichröder. The double connection to Rothschild and to Bismarck, and thereby the state, was a tremendous advantage to S. Bleichröder & Co. From "the best informed man in Berlin," his became "the greatest banking house in Berlin," and he, eventually, "the richest man in Germany."[55] At the time of the peace settlement between Germany and France in 1871, it was a matter of widespread antisemitic comment that the financial expert on both sides was a Jew, Bleichröder and Alphonse Rothschild.

Aside from heavy investment in railroad construction, German Jews were prominent in textiles, a traditional calling, first as retailers and progressively in manufacturing silk and cotton goods. They moved from textile manufacturing into chemical processes, sending some of their sons to technical schools to learn the science of dying, bleaching, and printing fabrics. Within a generation Jews were engaged in all aspects of the production and distribution of wool, linen, cotton, and chintz in spinning, weaving, knitting, and dying, and in ready-made clothes and suits. This last may or may not have been a Jewish invention, but Jews were pioneers in marketing "made-up" clothing. Jews also went into brewing and distilling, an offshoot from dealing in agricultural goods and foodstuffs supplied to armies. Having supplied cavalry horses to armies, an easy step for Jews was transportation, carriage service, horse-drawn municipal trams, and in time their electrified versions. The German wars of unification in 1864, 1866, and 1870 again saw the Jews in the field as war financiers and army contractors—on which they seemed to have a natural monopoly. The boom decades of the 1850s and 1860s—the *Gründerzeit*, age of the promoter and entrepreneur—were the heyday of Jewish banks in railway construction and military contracting, when the role of Jewish army suppliers was "hardly inferior in importance even to the 'cannon king' Alfred Krupp himself."[56]

With "the great depression" of the 1870s to 1890s, Jewish firms—paralleling a general phenomenon in the Western world—changed over from private family companies to joint-stock corporations. After the 1873 crash and the prospect of nationalization of the major lines, railway construction declined in importance; Jews took up the slack by opening up foundries to manufacture rails, rolling stock, parts and equipment, and eventually locomotives. In that age of the industrial tycoon, they participated in the wholesale business of coal, iron, other metals, textiles, and consumer goods. On a smaller scale, they were engaged in mining and metallurgy—especially in Silesia, an eastern province, economically unadvanced and so offering opportunities for development. Jews were strongly represented during that high tide of capitalism and entrepreneurship in the electrical and chemical industries, the paper and packaging business, publishing of newspapers and of books, and of course both private and corporate banks.

A remarkable example of Jewish enterprise was the General Electric Company (AEG) led by Emil Rathenau (1838–1915), which created a national electrical infrastructure in Germany. The electrical engineer Werner von Siemens (1816–1892), a gentile, was the inventor of the electrical generator, and his company of Siemens & Halske manufactured electrical apparatus and built electric railways and streetcar systems. After vegetating in various business activities, Rathenau recognized the potential of electricity and Siemen's generating system, and his firm, AEG, set about building transmission lines to provide electric power for lighting homes, offices, shops, factories, and streets. The two firms were relentless rivals between 1890 and 1910 in manufacturing electrical equipment of all kinds and the electrification of the country. They have been studied as contrasting examples of "German" or "Christian" or "gentile" as opposed to "Jewish" entrepreneurship. Yet, apart from personal idiosyncrasies and situational factors, no such archetypal differences emerge. They were both self-made men, tycoons, one having begun as a craftsman, the other a businessman, and they converged as great manufacturing entrepreneurs. Rathenau's Jewishness is not the key to understanding his economic behavior and success. Jewish economic behavior, whether AEG's or the German Jews' generally, depended on the general culture and on objective factors such as economic needs and social conditions much more than religious affiliations.

Notable developments in merchandising (most if not all of them Jewish innovations) and in the appearance of the department store occurred in the period, and were associated with the Grünfeld, Tietz, and Wertheim families. Their family-run stores featured high-quality goods at prices that were fixed, clearly marked, fair, and competitive (the antithesis of some age-old stereotypes), customer service, a soda fountain for customer enjoyment, stockroom controls, conveyer belts, elevators, illustrated catalogues and mail order service, advertising and salesmanship. They catered to an urban mass market, one that was especially directed toward the middle class. Although the department store originated in Paris or the United States, German Jews copied it and brought it to new heights of efficiency. In the process they generated much antisemitic detestation from their rivals who could not match the economies of scale and advertising promotion. Jews were active in export-import, overseas trade, international capital and commodity markets, and colonial enterprises. This was the age of the *Kaiserjuden* (the kaiser's Jews), when great Jewish bankers and financiers along with some major industrialists were welcomed at court, honored in various ways, and sometimes ennobled.

Clearly Jewish enterprise had diversified broadly since the early decades of the century. Jews were more in the mainstream than at the margins, and many operated "with conspicuous success within the new capitalist and industrial structures" of the half century preceding World War I.[57] While private banks and family firms declined, Jews flocked into the new managerial elite. These new men constituted an elite of talent rather than of wealth. They depended on salaries and did not own the companies they directed or the capital they managed. Many names of the old elite of wealth and status disappeared; the new men were more anonymous and less visible, inducing some historians to conclude that Jewish participation in the German economy declined. But that is not the case. A decline in private banks was offset by the number of directors, executive officers, chairmen, vice chairmen, and board members of joint-stock banks and industrial corporations. The organizing and leadership of the Disconto-Gesellschaft Bank, the Dresdener Bank, the Deutsche Bank, and the Berliner Handels-Gesellschaft tell a story of full-fledged Jewish participation in German banking and corporate activity. The new type is seen in Albert Ballin, a self-made man who, as chief executive of HAPAG shipping and passenger lines, turned that sleepy firm into one of the world's leaders and opened the way worldwide for German commerce and economic activity. A survey of Jewish participation in the German economy on the eve of World War I demonstrates that in the transition from private firm to joint-stock company, Jews retained their position and accounted for about one-fifth of the economic elite and leadership. That fact contradicts the assertions of antisemites like Hermann Ahlwardt and Heinrich Class, who accused Jews of controlling German economic life. While Jews held key positions, they did not dominate the German economy, for far more Christians were among the economic elite and Jews were notably absent from key areas such as heavy industry.

In the Weimar period following World War I, Jewish banks played an important part—thanks again to their international connections—in attracting much-needed foreign investment to Germany for the benefit of private industry, public utilities, and municipalities. The situation in Germany supported a revival of Jewish private banks, such as Warburg and Mendelssohn. At the same time the prominence of Jews in joint-stock banks peaked. They played an important part in the rationalization of German industry in the turmoil of World War I's aftermath and the great inflation of 1923 and in a second stage following the 1929 depression—doing much to organize the chemical combine IG Farben, HAPAG and Lloyd in maritime shipping, United Steel, Darmstädter and National Bank (Danat) in 1921 (taken over in 1931 by Dresdener Bank), the Diskonto Gesellschaft and Deutsche Bank under the presidency of Max Steinthal, and other conglomerates—and in reintegrating Germany into the world economy. The 1929 depression saw, as was generally true of the 1920s, the intensification of extreme nationalism and radical antisemitism, which had a deleterious effect on Jewish economic activity, yet it appears that Weimar was "the golden age of Jews in German banking."[58] It was only after the Nazis ascended to power in 1933 that the expulsion of Jews from the German economy became perilous, and it took until 1938—following a 1937 law decreeing that any firm with a Jew on its board would be considered "Jewish" and subject to "Aryanization"—that their expulsion was complete. Thus in the four or five generations since 1800, the German Jewish entrepreneur, as the economic historian David Landes remarked, had "traveled from the margins and interstices of the economy to its centre, and then back to the margin."[59]

## REASONS FOR THE SUCCESS OF GERMAN JEWS

In considering *why* the German Jews were so successful, one may begin by noting that they were far more important in Germany than their coreligionists in France, Britain, the Low Countries, or the United States; the German Jews' success was matched only in Austria-Hungary, where somewhat similar conditions prevailed. Thus Germany's relative underdevelopment, as compared to the Western nations, afforded Jews and other minorities economic opportunities. The doors of fortune also were more open to Jews and other outsiders because the business profession commanded less respect in Germany than elsewhere in Europe. The traditional aristocratic disdain for business and industry was, with little diminution by 1914, well nigh universal. "Freiherr von Schnuck," in a novel by Karl Immerman, hesitates to recoup the family fortune in industry: "Can I, as a nobleman of old family, justify myself in the eyes of my ancestors for participating in an enterprise which, when viewed clearly, has no other object but trade and commerce and profit, and which will be shared by all sorts of people of low origin?"[60]

Another factor often invoked, Jewish "marginality," saw Jews enter economic areas and activities disdained by gentiles. Thus Jews were pioneers and risk-takers in opening new fields or filling gaps in the economy. Yet marginality is limited in scope as an explanatory factor, since a remarkable number of German Jews sped from the margins into the economic mainstream. They were awarded honors by the state and were anything but pariah capitalists; moreover, Jewish pioneering tended eventually to fade out, since gentiles learned and followed their example, and what had been disdained or ignored became respectable and coveted. "[I]n modern times [the Jews] have done what they always had had to do; namely, pioneering in certain fields and lands where others had not staked out claims. . . . Overwhelmingly . . . the Jews have been pioneers and not competitors of the Gentile in the economic world; wherever the Gentile catches up, he easily seizes the power again."[61] Also, Jews preferred the family firm, an efficient and dynamic entity, some of them extending as dynasties over several generations, and one that partly shielded them from antisemitic contempt. When, by 1870, the family firm became less viable in competing with large joint-stock companies, Jews entered such companies in great numbers in managerial capacities—again, anything but the margins.

One of the decisive advantages of Jews was the national and international network of contacts and affiliation they enjoyed with their fellow Jews. This dispersed but cohesive religious and ethnic grouping was reinforced by apprenticeships served in Jewish firms, marriages, hiring and doing business with one's coreligionists—such solidarity ("clannishness" to antisemites) as was expressed by one of the English Rothschilds: "I enjoy Jewish characteristics and like doing business with Jewish people."[62] Such practices lasted until the 1860s and went far to assure Jews mutual confidence, fair dealing, and support. It was enhanced by a common language (Yiddish), customs, and law. It also was an efficient source of information and economic news. These were assets that gentiles did not have, or did not have in the same degree.

For centuries Jews had lived in a money economy and had learned to take cash and credit operations for granted as normal, natural, and familiar. In all the varied forms of trade and credit operations they had practiced, they had learned to think and act in monetary terms. They possessed expertise but also capital. They were dwellers on capitalist islands in the sea of a "natural" economy and "precapitalist" society.[63] Moreover, Jews were usually educated and literate, in contrast to most gentiles, a factor emphasized earlier in connection with the Middle Ages but just as relevant in the nineteenth century. Banking had early gained respectability among Jews, and reportedly it came second only to learning and "he who prays through study" for honor and status. The Rothschilds and many other great bankers exemplified the prestige to be garnered in the field: A mystique attached to them, they became barons, married into the nobility, and were received at court. Another powerful motivation followed from Jews' determination that they must not slip back into the poverty and degradation of the ghetto.

Judaism itself may have contributed to the Jews' economic success. The Bible is "neutral" with regard to getting and spending, the Talmud is "positively disposed towards economic activity and the profit motive," and "Judaism tended to sanction capital and capitalism" in sharp contrast to Christianity from the New Testament and Patristics on. The traditional Jewish way of life meshed with German opportunities to produce such remarkable results. "This was, in fact, a minority well prepared by religion and history to take advantage of opportunities." All the external factors invoked here were in the main peculiar to Germany, although shared in that same area of central Europe by Austria-Hungary to some considerable degree.[64]

## ANTISEMITIC REACTION IN GERMANY AND AUSTRIA

Jews, who wholeheartedly embraced German culture (the much-remarked "love affair"), were proud of their contributions to that culture and to economic life. But many Germans, viewing Jews as an alien "Asiatic race," or still harboring medieval anti-Judaic sentiments, resented their success and engaged in antisemitic polemics. These attacks grew vicious by 1873, when a worldwide depression hit Germany and Austria-Hungary, where years of feverish speculation and overexpansion of a superheated economy resulted in a sudden crash. As has happened so often, indeed predictably, in economic crises and downturns, scapegoats are needed, and antisemites quickly come to the fore. "Antisemitism rises as the stock market falls" went a German saying.[65] The *Krach*, "Black Friday," was immediately blamed on the Jews, who were highly visible on the exchanges and in the banks. It was portrayed as the "Jewish betrayal" of the "Christian Volk." It was certainly "traumatic"—psychologically and financially—for Jews who suffered terrible losses and paid the penalty for wild speculation, rash investment, and fraudulent promotion. Some Jews were involved in the financial chicanery, although "many Jewish investors were also ruined, and Christians were heavily involved in frauds, but there was no chance that the economic crisis would fail to be seen as the work of 'the Jews.'"[66] The fact that the Rothschilds escaped unscathed was attributed not to their prudence but to their conspiratorial insider connections with liberal politicians. Amid a great outpouring of antisemitic journalism and pamphleteering appeared one Otto Glagau. He blamed the 1873 collapse on "company and stock market swindles that are chiefly the work of Jews and Semites." Unlike many of his successors over the following decades, "I do not want to kill or slaughter the Jews." He did not even want to expel them or confiscate their property but simply to end their "domination." "I do want to hold them in check, fundamentally in check." That required that this "physically and psychologically most degenerate race" be disemancipated.[67] (Jews had gained emancipation by Bismarck's legislation in 1867 and 1869.) The antisemites relentlessly singled out Bleichröder as the head of the Jewish power juggernaut, taking Bismarck in tow, and through him inflicting on the country a *"Judenpolitik,"* so that policy and legislation were conducted by and for the Jews. That Jews were among the principal losers in the 1873 debacle got no notice

from the antisemites; the irrationality of Jews contriving the ruin of the economy, and thereby causing their own ruin, did not occur to them either.

In Austria-Hungary, too, the depression fueled racial-nationalist antisemitism and undermined political liberalism, on which Jewish hopes for fulfillment of emancipation depended. Over the next quarter century the brutally
antisemitic Christian Social party gained popular strength and won control of
Vienna, that "laboratory for every known species of anti-Semitism."[68] Emperor Franz Josef strove to stave off the ascent to the mayoralty of Vienna of
Karl Lueger, leader of the Christian Socials and a suave but radical antisemite,
whose popular support increased each time the emperor thwarted him from
becoming mayor. The emperor gave up after twice rejecting Lueger, who
served as mayor from 1897 to his death in 1910 and adhered to an officially
antisemitic policy.

But the Christian Socials had no monopoly on antisemitism in Austria. In
fact, from the 1870s to 1938 every political party in that country was antisemitic or used antisemitism. "Jewish predominance" was the single most persistent and pervasive issue in Austrian politics, serving to rally followers and
consolidate the party—it was the common denominator of politics. The antisemitic vocabulary featured the "parasitic," "cancerous," "usurious," "clannish," "anti-social," "disintegrating," "materialistic," "alien" Jews. The Social
Democrats and Communists—most of whose leaders were assimilated, "non-
Jewish Jews"—did not attack Jews as Jews but as "Jewish capitalists" responsible for "Jewish capitalism." Theirs was the legacy of Marx and the illusion that
antisemitism would disappear with the triumph of socialism and the extinction
of capitalism and *Judentum* (Jewishness). When German/Austrian Nazism
emerged, there was nothing novel or radical about its antisemitic ideology,
proposals, or decrees.[69]

After 1873 the leadership of the Jewish community made an effort to
rebut accusations of Jewish economic "control" and "conspiratorial" busi-
ness-financial collusion by those "clannish" Jews. Such defensiveness persisted to the end of the Habsburg era, in 1918. Many Jews converted, some
changing not only their religion but also their names so as to obliterate all
trace of Jewish origins. "In 1870, virtually the entire leadership of the Stock
Exchange had been visibly Jewish, and virtually all the great banks had been
visibly led by Jews. [Progressively after 1873] the degree of Jewish participation in the business world was hidden by a vast array of straw men and by
concerted efforts to avoid every appearance of Jewish control. At least one
Jew was still in a position of formidable influence in virtually every bank, but
in each one the power structure was different."[70] So despite rigorous efforts

by William McCagg to measure Jewish participation in economic life for the period after 1880, no systematic statistical basis for generalization is available, since it is not possible to distinguish Jewish from non-Jewish members of the economic elite. Nevertheless, Jews remained disproportionately prominent and productive in the economy. As a quip had it, Jews wanted to be distinguished but indistinguishable.

In the first decade of the twentieth century—Lueger notwithstanding, for he was thwarted from antisemitic enactments by Emperor Franz Josef and could not avoid awarding municipal contracts to Jewish firms—Jews flourished in Vienna as never before: 71 percent of the capital's financiers were Jews, 63 percent of its industrialists, 65 percent of its lawyers, 59 percent of its physicians, and over half of its journalists and editors. Despite the dislocations of World War I, the dissolution of the Habsburg Empire, and the severe inflation of the early 1920s, this state of affairs did not change materially, although "Jew" and "profiteer" long remained virtually synonymous terms. The great depression of 1929 was calamitous for the Jews in that they lost heavily—of the twelve Vienna banks that collapsed, ten were Jewish—and were subject to a tremendous upsurge of antisemitism.

The disproportionately large contribution of Jews to the growth of the German and Austro-Hungarian economies is a historical fact. Since the age of mercantilism and the court Jews, mercantilist policies had encouraged Jews in economic enterprise to make them "productive" and "useful" to the state. Such policies continued through Bismarck, whose relationship with Gerson Bleichröder was the classic one of ruler and court Jew, and into the twentieth century. Moreover, as appears in the memoranda of bureaucrats evaluating the services and merits of Jews nominated or chosen to receive various honors and titles, Jewish contributions to the economy were welcomed and appreciated; although not publicized, these reports constitute a counterchorus to the antisemites' recriminations. The importance of the Jews is seen particularly in their role in the banks, mobilizing and concentrating capital for investment, the development of the Berlin stock exchange (Jewish brokers had a decisive part from its founding), in financing the railways and German unification, and culminating in the consolidation of the Weimar economy. Jews played a salient role at every stage of the evolution of the German economy. They, therefore, became the targets of antisemites, nationalists, and volkish anticapitalists who condemned cities and heavy industry in their quest for the restoration of a golden age of peasant proprietors and unmechanized artisan production. To them Jews and "Jewish capitalism" were "alien" and "un-German." Many of these groups, as later the Nazis, plied the ludicrous distinction between *raffendes* (rapacious Jewish financial) versus *schaffendes* (creative German industrial) capital and, equally absurd, that between *nützlisches* (useful) as opposed to *schädlisches* (harmful) capital. Fearful defenders of old ways and aggravated competitors condemned Jews as cosmopolitan, antinational, unpatriotic, immoral, conspiratorial, and much else of that kind. Hence antisemites demanded quotas, disemancipation, expulsion, and the blocking of Ostjuden immigration. But even Kaiser Wilhelm II, who could be as antisemitic as anyone and in exile in the interwar period called for gassing the Jews, in 1912 rejected the demand for the Jews' expulsion by Heinrich Class, an antisemitic leader and Pan German. The kaiser replied that, if expelled, the Jews "would take away their enormous wealth and we would suffer a blow to our national wellbeing and working life that would throw us back to the conditions of a hundred years ago, and at the same time we would be expelled from the ranks of the civilized nations."[71] Even the economic historian Werner Sombart, hardly an admirer of Jews, acknowledged, "we shall have to admit that our economic development, as it took shape in the nineteenth century, would be quite unthinkable without the participation of the Jews. From the perspective of the modern evolution of capitalism, we observe the development of capitalistic methods and with them the release of strong productive forces . . . so that one cannot possibly avoid acknowledging the existence of Jewish economic elements as one of the greatest assets [of Germany's national economic development]."[72]

## GERMAN JEWS IN AMERICA

The German Jews who came to the United States from the 1830s to the 1880s made a comparable contribution to the nation's economic growth; in David Landes' words, they, too, and for some of the same reasons, "traveled from the margins and interstices of the economy to its centre," where they stayed, however, experiencing nothing remotely like German antisemitism or Nazi "Aryanization." The eleven Seligmans began things when their eldest brother, Joseph (1819–1880), arrived in Philadelphia in 1837. In little more than thirty years he had brought over the rest of the family and went from peddler's rags to the founding of a banking house of international standing and to be financial advisor to presidents. After a few years the brothers rented a store and then a warehouse; continuing as peddlers, they also sold wholesale to other peddlers and opened other stores in New York, St. Louis, and elsewhere. Joseph's merchandising principle was "Sell anything that can be bought cheaply, sold quickly at a little profit, small enough to place inside a pack and light enough to carry."[73] The gold rush brought the Seligmans to California, not for prospecting but to open a store to supply miners. That proved to be very profitable and opened the way to their becoming bullion dealers conveying gold to New York; the profits enabled them to become great merchants and then, the first of many German Jews to make the transition, bankers. Some "stayed behind" in merchandising and we know their names as department stores—Macy's, Bloomingdale's, Filene's, Abraham & Strauss, and a great many more—one or several in practically every American town and city. After the Civil War, during which J. & W. Seligman & Co. greatly increased its fortune supplying uniforms to the Union Army, the country caught "the railroad fever," which afforded bankers golden opportunities as dealers in railway securities at home and abroad as well as in transacting the numerous mergers, bankruptcies, and reorganizations. At one point the Seligmans, "the American Rothschilds" with a branch bank in Paris, Frankfurt, London, New York, San Francisco, and New Orleans, held investments in over a hundred railroad companies and sat on the boards of a great many of them. Other families—in those family enterprises the ties that bound were those of marriage and kinship; consider the Lehmans, Sachs, Goldmans, Loebs, Kuhns, Speyers, and Wolffs—followed much the same path from peddlers beset by ruffians throwing stones at "Christ killers" to bankers in top hats, except that none was invited to be secretary of the treasury, as Joseph Seligman was in the Grant administration. Horatio Alger served as tutor to Joseph's children, and it was the Seligman saga that inspired his rags-to-riches stories. A milestone of another kind occurred in 1877, when Joseph and his family arrived in his private railroad car in Saratoga for their annual vacation, only to be refused entrance to the Grand Union Hotel by order of its new administrator, Judge Henry Hilton, a fierce political foe of Joseph. A traumatic affair for him and American Jewry, it set off a tidal wave of antisemitism and was followed by the general exclusion of Jews from resorts, clubs, universities, business firms, and other institutions.

The Guggenheims also "started on foot" when the fourteen-member family arrived from Switzerland (though haling originally from Germany) in Philadelphia in 1848. They soon began to make their own wares, initially an improved stove polish, and eventually built up the greatest American fortune except perhaps for the Rockefellers. They, too, went west but became copper traders, a metal that was in great demand, as they anticipated, for telegraph and telephone wires. They got their first mine in the form of shares given to their father in lieu of payment of a bad debt. From there they went on not so much to buy mines to work but to buy or build smelters to smelt and refine lead, copper, and silver—the same strategy as John D. Rockefeller, who did not own an oil well but monopolized the refineries. Adolf Lewisohn, who arrived in the United States in 1867, did not set out as a peddler since he came from a wealthy family in Hamburg. He got into copper mining in Montana and had the railroad extended to carry the ore out from Butte. The struggle over control of copper and silver production ended up with the Guggenheims winning out, although the Lewisohns retained a large proportion of shares but not a controlling interest. By 1914 the Guggenheims' Smelting & Refining Co. had a dominant position in the world market; it drew the fire of, among others, Henry Ford and his antisemitic publications as a pro-German, conspiratorial monopoly exercised by "the triple copper monarchy of the Baruchs, the Lewisohns, and the Guggenheims."[74] Today the Guggenheims are remembered for their enormous philanthropic contributions and endowments of labs, university institutes, hospitals, foundations, and museums, most notably the Guggenheim Museum in New York, the nucleus of which was their own private art collection.

Jacob Schiff (1847–1920) was the scion of a wealthy family of bankers, scholars, and rabbis that traced its lineage to the fourteenth century in Frankfurt, where in the ghetto the family had long made its home in a building shared, half and half, with the Rothschilds. Arriving in the United States in 1865, Schiff soon joined the banking house of Kuhn, Loeb & Co., married a partner's daughter, and became the senior partner by the early 1880s. He took the firm into railroad investment, financing the Pennsylvania Railroad among others. His way of investing in railways was to study thoroughly how to run and finance railroads and gain firsthand knowledge by interviewing track men, engineers, and station masters, and then to immerse himself minutely in the details of a particular line. After an initial ferocious rivalry with the railway magnate Edward H. Harriman, the two men formed a working alliance in marketing railway shares in Europe and in the purchase, in 1897, of the Union Pacific line, which Schiff was instrumental in reorganizing and recapitalizing so that it became efficient, paid its debts, and was immensely profitable to both parties. The turn of the century saw the "battle of the giants," which pitted Harriman and Schiff against James J. Hill and J. P. Morgan for control of the Great Northern line; the outcome was more or less a draw, but Morgan had met his match and thereafter could not exercise the control over the nation's finances that he sought, and Kuhn, Loeb surpassed Seligmans as the largest Jewish investment house on Wall Street. In later years Schiff and Morgan sometimes cooperated in investment ventures at home and abroad, activities that proved to Ford that Morgan was a Jew.

Schiff waged his own war against tsarist Russia from the 1890s to 1917. He had long tried to use the prospect of loans as leverage for Jewish emancipation, but to no avail. In 1904 and 1905, Kuhn, Loeb funded Japan in its war against Russia. Schiff persuaded skeptics to go along, particularly his friend in London Sir Ernest Cassel (also of German origin). All told, four war loans and a fifth after the war were underwritten in New York, London, Berlin, and Paris with Schiff and Kuhn, Loeb at the hub of the action in floating the oversubscribed loans and in blocking Russia—the land of pogroms, "the enemy of all mankind"—from access to war credits. Although in bringing pressure to bear Schiff drew on an international network that included his brother Philip in Frankfurt, the Warburgs in Hamburg, and Cassel and Rothschilds in London, the boycott was less than successful, since Morgan was lured by the prospect of great profits and even some Jewish banking houses were tempted. Nevertheless, Russia was handicapped by obstacles and considerably higher interest rates than normal, and the Japanese haled Schiff as their savior, "the all-powerful Jewish banker."[75] In the aftermath a Russian minister of finance protested that "Our government will never forgive or forget what that Jew, Schiff, did to us. . . . He alone made it possible for Japan to secure a loan in America. He was one of the most dangerous men we had against us abroad." The Japanese were susceptible to the same myth of the "international Jewish bankers," but Japanese antisemitism, starting from the same premises as in Russia and the West, reached the opposite conclusion, that the Jews were not to be feared and hated rather admired, that the Japanese could form an "alliance" with all-powerful, world Jewry. While the myth was as remote from reality as ever, for once it served to help the Jews who found refuge rather than persecution in Japan during World War II. The myth of the conspiratorial bankers also dictated that Schiff and the American Jewish banking houses would be attacked as unpatriotic and pro-German during World War I. Schiff would not permit Kuhn, Loeb to subscribe to Allied war loans, unless Russia was excluded and did not get "one penny." "I cannot run counter to my conscience . . . for the sake of whatever advantage."[76] And although they strongly supported the Allied cause once the United States entered the war, Kuhn, Loeb and many other houses lost much business and declined significantly. With the Bolshevik phobia and the Red Scare that followed the Russian Revolution, the myth required that Schiff be responsible for financing the communist takeover—with $12 million! This fabrication was reiterated decade after decade, from Henry Ford, Father Charles Coughlin, and Gerald L. K. Smith to Pat Robertson, who embellished the calumny to assert that Schiff forked over $20 million in gold to underwrite the atheists.[77]

Schiff is more accurately remembered for his philanthropy, spending as much time giving away his money as in making it. In this he typified the German Jewish economic elite. Otto Kahn, a younger partner in Kuhn, Loeb who lavished millions on the Metropolitan Opera, explained that "I must atone for my wealth,"[78] but Jewish philanthropy was much more an expression of gratitude to a country that afforded immigrant Jews a fair chance. Julius Rosenwald, up from peddling and immensely rich through his leadership of Sears, Roebuck, was so inspired by Booker T. Washington's autobiography *Up from Slavery* that he committed enormous sums to building 5,437 schools and colleges for African Americans. Schiff's philanthropic ideas and practices were strikingly similar to those of his contemporary Andrew Carnegie and the "Gospel of Wealth," except that his inspiration to allocate surplus wealth for social good during his lifetime was religious rather than secular. He objected to bequeathing large sums to heirs because they seldom made contributions to society and often lapsed into a frivolous life. This was, in fact, frequently the fate of German Jewish dynasties after several generations: Great wealth and assimilation to the national life tended to undermine the "interlocking structure" that had assured "continuity of entrepreneurial skill" and commitment to the business.[79] One of Schiff's principal charities over thirty years were the two million Russian and Polish Jews who fled pogroms and poverty to make a fresh start. These downtown Jews were proletarians, quite different from their uptown coreligionists, who, though they helped them and worked hard to keep the doors of immigration open, took some time to overcome their prejudice against these Ostjuden. Their economic evolution is quite different from that of the German Jews. Thanks to the expanding economy of World War I and the 1920s, they went, as historian Henry Feingold puts it, "from class struggle to struggle for class," and by the end of World War II they had entered the middle class and produced another economic elite.[80] Whatever the similarities in development of German Jews and Ostjuden on either side of the Atlantic, those parallels ended with the Nazi regime and the sentence of annihilation.

## MYTHMAKERS AND "JEWISH ECONOMICS": MARX, SOMBART, AND FORD

The involvement of Jews in modern European economic development gave rise to several denigrating myths, often updated versions of medieval stereotypes, concerning their outlook and behavior. The Jews were castigated as greedy and materialistic predators eager to exploit and rob gentiles, behavior that was sanctioned by the Old Testament and the Talmud. In a Darwinian age in which racial explanations were widely employed, several theorists claimed that such traits were racially determined. Taking many a page from the *Protocols of the Learned Elders of Zion*, antisemitic publicists claimed that Jewish capitalists formed an international cabal to control the world's finances. Among numerous writers, some of them prominent, who helped shape these myths and impart to them "scientific" authority, two German theorists stand out: Karl Marx and Werner Sombart. Antisemites, both from the elite and the mob, used their conclusions to buttress their own bigotry.

Both these thinkers shared a common flaw: They had limited knowledge of key Jewish texts, particularly the Talmud and the vast rabbinical literature that commented on Jewish law and ethics. Consequently, their studies launched new stereotypes or fortified old ones. The Talmud, in which they were so deficient, propounds an apt warning: "'Scholars, be careful with your words,' for as it is said in Proverbs 18:21: 'Death and life are in the power of the tongue.'"[81] In the sharpest possible contrast to these German misinterpreters of Jews and Judaism, Henry Ford, the American automotive industrialist, was no intellectual. Ford never ceased to be the provincial farm boy, the prisoner of a one-room schoolhouse education and a rural Populist ideology that saw conspiratorial money men, particularly Jewish bankers, as oppressors of the farmer and other "little men."

## KARL MARX

Karl Marx (1818–1883) was born into a family that could boast of a long line of distinguished rabbis. But his father, an attorney, in order not to lose his livelihood and middle-class status, had himself baptized a Lutheran, and so was his son at age six or seven; his mother became a convert at a later date but was, apparently, a reluctant one. Marx grew up in a household where the family's Jewish extraction remained an unmentionable secret. Hence the personal acrimony that characterized his attitude toward Jews and Judaism, which was likely to have been reinforced by his Christian education at the Gymnasium (a former Jesuit academy where most of his fellow students were Catholics) in his native Trier in western Germany, as it was also by quarrels with his mother over money and over marrying a Christian. Many of Marx's formal works, especially the essay written in 1843 entitled "On the Jewish Question," and his personal letters and conversations brim over with contempt for *Judentum*, a term that can mean "the Jews," "Judaism," or "Jewishness," or all three at once; some consider these expressions of self-hatred his attempt "to produce a certificate of non-Jewishness."[82] No one would ever read Marx to learn about Judentum, since he was thoroughly ignorant of any and all of its manifestations. Nevertheless, his interpretation of Judaism and his pronouncements on Jews, together with his equation of Judentum with capitalism, has for a full century profoundly influenced socialist movements and the parties on the Left and, when they came into power, shaped their attitudes and policies toward the Jews, tragically so.

On Jewish subjects, Marx went to school not with Baruch Spinoza, Moses Mendelssohn, Moses Hess, Heinrich Heine, or any of the Jewish luminaries of his generation but with such classic denigrators of Jews and Judaism as Immanuel Kant, G. W. F. Hegel, D. F. Strauss, Ludwig Feuerbach, and Bruno Bauer. For Kant, the Jews were "a nation of swindlers," "a people composed solely of merchants," and "slaves of the law"; since the Old Testament has no concept of immortality, Jews lack a sense of "higher values," are materialistic, and thus are devoted only to material survival. According to Hegel, Judaism—"Jewish consciousness"—rendered the Jews, imprisoned as they were by their law, deficient in freedom and incapable of love; they stand "outside nature," are given to an ethic of "domination," and in their "stubbornness" have become a "ghost race" and "fossil nation"; history, once they had performed their providential task of preparing the ground for Christianity, passed them up and so doomed the "parasitic race" to "die." In this melange, one finds the nucleus of Jewish "egoism" so central to Strauss, Feuerbach, Bauer, Marx, and other Young Hegelians. To Strauss, author of a famous life of Jesus, the Jews were locked within the four walls of the law, the source of their egoism, what he called their "spiritual isolation"; he also chastised them for their inveterate "financial dishonesty." Nevertheless, Jews should be emancipated, but then gently made to disappear by intermarriage and abandonment of the law. To Feuerbach, author of the *Essence of Christianity*, the god of Judaism is egoism: "God is the ego of Israel." Feuerbach reduced Judaism to an anthropological formula of utilitarianism, egoism, and power domination, what he also called a "stomach religion." In this kind of opprobrium, he was followed by the equally arrogant and oracular Bauer and Marx, who also made egoism the essence of Judaism and who denounced Judaism for imparting a loathsome lust for gain to Christianity.[83]

In his essay "On the Jewish Question" published in 1844, Marx saw zeal for money as the essential feature of historic Judaism and the Jews of his day:

> Let us look at the real Jew of our time, the Jew of everyday life.
> What is the Jew's foundation in our world? Material necessity, private advantage.

What is the object of the Jew's worship in this world?
Usury/huckstering. What is his worldly god? Money.

Marx notes the seeming paradox that although the Jews are unemanci-
pated and without the vote, they nevertheless wield enormous political power:

> The contradiction between this actual political power and Jews' [lack of] po-
> litical rights is the universal contradiction between politics and the power of
> money. . . .
>
> The Jew has already emancipated himself in the Jewish way: "The Jew,
> who is, for example, merely tolerated in Vienna [a reference to the Roth-
> schilds], determines by his money-power the fate of the entire German Em-
> pire. The Jew, who is without rights in the smallest German state, decides the
> fate of Europe. . . ." [Marx is quoting Bauer.]
>
> This is no isolated fact. The Jew has emancipated himself in the Jewish
> fashion not only by acquiring money-power but also through money's having
> become . . . the world power and the Jewish spirit's having become the practi-
> cal spirit of the Christian peoples.

A cardinal thesis of Marx, obsessively repeated, is that Christianity has
been Judaized,

> because the materialistic spirit of Judaism has kept itself alive in Christian so-
> ciety and achieved there its highest expression. . . . Bourgeois society continu-
> ously brings forth the Jew from its own entrails. . . .
>
> Christianity sprang from Judaism; it has now dissolved itself back into
> Judaism.

In confirmation of Christianity's Judaization, Marx quotes an observer of
New England's "pious" and "free" citizens:

> "Mammon is the God of these people: they worship him not only with their
> lips but with all the powers of their bodies and soul. The earth in their eyes is
> nothing but one great stock exchange and they are convinced that they have
> no other mission here below than to become richer than their neighbors.
> Usury has taken hold of all their thoughts. . . ."
>
> Indeed, the materialistic rule of the Jew over the Christian world has in
> the United States reached . . . everyday acceptability. . . .

Marx keeps harping on the inescapably acquisitive, materialist basis of
Judaism:

Money is the zealous one God of Israel, beside which no other God may stand.

The God of the Jews has become secularized and is now a worldly God. The bill of exchange is the Jew's real God. His God is the illusory bill of exchange. The chimerical nationality of the Jew is the true nationality of the merchant, of the man of money.

Because of Judaism, money has become

the essence of man's life and work, which have become alienated from him. This alien monster rules him and he worships it. . . .

Only then [under the rule of Judaized Christianity] could Jewry become universally dominant and turn alienated man and alienated nature into alienable, salable objects, subject to the serfdom of egotistical needs and to usury.

Sale is the practice of alienation.

Jews are the embodiment of capitalism ("money-system") in action and the creators of all its evil consequences for humanity. Judaism is not a theology but the "commercial and industrial practice" of a "money-system." When capitalism is abolished it will no longer be possible to be Jewish, because the Jews' religious conviction will no longer have any object and the emancipation of the Jews from a money fixation, "usury" or "huckstering," will also mean "the emancipation of society from Jewry."[84]

Marx declared war on the Jews, Judaism, and Jewishness but never envisioned genocide. Yet his harsh condemnation of Jewry and all its works chimed in too readily with other voices demanding that "the Jew in the Jew must be done to death" or with proposals to cure "the Jewish disease"—trade and finance—by destroying the Jewish "commercial aristocracy."[85] In his later years Marx never retracted the brutally contemptuous condemnation of Jews and Judaism as capitalism personified, although he did soften his rhetoric and antisemitism ceased to be intrinsic to his worldview. In his last major work, *Das Kapital*, Jews and Judaism are hardly mentioned, for it is capitalism and the bourgeois, the capitalist economic system rather than individuals or a particular group, that are humanity's scourge. Yet Marx never ceased to bind Jews to the realm of finance, and one scholar has emphasized the "continuity" of Marx's animosity for Judentum in *Das Kapital* with the 1843 essay.[86] Almost all nineteenth-century socialists followed Marx in characterizing Jews as capitalists, as dominant in trade and finance, and as having an irredeemable predisposition for exploitation. His notion that Jewish emancipation was a minor matter, a mere detail of the emancipation of all humanity from capitalist society, strongly influenced socialist parties in his time and long after. For them, no special effort was necessary to combat antisemitism, since capitalism and antisemitism, having risen together, would disappear together with the triumph of socialism. For example, in 1893 German socialists passed a party resolution that they would not "waste the energy they needed for the struggle against the existing political and social order on a useless fight against a phenomenon [antisemitism] which stands and falls with bourgeois society."[87]

While the German and Austrian Social Democratic parties and the French Socialist party often denounced antisemitism as the way the ruling classes distracted attention from the real sources of the workers' exploitation onto the Jews and some socialist leaders decried antisemitism as "the stupid man's socialism," "the socialism of fools/simpletons/imbeciles," often they were inhibited by fear of antagonizing their worker members, many of whom were antisemitic. Others proposed utilizing antisemitism as a tactical weapon to rally the workers against their employers and "the bourgeoisie" at the ballot box.[88] Commenting on its capacity to generate extreme anti-Jewish hatred, historian Paul Lawrence Rose concludes that Marx's essay has "remained the chief source of socialist antisemitism," its influence "pernicious."[89] Ironically, Marx provided fuel for right-wing antisemites. Since he was himself derided as Jewish by friend and foe alike, parties of the Right defined Marxism as "Jewish," as he had defined capitalism and with some of the same kinds of calamitous effects in later times. Whatever his intentions were and whatever his unarticulated second thoughts may have been, Marx's essay was put to antisemitic use by Hitler and Nazi antisemites, Soviet antisemites* and their eastern European imitators, and Arab Islamic antisemites. To Julius Carlebach, the keenest student of Marx's relationship to Judentum, "Marx is a logical and indispensable link between Luther and Hitler."[90] Ruminating on Marx's essay, the German Israeli Marxist Franz Fink wondered "how one can consider objectively, as Marx's ideas should be considered, thoughts on Judaism which (however they were meant originally) sound like a justification for the murder of Jews? What Jew could forget the mass exterminations of 1943 when he reads the death sentence of 1843?"[91] In any event, neither Marx nor Marxism

---

* One instance is the notorious Trofim Kichko, who at the height of the campaign against "cosmopolitanism" in his 1963 diatribe *Judaism Without Embellishment* unleashed Marx's canards: "What is the [Jews'] secular god? Money. Money. Money, that is the jealous god of Israel." Quoted in William Korey, *Russian Antisemitism, Pamyat, and the Demonology of Zionism* (Jerusalem: Vidal Sassoon Center, Harwood Academic Publishers, 1995), 11. Kichko is reported to have collaborated with German occupiers of Ukraine in World War II.

affords a suggestive or illuminating, much less explanatory, analysis of Jewish economic prowess.[92]

## WERNER SOMBART

Werner Sombart (1863–1941) was an economic historian and academic who wrote on the bourgeoisie, the proletariat, capitalism, and German economic history. His *Jews and Modern Capitalism* (1911) sought to provide evidence in support of Marx's essay "On the Jewish Question." Sombart thus began his research with a thesis and "proved" it by selected evidence—much of it "trivial," "spurious," or "absurd" in "polyglot footnotes"—utilizing archetypes and stereotypes, and employing antisemitic sources such as Johann Eisenmenger and August Rohling; the data that contradicted his assertions, Sombart passed over in silence.[93] Like the anonymous authors of *The Secret Relationship between Blacks and Jews* (see chapter 6), Sombart cited Jewish sources to distort them and render his assertions more plausible. Purporting to speak universally of Jews in all places and times, Sombart in fact limited his inquiries to the Middle Ages and after, and to western and central Europe, thus leaving out of account the vast majority of Jews in eastern Europe and elsewhere. In his early career, capitalism was the enemy, and so he blamed it on the Jews in his notorious *Jews and Modern Capitalism*. In later life, when he became an enthusiastic Nazi, capitalism underwent rehabilitation and socialism-communism became the enemy, which he consequently blamed on the Jews. Throughout his life as a scholar, Sombart was given to oversimplification and exaggeration, and was driven by shifting ideological premises in his pursuit of *Homo Judaeus* as *Homo capitalisticus* and then *Homo communisticus*.[94] Although thoroughly flawed, like Marx's essay, *The Jews and Modern Capitalism* had an unwarranted influence and exacerbated the image of the villainous Jew.

Sombart's interpretation of Jewish capacity in business and finance is fundamentally racist: The race shaped and determined the religion. Together race and religion imparted to Jews a set of characteristics that fitted them, according to Sombart, to found capitalism and be its most successful and ruthless practitioners. Jews are a *"Händlervolk"* (a peddling people) in contrast to the Germans, a *Heldenvolk* (a race of heroes). When he came to take a more positive view of capitalism, Sombart indulged in a distinction between good capitalism, heroic German enterprise exemplified by the medieval Hanseatic League, and bad capitalism, which was, of course, "Jewish."

In chapter 12, entitled "Jewish Characteristics," Sombart assures the reader that he has consulted many "unprejudiced observers" such as Houston

Stewart Chamberlain (a notorious racial antisemite) and Karl Marx. Foremost
in the composition of the Jewish type is "the extreme intellectuality of the
Jew," which is far stronger in him than "physical (manual) powers." The Jewish genius is particularly apt for "calculating work" and "abstract thought."
But that Jewish genius is "one-sided," for it has little capacity for "feeling."
This makes the Jew incapable of mysticism or spirituality, for Judaism,
uniquely, looks askance on mysteries and thus reduces itself to pure "Rationalism," an icy creed for icy hearts. His "constant abiding in a world of abstractions" deprives the Jew of a sense of nature and the personal; Jewish law
"abolished personal relationships and replaced them by impersonal, abstract
connections or activities or aims." What a desiccated calculating machine is
the Jewish mind. Judaism's chief feature is rationalism: The Jews are "rational-
ists, both in theory and in practice"—Sombart seems never to have heard of
the Kabbalah, the vast corpus of Jewish mysticism.

Sombart described this "extreme intellectuality" at some length, because
"all the other Jewish peculiarities are rooted" in it. Following from it are the
Jew's "strong will," "moral and physical mobility," and "energy," these four
traits being the "corner stones of Jewish character" and of "special import in
economic life." In the economic realm, these characteristics manifest themselves as "extreme activity," as "adaptability which is unique in history," and as
Jewish "stubbornness" and "pliancy." We learn that the Jew's "adaptability" fa-
cilitates his readily overcoming "ethical or aesthetical" obstacles on his
worldly path; also expedient are his weak "personal dignity" and lack of conviction—"it means little to him to be untrue to himself." Sombart attributed
an ethical double standard to Jews that explained "the peculiar Jewish business
methods" in dealing with Christians: dishonest trading, cheating, introducing
the competitive in place of the just price, and extracting "usury."[95] And it turns
out that the Jew's vaunted intellectuality is only "shallow." But all of these features are assets "as applied to capitalism." Jews are coldly rational in calculating gain and averting loss no matter what the human costs. Affinities and
parallels abound in Sombart's exposition: There is, for example, "the parallel
between the feverish restlessness of Stock Exchange business . . . and the restless nature of the Jew." "Speaking generally [and in the Marxian terms of
1843], we may say . . . that the fundamental ideas of capitalism and those of
the Jewish character show a singular similarity. Hence we have the triple paral-
lelism between Jewish character, the Jewish religion, and capitalism."[96] Jewish
"characteristics" also explain the Diaspora. In Sombart's view, dispersion was
not imposed on the Jews but was "voluntary," the result of economic motives
and a reflection of the congenital "restlessness" of these desert wanderers of

antiquity. Their "inherent Nomadism or Saharaism" prepared them for the life of the restless and rootless merchant, who is not bound by traditional rules and codes of economic conduct. This is Sombart's rendering of the myth of the Wandering Jew, part of his fantasy that "throughout the centuries" the Jews have "remained a desert and nomadic people" who were not forced into exile and ghetto seclusion but chose these in pursuit of their capitalist destiny.[97]

In seeking to attribute capitalism to the villainous Jews, Sombart greatly exaggerated and oversimplified their importance. He held that Jews invented virtually all the tools and devices and institutions of capitalism, including capitalism itself, that product of "the spirit of Judaism." However, according to the greatest Jewish historian of the last century, Salo Baron, most of these instruments, "most of the new methods in business and public finance [were] already firmly established" by the time the Jews came on the scene, and "once actively engaged in their exploitation," the Jews and others such as the Puritans "contributed to their further growth in a more than proportionate degree."[98] No such subtleties for Sombart. To him, the "modern endorsable bill of exchange" came from Venice, "a Jewish town" where bill-brokering was in Jewish hands and so "must have been commenced by Jews." The same kind of logic establishes that securities or stock shares of standard denomination were introduced by Jews in the eighteenth century: "[I]ndirectly the evidence is fairly conclusive [since] Jews were great speculators. . . . A little reflection will show . . . that Jews must have had no small influence on the standardization of securities." So, too, with banknotes and the invention of the banking business: It may have been two Jews in Venice who established a bank there in 1400, or it may have been Marranos in Spain, but in any event "the fathers of the modern, impersonal banknote" could only have been Jews. Bonds for public debt and mortgages as instruments of credit "owe their origin [and 'modern form'] chiefly to Jewish influences"; not only that: "[C]an we possibly deduce modern credit instruments from Rabbinic law? I believe we can," avers Sombart, thus bringing capitalism and Judaism together once more in causal relationship. As for the institution of the stock exchange, it sprang up in those areas where bill-brokering was carried on; that is to say, "as the principal bill-brokers of the [early modern] period, the Jews must have had much to do with the establishment of the Stock Market [in the many cities where they arose]." In Berlin the stock exchange was "a Jewish institution from its very inception." As for the first appearance of stock market speculation, including commodity futures, it was in seventeenth-century Holland, and "the Jews were more prominent than others in this activity." "The predominance of Jews on the Stock Exchange of London"—following their readmission by Oliver Cromwell and the Revolution of 1688 that brought a Dutch prince to the throne as William III—"is perhaps more apparent than in the case of Amsterdam." In London they made stockbroking a profession. The Rothschilds are cited for the scale of their operations. With them "the stock market has become international," great international loans and transactions being treated by the Rothschilds as a family affair. "The age of the Rothschilds" was under way, and for Sombart the saying of the mid-nineteenth century, "There is only one power in Europe and that power is Rothschild," is simply the plain truth. The Jews were the railway kings as they were the monarchs of company promotion and the creators, in Sombart's mistaken view, of the joint-stock bank that lay behind all this activity. The inception of "this special banking activity" was "Jewish," namely, the Péreires' Crédit Mobilier and all their Jewish backers. Sombart invidiously points to the large number of Jews in the management of German industry by the end of the nineteenth century. Industries' dependence on the largely Jewish banks was, he explains, "the gap in the hedge through which the Jews could penetrate into the field of the production and transport of commodities, as they had done earlier in commerce and finance." Thus, continues Sombart, nearly a seventh of the board directors and nearly a quarter of board members, in a population where they are barely a hundredth, were Jews.[99] Much of what Sombart says is true enough and will be found in standard economic histories, but the role of the Jews is blown all out of proportion and the explanations offered of that role are unsubstantiated and undemonstrated, straying into popular stereotype and antisemitic myth: No Jews, no capitalism.

Sombart's eleventh chapter, "The Significance of the Jewish Religion in Economic Life," is where he is most clearly in Marx's ideological grip. He "avow[s] it right away: I think that the Jewish religion has the same leading ideas as Capitalism. I see the same spirit in the one as in the other."[100] Accordingly, the Jewish capitalist ethic requires that Eros be suppressed. Sombart—echoing Marx's dictum in the 1843 essay that Jewish marriage is an object of "commerce," women of "barter"—proceeds to reduce Jewish law and ritual to a mechanism for pressure-molding the family into an optimum unit for capitalist activity. Sexuality and marriage are regulated to sublimate libidinal desire into capitalist energy. As proof, though neither this nor the other numerous texts cited bear him out, Sombart quotes the famous statement, "A man should not be without a wife, nor a woman without a husband; both shall see to it that God's spirit is in their union." There is on the subject of sex and much else, Sombart goes on, "an almost unique identity of view between Judaism and Puritanism." For all its seeming cleverness, none of this stands up to analysis: Jewish attitudes toward love, marriage, and sex are not—as the pathbreaking sociologist of religion Max Weber (1864–1920) perceived in criticizing Sombart—puritanical or ascetic; Jewish regulation of these is not unique but common to most world religions; in other religions regulation of the sexual impulse is often more pronounced without supporting any disposition for economic endeavor.[101]

Antisemites, most notable among them Marx and Sombart, often have asserted that Judaism is a capitalist's religion, a creed that consecrates greed, that instills a capacity for rational calculation to gain profit and avoid loss, and so on. In chapter 11 Sombart features a vignette of "old Amschel Rothschild" who, having "'earned' a million on the Stock Exchange" that Friday turns for reflection to scripture; he finds much for smug satisfaction and very little to disquiet him, for worldly success is the Lord's blessing for the righteous, especially, according to Sombart, in Proverbs and Deuteronomy. Expectedly, Sombart simplifies matters terribly, reducing the Bible and Talmud to philistine justifications for money-grubbing. God and man are linked by a "businesslike connection" in which each person's deeds of good and evil are reckoned up in "a complicated system of bookkeeping," the one rewarded as profit, the other punished as loss.[102] Many historians have demonstrated that such expositions as Sombart indulges in here are more stereotype and caricature than analysis; according to the modern scholar Ellis Rivkin, "The notion that Jews let loose capitalism is one of those persistent myths that seem to grow with exposure."[103]

Their religion would make Jews agrarians: The Bible, Mishnah, and Talmud idealize agriculture in a marriage of land and people; every chance Jews have had they have taken it up again; they have not had many chances. The rabbis condemned the accumulation of wealth as an end in itself, the greatest Jewish philosopher of the Middle Ages Maimonides speaking for them when he said that "most of the damage done to people in the various states [of life] arises from the lust for money and its accumulation, and the excessive desire to increase possessions and honors."[104] True, there were no Jewish exponents of an ideal of poverty, such as long prevailed in medieval Christendom and led to the repression of economic activity, and Jewish sages regarded wealth honestly gained as a sign of divine favor. Nevertheless, they also insisted that wealth had to be honestly earned and they preached an ideal of moderation in its consumption and required manifold good works of philanthropy. That wealth was a means to a higher end is suggested by the proverb in fifteenth-century Germany that scholarship flourished there because most Jews earned their living in banking, which took relatively little time and energy away from studies, and with those not studying using their profits to support those who did. Maimonides was perhaps a trifle academic but reflective of the Jewish attitude when he advised the Jewish breadwinner to spend three hours a day earning a living and devote the rest to Torah study. Moreover, while private property was recognized by the rabbis, they hedged in its "rights" with a corresponding set of "responsibilities" to the poor, relatives, orphans, and the wider community. The ancient traditions of the sabbatical year (Deuteronomy 15:1–3) and of the jubilee year every half century (Leviticus 25) were never forgotten. Under the first, debts were canceled, which the rabbis later modified because few would make loans when there was no prospect of repayment and those who depended on loans suffered; the rabbis justified the change on the principle of "improving the human condition." Under the second a redistribution and equalization of wealth and land were effected and Hebrew slaves freed: And thus "you shall hallow the fiftieth year and proclaim liberty throughout the land unto all the inhabitants thereof" (Leviticus 15:10 and the Liberty Bell in Philadelphia). Although not enforced, indeed unenforceable, as binding legislation, the moral imperative of the sabbatical and jubilee years nevertheless served to quicken consciences. The rabbis fixed profit margins, setting a maximum of one-sixth, and they applied other socioeconomic restraints in the name of society and the "just price." For a long time they opposed the use of bills of exchange and other capitalist devices, giving way only to sheer necessity. Indeed, the Talmud's sanctioning of charity and philanthropy—rooted as it is in the greatest of all ethical teachers, the Prophets—was reinforced and never undermined. Such consumer protection or semisocialism (of which many more instances could be given) is radically inconsistent with the Sombartian notion of medieval Judaism as pure capitalism struggling to be born. What is so striking is to find that the rabbis, like the Christian canonists after them, were guided by the same principle, namely that all economic transactions must be governed by an ethical code; this was part of the Bible's command to moralize the whole of life in keeping with the divine will.

Sombart's accusation of a double moral standard, that Jews behave in one way toward fellow Jews and in another, less ethical way, toward gentiles, rests on Deuteronomy 23:20: "You may charge interest to a foreigner but not on a loan to a fellow-countryman." But Sombart and others who argued this way—including Max Weber, who in this case agreed with Sombart—generalized far too much on the basis of this one out of the 613 commandments. He seemed to think that it alone governed economic relations with the out-group and that it did so uniformly and unchangingly over the centuries since the Babylonian captivity. Over the centuries the rabbis interpreted this and many other biblical precepts in a multitude of ways. Both Weber and Sombart were decidedly at fault for failing to read the rabbis—had they pondered Rashi, Maimonides,

Nachmanides, Menahem Ha-Me'iri, David Kimchi, Don Isaac Abarbanel, Josel of Rosheim, Joseph Caro, Leone da Modena, among any number of others, they would have found that the sages vehemently forbade taking advantage of gentiles, that some commentators permitted charging interest to Jews and gentiles but forbade taking it from the Jewish or gentile poor, that far from being fixed and static there was an evolutionary development of rabbinical teaching on economic behavior, until by the sixteenth century and the emergence of "modern capitalism" necessity compelled *hahlakhic* (legal) modifications to enable Jews to make a living by collecting interest. If Sombart or Weber had troubled to acquire a firsthand acquaintance with five hundred years of rabbinical commentary and legal interpretation, both certainly would have found that dealing with strangers was not a matter of ethical indifference to Jews and that *strangers* had long ceased to be synonymous with *enemies*.[105]

Although Sombart makes little or no mention of them, there were, indeed, religion-based practices that may have affected Jewish economic activities *in some degree*. By partly segregating Jews from gentiles, keeping the Sabbath might have been an economic handicap, but from the mid-nineteenth century, its observance declined rapidly. On the other hand, withdrawal and rest in order to return with fresh energy may have been an asset. Sabbath observance also seems to have fortified family life. Keeping the dietary laws also kept Jews and gentiles apart and may have been an economic liability, but it too declined after 1850, or gave way to a compromise by which one kept kosher at home but not outside. Sobriety was certainly an economic asset, although there is no explicit religious requirement for it and it is not clear why alcoholism was rare among Jews. It did make for better health and family solidarity. Family stability is also an advantage. The role of women is not clear and still not much studied beyond the ideal wife and homemaker—who is a keen businessperson—of Proverbs 31:10–31; some women in the Middle Ages were the family breadwinners to enable the pater familias to concentrate on Torah study. Although reflecting no religious imperative, Yiddish was certainly useful as a way to communicate and keep secrets from one's gentile rivals, although its use declined with growing acculturation. To antisemites, however, neither Hebrew nor Yiddish was innocent. Martin Luther and a long line of mostly German antisemitic writers propagated the myth that Hebrew and Yiddish (defined as German masquerading to sound and look like Hebrew) were the "secret" and "hidden" languages of the Jews in trading and finance. According to such writers, the language of the Jews—the "quintessential thieves"—is the language of thieves, from which follows the supposed Jewish mendacity and chicanery in business dealings. Hence Emperor Joseph II's Edict of Toleration (1782), the pioneer document of Jewish emancipation, barred Jews from using Hebrew or Yiddish in commercial transactions, as did the Prussian Edict of Emancipation of 1812.[106]

More fundamental than language and other customs in shaping Jewish attitudes and practice was the Talmud. It takes a positive stance with regard to economic activity, in sharp contrast to the New Testament and Patristic theologians who were vigilant against, as they thought it to be, filthy lucre and serving Mammon, and thus incorporated a strong, mystical, antiworldly, antieconomic strain in Christian theology and ethics. The Talmud, by contrast, was written, compiled and edited, taught and interpreted for centuries by rabbis who were merchants, artisans, and professional men, knowledgeable and accepting of business and finance, in theory and practice. They were family men, and some of them earned their living as merchants and the like, so as to serve the community without pay. It may be that Judaism's affirmative outlook on the world—*Weltbejahung*, what Weber called being "accommodated to the world"—made Jews more rational, less mystical, and more focused on this life, and thus more likely to engage and be successful in economic activities *in some degree*. Also the Talmud, intricate in structure and intellectually demanding as it is, may have taught Jews to be logical, analytical, and rational *in some degree*. More significantly, however, in Talmud and Bible alike, getting and spending are far from being the primary or ideal purpose of life. Learning and wisdom were the jewels without price, which meant that Jews were literate and educated in civilizations where historically these assets for economic doings were rare.

In placing excessive emphasis on biblical inspiration and talmudic direction, Sombart leaves out of account the far more important factor in explaining Jewish economic performance, that the Jews were a small minority of strangers, tolerated but subject to prejudice and persecution. Jewish disabilities and minority status were dismissed out of hand by Sombart: "[T]hey were of no moment whatever for the economic growth of the Jews."[107] This is the most radically skewed and unfounded assertion in the whole book. He thereby forfeits the possibility of any kind of plausible explanatory matrix. Sombart thus passed over the fact that Jewish economic energies and activities, thwarted by guild exclusion, monarchical policies, the attitude of the church, and the like, had to be more dynamic and acute for Jews to survive in a hostile world.

In broad historical view, the Jews represented what the French historian Fernand Braudel called "civilizations of the diaspora type."[108] The Christian Armenians (wrongly styled "Jewish Christians" for their entrepreneurial pluck) played much the same role in the Ottoman Empire (and were the victims of ferocious persecutions from 1895 to 1920); from the early modern period they became international merchants, brokers, and bankers from Amsterdam to the

Philippines. The Chinese who are scattered about Southeast Asia and else-where fall into the same socioeconomic category and sometimes are called "the Jews of the East"; they, too, are often calumniated as being "aggressive" and "materialistic" as if they were all "rich middlemen" or "film magnates" of "un-limited acquisitiveness" who displace the natives in a conspiratorial "silent inva-sion." The massacre of ethnic Chinese and pillaging of their places of business, which accompanied the seizure of power in 1965 by General Suharto and his ouster in 1998 in Indonesia, are reminders of the age-old hatred and envy of a minority that is perceived as foreign and unduly privileged and prosperous. Other examples of dynamic minorities include the Banians, a Hindu caste of merchants and brokers in India for whom the Indian Ocean was what the Mediterranean was for medieval Jews; the Parsees of India, who fled from their native Persia when the Islamic Arabs conquered it and were renowned for a thousand years in the East for their commercial sagacity and spirit of enter-prise; the Indians—until they were expelled in 1972 by Idi Amin—from Uganda; and the Nestorian Christians in Egypt and Asia.

Each of these communities had several things in common: literacy, better education than the host society, and links with the outside world. What appears to be the key to the whole issue is education, or simply literacy, that fitted them to perform economic functions that the host society could not, initially, perform for itself. Until modern times most people, including some medieval kings, were illiterate. Since the first century B.C.E., when a system of mandatory elementary education was instituted in Judaea, Jews, in fulfillment of a religious obligation, normally were educated. A medieval Christian exegete who sought to refute Jewish interpretations of scripture nevertheless recognized that they prized edu-cation: "The Jews, out of zeal for God and love of the law, put as many sons as they have to letters, that each may understand God's law. A Jew, however poor, if he had ten sons would put them all to letters, not for [material] advantage as the Christians do, but for the understanding of God's law, and not only his sons, but his daughters."[109] Such education—he who "prays through study"—made Jews profound students of Torah, Mishnah, and Talmud, but also sharpened their fac-ulties and equipped them to carry on economic operations. This tradition of re-spect for education was put to great advantage in the nineteenth century by Jews newly emancipated from the ghetto.

A related issue, implicit in Sombart but one that he was unlikely to pur-sue, over which much mythmaking ink has flown, is Jewish intelligence. Ac-cording to the German publicist and diplomat Friedrich von Gentz (1764–1832), "Intelligence—that is the mortal sin of the Jews." The issue of the "the smart Jews" was raised anew by *The Bell Curve* furor—that controversial book published in 1994 by Richard Herrnstein and Charles Murray seeks to correlate intelligence, race/ethnicity, class structure, and environment. Although it is really not possible to say—only to speculate—that genetics and/or environment bestowed "superior" intelligence on Jews, Mark Twain thought that relentless economic competition had selected superior Jewish brains. Despite all obstacles put in their way, he said, the Jew "found ways to make money, even ways to get rich. . . . [T]he Jew without brains could not survive, and the Jew with brains had to keep them in good training and well sharpened up, or starve. Ages of restriction to the one tool which the law was not able to take from him—his brain—have made that tool singularly competent." How that brain power was transmitted and nurtured also has been a subject of discussion. Invoked to explain Jewish success and creativity are: child-rearing practices, universal education, the prestige of scholars and the preference for scholars as husbands, and marriage and family incumbent on men instead of celibacy enjoined on Christian clergy.[110]

Nowhere in Sombart's work is there so much as a hint that other peoples—the Armenians, Parsees, Chinese in Southeast Asia—functioned in similar ways. He eschewed any kind of comparative method, which would have shattered his whole interpretative scheme. Rather, he persisted in an a priori racial-religious explanation of Jewish economic behavior as well as in his Marxian formula that capitalism is nothing more than the workings of the "spirit of Judaism." Nor did Sombart consider some obvious factors. The sociological fact that for centuries they were barred from artisan guilds and excluded from agriculture by being deprived of land might be expected to explain, in large part, why Jews concentrated their efforts on those aspects of economic activity that utilized "human" rather than "natural" forces, with a decided preference for "mental" and "intellectual" over "physical" labor as well as for self-employment in the professions and private businesses over wage employment.[111] A much sounder answer to these questions is that of Thorstein Veblen, an American economist and economic historian who was a contemporary of Sombart. He attributed the Jews' startling creativity, first, to their being "a nation of hybrids" rather than Sombartian "inbreds," and, second, to their minority status. It was the creative tension of "divided [cultural] allegiance," one foot in the Jewish community and the other "within the gentile community of peoples," that generated "the skeptical frame of mind," the "release from the dead hand of [the] conventional," that are fertile, according to Veblen, of innovation and pioneering.[112]

Sombart began with far greater knowledge of Judaism, of Jewish history and texts than Marx did, but he also began with Marx's ideological presuppositions and ended with decking out familiar anti-Jewish prejudice and polemic with scholarly garb and justification. Jews, because Judaism was "the spirit of capitalism," had played the decisive role in erecting the capitalist system; yet, uncannily, they and their religion had a decisive role in the development of socialism-communism and they were bent on destroying capitalism, their own creation. From either perspective, for Sombart Jews remained culpable and villainous. In his youth he had been a student of the antisemitic and nationalistic historian Heinrich von Treitschke, and Volkish nationalism appears to have been the one constant ideological element of his outlook. With Max Weber it may be said that despite Sombart's fundamental misreading of the phenomenon, "one fact could not be seriously questioned, namely that Judaism played a conspicuous role in the evolution of the modern capitalistic system."[113] But one is not dependent on Sombart to come to that realization; rather one is conscious that the beginning student is simply likely to be badly misled by *The Jews and Modern Capitalism*. It remains perplexing why serious scholars took what David Landes calls a "hoax" so seriously so long.[114]

## HENRY FORD

Although he did as much as anyone to revolutionize American society, Henry Ford (1863–1947), a rural Protestant, retained a provincial outlook all his life. He supported a back-to-the-soil movement; urged a McGuffey curriculum; condemned cities, bankers, the East, and Wall Street; and had a simplistic approach to social issues: "All the world needs for the guidance of its life could be written on two pages of a child's copybook."[115] He treasured McGuffey's readers and extolled them all his life for their great lessons, most especially no. 59 in the *New Fifth Eclectic Reader*, "Shylock, or The Pound of Flesh."[116] While he was a master mechanic with a genius for coordinating production on the assembly line, this uneducated and unread man felt empowered to pronounce oracularly on any and every subject under the sun. Given his enormous wealth as one of the richest men in the world and his folk-hero status as auto wizard and author of the five-dollars-a-day wage, Ford's deliverances were accepted as revealed truth. This "simple man, almost primitive in his general outlook,"[117] took up "the Jewish question" with the most devastating effect.

On the eve of launching his antisemitic crusade in 1920, Ford vouchsafed to an interviewer: "International financiers are behind all war. They are what is called the international Jew: German Jews, French Jews, English Jews, American Jews. I believe that in all those countries except our own the Jewish financier is supreme . . . here the Jew is a threat." He was convinced the "Jewish capitalists" started World War I and were responsible for all the "thieving and robbery" in the United States.[118] Ford shared Marx's view that "The Jew is a mere huckster, a trader who doesn't want to produce, but to make something [profit] out of what somebody else produces. Our money and banking system is the invention of the Jews, for their own purposes of control, and it's bad. Our gold standard was founded by Jews; it's bad."[119] Likewise, Jews invented capitalism, the stock market, and economics: "The whole science of economics, conservative and radical, capitalistic and anarchistic, is of Jewish origin."[120] In his own eyes Ford was no capitalist or "super-capitalist" but an "industrialist" or "manufacturer." Ford could rail at the Guggenheims' Smelting & Refining Co. as a villainous Jewish international firm, without ever seeing himself as the classic example of an international capitalist entrepreneur, grasping more and more widely at opportunities to plant his factories in country after country and reap great profits from six continents. He controlled "the flow of materials" from the raw state to the finished manufactured product that was distributed by his network of markets and agencies; his empire included rubber plantations, coal and iron mines, steel and glass plants, ships and shipbuilding, a railroad, and airplane manufacturing. He had branches, assembly plants, distribution centers worldwide: Canada, Australia, England, Holland, Belgium, Italy, Scandinavia, Japan, Latin America, Soviet Russia, and Nazi Germany.

The *Protocols of the Learned Elders of Zion* came to Ford's attention by 1919. For him it was the golden key and missing link, a flash of confirmation of his farm-bred prejudices and Populist phobias, broadening and deepening and justifying them. The *Dearborn Independent*, his weekly newspaper that was the vehicle in his war on the Jews, cited the *Protocols* repeatedly as proof and confirmation of its accusations. Ford himself was not literate enough to write the ninety-one articles that ran in the *Independent* from May 1920 to January 1922. Three men were Ford's instruments. Ernest Liebold, the friend of Hitler's future vice-chancellor Franz von Papen to whom he provided antisemitic propaganda materials, was American-born of German parents and Ford's personal secretary; he was Germanophile and antisemitic, vowing that "When we get through with the Jews there won't be one of them who will dare to raise his head in public."[121] William J. Cameron, in whose office Ford sat almost every day whether to direct or learn the direction of the next edition and even of what purported to be Ford's own weekly column, was the principal author of the articles; he was a lay preacher and became president of the Anglo-Saxon Federation, which proclaimed Anglo-Saxons to be "the true Israel" and Jews usurpers. Boris Brasol had been a tsarist army officer and member of its secret police as well as the infamous Black Hundreds, which spread vile tales about Jews and periodically killed and maimed Russian Jews in brutal pogroms. Brasol was instrumental in bringing the *Protocols* to America and to Ford's attention. Since 1918 he had been in Washington circulating the *Protocols*, in an effort to discredit the Russian Revolution, and had a hand in publishing *The Protocols and World Revolution* in 1920, with a lengthy preface by himself. If not a member of Ford's inner circle, Brasol was always welcome in Dearborn. He boasted that his writings "have done the Jews more injury than would have been done to them by ten pogroms" and said he anticipated having "the biggest pogroms and massacres here," that he would "write and . . . [thus] precipitate them."[122]

Ford always insisted, employing the royal "We," that "We are not anti-Semitic," but almost in the same breath could utter, "We [in America] will never get rid of our troubles until we get rid of the Jews."[123] He intended his anti-Jewish crusade, which he expected would take five years, to be "educational" and "cleansing," to induce Jews "to clean up their act."[124] Ford's abrupt decision to call a halt with article 91 in the *Dearborn Independent* may have been due to a steep decline in car sales in areas with large Jewish populations like New York, although there was no organized Jewish boycott, or because he had presidential aspirations. In any event, his rhetoric—he repeatedly stated that the *Protocols* "fit with what is going on. . . . And have fitted the world situation up to this time"—remained crude and acerbic, if less public. "Research" and accumulation of "sources" on "the Jewish question" continued and the *Independent* went on publishing antisemitic articles: for example, a series attacking Aaron Sapiro (founder of the National Council of Farmers' Cooperative Marketing Associations and counsel to many farm coops) as conspiring to take over and control American agriculture through the farmers' cooperative movement and Paul Warburg (obviously one of those German Jewish bankers) for his part in creating the Federal Reserve System and conspiring to use that "legal private monopoly" to control American banking and finance.[125] Only after this "second wave" and lawsuits was the *Independent* finally closed down in 1927.

Ford was a great hero to Hitler and the Nazis from the early 1920s. There was a life-size portrait of Ford in Hitler's office. Ford's publication, the *International Jew*, a reprint of the articles published in the *Independent*, was translated into German; it was emblazoned with Ford's and Hitler's names and photographs on the cover and was a main item in party sales of books and pamphlets. The prodigious antisemitic publisher and writer Theodor Fritsch published *Der Internationale Jude*, which was distributed "by the carload" in German-speaking Europe and was reportedly in its twenty-ninth printing by

1933. "We look to Heinrich Ford as the leader of the growing Fascist movement in America," Hitler said admiringly and boasted that he received financial support from Ford; in 1931 he acknowledged to a reporter for the *Detroit
News*, "I regard Henry Ford as my inspiration."[126] In July 1938 Hitler awarded
Ford on his seventy-fifth birthday Germany's highest honor for foreigners, the
Grand Cross of the German Eagle, which Ford accepted enthusiastically from
the German consul in a resplendent public ceremony in Detroit, rejecting all
pleas to refuse or return it.* Ford's own admiration for Hitler expressed itself
in various ways. He sent Hitler a fiftieth birthday present of 50,000 marks in
April 1939 and as late as the summer of 1941 was still supportive of Hitler and
the German cause.

In *Mein Kampf*, it has been noted, "Hitler plagiarized from Ford, lifting
his reasoning and some times the very words which appeared in the *Dearborn
Independent*."[127] Much the same applies to a 1924 pamphlet by Dietrich Eckart
and, possibly as coauthor, Hitler, *Bolshevism from Moses to Lenin: A Dialogue between Adolf Hitler and Me*, in which Ford is cited several times, as is Sombart.[128] Ford is the only American cited in *Mein Kampf*, where Hitler assails
international Jewish bankers: "Every year they [the Jews] manage to become
increasingly the controlling masters of the labor power of a people of
120,000,000 souls; one great man, Ford, to their exasperation still holds out
independently there even now." The editors of this American edition comment: "These reflections are copied, for the most part, from the *Dearborn In-*

---

* In 1937 Hitler awarded IBM chairman Thomas J. Watson the Merit Cross of the
German Eagle, which he reluctantly returned only in 1940. Both Ford and IBM, and
many American corporations with branches in Germany, pursued their profits, greatly
contributed to the Third Reich's economic and military strength, and ignored evidence
of persecution and genocide. IBM's subsidiary Dehomag placed its Hollerith punch-
card sorting machines—as well as indispensable maintenance and spare parts—at the
disposal of the Nazi regime to the end of the war. IBM subsidiaries were built in countries as Hitler conquered them, and thus IBM made the tracking and destruction of Europe's Jews fast and efficient, resulting in higher casualties, an illuminating example in
the death process of technology, a hallmark of the Holocaust. According to Edwin
Black, *IBM and the Holocaust: The Strategic Alliance between Nazi Germany and America's
Most Powerful Corporation* (New York: Crown, 2001), 107, 113, "Jews could not hide
from millions of punch cards thudding through Hollerith machines, comparing names
across generations, address changes across regions, family trees, and personal data
across unending registries," and Dehomag facilitated "Aryanization" of property by its
capacity to "cross-reference account numbers on bank deposits with census data, including grouping by profession and industry." Black exaggerates IBM's significance in
the Holocaust—Hitler would have implemented it with or without IBM; its record was
no worse than Ford's and other American corporate branches that used slave labor.

*dependent*, Mr. Henry Ford's newspaper. Much of the anti-Semitic propaganda once disseminated by this journal is still [late 1930s] current in Germany."[129] It was all too fitting for Fritsch to gloat that the banner of antisemitism had been passed from Ford to the Führer: "Adolf Hitler under the symbol of the swastika took over the fight against Judah in the spring of 1933."[130]

There are some striking parallels between Ford and Hitler, aside from taboos on tobacco, alcohol, and meat. Both believed that: Race is the decisive factor in history; superior and creative races are engaged in a life-and-death struggle with degenerate, evil races; and history and biology necessitated maintaining Aryan/Anglo-Saxon purity. Both maintained that: Commercial and financial Jews were a grave threat to agrarian virtues; Jewish influence on culture was baneful and corrupting; Jews controlled the press and used it to undermine religion and morals to further Jewish domination. For both Ford and Hitler, Bolshevism and Judaism were synonymous, and both claimed that Jews made the revolution and were ruling Russia. Both also held that Jewish capitalists and Jewish labor organizers worked hand in glove to enslave and exploit in the manner of the *Protocols*. In Ford's rendering, "You probably think the labor unions were organized by labor, but they weren't. They were organized by those Jewish financiers. . . . It's a great thing for the Jew to have on hand when he comes around to get his clutches on an industry."[131] Ron Rosenbaum notes perceptively that while historians have searched out "an exhaustive array of nineteenth-century German anti-Semitic predecessors to Hitler, there is perhaps an even more important *American* source of Hitler's hatred of Jews. A crucial source of his vision of a Jewish world conspiracy and a perhaps crucial source of funding for Hitler's own conspiracy to seize power: Henry Ford. It's remarkable how easily—or conveniently—Ford's contribution to Hitler's success has been lost to memory in America. It wasn't lost to Hitler. . . ."[132]

Faced with libel suits for slandering Jews and trying to avoid taking the witness stand, in 1927 Ford agreed to out-of-court settlements and a public apology and retraction of his antisemitism. In the 600-word statement, Ford admitted the spuriousness of the *Protocols:* "I confess that I am deeply mortified that this journal . . . has been made the medium for resurrecting exploded fiction, for giving currency to the so-called *Protocols of the Wise Men of Zion*, which have been demonstrated, as I learn, to be gross forgeries, and for contending that the Jews have been engaged in a conspiracy to control the capital and the industries of the world."[133] That all sounded solemn and heartfelt—"a death blow" to antisemitism, exulted the Jewish *Forward*—but it turned out to be only a tactical turn in Ford's antisemitic course.[134] Until World War II,

Ford continued his antisemitic divagations, only more covertly, through the magazine *Destiny*, edited by the selfsame Cameron. It was the vehicle of the Anglo-Saxon Federation of America, through which Ford appears to have extended his antisemitic empire of prejudice and calumniation by giving moral and financial support to William Dudley Pelley and the fascist Silver Shirts, the Reverend Gerald Winrod and his antisemitic Defenders of the Christian Faith, various German American Nazi groups, and Father Charles Coughlin, with whom Ford shared an obsession with international Jewish bankers. The Catholic Coughlin published the *Protocols* in his paper *Social Justice* and averred that "Mr. Ford did retract his accusations against the Jews. But neither Mr. Ford nor I retract the statement that many of the events predicted in the *Protocols* have come to pass." Ford said of Coughlin's Protestant counterpart, the Reverend Gerald L. K. Smith, radio sermonizer against the New Deal as the "Jew Deal," "I wish Gerald L. K. Smith could be president of the United States."[135] Although he burned five truckloads of the *International Jew*, it continued to be published with Ford's name on the title page in Germany, Britain, and the United States, where the Ku Klux Klan and other groups long after circulated it; it had been translated into sixteen languages, including Arabic, and was distributed by the millions in Europe, Latin America, and the Middle East. (Since neither the *Independent* articles nor the *International Jew* had ever been copyrighted—no doubt deliberately—Ford could not legally stop republication.) "I do not want any harm to come to them [the Jews]," he had said in 1922 in ending the series of articles in the *Independent*, but he continued to do enormous harm.[136] True to his antisemitic self, he was convinced that "international Jewish Bankers" triggered World War I, "pushed" the United States into the war in 1917, dictated the Versailles peace settlement in 1919; and, in 1940, he was further convinced that Hitler and Mussolini were "puppets upon whom someone is playing a dirty trick," namely the conspiratorial Jews.[137] That someone of Ford's standing endorsed antisemitic conspiracy fantasies no doubt convinced a great many people of their truthfulness. "All in all," in the considered judgment of the renowned student of myth Norman Cohn, "*The International Jew* probably did more than any other work to make the *Protocols* world-famous."[138]

## CHAPTER 5

# DENYING THE HOLOCAUST

## A NEO-NAZI MYTHOLOGY

FOR TWO MILLENNIA SCURRILOUS MYTHS about Jews abounded in Christian lands. We have seen how the medieval Christian myth of the Jew as Satan's agent conspiring to destroy Christendom helped spawn the modern nationalist myth of a Jewish cabal plotting to rule the planet. This myth and others about Jews, including their racial inferiority, were widely believed by many people and unashamedly propagated by members of the cultural elite—all this in a scientific age that had experienced the critical spirit of the Enlightenment. The Nazis employed these myths to justify their war against the Jews: They were cleansing Europe of parasitical subhumans who threatened the fatherland. The zeal and brutality displayed by both the SS and ordinary Germans involved in the extermination process attest to the immense impact these myths had on people's thinking.

The systematic slaughter of two-thirds of the Jewish population of Europe shamed many people and awakened them to the evilness and danger of anti-Jewish myths. It also spurred a growing Christian-Jewish dialogue that has fostered greater understanding and tolerance. As a result, the propagation of old myths about Jews has greatly abated in Western lands, at least in respectable circles. Nevertheless, antisemitism still has the capacity to ignite people's meanest feelings and distort thinking, as in the disturbing phenomenon of Holocaust denial.

A number of writers, some of whom are or have been affiliated with academic institutions, have deliberately and cruelly manufactured a new myth—that of Holocaust denial. These people argue that during World War II the Germans had no policy of extermination; the Jews invented the Holocaust to gain world sympathy for Zionism and to wrest enormous indemnity payments from innocent Germans. Using their putative capacity for conspiracy, financial power, political influence, and control over the media, say the deniers, Jews have managed to dupe the world.

In the tradition of earlier antisemites, Holocaust deniers intend to inflict maximum pain on Jews, for they know that the Holocaust touches the Jewish soul like few other issues. Antisemitic and neo-Nazi movements throughout the world have gleefully adopted the cause of Holocaust denial—anything to hurt the Jew. Through their own productions—books, pamphlets, video cassettes, comic books—the Internet, advertisements in college newspapers, and radio and television programs that give them an audience in the interest of "fairness and free speech," they disseminate this new antisemitic myth. For many of these Jew-baiters it is also a way to profiteer.

Holocaust denial, which flies in the face of all documentary evidence, including the testimony of eyewitness survivors, perpetrators, and bystanders, demonstrates anew the fragility of human reason and the seemingly limitless capacity of the mind to embrace the most grotesque beliefs. It is still another illustration of the power of antisemitism to drag the mind into the murky waters of the irrational.

Let us suppose that some white racist produced a book denying that blacks were once slaves in this country. In the preface he summed up his position:

> I have written this book because I feel that I have a moral duty to expose a great hoax that continues to do great harm to the American people. Contrary to everything we have been told, bondage slavery never existed in the United States. Blacks invented the myth that their ancestors were enslaved in order to wrench welfare payments and affirmative action programs from the government. The Africans that Europeans and Americans brought to the New World came voluntarily seeking a better life, and were fortunate to be given this opportunity. The accommodations of Africans on the ships crossing the Atlantic were no worse than those of the crew, and they were encouraged to sing and dance. But unlike European immigrants, Africans, many of whom still retained their savage ways, were unable to fend for themselves in the American colonies; in order to survive, they asked to be placed with caring families who provided them with food, and shelter, and work. Most blacks were satisfied with this arrangement, but occasionally the authorities were compelled to use

force against criminal blacks. It is unfortunate that the North, whipped into a frenzy by the lies and distortions of black rabble-rousers and their Abolitionist dupes, launched an unjust war against the South. Since the Civil War, blacks have engaged in a vile conspiracy to misrepresent the antebellum labor system by calling it slavery. Everywhere they have cunningly forged documents and planted misleading information that continue to deceive gullible historians. So great is their power that they were able to pressure white plantation owners and their descendants to confirm this myth, even though they knew in their hearts it was untrue. I have only one reason for writing this book—to present the truth to the world. Those who fear the truth, or are victims of a well-orchestrated black propaganda campaign, will call me a racist. But I will persist in my struggle, which I regard as a sacred duty.

The arguments advanced by Holocaust deniers are just as grotesque and their motivation just as fraudulent and mean-spirited. But one of the painful lessons of recent history is that the most absurd and hateful ideas, cleverly packaged and tirelessly repeated, do have an effect on people, particularly when Jews are the target.

## THE MYTHMAKERS

Over the past twenty years Holocaust denial has become a major propaganda tool of the extreme Right in many lands, and its propagation has become a growth industry. The inventors and disseminators of the myth have varied motives. Many are outright fascists or neo-Nazis, captivated by the idea of a powerful national-racial community, and admirers of Hitler, the self-made leader who unified and gave hope to a defeated and dispirited people. They are right-wing German nationalists or philo-Germans who want to rehabilitate Germany's reputation tarnished by the crime of genocide. By absolving the Third Reich of systematic mass murder, including more than a million Jewish children, these Nazi apologists hope to increase fascism's appeal for today's world, enhance Hitler's stature, and reinvigorate German nationalism. The same outfits that promote Holocaust denial also distribute audiocassettes of Nazi marching songs, videocassettes glorifying life in the Third Reich and German victories in the war, and the *Protocols of the Learned Elders of Zion*, the classic antisemitic libel. No doubt the sentiments of Willis A. Carto, a leading Holocaust denier, are shared by his colleagues:

Hitler's defeat was the defeat of Europe. And of America. How could we have been so blind? The blame, it seems, must be laid at the door of the international

Jews. It was their propaganda, lies, and demands, which blinded the West to
what Germany was doing. . . . If Satan himself, with all of his superhuman genius and diabolical ingenuity at his command, had tried to create a permanent
disintegration and force for the destruction of the nations, he could have done
no better than to invent the Jews.[1]

Virtually all deniers harbor a devouring hatred for Jews, which, depending
on the circumstances, they either disguise or flaunt. They refer to Jews as the
"traditional enemy" and view Zionism as an evil ideology and Israel an illegitimate state whose extinction they welcome. By denying the Holocaust, they
delegitimize Israel, which the international community, shocked and shamed
by the Nazi horrors, had helped to create. Deniers are obsessed with the
grotesque and stale theme of an international Jewish conspiracy; for them the
Holocaust is still another evil ploy by Jews in their drive for world power.
Some deniers seek recognition and a place in history as crusading iconoclasts,
for they know that Jewish conspiracy theories attract an audience.* They are

---

* Throughout the world Jew-haters have gleefully added Holocaust denial to their arsenal of antisemitic myths. In 1998, for example, a nationalist Ukrainian newspaper argued that concentration camps were really intended to save Jewish lives—an expression
of Nazi humanitarianism, if you will. "There were no crematoriums or gas chambers in
German concentration camps. These 'death factories' were rather a cunning way to
save Zhids [a traditionally insulting reference for Jews] than the means of [their] elimination" (*Forward*, July 17, 1998, 4). Holocaust denial is particularly onerous in Muslim
countries, where it is used to undermine Israel's legitimacy. If there were no Holocaust,
it is argued, then the sympathy for the Jews that led the United Nations to vote for the
partition of Palestine in 1947 was misplaced. Moreover, fabricating a tale about gas
chambers demonstrates the monumental wickedness of Zionist Jews, the enemy of
Islam. On September 3, 1997, an article in the official Palestine Authority newspaper
referred to the Holocaust as the "forged claims of the Zionists regarding the alleged
acts of slaughter perpetrated against the Jews" (*Jerusalem Post*, International Edition,
January 31, 1998, 8). Another article on July 2 in the Palestinian newspaper *Al Hayat al
Jadida* referred to the Holocaust as a "deceitful myth." It accused the Jews of disseminating "frightful pictures of mass executions and invent[ing] the shocking story of the
gas ovens, where Hitler allegedly burned them" (*New York Times*, International, July 24,
1998). In 1998 Roger Garudy, a French writer and convert to Islam, was found guilty of
racial defamation and inciting hatred for his 1995 book that denied the Holocaust—
France, Germany, and other countries have laws against Holocaust denial. During the
trial there were rallies in several Middle Eastern cities in support of Garudy, and six
hundred Iranian journalists signed a statement backing him. In the summer of 1996
Garudy toured Muslim lands, meeting with dignitaries and addressing major literary
and intellectual groups that acclaimed his work. On March 4, 2000, a writer for *Al-
Gumhuriga*, an Egyptian paper, wrote: "Zionist propaganda continues, even today, to
raise the issue of the Nazi crematoriums for Jews, although historical evidence, revealed by renowned German, British, and French historians, proved that claims that

ideologues who have discovered a belief system and a mission—exposing the lies of Jews and the distortions of academics who have been duped by them.

Holocaust deniers take two positions toward Nazi antisemitism. Sometimes they try to justify it, claiming that the Nazis were only reacting to Jewish offenses against the German people. In a repeat of the Third Reich's propaganda, they argue that the Jews were responsible for Germany's misfortunes during the Weimar era, and once Hitler came to power, Jews throughout the world declared war on the Third Reich and incited Western states against the Nazi regime. In self-defense against Jewish spies, provocateurs, propagandists, black marketeers, and communist subversives—and to protect the Jews themselves from the legitimate anger of the German people and the nations invaded by Germany—it was necessary to deport them to concentration camps, which were only labor camps. (Some say they were like resorts with educational and recreational facilities.) Germans incarcerating Jews in "resettlement" camps, say the deniers, was no different from American soldiers interning Japanese Americans during the war. In both instances, governments regarded these people as aliens who threatened national security. On the day after the war began, had not Chaim Weizman, president of the Jewish Agency for Palestine, written to British prime minister Neville Chamberlain, assuring him that Jews throughout the world sided with Britain in their struggle against Nazi Germany? By "declaring war against Germany," international Jewry was responsible for the actions taken against European Jews by the Third Reich. If some Jews suffered mistreatment in the camps, say the deniers, it was due to the criminal behavior of fellow prisoners; the Germans staffing the camps were under strict orders not to abuse prisoners. The pictures of dead, dying, and starving inmates taken when Americans entered the camps are misleading. These deplorable conditions were not due to German neglect but to typhus and the inability of the Nazis to transport food into the camps because of the Allied bombings.

Recognizing that attempts to vindicate the Nazis' antisemitism and their behavior toward Jews hamper their credibility, several deniers, in a tactical maneuver, now maintain that the Nazis did mistreat Jews, but conditions were not nearly so bad as the wailing Jews complain: There was no policy of liquidation, no gassings, no systematic mass shootings of innocent civilians; and the percentage of Jewish dead was not disproportional to what one would expect in a war that engulfed Europe for six years. Consistent with this charade, the

---

such crematoriums existed in Nazi detention camps are jokes" (*Forward*, March 31, 2000, 6). These are far from isolated examples.

deniers dismiss the idea that they harbor anti-Jewish feelings and even claim to deplore antisemitism.

Paul Rassinier, one of the earliest Holocaust deniers and a revered figure in Holocaust denial circles, is a paradox. A former communist turned socialist, he served with the French Resistance during the war. After being captured by the Nazis he was imprisoned in Buchenwald, a notorious concentration camp located in Germany. (It was not an extermination camp—they were all located in Poland.) Rassinier admitted that his contact with the SS while a prisoner had led him to think favorably of Nazism and French collaborators. Despite his firsthand experience with Nazi brutality and Jewish suffering (although he had no direct knowledge of the death camps in Poland and the murder squads operating in the Soviet Union), Rassinier became preoccupied with discrediting the testimony of concentration camp survivors, absolving the Nazis of guilt, and demonstrating that the Holocaust was a hoax perpetrated by Zionists who conspired with survivors and Jewish historians. Like the Nazis, Rassinier was obsessed with the idea of an international Jewish conspiracy. Exemplifying the greed for which Jews are well known, he said, Zionists invented the myth of genocide to extort reparation payments from Germany. For Rassinier and other antisemites, Jews, acting in unison, had long been tightening their grip on international finance. The money extorted from Germany would facilitate their plan for domination of world finances. "Today speaking metaphorically, the aim is the gold of Fort Knox. If the plan should succeed—and all that is needed is for the American branch of international Zionism to get its hand on Wall Street—the Israeli home-port of the Diaspora would become . . . the command post of all the world's industry. . . . Then at the very least, it could be said that the designation 'Chosen People,' which the Jews claim for themselves, would assume it [sic] full significance."[2]

Holocaust deniers rely heavily on the writings of another French national, Dr. Robert Faurisson, who taught French literature at the University of Lyons until he was suspended in 1978 for his distortions and falsifications of the Shoah. Faurisson participates in Institute for Historical Research (IHR) conferences and contributes to its journal. In 1979 he wrote in Le Monde, the French newspaper: "[T]he number of Jews destroyed by the Nazis is zero. The genocide against the Jew never happened."[3] In 1980, in a radio interview, he summarized his position: "The alleged Hitlerian gas chambers and the so-called genocide of the Jews form a single historical lie whose principal beneficiaries are the State of Israel and International Zionism and whose principal victims are the German people, but not its leaders, and the Palestinian people in its entirety."[4] In 1981 Faurisson stood trial for willfully distorting historical documents; for slandering Léon Poliakov, a leading authority on the history of antisemitism, whom he accused of fabricating sources to perpetuate the legend of the gas chambers; and for inciting racial hatred. The court fined him and ordered him to pay damages. In 1995 French judges convicted and fined him again for contesting the existence of the Holocaust. In a devastating critique of Faurisson, Pierre Vidal-Naquet, the distinguished French classicist who lost both his parents in Auschwitz, labeled him an "assassin of memory" who maliciously falsifies history for antisemitic ends.*

The center of Holocaust denial, which is now an international movement, is the Institute for Historical Research.** Founded in California in 1979 by Willis A. Carto, IHR disseminates Holocaust denial literature and Nazi books, pamphlets, tapes, and videocassettes throughout the world. It attracts Nazi sympathizers and people actively affiliated with far Right groups in several countries; several figures with past affiliations to the Third Reich attend IHR gatherings and contribute to its journal. One such person is H. Keith Thompson, a wealthy American businessman and Yale alumnus. During the war, as a young man, he had spied for the Germans; after the war, he fought to free Nazi war criminals, aided Nazis to escape from Europe, and worked with neo-Nazi organizations in Germany and the United States. Addressing an IHR meeting in 1983, Thompson drew a standing ovation when he urged the audience to "stand by the Third Reich." In 1987 Thompson arranged for SS Major General Otto Ernst Remer, an unrepentant Nazi who was held in awe by the far Right, to deliver the keynote address at an IHR conference. At the time Remer, who died in 1997, was having legal problems with the West

---

* One illustrative example of Faurisson's nefariousness is his claim that not until he first read Rassinier in 1960 did he become interested in the Holocaust and only after years of research and reflection was he convinced of its falsity. The author of a work on Rassinier reveals that Faurisson's antisemitic and pro-Nazi leanings were already evident in the late 1940s when he was a young student and that his familiarity with Rassinier and other negationists antedated by several years that moment of discovery he claims occurred in 1960. See Richard J. Golsan's introduction to Alain Finkielkraut, *The Future of a Negation*, trans. Mary Byrd Kelly (Lincoln: University of Nebraska Press, 1998).

** In her admirable work, *Denying the Holocaust: The Growing Assault on Truth and Memory* (New York: Free Press, 1993), Deborah Lipstadt described the background of key figures associated with IHR. In *The Beast Reawakens* (Boston: Little, Brown, 1997), an examination of right-wing extremism worldwide, Martin A. Lee discusses in even greater detail these Nazi sympathizers and Jew-haters. And most recently, Michael Shermer and Alex Grobman, *Denying History* (Berkeley: University of California Press, 2000), provide additional background material on the deniers.

German government for denying the Holocaust and making crude and injurious references to Jewish suffering during the war. Participants in the conference received Remer warmly and applauded every reference to Hitler and National Socialism.

In a bid for respectability, IHR claims that it consists of revisionist historians who employ the tools of scholarship to rectify a mistaken and fraudulent interpretation of the Jewish experience during World War II. To maintain the appearance of scholarship, they hold conferences, publish books, and issue the *Journal of Historical Review*, which has a scholarly format. In reality, the people associated with IHR, as backers, administrators, or contributors to the journal, are not in the least concerned with the standards of scholarship—accuracy and objectivity—but with maligning Jews and defending the Third Reich. They are not an association of historians but a sect whose central dogmas are hatred of the Jew and admiration for Hitler and the Nazi regime.

The first director of IHR was "Lewis Brandon," who, it was later revealed, was really William David McCalden, a man active in British neo-Nazi organizations. He was denied membership in the English National Union of Journalists because he edited racist publications that openly spouted racial bigotry. In his appeal, McCalden maintained that fostering racial discrimination was a legitimate concern for journalists. In 1984 he quit IHR because of differences with Willis A. Carto, the organization's founder; a few years later he died of AIDS.

In 1957 Carto founded the right-wing extremist Liberty Lobby, which conservative thinker William F. Buckley has described as "a hotbed of anti-Semitism." The *Spotlight*, the Liberty Lobby's tabloid newspaper, focuses on familiar antisemitic themes: Holocaust denial—a "profitable hoax" it calls the Shoah; the wickedness of Zionism and Israel; Jewish control of American financial and foreign policies; and defense of Germany's reputation, which, it says, has been besmirched by Jewish propaganda. On this last point, Carto has argued that Jews were responsible for America's misguided policy toward Nazi Germany and its failure to enter into an alliance with the Third Reich. (The *Spotlight* also attacks blacks—it denounced Martin Luther King, Jr. as a "hypocritical communist," expressed admiration for Skinheads, and whitewashed the Ku Klux Klan.)

Carto's political philosophy was shaped to a large extent by Francis Parker Yockey, who some researchers refer to as "America's Hitler." In *Imperium—Philosophy of History and Politics* (1948), which he dedicated to Hitler, Yockey called for Western "Aryan states," guided by a National Socialist ideology, to protect Western civilization from an alien and corrosive Jewish influence; advocated the expulsion of Jews from Europe; and claimed that in postwar Europe Jews, many of them black marketeers, had deliberately falsified photographs and written accounts of their experiences in concentration camps that were really fantasies.

In 1962 Noontide Press, recently acquired by Carto, reissued *Imperium;* the reprint contained a lengthy and laudatory introduction by Carto. Noontide Press keeps in circulation the *Protocols of the Learned Elders of Zion* and Henry Ford's *The International Jew*, and also publishes more recent antisemitic works, including the English translations of Rassinier's books. Antiblack books are also prominently represented in its listings.

In 1993 a bitter dispute led to Carto's ouster from IHR. Senior officials denounced his dictatorial management style and accused him of financial improprieties; at stake was a $7.5 million bequest by a Swiss woman to the Legion for the Survival of Freedom, the IHR's parent company. In 1996 a San Diego judge, ruling that Carto had misappropriated money from the bequest, ordered him to pay $6.4 million to the group controlled by his rivals. The decision is being appealed. The dispute also involved a substantive issue: Carto wanted the *Journal of Historical Review* to abandon its singular concern with Holocaust denial and treat other issues of concern to the extremist Right. After losing control over the IHR, Carto inaugurated *The Barnes Review*, which tried to appeal to the far Right. In addition to spewing the deniers' message, it also publishes articles defending Hitler, praising the fascist and antisemitic poet Ezra Pound, denouncing Israel, and warning against Third World immigration into North America. Well-known Nazi sympathizers and antisemites contribute articles. In May 1998 the Liberty Lobby filed for Chapter 11 bankruptcy reorganization; Carto and his wife, seeking personal protection, filed under Chapter 7.

Austin J. App (d. 1987), who earned a Ph.D. in English literature at the Catholic University of America, taught at the University of Scranton and LaSalle College. Of German descent, App during the 1930s was active in far Right German American organizations, and after the war he fought to remove the moral stigma with which Germany had been stamped because of its war crimes. In 1973, he published a brief work with the revealing title, *The Six Million Swindle: Blackmailing the German People for Hard Marks with Fabricated Corpses.* And the following year he published *A Straight Look at the Third Reich.*

App blamed American intervention in the war on "Zionists and Talmudists," who had unjustly railed against Hitler, and denounced accounts of German atrocities as a Jewish fabrication. The true victims of the war, he said, were German soldiers and civilians, whom the Allies, urged on by "barbarous"

Jews, abused unmercifully. App maintained that Nazism was essentially a form
of positive Christianity. National Socialism and Hitler have been victims of
"the crudest, the dirtiest, the vilest character-assassination! Only moral cripples would stoop to it, and only a brainwashed public would believe it. . . .
Even if the wartime atrocities alleged against the Third Reich were factual
(and they are not), they still would not be valid grounds for rejecting National
Socialism."[5]

The Nazis only wanted Jews to emigrate, says App, which "is what every
civilized country has wanted, . . . namely to get the Jews out of their hair."
The Nazi policy of emigration was "quite in tune with the historical and civi-
lizing development of Europe," for Jews "subvert . . . Christian culture." Jews
and "gypsies are historically the only earthly tribes whom no country ever
wanted or wants." In the United States the Jews "now control the media and
the money—and sex education and pornography. . . . They are grand larce-
nists and subversives" who have turned New York into "a Jewish Sodom and
Gomorrah."[6]

Dr. Arthur Butz, an electrical engineer who writes for the *Journal of Historical Review*, teaches computer science at Northwestern University. In *Hoax
of the Twentieth Century*, published in 1976 by Noontide Press, Butz skillfully
used a scholarly façade—footnotes, extensive bibliography, and references to
some leading books in the field, to principal research centers, and to collections of archives—in order to camouflage an antisemitic tract. In 1990 two dis-
gruntled parents withdrew their thirteen-year-old daughter from an Illinois
classroom because they objected to the way the Holocaust was taught. To support their case, they used *Hoax* as a reference, prompting Peter Hayes, who
teaches modern German history at Northwestern, to give this astute evaluation of Butz's book: "It presents the history of the Holocaust as Heinrich
Himmler . . . wanted people to believe it occurred. Butz accepts the camou-
flaging vocabulary of Nazi sources at face value, rejects all other written and
eyewitness records . . . and thus concocts an account that virtually all professional historians have rejected."[7]

A member of the *Journal of Historical Review*'s editorial board, Ditlieb
Felderer, a Swedish citizen of Austrian birth, publishes and disseminates antisemitic literature, including pornographic pictures designed to humiliate
Holocaust survivors. In 1983 he was sentenced to ten months in prison for distributing hate material. The IHR reprinted and distributes his book, which
claims that Anne Frank's diary was a hoax. He has also organized trips to concentration camp sites in Poland, instructing the tourists on the "truth" of what
had occurred there.

An oft-referred to work by deniers is *Did Six Million Really Die? The Truth at Last.* First published in 1974, the booklet has been widely circulated in Europe, the United States, and the Middle East. The author, Richard Harwood, it was later learned, was really Richard Verrall, former deputy chairman of the National Front, a British neo-Nazi organization that attacks the Jews for corrupting the racial and cultural heritage of Britain and Europe. Hugh Trevor-Roper, the distinguished British historian, commented succinctly on the pamphlet: "My judgment of it is that, behind a simulated objectivity of expression, it is in fact an irresponsible and tendentious publication which avoids material evidence and presents selected half-truths and distortions for the sole purpose of sowing anti-Semitic propaganda."[8]

In his numerous books on World War II, published by respectable houses, British historian David Irving sought to cleanse Hitler's image and to relativize Nazi war crimes—they were no worse than the deeds committed by the Allies, for example, the firebombing of Dresden. Irving blamed Britain's decline on its misguided decision to go to war with Nazi Germany; in 1977, on a BBC program, when asked if he considered Hitler evil, Irving responded: "He was as evil as Churchill, as evil as Roosevelt, as evil as Truman."[9] Nor did he view Hitler as a pathological Jew-hater. Before 1933, Irving maintained, Hitler employed antisemitism in a tactical way to win support; once in power, however, "he became a statesman and then a soldier. . . . And the Jewish problem was a nuisance to him, an embarrassment."[10] Several years later Irving described Hitler as "probably the biggest friend the Jews had in the Third Reich, certainly when the war broke out. . . . He was the one who was doing everything he could to prevent things nasty happening to them."[11]

Initially, Irving did not deny the Holocaust, maintaining that it was Himmler who, unknown to Hitler, ordered the extermination of the Jews. But increasing association with Holocaust deniers and the far Right (and a more than latent antisemitism) led him to identify with the deniers' position. In 1988 he began to argue that Jews were not systematically slaughtered in accordance with the policy and directives of the Third Reich but were unfortunate victims of diseases that ravaged the concentration camps or were killed by SS units acting on their own and not carrying out orders from Berlin. He also denied that Jews were murdered in gas chambers: "[T]o the best of my knowledge, there is not one shower bath in any of the concentration or slave labor camps that turns out to have been some kind of gas chamber."[12] And he simply dismissed the eyewitness testimony of Jewish survivors, whom he categorized as liars, psychiatric cases, and extortionists. In 1990 he told an audience at Latvian Hall, Toronto, that Jews even had themselves tattooed with numbers to bolster their claims that they were survivors and therefore entitled to compensation. Be sure "that it's not a number which anyone has used before," he told his laughing listeners, playing to his audience's prejudices. Over the years Irving continued to lace his speeches with crude and hurtful statements, which British historian Richard J. Evans describes as "the classic language that I had encountered in reading texts from German anti-Semites from the late nineteenth century on."[13]

By denying that the Nazi regime planned and organized the extermination of European Jewry and by minimizing the number of Jews murdered, Irving and his fellow deniers intend to convey that the murder of Jews was only a by-product of a vicious war, that Jewish suffering was no greater than that endured by others during World War II, that, in fact, the "story [of the Holocaust] was but a legend."[14]

In 1989 Irving's firm, Focal Point Publications, printed *The Leuchter Report*, which purported to provide scientific evidence that no gas chambers were used to kill people in German concentration camps. It was soon learned that the author, Fred Leuchter, lied about his engineering background—he had none; moreover, under expert analysis, both his methodology and conclusions were discredited. In his introduction, Irving expressed hope that the report would enlighten people who have been "swindled" and "duped" by a "well-financed and brilliantly successful publicity campaign." Fined in Germany for preaching Holocaust denial, Irving urged the court "to fight a battle for the German people and put an end to the blood lie of the Holocaust which has been told against this country for fifty years."[15] He participates actively in IHR conferences and has addressed adoring neo-Nazis at rallies in Germany and Argentina, asserting that the Holocaust is "a major fraud. . . . There were no gas chambers. They were fakes and frauds."[16] Irving said that in a second edition of *Hitler's War*, his major work, he would remove all references to the Holocaust, which he now sees as a "legend [and] a blood libel against the German people."[17]

Such behavior prompted Alan Bullock, the distinguished British historian and author of the classic *Hitler: A Study in Tyranny*, to say of Irving: "Strange little rascal, he whips it up, and he *knows he's doing it*."[18] In an interview in 1996 with Ron Rosenbaum, Irving, in Rosenbaum's words, maintained "that there was some deliberate killing of Jews, perhaps a hundred thousand or so,* but

---

* Irving is inconsistent on the number of Jewish victims, as Shermer and Grobman note in *Denying History*, 50: "In a 1994 interview he estimated that 600,000 Jews were killed in World War II, but on a July 27, 1995, Australian radio show, Irving admitted that

mainly wildcat, unauthorized actions in the blood heat of the fighting on the eastern front. And as for the concentration camps, they were really there for concentration, not killing."[19] In his highly regarded *Hitler of History*, John Lucas described Irving's books as revealing "a gradual progression from partial exoneration, through rehabilitation, to the virtual elevation of Hitler to a level of historical and moral greatness." In his books and his personal behavior, particularly in addressing neo-Nazi groups, Irving "has revealed himself to be an unrepentant admirer of Hitler."[20] Several historians have praised Irving for his extensive research into Nazi archives and his ferreting out of obscure diaries and private correspondence from the German side of World War II, about which he has extensive knowledge. However, his hard-to-disguise admiration for Hitler has distorted his judgment, particularly when it comes to the persecution of Jews.

Irving sued Deborah Lipstadt and her publisher, Penguin Books, for libel because she claimed that he is not a historian but a Hitler partisan and dangerous propagandist for Holocaust denial. Such an accusation, he said, ruined his reputation and wrecked his career. At the trial held in London in early 2000, expert testimony demonstrated conclusively that Irving manipulated data to minimize and disguise the atrocities committed by the Third Reich. Declaring that Irving is a racist and antisemite, Mr. Justice Charles Gray ruled against him. Richard J. Evans, a specialist in modern German history with a broad background in archival research, was one of several authorities commissioned by the defense to serve as an expert witness. Evan's testimony was a significant factor in Justice Gray's decision. A year after the trial, Evans published *Lying about Hitler: History, Holocaust and the David Irving Trial*, which employs the trial to show "how we can tell the difference between truth and lies in history."[21] In instance after instance Evans exposed how Irving misquoted sources, "misrepresented data, . . . skewed documents [and] ignored or deliberately suppressed material when it ran counter to his arguments."[22] Irving's claim that

> Hitler did not know or approve of actions against Jews . . . clearly rested on a
> substantial number of falsehoods. . . . [W]hen I followed Irving's claims and

---

perhaps as many as four million Jews died at the hands of the Nazis: 'I think, like any scientist, I'd have to give you a range of figures and I'd have to say a minimum of one million, which is monstrous, depending on what you mean by killed. If putting people into a concentration camp where they die of barbarity and typhus and epidemics is killing, then I would say the four million figure because, undoubtedly, huge numbers did die in the camps in conditions that were very evident at the end of the war.'"

statements back to the original documents on which they purported to rest . . . Irving's work in this respect was revealed as a house of cards, a vast apparatus of deception and deceit. Lipstadt was therefore right to describe Irving as a Hitler partisan who manipulated the historical record in an attempt to portray his hero in a favorable light.[23]

Seeking to generate publicity, at its first convention the IHR offered a reward of $50,000 to anyone who "could prove that the Nazis operated gas chambers to exterminate Jews during World War II." When the media ignored this ploy, the IHR sent letters to survivors prodding them to accept the challenge. Mel Mermelstein, an Auschwitz survivor whose mother and sisters perished in the gas chambers and whose father and brother died in one of Auschwitz's satellite camps, took the dare. When the IHR said that the tribunal judging the case would consist of Faurisson, Butz, and Felderer, three members of its board, Mermelstein sued. In an attempt to torment Mermelstein, David McCalden wrote him: "I notice that you go under two names: Mermelstein and Memmelstein. Having two names would indicate that you have been gassed at least twice, possibly also receiving double pension for your execution."[24] In 1985 the Los Angeles Superior Court, recognizing that the gassing of Jews at Auschwitz was a historical fact not subject to dispute, awarded Mermelstein the $50,000 award and an additional $40,000 for pain and suffering. The IHR also had to issue him an apology.

Aspiring to reach college students, in 1987 the deniers organized the Committee for Open Debate on the Holocaust (CODOH), which has placed full-page advertisements in college newspapers stating their position. Coordinating this campaign are Bradley Smith* and Mark Weber, who was replaced in 1990 by Dr. Robert Countess. All three are associated with IHR; Mark Weber also had a long-standing relationship with the National Alliance, an extremist neo-Nazi and white supremacist group. He is now editor of the *Journal of Historical Review* and director of IHR.

Their ads carefully avoid overt antisemitic language and Nazi sympathies, knowing that such displays will deny them the legitimacy they crave. The only objective of revisionists, say the ads, is to submit the Holocaust to open inquiry and free debate that have hitherto been blocked by influential pressure groups, "Thought Police" who are fearful of a heretical view. Smith and Weber know that such words will appeal to unseasoned and impressionable students with little knowledge of the past. Moreover, when a paper rejects

---

* Not to be confused with Bradley F. Smith, a very able historian.

their ad, they try to claim violation of the First Amendment.

While many college newspapers have refused to accept the deniers' ads, several have printed them, arguing that even the most hateful views have a right to be heard. (In 1997 twenty colleges printed the advertisement or a denier opinion piece; in 1998 the figure was twenty-six.) Some editors, admitting that they would not print overtly racist or sexist ads, held that Smith's ads do not malign Jews. The editor of the *Duke Chronicle*, which ran the ad, was even more deluded; the revisionists, she said, were "reinterpreting history" and their views were part of an ongoing "scholarly debate."[25] A more fitting evaluation came from the *Harvard Crimson*, which rejected the ad, denouncing it as "vicious propaganda based on utter bullshit that has been discredited time and time again." The revisionists' view was not just "moronic and false," it was also a deliberate attempt "to propagate hatred against Jews."[26]

Deniers insist that they are serious researchers engaged in an honored historical enterprise—marshalling evidence to challenge a traditional view; they describe themselves as "revisionists" prepared to refute the erroneous and biased interpretations of "exterminationists" who have dominated the field. Knowing the right words to use, they say that their revisionism "is a scholarly process, not a doctrine or an ideology."[27] Hoping to gain recognition and entrance into the mainstream of historical discourse, they press for discussion and debate with academic scholars. But the profession dismisses them as purveyors of hate. In December 1991 the governing council of the American Historical Association (AHA) officially condemned the deniers, declaring "No serious historian questions that the Holocaust took place."[28] And in 1994 an AHA press release stated that "the Association will not provide a forum for views that are, at best, a form of academic fraud."[29] The Organization of American Historians has taken similar action. When rebuffed by the profession, deniers protest that their opponents are afraid of the truth. They see themselves, in the words of Butz, as "a handful of lone individuals of very meager resources,"[30] braving intimidation and persecution for a noble cause.

In the fifth century B.C.E. Socrates urged his fellow Athenians to think rationally about the problems of human existence and supplied a method of inquiry, dialectics or logical discussion, as the avenue to knowledge. But a precondition for a dialogue is an open mind, a willingness to examine ideas critically; confront illogical, inconsistent, dogmatic, and imprecise assertions; and form and alter conclusions on the basis of knowledge. One cannot, for example, enter into dialogue over the question of time with religious fundamentalists committed to the belief that the universe was created six to ten thousand years ago, a few days before God created Adam and Eve. When confronted with astronomical evidence indicating that the universe is some twelve or more billion years old, vast geological evidence that the earth itself is some five billion years old, and fossil evidence that complex forms of life go back hundreds of millions of years, they either fault the evidence and dating techniques or, as a last resort, maintain that God planted this evidence to test our faith.

It is also purposeless to engage in dialogue with neo-Nazis, who distort, manipulate, alter, and interpret facts to accord with an antisemitic worldview and simply ignore other facts that cannot be bent to fit their agenda.* No discourse is possible with people who mock survivors of Auschwitz and seek to disguise hate, myth, and delusion behind the respected historical enterprise of revisionism. Their fundamental aim is to sanitize the Nazis and make Jews the real villains of World War II. An appeal to neither logic nor to decency will lead these people to abandon their delusional view of the Jew and the Holocaust: The true believer does not easily break with a faith that gratifies deeply seated emotions. It would be a terrible mistake to engage in a dialogue with members of the Holocaust denial sect, for this would grant these purveyors of "gutter history" a measure of respectability and legitimacy.

Historians do debate certain questions related to the Holocaust—for example, whether it was Hitler or SS leaders, seeking to prove their dedication to the Führer and their commitment to Nazi ideology and values of the Third Reich, who initiated the mass exterminations; the degree of Jewish resistance; and the extent to which German citizens and other bystanders knew what was happening. And they are open to and do engage in *genuine* revisions on the basis of new findings—for example, reducing the number of French Jews deported to the camps from 120,000 to 75,121 (of whom 2,564 returned) and reducing the number of Jews murdered at Auschwitz from some 2 million to about 1 million. They now dismiss the view that there were gas chambers at Dachau concentration camp, which was located on German soil. While many people, Jews and non-Jews, perished at Dachau, the Germans used gas cham-

---

* Austrian historian Brigitte Bailer-Galanda says that these revisionists "not only distort the number of murdered Jews cited in serious historical works but even construct 'evidence' by citing nonexistent letters of the International Committee of the Red Cross, using pseudostatistics about the Jewish population of the world, or willfully misinterpreting statistics about the number of deaths in concentration camps." She elaborates on the Red Cross: "One standard argument is that the International Red Cross stated that only 300,000 Jews died in the course of National Socialist persecution. This lie has been repeated for decades, despite the fact that the Red Cross repeatedly has formally denied ever publishing such a statement." "'Revisionism' in Germany and Austria," *Antisemitism and Xenophobia in Germany after Unification*, ed. Hermann Kurthen, Werner Bergmann, and Rainer Erb (New York: Oxford University Press, 1997), 177, 182.

bers only in several camps built in Poland. The earlier view that the SS was entirely responsible for carrying out the Final Solution has also been revised. It has now been established that the SS did not act alone, that ordinary German police battalions were actively engaged in the killing operations, and that the German army was also a willing participant. Scholars had revised their estimates of Jewish dead, lowering by several hundred thousand the generally accepted figure of 6 million. But based on recently released documents from the archives of the former Soviet Union and its one-time satellites, it now appears that the figure may well exceed 6 million.

While students of the Holocaust debate certain issues and revise views based on new findings, none of them doubts that it happened. The annihilation of European Jewry, like World War I, is an irrefutable fact of history, a gruesome descent into the irrational that still haunts us. The Holocaust is not an issue that can have two sides—one exterminationist and the other revisionist—as the deniers would have it. To propose this, to suggest that the Jews were not victims of Nazi genocide, is obscene but not totally implausible, given the history of antisemitic myths and the pathological hatred that people have had for Jews over the centuries. Gavin I. Langmuir, a distinguished student of religion and antisemitism (and a non-Jew), succinctly says of the deniers: "If I encounter individuals who deny that anything like [the Holocaust] happened, I can only assume their individual irrationality, their cynical political immorality, or the irrationality of their social indoctrination."[31]

Among the several ploys used by deniers, three stand out: mishandling new findings, mishandling sources, and mishandling the views of scholars. Whenever scholars effect a correction, the deniers rush in claiming that another fabrication about German atrocities has been exposed and soon the facts will compel historians to abandon all the "vile falsehoods" they have been propagating about extermination. For example, after the war it was claimed that the Germans had drained away human fats from the crematoria victims to manufacture soap. The soap story, which historians dismissed as false around 1975, was not an unreasonable assumption since the Germans harvested the victims' gold tooth fillings, which was melted down into gold bars, and their hair, which was used in mattresses. Moreover, camp guards were notorious for taunting prisoners that "You'll be up the chimney flue this afternoon" or "You'll be soap tomorrow." Historians learned that "RIF" or "RJF," which was imprinted on bars of soap, was not an acronym for "pure Jewish soap" (Reines Jüdisches Fett) but for "Reich Center for Industrial Fat Provisioning" and that the technology for making soap from human fats (apparently the Germans carried out such experiments but not on a mass scale) was not known before

1945. To the deniers, the historical profession was knowingly promoting lies until forced to abandon them by the facts. But the facts were established by legitimate historians, working to rethink and correct, as they always do; the deniers had nothing to do with this or any other correction or revised interpretation in our understanding of the Holocaust.

To support their claim that there were no gassings or gas chamber installations at Auschwitz, the deniers cite a Nuremberg Military Tribunal document, NI-11696, an affidavit of a British military sergeant who was a prisoner of war in Auschwitz for several years. Not surprisingly, the sergeant's testimony contradicts the deniers completely. The relevant passage reads:

> Although I had heard that conditions were bad, I at first did not believe it. I made it a point to get one of the guards. . . . For a few cigarettes he pointed out to me the various places where they had gas chambers and the places where they took them down to be cremated. Everyone to whom I spoke gave the same story, the people in the city of Auschwitz, the SS men, concentration camp inmates, foreign workers, everyone said that thousands of people were being gassed and cremated at Auschwitz, and that inmates who worked with us and who were unable to continue working because of their physical condition and were suddenly missing, had been sent to the gas chambers. . . . Even among the Farben employees to whom I spoke, a lot of them would admit they knew about the gassing. . . . It would be utterly impossible not to know. Everyone knew from the civilians to the top dogs. It was common talk.[32]

In *Why Did the Heavens Not Darken?* Arno Mayer, a prominent historian of modern Europe, commented on the gas chambers:

> Sources for the study of the gas chambers are at once rare and unreliable. Even though Hitler and the Nazis made no secret of their war on the Jews, the SS operatives dutifully eliminated all traces of their murderous activities and instruments. No written orders for gassing have turned up thus far. The SS not only destroyed most camp records, which were in any case incomplete, but also razed nearly all killing and cremating installations well before the arrival of Soviet troops. Likewise, care was taken to dispose of the bones and ashes of the victims.[33]

Mayer, of course, is not saying that there were no gas chambers. However, when the deniers cite this passage, they quote only the first sentence— "Sources for the study of the gas chambers are at once rare and unreliable"— implying that a respected history professor supports their position.

Holocaust deniers may have had some marginal success in reaching people who were not already infected with the antisemitic virus, but they have made no inroads with historians or governments. No scholarly conference invites them; no national or international committee investigating the plundering of Jewish wealth and property during the war requests their advice. Interfaith groups dedicated both to understanding the historical roots of Christian anti-Judaism and to teaching tolerance regard the deniers as abhorrent hatemongers. Educational groups in several countries preparing Holocaust curriculums for students shun them, and several countries, including Germany, Belgium, Italy, Sweden, Australia, and New Zealand, have made it illegal to propagate the insidious myth of Holocaust denial.

## THE MYTH

It is not our purpose here to refute in a systematic way what Holocaust deniers say. There exists a massive and rapidly growing literature on the Holocaust; very able historians from many lands and of various persuasions, utilizing an array of sources, particularly the official records of the Third Reich and increasingly of eastern European lands, have described the systematic murder of European Jewry. Nowhere in their writings do they refer to Holocaust deniers, except perhaps as an aside to express their disdain for them. No historian—except those with neo-Nazi leanings and affiliations—endorses the so-called revisionist position. Here we want only to examine some views advanced and procedures employed by the deniers. (For more detailed critiques of the deniers, the reader is referred to the works of Deborah Lipstadt and Pierre Vidal-Naquet.) The denialist position can be reduced to several elemental points.

*1. The Third Reich had no policy of extermination. German records from the war and statements by German officials that point to mass murder have been wrongly interpreted or are forgeries. The testimony and confessions of Nazis in the various trials held between 1945 and 1963 are not trustworthy—they were obtained through torture, threats, or the hope of a lighter sentence.*

In the deniers' eyes, the Nuremberg trials, conducted immediately after the war for leading Nazis implicated in war crimes were simply the revenge of the victors. They offer this reason for dismissing as untrustworthy and fraudulent the enormous amount of documents assembled by the prosecution. Germans who confessed to war crimes, say the deniers, were really innocent; they told their captors what they wanted to hear, including admissions of guilt, because this was their only way of getting a reduced sentence. For the deniers, the Nuremberg trials were little better than Stalin's show trials of the 1930s in which innocent people confessed to the most absurd charges.

That the thousands of documents assembled by the prosecution continue to be used by historians researching the history of the Third Reich is a good indication of their value and authenticity. Moreover, the defendants at Nuremberg did not deny the mass murder of European Jews—the evidence was too overwhelming for such absurdity. Rather, their defense was simply that they were following orders. Similarly, Adolf Eichmann, a key administrator of the Final Solution, testified in Israel that he was responsible only for deporting Jews to the death camps, not for killing them; the "extermination machinery," he said, was the responsibility of another authority.

The Nazis employed innocuous terminology—"cleansing," "special action," "special treatment," "resettlement," "selection," and "Final Solution"—to disguise genocidal operations. But on October 4, 1943, Heinrich Himmler, Reichführer-SS, unambiguously told an audience of SS generals that the Jews were being annihilated:

> I also want to talk to you, quite frankly, on a very grave matter. Among ourselves, it should be mentioned quite frankly, and yet we will never speak of it publicly. . . . I mean the clearing out of the Jews, the extermination of the Jewish race. It's one of those things it is easy to talk about. "The Jewish race is being exterminated," says one party member, "that's quite clear, it's in our program, elimination of the Jews, and we're doing it, exterminating them." And then come 80 million worthy Germans, and each one has his decent Jew. Of course, the others are vermin, but this one is an A-1 Jew. Not one of all of those who talk this way has witnessed it, not one of them has been through it. Most of us must know what it means when 100 corpses are lying side by side, or 500, or 1000. To have stuck it out and at the same time, apart from exceptions caused by human weakness, to have remained decent fellows, that is what has made us hard. This is a page of glory in our history which has never been written and is never to be written. We have taken from them what wealth they had. . . . We had the moral right, we had the duty to our people, to destroy this people which wanted to destroy us. . . . [W]e have exterminated a bacterium.[34]

Butz's interpretation of this speech is a good illustration of the deniers' approach. First he expresses doubt that the transcript of the speech is genuine. But even if these are Himmler's words, says Butz, they have been misinterpreted: "[B]y '*Ausrottung*' Himmler merely meant 'uprooting' or some form of elimination less drastic than killing. . . . The corpses referred to could easily be interpreted as German corpses produced by the Allied air raids, which the Nazis often claimed the Jews were ultimately responsible for."[35]

*2. Most Jews killed by the Einsatzgruppen were spies, partisans, or criminals against whom the Germans engaged in legitimate acts of retaliation.*

The first stage of the Final Solution was carried out by the Einsatzgruppen—special units of SS trained for mass murder who followed on the heels of the German army into Soviet Russia. Moving systematically into captured villages and towns, the Einsatzgruppen rounded up Jewish men, women, and children and herded them to execution grounds. The victims, standing naked in front of pits, were slaughtered with machine-gun and rifle fire. The dead and dying were then covered with earth. Streams of blood flowed and, for a time, as one survivor recalled: "The pits heaved and sank, heaved and sank, these were the last convulsions of the dying."[36] Aided by Ukrainian, Lithuanian, and Latvian auxiliaries, along with contingents from the Romanian army, the Einsatzgruppen massacred some 1 to 1.4 million Jews. Units of the regular German army, the Wehrmacht, actively participated in the rounding up of Jews and sometimes in the actual shootings.

Our knowledge of the Einsatzgruppen comes from eyewitness accounts of Jewish survivors and non-Jewish observers; the testimony after the war of SS participants in the mass murder; and reports filed by the four Einsatzgruppen. Helmut Krausnick, a German historian who has examined these reports, writes:

> From 15 August 1941 the *Einsatzkommando* (according to its own "general report") was also shooting Jewish children almost daily: for instance, in the operation carried out in Moletai and Utena on 29 August 1941, "1,460 Jewish children" were put to death in addition to 582 Jewish men and 1,731 Jewish women. Under the heading "Executions up to 1 February 1942," . . . the following figures were given: communists, 1,064; guerrillas, only 56; mentally unsound 653; Poles, 44; Russian prisoners-of-war, 28; gypsies, 5; Armenians, 1; Jews, 136,421! These figures were reported by Einsatzgruppe A, which had already executed 229,052 Jews. Einsatzgruppe B reported 45,467 shootings by 14 November 1941; Einsatzgruppe C, 95,000 by the beginning of December 1941; and Einsatzgruppe D, 92,000 by April 1942. To these figures must be added a further 363,211 shootings carried out during the months of August to November 1942 in Ukraine, South Russia, and the province of Bialystock, as reported to Hitler by Himmler himself.[37]

In his report of December 1, 1941, SS Colonel Karl Jäger, commander of an Einsatzkommando, described the killing operations:

> The decision to free each district of Jews necessitated thorough preparation of each action as well as acquisition of information about local conditions. The Jews had to be collected in one or more open towns and a ditch had to be dug at the right site for the right number. The marching distance from collecting points to the ditches averaged about 3 miles. The Jews were brought in groups of 500, separated by at least 1.2 miles, to the place of execution. . . . Distances to and from actions were never less than 90–120 miles. Only careful planning enabled the Commandos to carry out up to 5 actions a week and at the same time continue the work in Kovno without interruption. Kovno itself, where trained Lithuanian [nationalists] . . . are available in sufficient numbers, was comparatively speaking a shooter's paradise.[38]

Lest this clinical account disguise the agony of Jewish suffering and the brutality of the Nazi murderers, here is a description of a typical liquidation. On October 5, 1942, Hermann Graebe, a German engineer, witnessed the slaughter of the Jewish inhabitants of Dubno in Ukraine:

> The people who had got off the trucks—men, women, and children of all ages—had to undress upon the order of an SS man, who carried a riding or dog whip. An old woman with snow-white hair was holding a one-year-old child in her arms and singing to it and tickling it. The child was cooing with delight. The parents were looking on with tears in their eyes. The father was holding the hand of a boy about ten years old and speaking to him softly; the boy was fighting his tears. The father pointed to the sky, stroked his head and seemed to explain something to him. At that moment the SS man at the pit shouted something to his comrade. The latter counted off about twenty persons and instructed them to go behind the earth mound. . . . I walked around the mound and found myself confronted by a tremendous grave. People were closely wedged together and lying on top of each other so that only their heads were visible. Nearly all had blood running over their shoulders from their heads. Some of the people were still moving. Some were lifting their arms and turning their heads to show that they were still alive. The pit was already two-thirds full. I estimated that it contained about a thousand people. I looked for the man who did the shooting. He was an SS man, who sat at the edge of the narrow end of the pit, his feet dangling into the pit. He had a tommy gun on his knees and was smoking a cigarette. The people, completely naked, went down some steps and clambered over the heads of the people lying there to the place to which the SS man directed them. They

lay down in front of the dead or wounded people; some caressed those who were still alive and spoke to them in a low voice. Then I heard a series of shots. I looked into that pit and saw that the bodies were twitching or the heads lying motionless on top of the bodies that lay beneath them. . . . The next batch was approaching already. . . . I swear before God that this is the absolute truth.[39]

The deniers' reaction to such evidence is twofold. First they maintain that the Einsatzgruppen's reports are "spurious," most likely forged by YIVO (Institute for Jewish Research) and the Soviets. Second, they insist that the Einsatzgruppen were simply soldiers fighting dangerous partisans; in such a dirty war, it is to be expected, as Vietnam demonstrated, that some innocent women and children would be killed inadvertently. The Einsatzgruppen, the deniers insist, had no orders to kill Jews just because they were Jews. "Common sense alone would reject the notion that the Einsatzgruppen, which had a total of 3,000 men, as a matter of general policy, spent their time and effort pursuing objectives unrelated to military considerations."[40]

But, of course, if "common sense alone," rather than a murderous ideology, had prevailed, Nazi racial antisemitism, which regarded the Jew as a dangerous "subhuman" responsible for all Germany's ills, would have attracted few believers. Common sense also demanded that one does not murder people whose labor could be utilized for the war effort. Yet despite the protests of some high-ranking officers and officials in the army and the armaments industry, the SS sent Jewish workers, many of them skilled, to the death camps, and when Germany's military plight was desperate, the SS still diverted military personnel and railway cars to deport Jews to the gas chambers of Auschwitz. They did this in defiance of common sense because they viewed the annihilation of the Jews as a prime war aim that warranted their total commitment.

And our common sense should dismiss as absurd the allegation that the Einsatzgruppen's reports methodically listing the number of Jews killed in each action were really fabricated by a Jewish group, which then planted the more than 2,900 pages in Gestapo headquarters in Berlin, where they were found on September 3, 1945. More than a year later the actual contents of the reports were discovered, and in 1947 they were used as evidence in the trial of twenty-four Einsatzgruppen leaders. The leaders themselves attested to the genuineness of the reports, and no historian has ever questioned their authenticity, although one might point to an occasional inaccuracy. Finally, our common sense recoils in disgust at the suggestion that the tens of thousands of murdered Jewish children, many of them infants, were dangerous partisans.

*3. No gassings took place at Auschwitz or the other camps set up by the
Germans. Auschwitz was an industrial complex, not an extermination camp.
The so-called gas chambers were really showers or delousing rooms. The Zyklon
B gas stored at Auschwitz was used to kill lice on clothes, not people. The
affidavits of Commandant Rudolf Höss and others are lies or fantasies. German
records of Auschwitz deaths, says Carto, "show that no more than 120,000
persons of all religions and ethnicity died at Auschwitz. . . . The cause of
death . . . usually was old age. But many died from disease, such as typhus,
which the Germans combated with an insecticide, Zyklon B."[41]*

Some 2.5 to 3 million Jews were gassed in the Nazi death factories—Chelmno,
Treblinka, Sobibor, Belzec, Majdanek, and Auschwitz-Birkenau—built in
Poland. The documentary evidence for gassing of Jews in extermination
camps located in Poland is scanty in comparison to the evidence confirming
the mass shootings by Einsatzgruppen, whose commanders regularly sent extensive reports to Berlin to demonstrate that they were carrying out the state's
policy. The SS destroyed documents and the gas chambers to hide their crime.
Surviving German documents show that hundreds of thousands of Jews were
transported to Belzec, Sobibor, and Treblinka. (Auschwitz is discussed below.)
About a hundred escapees survived the war; the others just disappeared. Although no German document states what happened to them, the testimonies
of a substantial number of eyewitnesses confirm that the Jews perished in gas
chambers. These eyewitnesses include (1) Nazi personnel stationed at the
camps*; (2) German visitors who observed the killing process; (3) Ukrainian
prisoners of war recruited and trained to serve as guards; (4) Poles who lived
near the camps; and (5) the handful of Jews who managed to escape. Christopher Browning, who has examined these testimonies, describes their meaning
and, in the process, demolishes the deniers' tactic of dismissing eyewitness accounts completely if they contain the slightest discrepancies:

> Once again, human memory is imperfect. The testimonies of both survivors
> and other witnesses to the events in Belzec, Sobibor, and Treblinka are no
> more immune to forgetfulness, error, exaggeration, distortion, and repression
> than eyewitness accounts of other events in the past. They differ, for instance,
> on how long each gassing operation took, on the dimensions and capacity of

---

* The testimonies of twenty-nine Germans stationed at these camps are particularly revealing. Put on trial in the 1950s and 1960s, none of them denied that Jews were murdered in gas chambers, and in testimonies given under oath they described in detail the
process of industrialized mass murder.

the gas chambers, on the number of the undressing barracks, and on the roles of particular individuals. Gerstein, citing Globocnik, claimed the camps used diesel motors, but witnesses who actually serviced the engines in Belzec and Sobibor (Reder and Fuchs) spoke of gasoline engines. Once again, however, without exception all concur on the vital issue of dispute, namely that Belzec, Sobibor, and Treblinka were death camps whose primary purpose was to kill in gas chambers through the carbon monoxide from engine exhaust, and that hundreds of thousands of corpses of Jews killed there were first buried and then later cremated.[42]

Auschwitz-Birkenau, the largest of the death camps, began as a concentration camp for Poles, who were later joined by Soviet prisoners of war. In the summer of 1941, Himmler told Rudolf Höss, the camp commandant, about his new plans for Auschwitz: "The Führer has ordered the Final Solution of the Jewish question. We the SS have to carry out this order, this mission. The existing extermination sites in the East [most likely a reference to the Einsatzgruppen] are not in a position to carry out these intended operations on a large scale. . . . I have, therefore, chosen Auschwitz for this purpose. First of all, because of the advantageous transport facilities, and secondly because it allows this area to be easily isolated and disguised."[43]

Our information about the mass murder at Auschwitz comes from many sources:

- German documents, including technical drawings, related to the construction of gas chambers and crematoria for Auschwitz, and to the shipment of Zyklon B gas to the camp
- Aerial photographs taken by the Allies that show gas chamber/crematorium complexes
- Reports by escaped prisoners and accounts smuggled out of the camp, particularly by the Polish Resistance
- The testimony of prisoners who survived
- Accounts discovered after the war that had been buried for safekeeping by the Sonderkommando (chiefly Jewish prisoners assigned to removing the corpses from the gas chambers and disposing of them in the crematoria)
- The testimony of SS functionaries stationed in the camp, including Commandant Rudolf Höss; Pery Broad, an SS official connected with the Gestapo; and Johann Paul Kremer, an SS doctor who participated in the selection of victims for the gas chamber (A very cultivated man,

Kremer also held a Ph.D. in philosophy, was fluent in several languages, and was a professor of anatomy at the University of Münster.)

Rudolf Höss was Auschwitz's commandant from 1940 until late 1943. Reassigned in November 1943 to a key position administering the whole network of concentration camps, he returned to Auschwitz in mid-1944 to supervise the liquidation of Hungarian Jews who were arriving in huge numbers. With the Soviets advancing rapidly, on November 25, 1944, Himmler, seeking to obliterate the evidence of SS crimes, ordered the destruction of the installations of extermination. Höss presided over the dismantling and demolition of the facilities. While much of the physical evidence of the extermination complex was destroyed, much remained, including walls and floors of underground gas chambers, parts of furnaces, and the rails built into the floors over which corpses were delivered to the furnaces.

In his sworn declaration made to the International Military Tribunal at Nuremberg, Höss described the killing operations:

> It took from three to fifteen minutes to kill people in the death chamber, depending upon climatic conditions. We knew when the people were dead because their screaming stopped. We usually waited about one-half hour before we opened the doors and removed the bodies. After the bodies were removed our special Kommando [the Sonderkommando] took off the rings and extracted the gold from the teeth of the corpses. . . . The way we selected our victims was as follows. We had two SS doctors . . . examine the incoming transports of prisoners. . . . Those who were fit to work were sent into the camp. Others were sent immediately to the extermination plants. Children of tender years were invariably exterminated since by reason of their youth they were unable to work. . . . We endeavored to fool the victims into thinking that they were to go through a delousing process. Of course, frequently they realized our true intentions, and we sometimes had riots and difficulties due to that fact. Very frequently women would hide their children under clothes, but of course when we found them we would send the children in to be exterminated.[44]

In jail awaiting execution after his conviction, Höss wrote his autobiography confirming his earlier testimony.

In the war crimes trials, Kremer testified that when the gas was poured into the sealed chamber, the "shouting and screaming of the victims could be heard through that opening and . . . they fought for their lives. These shouts lasted . . . several minutes, though I cannot give a precise estimate."[45]

Broad, who was convicted at the Auschwitz trials held in Frankfurt am Main from 1963 to 1965, testified that "Auschwitz was an extermination camp, the largest such camp in history,"[46] and he described the mass murder in the gas chambers that he witnessed: "As soon as the last person had entered, the SS guards disappeared. . . . Suddenly the door was closed; it had been gas-proofed with rubber and reinforced with iron fittings. Those inside heard the heavy bolts being secured. A deadly, paralyzing terror gripped the victims. They started to beat on the door, hammering it with their fists in helpless rage and despair."[47]

Anna Pawelczynska, a Polish sociologist and a non-Jewish survivor of Auschwitz, described the camp:

> First place in this sequence of dying was assigned to prisoners of Jewish descent . . . and the proof was their mass murder through the use of assembly-line techniques . . .
>
> Selection was carried out by German doctors, who designated those capable of work. . . . Those considered incapable . . . were delivered up to immediate death. . . . The camp staff . . . perfect[ed] the technology for killing as many people as quickly and as efficiently as possible. On top of this some of the SS who took part in the mass murders carried out their duties by thinking up individual little amusements which fulfilled a sadistic need. Documents that have been preserved, especially documents of the *Sonderkommando*, made up of forced prison labor and mostly of Jewish origin, describe in detail the techniques of the gas chambers, the crematory ovens, and the obliteration of the traces of industrialized genocide.[48]

Auschwitz consisted of two main camps, Auschwitz I and Auschwitz II–Birkenau; around them were constructed some fifty satellite camps, in which inmates worked as slave laborers for the German armaments' industry. The working pace at the factory and the ill treatment by guards were so brutal, reported a physician and inmate, that "while working many prisoners suddenly stretched out flat, turned blue, gasped for breath, and died like beasts."[49]

Deniers insist that Auschwitz was no more than a large industrial center producing for the German war effort. But if Auschwitz were simply an industrial complex, why were babies and young children sent there? And how do we account for their sudden disappearance? And what happened to those Jews whose names appeared on the list of deportees from various ghettos and collection centers, but not on the list of those registered as new arrivals at the camp? The unregistered, of course, after being disgorged from the cattle trains, did not survive the selection process. They were immediately gassed, as

were the babies and young children. The Nazis only recorded the names of
those deportees who were permitted to live—at least for a while—in that
inferno.

To support their claim that Auschwitz was not an extermination camp,
the revisionists twist and dodge facts and distort the meaning of words—just
as they do in their interpretation of the Einsatzgruppen and Himmler's
speech at Posen. Pierre Vidal-Naquet graphically illustrates this point, using
passages from the diary of Dr. Kremer, who was at Auschwitz for several
weeks in 1942. Kremer recorded in his diary eleven "special actions," the
Nazi euphemism for the roundups, beatings, shootings, and, in this instance,
gassing of victims. On September 2 he wrote: "I attended a special action for
the first time, outdoors, at three o'clock. In comparison, Dante's *Inferno*
seems almost a comedy to me. It is not for nothing that Auschwitz is known
as an annihilation camp." On October 12 Kremer attended "a special action
for people coming from the Netherlands (1,600) persons. Frightful scenes."
And on October 18: "I attended the eleventh special action (Dutch). Horrid
scenes, with three women begging for their lives."[50] Faurisson, the perverse
literature professor, deconstructs Kremer's diary entries, maintaining that
"special action" only means separating those afflicted with typhus from the
healthy; and, continues Faurisson, it is because typhus kills that Kremer
called Auschwitz an "annihilation camp."[51]

The deniers insist that since physical evidence is lacking for the existence
of openings on the roof of the chambers through which gas was supposed to
be released, these structures were not used as homicidal gas chambers. In December 1944 and January 1945, with the Soviets advancing, the Germans dismantled and blew up the crematoria where the gas chambers were located to
obliterate the evidence of what they had done. After the war the Poles reconstructed parts of the killing apparatus so that the Nazi deeds would not be
erased from memory. Some of the rubble from the original structures still remains, but from these remnants it is impossible to provide physical evidence of
the openings in the roof through which the gas had been inserted. Eyewitness
accounts, including the drawings from memory of a surviving Sonderkommando, who was a skilled draftsman and painter, and aerial photographs taken
by Americans in the summer of 1944 attest to the existence of these openings.
And, given all the overwhelming evidence that Jews were liquidated by gas at
Auschwitz and other camps, what does it really mean that evidence for the
openings is limited? It means something only to someone who maliciously operates from a preordained conclusion and dismisses and manipulates facts that
do not accord with this position. This is typical of the deniers. If a survivor

errs in his or her recollections, then the testimony of all survivors is disqualified. If after the war a Nazi official lied about any aspect of the crimes committed against Jews—usually to minimize his involvement—then the testimony of all Nazi officials is dismissed. If any captured Nazi could be shown to have been mistreated, then anything said about the Holocaust by all captured Nazis is invalid.

A telling example of the Holocaust deniers' assault on truth is *The Leuchter Report*. In 1988 Fred Leuchter Jr. was hired by Ernst Zündel, a German national residing in Canada, to gather evidence from concentration camp sites in Poland that would prove that Jews were not murdered in gas chambers. At the time Zündel, coauthor of *The Hitler We Loved and Why* and a leading exporter from Canada to the United States and Germany of Nazi memorabilia and antisemitic and Holocaust denial literature, was on trial for publishing and distributing Harwood's *Did Six Million Really Die?* Zündel was being prosecuted for violating a Canadian statute which makes it a criminal offense to disseminate knowingly false information harmful to the public interest—in this instance, the lie of Holocaust denial. Leading Holocaust deniers including Faurisson, Smith, and Irving traveled to Canada to assist Zündel with his defense.

During his eight-day stay in Poland, Leuchter visited Auschwitz-Birkenau and Majdanek, gathering "evidence" that would aid the deniers' case. His report concluded that Jews were not murdered in gas chambers at these camps. Deniers, who heralded Leuchter as an engineer with expertise in gas chambers and his report as "the first forensic examination of Auschwitz," were gleeful.

Leuchter's credibility, however, was quickly destroyed when he testified in Zündel's defense as an expert witness. In the prosecution's cross-examination, Leuchter revealed that he had misrepresented himself as an engineer. He held an undergraduate degree in history, not engineering, had taken only basic college chemistry and physics courses, and had no specific training in toxicology. The court also discredited his methodology and conclusions. Zündel was sentenced to nine months' imprisonment. His conviction was later overturned when the statute under which he was indicted was declared unconstitutional.

Since then the Canadian Human Rights Commission has brought further accusations against Zündel and barred him from access to the Internet, which he utilized to distribute great quantities of Holocaust denial literature and antisemitic material, including his own concoctions and IHR publications. The case against Zündel hinged on demonstrating that the ideological stereotypes he employs in attacking Jews replicate antisemitica that date back to the Middle Ages, that his propagating of antisemitic propaganda constitutes a historically proven danger to a distinct and recognizable group of people. Zündel left Canada in 2001 and now operates freely in the United States.*

After Zündel's first trial, *The Leuchter Report* was totally demolished by Jean-Claude Pressac, a French pharmacologist and independent scholar. At first Pressac, a non-Jew, flirted with Holocaust denial, but after visiting extermination sites, exploring the archives, and entering into a dialogue with Faurisson, he dismissed as nonsense and "nihilism" the deniers' position on gas chambers at Auschwitz. In *Technique and Operation of the Gas Chambers* (1989), Pressac assembled a multitude of documents—letters, telegrams, memos, blueprints, diagrams, and photographs relating to the construction and operation of gas chambers at Auschwitz. His later work, *Les Crématoires d'Auschwitz: La machinerie du meurtre de masse* (1993), which was based on exhaustive archival research, described in minute detail the evolution and utilization of the Nazi technology of extermination at the death camp. A trained scientist, unlike Leuchter, Pressac treated Leuchter and his "findings" with contempt in his article, "The Deficiencies and Inconsistencies of the Leuchter Report."

Leuchter, with hammer and chisel, gouged brick fragments from the gas chambers, an illegal and reprehensible act for the site is now a museum often visited by mourners reciting memorial prayers for their murdered relatives. The concealed samples were smuggled out of Poland and later tested to determine the residual cyanide level. The tests showed that the places that were used to gas people retained only minute traces of cyanide; yet the areas where clothing was deloused showed traces 150 to 1,000 times greater. To Leuchter, this proved that Auschwitz had no homicidal gas chambers, only delousing gas chambers. Pressac filled in what Leuchter suppressed or did not know:

> Lice have a much higher resistance to hydrocyanic acid (HCN) than humans do. A hydrocyanic gas concentration of 0.3 g/m3 [grams per cubic meter]—a lethal dose—is immediately fatal to a man, while killing lice requires a concentration of 5g/m3 for a period of at least two hours. . . . The dose used at Birkenau . . . was lethal 40–70 times over (12–20 g/m3), which infallibly killed a thousand persons in less than *5 minutes*. . . . Afterwards the place was aired

---

* At the invitation of counsel for the Human Rights Commission, the authors participated in the proceedings against Zündel. Some of the material appearing in this book was made available to counsel, and Frederick Schweitzer testified on the stand. His efforts were also instrumental in persuading the tribunal to reject Robert Countess, Robert Faurisson, and Mark Weber as "expert witnesses" on the Holocaust and related subjects. The hearing concluded February 28, 2001, and the tribunal's decision was issued January 18, 2002; for fuller details and excerpts from the decision, see Appendix II.

out by means of (either artificial or natural) ventilation. . . . The HCN was in physical contact with the gas chamber walls for no more than ten minutes a day. . . . In the delousing chambers. . . . [t]he walls were impregnated with hot HCN for at least 12 hours a day.[52]

But the deniers still had to explain why even small amounts of cyanide traces were found in places where, according to them, there never were homicidal gas chambers. If the deniers were correct, not even minute traces of cyanide should be found in the bricks. Faurisson, who had recommended Leuchter to Zündel and consulted with him, tried to unravel the paradox. Following is Pressac's evaluation of Faurisson's explanation:

> He draws upon one of the most often-used lies in explanation: The minute traces come from the fact that the "morgues" were sometimes disinfected with Zyklon-B. [The term "morgues" in the crematorium blueprints denotes ground-level rooms to be used ostensibly for this purpose but in reality they were intended for and used as homicidal gas chambers. Faurisson still insists they really were morgues.] Hydrocyanic acid is used first and foremost to exterminate such vermin as insect pests and rodents. Classified as an insecticide and vermin killer, it has no bactericide or germicide properties for use as an antiseptic. . . . [A] morgue is not disinfected with an insecticide or vermin killer like hydrocyanide acid, as Faurisson foolishly claims, which would be as much use as a poultice on a wooden leg. Leuchter, who claims to be scientifically trained, whereas Faurisson is not, similarly used this stupidity in his report.[53]

The Sonderkommando removed the bodies from the gas chamber and placed them on carts that moved on rails to the incinerator ovens. Both Faurisson and Leuchter claim that homicidal gas chambers and cremation ovens could not be housed in the same facility, because the gas released from the open doors combined with the air from the lit ovens would have caused an explosion powerful enough to destroy the building. Pressac also destroys this claim:

> . . . upon contact with a flame there is an explosion if the concentration of hydrocyanic acid in air comprises between 67.2 g/m3 and 480g/m3. Below 67.2g/m3 there is no risk, nor is there any at greater than 480 g/m3, because there is not enough remaining oxygen for burning to begin. The SS used doses of 5 g/m3 in delousing and 12–20 g/m3 in killing, well under the 67.2 g/m3 threshold. Their gas chambers and crematoriums were not about to explode. Leuchter's "impartial" opinion is based upon an incorrect calculation.

This twisted idea comes from Faurisson. It is appalling that Leuchter should have backed it up without checking it out for himself.[54]

The points just discussed constitute a portion of Pressac's technical analysis of *The Leuchter Report*. His scientific temperament offended by Leuchter's faulty techniques and erroneous conclusions, Pressac did not hide his contempt:

> The work's lamentable level of professionalism conforms to the customary standards of nihilist [Holocaust denial] publications. Based on misinforma-tion, which leads to false reasoning and misinterpretation of data, "The Leuchter Report" is unacceptable. It . . . ignor[es] the most straightforward of historical data, and founders in gross errors of measurement. . . . Leuchter lied about his source documents. . . . Besides, he carefully avoided consulting the historical material available at the [Auschwitz] museum archives. . . . I cannot contain my indignation at such a "work," which is not even worth the wastebasket it will end up in. Leuchter has disgraced the title of engineer. . . . Leuchter is the victim of his own errors: layout errors, location errors, meas-urement errors, drawing errors, methodology errors and historical errors. Based on fake knowledge, inducing fake reasoning and leading to false inter-pretations—"The Leuchter Report" is inadmissible. . . . [It] lands in the cesspool of pretentious human folly.[55]

Serious scholars dismiss *The Leuchter Report* as rubbish. But consistent with their charade, the deniers disseminate it widely and continually refer to it as proof of their case. The discredited David Irving called its results "shatter-ing" and "truly astounding." This is tantamount to Goebbels quoting the *Pro-tocols of the Learned Elders of Zion* to justify Nazi antisemitism. And if the history of the *Protocols* is any indication, *The Leuchter Report* will have a long life and win converts.

### 4. Only a small percentage of European Jews perished in the war.

A question-and-answer leaflet prepared by the IHR and translated into several languages says that about 300,000 Jews perished in concentration camps and their deaths were due not to German policy but to recurring outbreaks of ty-phus, which took the lives of many Europeans during the war, and to Allied bombings, which destroyed supply lines, making it impossible to provide in-mates with food and medical care. Rassinier had estimated 1 million Jewish dead, a figure that Butz considered rather high but possible.[56]

But then why do so many Jews mourn the loss of so many loved ones? Where are these missing Jews? Rassinier suggested a working hypothesis to account for the missing Jews. The majority of the Jews in Lithuania and Ukraine and many Polish and Romanian Jews, he said, were evacuated to Central Asia by the Soviet army, and after the war, they secretly made their way across China and the Pacific Ocean to North and South America, where they reside today. Butz offers his own solution. Jewish men were conscripted for labor tasks, "for what was undoubtedly intended by the Germans to be a period of limited duration. . . . Under such conditions it is reasonable to expect that many of these lonely wives and husbands would have, during or at the end of the war, established other relations that seemed more valuable than the previous relationships. In such cases, then, there would have been a strong motivation not to reestablish contact with the legal spouse."[57] Irving claims that after the war Jews were "whisked into new homes, lives, and identities in the Middle East, leaving their old, discarded identities behind as 'missing persons.'"[58]

By claiming that not 6 million but fewer—in some instances they say far fewer—than 1 million Jews perished, deniers aim to relativize the Holocaust to simply one of many atrocities committed in a brutal conflict, that, for example, what befell the Jews was no worse than the terror bombing of German cities by the Allies, a comparison often made by David Irving. For instance, historians conclude that about 1,100,000 Jews perished at Auschwitz, most of them in gas chambers. In a speech delivered in 1992 in Toronto, Irving claimed that over a four-year period, no more than 100,000 died there, 75,000 from epidemics, 25,000 by hanging or shooting. Besides fraudulently minimizing the number of deaths, Irving considered Auschwitz a lesser crime than the firebombing of the German town of Pforzheim by the Allies in February 1945: " . . . twenty-five thousand civilians . . . [Richard Evans notes that the Statistical Office of the City of Pforzheim estimated the number of deaths as 17,600] burned alive in twenty-five minutes! In Auschwitz it was a crime committed over four years. You don't get it spelled out to you like this, except by us, their opponents. When you put it into *perspective* like that, of course, it diminished their Holocaust—that word spelled with a capital letter."[59]

It is not unusual for some Jewish survivors to light memorial candles for fifty, seventy, or even a hundred relatives who perished in the Holocaust. These people witnessed horrors and endured pain that still baffle belief. It should be comforting to these survivors to learn that their loved ones did not perish in the Polish ghettos from planned and gratuitous mistreatment; they were not clubbed to death in Vilna, gassed at Treblinka, Sobibor, or Auschwitz, or machine-gunned in Ukraine; they did not die in the brutal death marches from Auschwitz and other camps to Germany near the end of the war. They are probably living in Israel or the United States, reluctant to reestablish their old identities!

*5. Chronicles written by Jews during the war describing their ordeal and*
*photographs of mass executions are disqualified as evidence—they are either*
*forgeries or have been so tampered with as to make them invalid. The*
*testimonies of Jewish survivors after the war are either lies or fantasies. Jewish*
*historians who write about the Holocaust, too, cannot be trusted, for they*
*fraudulently manipulate data to perpetuate the hoax of the 6 million.*

What we have here are a new version of the myth of the Jewish conspiracy that
outdoes in fantasy, paranoia, and meanness all its predecessors and a reprise of
the hoary accusation—as old as the gospel of John 8:44–47—of Jewry's addic-
tion to lying and deception, part of its armory of manipulation and destruction.
One marvels at the extraordinary talents attributed to the Jewish leaders who
orchestrated this plot and manufactured such falsehoods. They got millions of
Jews living in many lands, with a passion for words and a proven record for
quarrelsomeness—just look at Israeli politics!—to submit to this scheme and to
keep it secret for more than fifty years; they made up the most gruesome atroc-
ity stories and coached thousands of Jews to tell them properly; they planted
forged documents—the prosecution in the Nuremberg trials alone assembled
197,113 pieces of evidence—in virtually every country occupied by the Nazis,
even passing off pictures of "piles of German women and children killed in Allied bombing raids . . . as dead Jews"[60]; they convinced thousands of Germans,
many of them former Nazis, to attest to the existence of crimes that they knew
were never committed and compelled German statesmen to agree to pay hundreds of millions of dollars in reparations to Jews whom they knew had lied
about suffering at German hands; in the same vein, more than fifty years after
the war they tricked Swiss banks to pay compensation for their role in converting plundered gold, including gold fillings extracted from death camp victims,
into Swiss francs that helped finance the German war effort, and for denying
survivors' heirs access to numbered accounts because they could not provide
death certificates for relatives who had perished in Auschwitz and the other
death camps; they arranged for thousands of non-Jewish victims and witnesses
to Nazi brutality to lend credence to the hoax; they duped the awarders of the
Nobel Prize to grant one to Elie Wiesel, an Auschwitz survivor, for his moving
books on the Holocaust, which draw on his own experience; and they duped
and continue to hoodwink researchers who provide scholarly support for the
"plot." And, most recently, they deluded the Vatican to issue in March 1998 *We*
*Remember: A Reflection on the Shoah*, which states:

> This century has witnessed an unspeakable tragedy, which can never be for-
> gotten: the attempt by the Nazi regime to exterminate the Jewish people,

with the consequent killing of millions of Jews. Women and men, old and young, children and infants, for the sole reason of their Jewish origin, were persecuted and deported. Some were killed immediately, while others were degraded, ill-treated, tortured and utterly robbed of their human dignity, and then cruelly murdered. Very few of those who entered the Camps survived, and those who did, remained scarred for life. This was the *Shoah*. It is a major fact of the history of this century, a fact that still concerns us today.[61]

Deniers simply dismiss as untrustworthy the leading Jewish historians—propagandists and mythologizers, they call them—engaged in Holocaust studies. In attempts to discredit Jewish scholars, they deliberately and malevolently lie and distort facts. For example, Rassinier refers to an article written by Hannah Arendt, a prominent American political theorist and refugee from Nazi Germany. Arendt, he says, "coolly inform[ed] us that three million Polish Jews were murdered during the first days of the war." Such a statement would, of course, make Arendt seem irresponsible. But what she really wrote was that "three million Polish Jews had been in the process of being massacred ever since the first days of the war."[62]

Deniers engage in a similar underhandedness to discredit chronicles written by Jews during the war. For example, Emanuel Ringelblum, a Polish Jewish historian, kept a diary so the world would have a record of the torment of the Jews in the Warsaw ghetto; the document, carefully hidden, survived his execution by the Germans. In *Did Six Million Really Die?* Harwood dismisses the diary as "a worthless historical document,"[63] because it was first published in communist Poland. For a similar reason, deniers reject the accounts written by the Sonderkommando of Auschwitz, which were buried for safekeeping and discovered after the war. Describing precisely the procedure of extermination, these documents concur with the information obtained from other sources. Faurisson does not try to deal with them but simply rejects them as "manuscripts—miraculously—rediscovered."[64]

A particular irritation to the deniers is *The Diary of Anne Frank*, the autobiographical description of a sensitive young girl's ordeal hiding from the Nazis. Anne Frank's words and her capture and death in a concentration camp have moved hundreds of thousands of readers throughout the world. Deniers have tried to discredit the book by claiming that it was really written after the war by Otto Frank, Anne's father, in collaboration with a New York scriptwriter. Therefore, it is "just one more fraud in a whole series of frauds perpetrated in support of the 'Holocaust' legend and the saga of the six million."[65] Otto Frank brought charges in German courts against these detractors several times and won. To put an end to these accusations, the Netherlands

State Institute for War Documentation, which was given the diary after Otto Frank's death in 1980, subjected the handwriting, paper, glue, binding, and ink to a full battery of scientific tests. It concluded that the diary was authentic: It was written by one person during the war years, and the emendations made after the war by Anne's father and others—grammatical corrections and the deleting for the sake of propriety of some references to sex and private family matters—were not substantive; they did not alter the meaning of Anne's entries in her diary. The institute then published a 714-page authoritative edition of the diary, which included Anne's original, the edited published version, and the results of the investigation. But still the deniers, whose concern has never been accuracy and truth but propagating an antisemitic myth, continue to denounce the diary as a hoax.

To deny the existence of gas chambers and extermination squads—to claim that survivors of the Holocaust fabricated a tale of genocide—is another expression of the Jew as an evil conspirator. As such it is consistent with all the other antisemitic myths that helped to produce the Holocaust. Jews have always been astonished at the utterly bizarre content of antisemitic myths; they have found it incomprehensible that to their tormentors these myths were unassailable truths. If Nazis, with immense moral fervor, could drive Jews into gas chambers, we should not be surprised that their spiritual descendants, with equal conviction and wickedness of spirit, believe that Jews fabricated a tale of mass murder. For them, the Jews are capable of any enormity. Ditlieb Felderer reveals what the deniers really think of Jews and how they have recycled virtually all the myths about the Jews that are the subject of this book:

> All the way back in antiquity the Zionists have peddled their ware, a disease far worse than the leprous plague. In this way they have brought havoc, confusion, butcheries, cruelties and death to millions of innocent people. Wherever they have tread—crime, corruption, perversion and pornography has come. Whoever has aligned himself with them has finally become the victim of their crime and succumbed to their satanism. The Zion-racists continue on to our present day to whore their race merchandise, often under the guise of equality, brotherhood and democracy. In truth, their form of "democracy" is no other thing but a chronic state of democracy—a rule by incarnated demons.[66]

For the deniers, faking a tale of systematic mass murder—and succeeding at it—is perfectly consistent with the behavior of "incarnated demons." But it is also likely that the deniers are fully aware of the Nazis' genocidal behavior toward the Jews. What really disturbs them about Auschwitz is not the actual extermination but the barrier its image as a death factory poses to winning mass support for the rehabilitation of Hitler and Nazi ideology, including Jew-hatred. H. Keith Thompson's words at an IHR conference are revealing: "If, in the end, the Holocaust did take place, then so much the better."[67] In support of their position, revisionists often refer to *The Auschwitz Lie*, written by Thies Christophersen, a former SS guard at Auschwitz-Birkenau.* Not only did Christophersen, who died in 1997, deny the existence of gas chambers and mass killings, he also described the notorious death camp as a sort of resort where prisoners, after work, could swim, listen to music in their rooms, or visit a brothel. Later he was captured on videotape—he mistakenly thought the interviewers were fellow neo-Nazis—confessing that he had lied about the gas chambers because of loyalty to the SS and his desire to protect Germany's honor. The videotape was first broadcast in Sweden in September 1991; in the following months it was shown in most European countries, to the embarrassment of Christophersen and his neo-Nazi colleagues.

Addressing an SS reunion in Bavaria, General Otto Ernst Remer, who openly denied the Holocaust, provided another insight into the deniers' mindset. Removing from his pocket a gas-filled cigarette lighter, observed a reporter from *Stern* magazine, Remer "pressed carefully on the release so that the gas escaped slowly. 'What is that?' he asked sniffing it, and then he gave the reply: 'A Jew nostalgic for Auschwitz.'"[68] The remark, intended to prompt laughter from the former SS men, which it did, also reveals the utter cynicism and malevolence of the deniers, as does Remer's comment to Martin E. Lee, the author of *The Beast Reawakens*. After lauding Hitler and voicing a fanatical hatred for Jews, the old Nazi told Lee that Jews "are our deadly enemies. They have no business being here. They all must be killed."[69] What this Holocaust denier really meant is that the job started by the Nazis should be finished.

The Nazi years demonstrated the human being's infinite capacity for depravity; but it demonstrated something else of equal importance—the mind's infinite capacity for mystification and the seeming helplessness of reason to prevent this regression to myth, paranoia, and demonization. It would be absurd to give Holocaust deniers a forum to uphold the principle of a marketplace of ideas in which all voices are heard. Are scientists expected to debate

---

* In 1986 Christophersen fled to Denmark to escape prosecution by German authorities for denying the Holocaust. In 1994 protesters forced him to leave Denmark. He went to Switzerland but was ordered out. Arrested in Germany in January 1997, he was quickly released because he was near death from kidney cancer. He died several weeks later.

so-called researchers who subscribe to the theory of a flat earth or, as Vidal-Naquet wondered, with proponents of the theory that the moon is made of Roquefort cheese? Similarly, in the interest of free speech, are college newspapers required to accept ads placed by advocates of pedophilia or female genital mutilation? Rather than being granted a forum, the deniers should be exposed and studied as living examples of the enduring strength and danger of mythical thinking, another demonstration of the inability of the mind to predominate over the dark and mysterious forces of the irrational, another reminder of the capacity of Jew-hatred to warp judgment and pervert morality. Exposing and condemning these hatemongers and charlatans constitute a victory for reason and humanity and a vindication of memory.

## CHAPTER 6

# ANTISEMITIC MYTHS
# BLACKWASHED

## THE NATION OF ISLAM INHERITS A DEVIL

IN A SPEECH AT KEAN COLLEGE IN NEW JERSEY on November 29, 1993, Muhammad Khallid, then a national spokesman for the Nation of Islam, launched a vicious attack against Jews that was reminiscent of Nazi propagandists. Jews, he said, controlled the White House and the Federal Reserve System, Hollywood, and the media. Their behavior in Germany forced Hitler to act the way he did. Jews, he continued, used the civil rights movement to exploit blacks, and they continue to exploit black athletes and entertainers. To the familiar accusations of parasites and exploiters that antisemites have traditionally hurled at Jews, Khallid added a rarely used one—cannibals: "You are a European . . . people who crawled around on all fours . . . , eatin' juniper roots and eatin' each other."[1]

Khallid's tirade was not a singular event. In recent years black organizations at several colleges have paid handsome fees to Khallid and other openly antisemitic guest lecturers. The Nation of Islam has published and circulated antisemitic literature and Minister Louis Farrakhan, the Nation's leader, has on numerous occasions disparaged Jews. Several African American spokesmen, particularly those associated with the Nation of Islam, have demagogically adapted and exploited classic antisemitic images and conspiracy theories to further their own ends. This is the surest indication that the black-Jewish

alliance, which had waged a successful struggle for civil rights, has largely collapsed. Before we examine current black antisemitism, particularly as voiced
by Louis Farrakhan, let us survey the historic partnership between blacks and
Jews and the ensuing rift.

## THE PARTNERSHIP ESTABLISHED
## AND DISSOLVED

Having suffered from persecution in Europe, many Jewish immigrants to the
United States were attracted to liberal ideals that stressed equality, toleration, the inviolability of the human person, and a humane concern for people. Respect for these ideals led many Jews to identify with the plight of
American blacks who were treated unequally and unjustly. Examples of Jewish support for black people and African American causes abound. In the
opening decades of the twentieth century, Jewish philanthropists, including
the Schiffs, the Lehmans, the Warburgs, James Loeb, and Julius Rosenwald,
contributed substantial sums to Tuskegee Institute, a famous black college;
its best known teacher Booker T. Washington urged Paul M. Warburg to sit
on Tuskegee's board. Financial backing by Rosenwald helped the Urban
League get started, and the Rosenwald Fund created in 1917 provided assistance to many black writers and performers, including singer Marian Ander-
son, historian John Hope Franklin, psychologist Kenneth Clark, and writers
Ralph Ellison and Langston Hughes. In 1909 members of the German Jewish elite helped to found the National Association for the Advancement of
Colored People (NAACP), and from 1913 to 1919 Joel Spingarn (a distinguished academic and historian of literary criticism) served as its chairman
and was president many years until his death in 1939. Over the years several
Jewish attorneys provided legal services without pay, and during the depression Jewish philanthropy kept the financially troubled organization from
going under.

Largely Jewish labor unions, unlike some other unions, welcomed black
membership, and Jewish labor leaders urged an end to discrimination in
unions and assisted A. Philip Randolph in organizing the nation's sleeping car
porters, which became an active political force in the fight for equal rights.
Jewish newspapers denounced racial discrimination, spoke out strongly
against lynching, and actively campaigned to reverse the verdict in the famous
Scottsboro case of the 1930s in which an Alabama court sentenced to death
eight black youths who were falsely accused of raping two white women.
Largely through the efforts of Samuel Liebowitz, a New York attorney, the

youths won an appeal and eventually were acquitted. Jewish scholars Philip Foner, Herbert Aptheker, and Melville J. Herskovits pioneered in the study of black history.

In the 1950s and 1960s various Jewish organizations and numerous Jews acting individually joined with blacks in the civil rights struggle. The American Jewish Congress (AJC) and the Anti-Defamation League (ADL) collaborated with the NAACP to challenge discrimination in the courts. Attorney Jack Greenberg, head of the Legal Defense Fund of the NAACP, was instrumental in assisting Thurgood Marshall to win the case of *Brown v. Board of Education of Topeka, Kansas,* that ended the legal basis of public school segregation. Jewish labor leaders contributed their organizational skills to the movement, and probably more than half of the lawyers representing civil rights workers were Jews. Jews donated more than half the money raised by civil rights organizations. They were also active in the front lines—the freedom rides, sit-ins, and protest marches—constituting about two-thirds of the white Freedom Riders traveling in the South in the summer of 1961 to promote desegregation and probably half of the summer volunteers in the black voter registration drive in Mississippi in 1964. Many of the participants were rabbis, and yarmulkes—"freedom hats" as they were called—became something of a symbol of the struggle. Two Jewish volunteers, Andrew Goodman and Michael Schwerner, were murdered with James Chaney, a black, by racists in Mississippi. In that same year, seventeen white rabbis were jailed with Dr. Martin Luther King, Jr., in St. Augustine, Florida, for participating in an antisegregation demonstration.

Jewish participation in the cause of black civil rights started earlier and was significantly greater than that of any other definable white group, a fact acknowledged by Dr. King and other black leaders. In 1965 Dr. King asked:

> How could there be anti-Semitism among Negroes when our Jewish friends have demonstrated their commitment to the principle of tolerance and brotherhood not only in the form of sizable contributions, but in many other tangible ways, and often at great personal sacrifice? Can we ever express our appreciation to the rabbis who chose to give moral witness with us in St. Augustine during our recent protest against segregation in that unhappy city? Need I remind anyone of the awful beating suffered by Rabbi Arthur Lelyveld of Cleveland when he joined the civil rights workers there in Hattiesburg, Mississippi? And who can ever forget the sacrifice of two Jewish lives, Andrew Goodman and Michael Schwerner, in the swamps of Mississippi? It would be impossible to record the contributions that the Jewish

people have made toward the Negro's struggle for freedom—it has been so great.*[2]

So obvious was the partnership that Mississippi Senator Theodore Bilbo, a spokesman for white supremacists, declared: "The niggers and the Jews of New York are working hand in hand."[3] Enraged racists bombed Jewish facilities, including temples, in several southern cities.

The reasons for Jewish involvement in the civil rights movement are varied. No doubt Jews believed that by combating bigotry against blacks, they were helping to create a more tolerant and open society in which antisemitism would diminish. In the 1950s and 1960s Jews still were being denied positions in major law and financial firms, and quotas on their entry into certain law and medical schools had not been entirely abandoned. At the same time, many Jews were also idealists, genuinely committed to liberal principles and the ancient prophetic message of social justice. Moreover, their own history of victimization led them to empathize with black suffering.**

Jews remembered all too well discriminatory practices that excluded them from prestigious colleges and universities and executive positions with major corporations and denied them access to homeownership in certain neighborhoods and membership in certain clubs. Moreover, the Holocaust, still very fresh in the mind of Jews, made the need to resist racial injustice a compelling moral obligation. As the African American scholar of the Holocaust Hubert Locke writes, two very diverse peoples, "who yet have endured the common experience of bigotry and oppression, have far more to unite than to divide them. . . . The history of Western societies suggests that the racial antipathy of which both minorities have been victims is indiscriminate in its targets and that minorities who are not wise enough to work together for a common and beneficial destiny run the grave risk of suffering a similar fate."[4]

While Jews could identify with an oppressed minority, profound differences between the two groups ultimately served to pull them apart. The so-

---

* Dr. King also gave his support to the Jewish community. He denounced antisemitism in the Soviet Union, praised the aim of Zionism to return Jews to their biblical homeland, and expressed his support for Israel in the Six Day War.

** For the same reasons, Jews were more likely than other white South Africans to oppose apartheid, as Nelson Mandela noted: "I have found Jews to be more broadminded than most whites on issues of race and politics, perhaps because they themselves have been victims of prejudice." Nelson Mandela, *Long Walk to Freedom* (Boston: Little, Brown, 1994), 62.

cioeconomic status of Jews in recent decades and their historical experience in America were far different from that of blacks. Jews achieved extraordinary success in American society, whereas a significant percentage of blacks remained mired in poverty. And whereas in the 1960s and after, the barriers to Jewish advancement had been reduced to only an occasional stumbling block, blacks, despite considerable progress, continued to struggle against enormous obstacles, including the psychological legacy of slavery, segregation, lynching, sharecropping, and the ongoing bigotry of white Americans. Having themselves climbed out of poverty and utilized public education to full advantage, Jews would become impatient with a black underclass mired in welfare, illiteracy, and illegitimacy. "Why can't they lift themselves up the way we did?" would become an all-too-common, but naive, response of middle-class Jews to the awesome plight of the ghetto poor.

Thus even during the years that Jews and African Americans were forging a successful alliance, friction, and even hostility, existed between the two groups. Like other Christians, blacks were exposed to the negative image of Jews found in the New Testament and perpetuated directly or indirectly from the pulpit. And Jews were not unaffected by the antiblack sentiments that pervaded American society. As Jews and blacks rubbed shoulders in northern cities, particularly after World War II, additional causes for tension emerged. Blacks accused Jewish landlords of rent gouging, Jewish store owners of selling shoddy merchandise at high prices and not hiring blacks, and Jewish housewives of demeaning black domestics. And Jews, like other whites, were troubled by the influx of blacks into their neighborhoods. Generally Jews were less opposed to integrated neighborhoods and schools than other definable white groups, and, unlike some white ethnics, they never resorted to violence to keep blacks out. Nevertheless, like other whites, many Jews, citing black crime and decaying schools, fled, often to the growing suburbs. The riots that devastated several American cities in the 1960s and 1970s caused many Jews to retreat from their espousal of black causes. The scenes, graphically depicted on television, of blacks trashing shops, many of them owned by Jews, and carting away stolen merchandise exacerbated feelings about black criminality. And in subsequent years, the rapid deterioration of formerly Jewish working-class and middle-class neighborhoods now inhabited predominately by blacks and the proliferation of urban black street criminals, whose victims not infrequently were Jews, led more and more Jews to sympathize less with the plight of the black underclass.

But what really split the alliance of blacks and Jews was the growing influence of black militants who rebelled against integration and called for black

nationalism and "Black Power." In their denunciation of whites, militants increasingly singled out Jews as the principal enemy of black people. When
these militants postured with weapons, praised violence as liberating, and engaged in antisemitic rhetoric, they seemed like black fascists to Jews. When
they defended the burning and looting in the cities as guerrilla warfare against
oppressors and colonizers, Jews, like other Americans, saw them as wild-eyed
fanatics who threatened American society.

Among other things, advocates of Black Power demanded that whites be
excluded from black civil rights organizations, that blacks control predominately black public schools, and that black children be taught from an Afro-
centric viewpoint by black teachers. On college campuses, they demanded
separate living facilities for blacks and the establishment of black studies programs headed and staffed only by blacks. One of the worst examples of such
fervor occurred at Harvard in the mid-1980s when militant black students
protested the appointment of Jack Greenberg as coteacher of a course on race
and law. (The other instructor, Julius Chambers, head of the NAACP Legal
Defense Fund, was black.) In his long association with the NAACP, Greenberg had helped to win several school desegregation cases, organized the defense of civil rights demonstrators, launched a program to provide legal
services for poor blacks, and raised considerable sums for the financially hard-
pressed organization. Ironically, he also criticized Jewish organizations for op-
posing affirmative action. Although the militants' demand that an African
American instructor replace Greenberg was rejected, the incident offended
Jewish sensibilities.

Three incidents that exemplified the growing hostility of blacks toward
Jews and the growing disillusionment of Jewish liberals occurred in New York
City. One was the conflict that engulfed the schools of Ocean Hill–Brownsville
in the late 1960s. The other two incidents took place in the early 1990s—the
Crown Heights riot and the antisemitic harangues of Leonard Jeffries, chairman of the Black Studies department at City College (CCNY). During each of
these incidents, numerous callers to black radio stations maligned Jews in hateful, stereotypical ways.

In 1968 city authorities, seeking to give blacks greater voice in black
neighborhoods, empowered local school boards. In the predominantly black
school districts of Ocean Hill–Brownsville, the community board appointed
Rhody McCoy, a militant black, as superintendent. He immediately dismissed
nineteen white teachers and supervisors, eighteen of them Jewish, on flimsy
charges. The largely Jewish United Federation of Teachers (UFT), headed by
Albert Shanker, demanded that the teachers be reinstated. Shanker reasoned

that if McCoy got away with these firings, then no teacher's job would be secure, the carefully crafted examination system for hiring and promotions
would be undermined, and the UFT, whose job it was to protect teachers,
would suffer a major defeat. When McCoy refused, the UFT called a strike
that closed down the schools for two months. During these tense days, some
blacks hurled cruel antisemitic epitaphs at teachers walking the picket lines.
Several of these tormenters were affiliated with Sonny Carson, a particularly
notorious hatemonger. On several occasions prior to the strike, he and a gang
of thugs had invaded the schools to menace white teachers. "The Germans did
not do a good enough job with the Jews" was one of their torments.

Shanker publicized antisemitic leaflets distributed by black radicals, including one that called for black children to be taught by African Americans
rather than "Middle East Murderers of Colored Peoples." After the strike, a
black talk show host had as his guest Leslie Campbell, a militant teacher from
a troubled junior high school in the Ocean Hill district. Campbell, who had
been fostering black nationalism and inciting violence among his students,
read a poem written in his office by one of his protégées. Dedicated to Albert
Shanker, it read: "Hey Jew-boy with that yarmulke on your head, / You pale-
faced Jew boy—I wish you were dead." Several days later another militant
teacher appeared on the same show and added this thought to the cauldron:
"As far as I'm concerned more power to Hitler. He didn't make enough lamp-
shades out of them. He didn't make enough belts out of them."[*5] Disgusted by
such displays of raw antisemitism, many Jews pulled further away from the already fracturing black-Jewish alliance.

In August 1991 a car, part of the entourage escorting the head of a Hasidic
sect to his home in Crown Heights, Brooklyn, ran a red light and struck Gavin
Cato, a seven-year-old black child. A private ambulance driven by a Hasidic
driver arrived to take the child to the hospital. With a city ambulance in sight
and the angry crowd threatening the driver of the automobile that hit Gavin—
he had already been beaten and his wallet stolen—the police ushered him into
the ambulance and ordered it out of the neighborhood. A minute later the city
ambulance rushed Gavin to the hospital, where he died. Immediately rumors
spread that the Jewish driver had deliberately hit Gavin, that the boy lay dying

---

* It is a striking irony, noted by Hubert Locke, *Learning from History*, 39–41, 103–4,
that Nazi German theories of racial superiority and genocide derived in part from German pseudoanthropological studies of Africans in what was then German Southwest
Africa (Namibia), 1880s to 1914; this history and the fact that the Germans treated the
few blacks they had access to as they did Jews persuades Locke that African Americans,
rather than denigrate the Holocaust, ought to be as keen students of it as are Jews.

while the Jewish ambulance service tended only to the Jewish driver, and that
the police refused to arrest him. Several hours later some twenty black youths,
shouting "Kill the Jew!" attacked Yankel Rosenbaum, a visiting Hasidic
scholar from Australia. Stabbed by Lemerick Nelson, Jr., Rosenbaum later
died in the hospital. (With better care most likely he would have survived.) For
the next four days blacks, often spewing antisemitic slogans, including "Heil
Hitler," surged through the Hasidic section, attacking homes, stoning and
beating people, setting fires, and looting stores. The terrified Jews appealed to
the police for protection, but Mayor David Dinkins and his black police com-
missioner did not call out the police in force until the fifth day. It was specu-
lated that Dinkins, a black who always had congenial relations with Jews, felt
that a massive police response would have alienated his black constituents.
Some black spokespersons from the area said that the riots were a response to
years of mistreatment that they suffered at the hands of the insular Hasids. To
the Hasids, many of them Holocaust survivors, the riot was nothing less than a
pogrom, reminiscent of what their relatives had faced in tsarist Russia when
mobs periodically attacked Jewish neighborhoods while the authorities looked
the other way. Equally distressing to Jews was the relative silence of the black
community during and immediately after the outrages.

  Also in 1991, Professor Leonard Jeffries, Jr., told an approving audience
of black educators and artists that the Jewish moguls of Hollywood had conspired with the Mafia to spread negative images of blacks in their films and
that Jews were the principal financiers and organizers of the Atlantic slave
trade. In the furor that followed, several distressing things were learned about
Jeffries. He had been appointed in 1972 both chairman and full professor immediately after receiving his Ph.D. degree from Columbia University. (For an
unpublished scholar to receive a full professorship in a major institution so
soon after earning a doctorate is virtually unheard of.) He never published,
staffed the department with militant cronies, paraded about campus with an
entourage of posturing and menacing neighborhood blacks, was frequently
absent, late to class, and negligent in handing in grades, and propagated
bizarre racist theories about whites and historical nonsense about Jews. And
on campus, both inside and outside the classroom, Jeffries conducted himself
like a thug and a huckster.

  James Traub, who sat in Jeffries' classroom and wrote a revealing article
for *The New Yorker,* reported that he taught that white people are less humanistic than blacks because they evolved in a cold climate that hardened their
hearts. According to Jeffries' anthropology, black people, because they are
"sun people," are endowed with a "humanistic, spiritualistic value system,"

whereas Europeans and Americans—"ice people"—are "egocentric, individualistic, and exploitative." Jeffries attributed blacks' moral superiority to the melanin, which accounts for pigmentation, that they possess.[6] Jeffries engaged in angry tirades in which he denounced whites for conspiring to destroy blacks with the AIDS virus and for spreading homosexuality, which undermined African manhood.

Jews, who once predominated at CCNY and whose academic achievement had earned CCNY the appellation "the proletarian Harvard," were enraged that this venerable institution was now providing a platform for an openly antisemitic bigot. Jeffries continued his infractions of ordinary college rules, but the college authorities, fearful of violence from the black neighborhood in which City College is located, were reluctant to take action. However, in 1992, after his outrageous speech before black educators, he was dismissed as chairman of the Black Studies department but was reinstated after a court ruled that his freedom of speech had been violated. In 1995 the college, because of financial stringency, reduced the Black Studies department to a mere program, and Jeffries was transferred to the Political Science department, much to the dismay of its faculty.

Another incident that widened the rift between the two groups occurred in 1984 when Jesse Jackson, who was then seeking the nomination of the Democratic party for president, in an aside to a black reporter, Milton Coleman, said of a section of Chicago: "Jewtown is where Hymie gets you if you can't negotiate them down."[7] Then to complete the thought he referred to New York City as "Hymietown." When Coleman made these remarks public, Jackson first denied them and then apologized. Many Jews, who already were antagonized by the sympathy he had expressed for the Palestine Liberation Organization (PLO), were reluctant to accept Jackson's apology for this unfortunate remark. On their part, blacks thought that Jews came down much too hard on their champion, particularly since he apologized. "Don't Jews believe in forgiveness?" they protested. In 1979 Andrew Young, the American ambassador to the United Nations and the most prominent African American in the Carter government, was compelled to resign when he violated policy by meeting with representatives of the PLO; Jackson dubbed Young's departure a "capitulation to the Jews" and contended that "the real resistance to black progress has not been coming from the Ku Klux Klan but from our former allies in the American Jewish community."[8] In subsequent years Jackson apparently overcame his anti-Jewish antipathies and has been stalwart in combating antisemitism.

A continuous source of friction between African Americans and Jews is the forceful opposition of many influential Jews, loosely called neoconservatives, to racial preferences for admission into elite universities, medical schools, and law schools; for hiring and promotions in business; and for gaining government contracts. For blacks, affirmative action is a just and appropriate way of moving blacks into the mainstream of American society after years of being held down. Most whites oppose affirmative action, which they regard as reverse racism. It is likely that Jews disproportionately favor it, as they do other liberal measures. Nevertheless, like other opponents of affirmative action, Jewish opponents argue that it is simply unjust for an educational institution to admit a black—which in practice means excluding a white or an Asian— who scores significantly lower on entrance examinations than a nonblack candidate chiefly because of his or her color. Moreover, Jews fear that a policy of racial preferences threatens the merit system that has been their avenue into the civil service and the professions. In the early part of the twentieth century, discriminatory quotas, both official and unofficial, had placed ceilings on Jews entering leading universities, medical and law schools, and the professions. Jews, who constitute 1.5 percent of the population in the United States, hold a disproportionate number of positions in medicine, law, college teaching, and the media. Jews interpret this as the fruit of ambition, hard work, and a merit system that they do not wanted tampered with. Placing their trust in the free marketplace and the merit system, Jews fear that any program of racial preferences would degenerate into odious quotas that would limit their access to the professions. Black supporters of affirmative action have never argued that Jewish representation in the professions should reflect the number of Jews in the country and mainstream black organizations hold that Jews, who share a history of suffering, should be more sympathetic to the needs of blacks on this issue.

The Arab-Israeli conflict has also contributed to tensions between blacks and Jews. Increasingly black intellectuals (but not most black members of Congress), identifying with Third World liberation movements, have viewed the Palestinians as victims of an imperialist and even racist Zionist ideology. They see the fact that the United States tends to support Israel as another indication of the nefarious power possessed by American Jews. Blacks were also angered by Israel's refusal to join the international economic boycott against South Africa to compel it to abandon its apartheid policy. American Jews resented strongly the identification of Zionism with racism, and they wondered out loud why American blacks made a point of singling out Israel and ignoring black African and Muslim Arab lands whose commercial relations with South Africa far surpassed that of the Jewish state.

## LOUIS FARRAKHAN AND THE NATION OF ISLAM

It is within this context of deepening alienation between African Americans and Jews that Minister Louis Farrakhan, head of the Nation of Islam, has gained notoriety. Beginning in 1984, Farrakhan and his spokesmen deliberately aroused receptive black audiences with antisemitic rhetoric. Ironically, the Nation of Islam, which urges blacks to liberate themselves from a decadent European civilization, employs and propagates classic European anti-Jewish imagery and myths. It has recycled and updated for black listeners the traditional canards disseminated by European Christian antisemites, often with the same venom shown by earlier generations of European Jew-haters. Before discussing Farrakhan's antisemitic campaign, it is necessary to provide some background to the man and his movement.

Born in 1933, Louis Farrakhan was baptized Louis Gene Walcott and grew up in the Roxbury suburb of Boston, where his mother, a native of the West Indies, worked as a domestic. As a youngster Gene—as he was commonly called—studied violin with a Russian Jewish teacher. He quickly demonstrated a gift for music and a passion for the instrument, often practicing several hours a day. He was also intelligent, earning admission into the elite Boston Latin School; for whatever reason, after one year he transferred to English High, also a superb school, where he distinguished himself academically and ran on the track team. While still in high school, Gene sang calypso in black nightclubs, using the name "the Charmer." After graduation he attended a black college, Winston-Salem Teachers' College, where he organized a traveling calypso band. In 1952 Walcott married Betsy Ross, a young woman from his Roxbury neighborhood; with a baby on the way, Walcott dropped out of school and concentrated on performing. While appearing in Chicago, he attended the Nation of Islam Savior's Day convention and heard Elijah Muhammad, the sect's leader, address the faithful. Impressed with Muhammad's words and demeanor, Walcott joined the movement and later, after hearing Malcolm X preach, became an enthusiastic devotee.

The Nation of Islam was founded during the depression by one Wallace D. Fard. At times he was described as a light-skinned black; other times, as a white man or an Arab. In the 1960s it was discovered that Fard, under the name Wallace Ford, had served three years in San Quentin for selling drugs. After his release, Ford sold silks door to door in the Detroit ghetto and took his new name. In the homes of his customers, he lectured on African history and culture. Fard's lectures, intended to give poor and oppressed blacks a sense of dignity, gained him a following. He soon rented a hall and founded a church, the Temple of Islam. One of Fard's followers, stirred by his mentor's teachings, killed a man in what was described as a human sacrifice. Fard was arrested and invited to leave Detroit after reportedly confessing to the police that his church was a moneymaking racket. He was never seen again. After Fard's departure, the movement came under the leadership of Elijah Muhammad, formerly Elijah Poole, who had been so swayed by Fard that he considered him God in human form—at times Fard had referred to himself as the "Supreme Ruler of the Universe"—and did not doubt the truth of Fard's message.

Fard told his audience of poor, alienated, and angry blacks, who had good reason to hate white America, that he came to them from the holy city of Mecca with a message of worldly redemption: Black people were inherently moral, noble, strong, and intelligent, whereas white people were by nature immoral, wicked, and puny in body and mind. He spun a mythological tale designed to create true believers among his followers. As related by Malcolm X, in the beginning, "after the moon separated from the earth," black people, the first human beings, "founded the Holy City of Mecca. Among the black race were twenty-four wise scientists. One of the scientists . . . created the especially strong black tribe of Shabazz from which American Negroes, so-called, descend." Among some dissatisfied blacks there was born a Mr. Yacub, who "was born to cause trouble, to break the peace, and to kill. . . . At the age of eighteen, Yacub had finished all of his nation's colleges and universities. . . . Among many other things, he had learned how to breed races scientifically." Because of his wickedness, Yacub was exiled to the island of Patmos with 59,999 of his followers. Seeking revenge, Yacub, known as "big head scientist," decided "to create . . . a devil race—a bleached-out white race of people." The process, carried on by generations of his successors, took several hundred years. But eventually the island of Patmos was inhabited only by

> these blond, pale-skinned, cold-blue-eyed devils—savages, nude and shameless; hairy, like animals, they walked on all fours and they lived in trees. . . . Six hundred more years passed before this race of people returned to the mainland among the natural black people [and within six months] this devil race had turned what had been a peaceful heaven on earth into a hell torn by quarreling and fighting.
>
> But finally the original black people recognized that their sudden troubles stemmed from this devil white race, that Mr. Yacub had made. They rounded them up, put them in chains. With little aprons to cover their nakedness, this devil race was marched off across the Arabian desert to the caves of Europe.[9]

Ultimately blacks would defeat their white oppressors, gain power throughout the world, and restore the paradisiacal Eden that they had enjoyed before Yacub had created these white demons.

To Elijah Muhammad, Fard's tale constituted divine revelation. And Gene Walcott, who took the name Louis X and then Louis Farrakhan, subscribed to Fard's theology and regarded Muhammad as an apostle. Farrakhan, who established a successful temple in Boston, endorsed the Nation of Islam's strict prohibitions against drugs, adultery, and foul language, and spread its gospel of black separatism and self-sufficiency. Demonstrating a quick mind and oratorical skill that captivated audiences, Farrakhan's star was rising.

Starting in the 1960s, the Nation was torn by crisis. Members of Elijah Muhammad's immediate family, some of them now serious students of Islam, recognized that Muhammad's theology had little to do with the religion of Islam. Second, Muhammad had avariciously sequestered money from the Nation of Islam to lavish luxuries on himself and his family. Then it was discovered that Elijah had sired thirteen children with six Nation secretaries, whom he threatened with physical harm if they revealed his paternity. These moral lapses and the strong-arm methods of the Fruit of Islam, the Nation's paramilitary unit that was staffed with many ex-convicts, led many people to defect and to request police protection. The most prominent defector was Malcolm X, who had become a national figure. After a pilgrimage to Mecca, Malcolm, influenced by Islam's universalism that draws no distinctions on the basis of color, denounced Muhammad as a fraud and publicly condemned his racism as inimical to true Islam. (Traditional Muslims had regarded Nation of Islam theology—deifying Fard and viewing Elijah Muhammad as a prophet or a messiah—as heretical.) Siding with his mentor, Farrakhan attacked Malcolm as a traitor and said he was "worthy of death." To this day there is suspicion that Farrakhan had a hand in Malcom's assassination.

The assassination of Malcolm in 1965 by members of the Nation of Islam was followed by several other murders and beatings of Muslim dissidents and the killing of Nation officials by disaffected former members. This sectarian gang warfare reached a gruesome pinnacle in 1973 when a group broke into a dissident's home and murdered seven people, including three infants and a ten-year-old boy. Meanwhile, the Nation of Islam's image was further tarnished by the accounts of former members describing brutal beatings and financial extortion.

After Elijah Muhammad's death on February 6, 1975, his son Wallace took over leadership of the Nation, to the chagrin of Farrakhan, who aspired to the honor and the power. To forestall any insurrection in the Nation of

Islam's ranks, Wallace transferred Farrakhan from New York to Chicago, the Nation's headquarters, where he could be observed; and to show Farrakhan who was boss, Wallace appointed him minister of a dingy temple. Wallace also broke with his father's racist, demonological, and separatist worldview. In an extraordinary about-face, he declared that whites were not devils but fully human, abandoned the demand for a black territorial base within the United States, and denied that Fard was divine and his father a prophet. He terminated the Nation of Islam and urged his followers to associate with mainstream Islam. Under the name W. Deen Mohammed (spelled differently from his father's name), he is now viewed as the respected leader of African American Muslims, as symbolized by his leading the Senate in prayer in February 1992. Imam Mohammad has disavowed antisemitism and maintained cordial, if not friendly, relations with Jewish groups. His followers greatly outnumber Farrakhan's group, which is estimated to have only between ten and twenty thousand members.

At the end of 1977, Farrakhan quit Wallace's church and revived the Nation of Islam. He restored Fard Muhammad as Allah, Elijah Muhammad as the messenger of Allah's teachings, and the myth of Yacub. When Farrakhan was asked in 1996 whether the tale of Yacub was truth or a metaphor, he replied: "It is not, in our judgment, metaphorical. . . . Personally, I believe that Yacub is not a mythical figure—he is a very real scientist."[10] Like his mentors, he rejected the integrationist ideals of Martin Luther King, Jr., and called for an American society in which whites and blacks are completely separated; and, like them, he proclaimed the solidarity of black people as his goal.

In recent years Farrakhan has sought to become a national black leader. Toward this end he has urged blacks of all faiths to join hands and has softened his antiwhite rhetoric. One illustration of Farrakhan's elevated status among black people is the unwillingness of many black leaders, including Jesse Jackson, to renounce him when he taunts Jews. Jackson, who had accepted Farrakhan's support when he sought the Democratic party nomination in 1984 and 1988, has criticized Farrakhan's antisemitism but not the man who uttered the hateful remarks. Jackson and other black leaders know that to do so would be perceived in the black community as surrendering to the white man. In 1993 Kwasi Mfume, then chairman of the Congressional Black Caucus, the association of African American members of Congress, pledged that the Caucus would enter into a "sacred covenant" with all black organizations, including the Nation of Islam, that support self-help and self-improvement for black people. The meaning of this pledge is obvious, as Robert Singh, author of a recent study of Farrakhan, notes: "[I]ts implicit message was that the issues of anti-Semitism and black racism that continued to shroud Farrakhan and his organization in a negative veil of the vilest bigotry were essentially secondary to the formulation of a common national black American political agenda."[11]

Another indication that Farrakhan was gaining legitimacy as a national black leader was the entente he forged with Betty Shabazz, Malcolm X's widow. What prompted Shabazz, who had earlier incriminated Farrakhan in her husband's assassination and had never forgiven him for it, to consummate an accommodation with the Nation of Islam leader was the arrest in early 1995 of her daughter, Qubillah Shabazz, for conspiring to assassinate Farrakhan in an act of revenge. Apparently a deal was struck, for the charges against Qubillah were dropped. And most important for Farrakhan's agenda was the healing of the rift that had divided blacks after the assassination of the immensely popular Malcolm. The opposition to Farrakhan on this issue had been effectively neutralized.

The extraordinary success of the Million Man March on October 16, 1995, which Farrakhan initiated and organized, confirmed his place in the ranks of black political leadership. Some 400,000 black men—some estimates are significantly higher—converged on the nation's capital at Farrakhan's request—more than twice the number that attended Martin Luther King's historic march in 1963. Joining them were numerous African American dignitaries, including Jesse Jackson, several congressmen, academics, and Rosa Parks, an icon in the civil rights struggle. Many of the participants, particularly the noteworthies, claimed that it was solidarity with fellow blacks and a hope of black spiritual renewal, and not Farrakhan the man or his antiwhite and antisemitic message, that brought them to Washington. The demonstration, for which Farrakhan delivered the keynote address, was a spectacular indication that he was a prominent African American leader.

In 1996, several months after the triumph of the Million Man March, Farrakhan embarked on a World Friendship Tour of Africa and the Middle East that included visits with the notorious dictators of Libya, Nigeria, and the Sudan, and fundamentalist clerics in Iran. Farrakhan's support of these regimes has somewhat sullied his reputation among politically aware African Americans. He has accepted millions of dollars from the Libyan dictator Muammar Gadhafi and praised both the clerical rulers of Iran for their attacks on the "Great Satan," as they refer to the United States, and the fundamentalist Islamic leadership of Sudan, whose human rights violations include tolerating the persecution and enslavement of tens of thousands of black African Christians and animists. Indeed, Farrakhan has refused to speak out against slavery in the Sudan despite mounting and irrefutable evidence. Similarly, in his concern for black solidarity, he simply ignores the human rights violations that plague many African lands.

Several reasons account for Farrakhan's popularity. First the man himself. Attractive, bright, and a compelling orator, he has charismatic qualities that appeal to many black people. Second, even black people who dismiss his theology are impressed by his call to replace black dependence on whites through black-self-help, black entrepreneurship,* and black pride; by his denunciation of criminal behavior, gang violence, and drug abuse among blacks; by his campaign against out-of-wedlock teenage births and neglectful fathers that have plagued black communities; by the seeming success of his organization in rehabilitating ex-convicts; by his unflinching attacks on past and present injustices committed against black people; and by his militant in-your-face response to his white detractors. Third, Farrakhan commands the attention of downtrodden and alienated blacks for whom the hopes of the civil rights

---

* Yet the Nation of Islam's business ventures, which include a toiletry company, security companies, a produce farm in Georgia, and a restaurant in Chicago, have not been models of success, at least through March 1995. At that time, in an article subtitled "The Nation of Islam's Mission is Mired in a 10-year Heap of Unpaid Bills," the *Washington Post* reported: "The nation and a variety of businesses and properties linked to it are beset by financial problems. They have accumulated a 10-year record of debt and troubled management that is in sharp contrast with Farrakhan's stated goal of black economic empowerment" (Lorraine Adams, "A Dream Past Due," *Washington Post National Weekly Edition*, September 9–15, 1994, 6). A much more extensive investigation was conducted by David Jackson and William Gaines, who wrote a series of articles for the *Chicago Tribune* in March 1995. They reported that a soap and cosmetic company, subsidized with $5 million from Gadhafi and launched with delirious hopes, slid into unaudited and unreported losses, hiding from creditors and begging for even more donations from the faithful poor on whose backs these ventures weigh heavily. Leonard Searcy Muhammad, the tsar of most Nation-associated enterprises, is noted for business failure. A bankrupt chicken business brought him into litigation; in the court papers he was accused of "fraud, dishonesty, incompetence, and gross mismanagement" (March 14, 1995, 10). The Abundant Life Clinic, headed by Dr. Abdul Alim Muhammad, who holds that "white people is equal to dogs and horses," sold for profit a drug purported to cure AIDS, despite tests demonstrating that the drug is useless for treating AIDS, a conclusion backed by the U.S. government and the World Health Organization. After analyzing all of Farrakhan's business operations, Jackson and Gaines concluded that "Nation-affiliated companies are riddled with debt, failure, and fraud" (ibid.). Nevertheless, Farrakhan, his family, and his inner circle live in lavish luxury, enjoying custom-made automobiles, palatial homes, and resplendent clothes. In response to the articles, Farrakhan did not provide audited financial statements or answer the charges with relevant data. Rather, he presented himself as a victim of a global conspiracy, pursued by a "secret government made up of the media, international bankers [code term for Jews] and federal agencies," which are all "destined to disgrace and total destruction" (ibid., March 20, 11).

movement seem impossible dreams and traditional civil rights leaders are failures. Farrakhan is the leading voice of black rage in America. Years earlier
Martin Luther King, Jr., had anticipated such a tragic development and fought
to avert it:

> I stand in the middle of two opposing forces in the Negro community. One is
> a force of complacency.... The other force is one of bitterness and hatred,
> and comes perilously close to advocating violence. It is expressed in the vari-
> ous black nationalist groups that are springing up all over the nation, the
> largest and best known being Elijah Muhammad's Muslim movement. This
> movement is nourished by the frustration over the continued existence of
> racial discrimination. It is made up of people who have lost faith in America,
> who have absolutely repudiated Christianity, and who have concluded that
> the white man is an incurable "devil." I have tried to stand between these two
> forces, saying that we need not follow the "do-nothingism" of the complacent
> or the hatred and despair of the black nationalist.... And I am further con-
> vinced that if our white brothers dismiss us as "rabble rousers,"... millions
> of Negroes, out of frustration and despair, will seek solace and security in
> black nationalist ideologies, a development that will lead inevitably to a
> frightening racial nightmare.[12]

## ANTISEMITIC DEMAGOGUERY

It was in 1984 that Farrakhan began to show overt hostility to Jews and employ traditional antisemitic imagery. After his gaffe about "Hymietown,"
Jackson had received numerous death threats, some of them no doubt from
radical fringe Jewish groups. On February 25, standing next to Jesse Jackson,
Farrakhan warned there would be retaliation if Jackson were harmed. Two
weeks later he warned the black reporter Coleman who had released the
story: "One day soon we will punish you with death."[13] Then on a radio
broadcast on March 11 he called Hitler "a very great man" for uplifting his
people. A month later he described Hitler as "a great man, but also wicked—
wickedly great." In fairness to Farrakhan, the media and Jewish spokesmen
took this remark out of context, giving the impression that Farrakhan was ex-
tolling Hitler. By "great," as Farrakhan has stated frequently, he only meant
that Hitler was a prominent and influential historical figure. In June of the
same year he declared that Israel will "never have ... peace, because there
can be no peace structured on injustice, lying, and deceit and using the name
of God to shield your dirty religion under his holy and righteous name."[14]
On August 18, speaking in Washington D.C., Farrakhan asked the audience

what should happen to black leaders who seek Jewish support. When someone shouted, "Kill them," Farrakhan replied: "I didn't say it. I just seconded
the motion."*

Farrakhan quickly grasped that playing the antisemitic card would generate much publicity for him and would appeal to numerous blacks who harbored anti-Jewish feelings; moreover, standing up to the criticism that was
certain to follow—by demonstrating that he was not a black man to be trifled
with—would gain him the respect of many blacks. On October 7, 1985, Farrakhan addressed an overflow crowd of some 25,000 at Madison Square Garden in New York City, a resounding sign that he was now a black spokesman
of prominence. The focal point of his speech was not economics as promised
but Jew-bashing, and the audience loved it. First the ancient charge of deicide
that Christian churches have been struggling to eradicate: "Who were the enemies of Jesus?" Farrakhan asked: "Jews! Jews! Jews!" was the crowd's thun-
derous response.[15] There was also the familiar myth of Jewish power and a
Jewish conspiracy: "The Jewish lobby has a stranglehold on the government of
the United States."[16] He also accused Jews of plotting his death: "The germ of
murder is already sewed into the hearts of the Jews in this country." Linking
himself to prophets of God supposedly killed by Jews, he warned "But if you
rise up to try to kill me, then Allah promises you that he will bring on this generation the blood of the righteous. All of you will be killed outright." And in
what journalist Milton Kramer called "an exquisitely crafted stab-through-the
heart-phrase," he added "You cannot say 'Never Again' to God, because when
He puts you in the oven, 'Never again' don't mean a thing."[17]

Perhaps the most distressing feature of Farrakhan's speech was not his
hateful words—one expects this from a demagogue playing to the crowd—but
the glee with which his audience received them. Whenever he stuck it to the
Jews, people reacted jubilantly: "Tell 'em Brother" was an oft-heard response.
Witnessing the spectacle was Julius Lester, a black convert to Judaism, who
was then director of the African American Studies program at the University
of Massachusetts, Amherst. He commented on the symbiotic relationship between the orator and the crowd: "The audience greeted each anti-Semitic
thrust by rising to its feet, cheering, arms outstretched at 45-degree angles, fist
clenched. As this scene repeated itself throughout the evening, I wondered, Is
this what it was like to be at the Nuremberg rallies in Nazi Germany?"[18]
Equally distressing was the unwillingness of black spokespersons to criticize

---

* All quotations not endnoted are from the numerous reports issued by the Anti-
Defamation League, which monitors the activities of antisemites.

Farrakhan, an ominous sign that Jew-hatred was becoming increasingly acceptable for blacks.

In succeeding years Farrakhan spewed forth a barrage of antisemitic remarks that were adaptations of centuries-old canards, which had caused the Jewish people great suffering. What follows is just a sampling. On January 26, 1990, in Oakland, California, in an obvious attempt to present himself as a messianic figure and to capitalize on an ancient hatred, he declared that "The same enemies that hated Jesus hate Farrakhan. Jesus was hated by the Pharisees and the Jews. I am hated by the same." At Michigan State University, on February 18, he employed the language and imagery of medieval Christian Jew-haters, accusing Jews of "sucking the blood of the black community." On March 1 he reiterated the stale tale of the Jewish conspiracy. The *Washington Post* reported that in an interview held several days earlier, Farrakhan said that Jews are part of "a small clique who use their power and their knowledge to manipulate the masses against the best interests of the people."[19] On March 3 the *Washington Post* editorialized: "[Farrakhan] says he met a Jewish man who described to him the small clique of which he is a member and which cleverly manipulates opinion all over the world ('85 percent of the masses of the people of earth are victimized by a small clique who use their power and their knowledge to manipulate the masses against the best interests of the people')."[20] By fixating on Jewish bankers and financiers purported to control governments and dictate policy, Farrakhan, of course, propagates a conspiracy myth that puts him in the company of Goebbels, the *Protocols of the Learned Elders of Zion*, and radical conservative nationalists in many European lands since the late nineteenth century. On June 22, 1994, *The Final Call*, the Nation of Islam's newspaper, published an article written by Farrakhan that revived the classic anti-Judaic myth that responsible Christian leaders have denounced and excised from Christian teachings. Jewish conspirators, said Farrakhan, plotted to kill Jesus and for such a wicked crime the entire Jewish people must bear responsibility.

An incident illustrating the attraction of Farrakhan's antisemitism occurred in Chicago. On May 2, 1988, the *Chicago Tribune* reported that Steven Cokely, a Farrakhan sympathizer who had been appointed an aide to acting mayor Eugene Sawyer in late 1987, had from 1985 to 1987 given four speeches at the Final Call, Farrakhan's Chicago headquarters, that included ugly antisemitic remarks. An article in the *New Republic* summarized what Cokely said: "Cokely had vehemently attacked both Jesse Jackson and [Mayor] Harold Washington for retaining Jewish advisers. He had alleged that Jewish physicians were injecting black children with the AIDS virus. . . . and accused

Jews of creating a 'secret society,' the purpose of which is to form a world government controlled by Jews that would oppress blacks. 'The Jew,' Cokely had stated, 'hopes to reign forever.' . . . The tapes of Cokely's speeches remain on sale at the Final Call."[21]

Several black columnists denounced Cokely's raw bigotry, but black local government officials failed to repudiate him and only belatedly and reluctantly did Mayor Sawyer dismiss him. A *Chicago Tribune* poll showed that 92 percent of blacks believed that Cokely's dismissal was warranted, an encouraging sign. After his dismissal, Cokely accepted a position with Farrakhan, who defended him. Jewish officials, said Farrakhan, were offended only because "Cokely spoke the truth and . . . the truth hurts. . . . I know if he said it, he got the stuff to back it up." *The Final Call* supported Cokely and endorsed his bizarre conspiracy theories. An editorial on May 27 maintained:

> Brother Steve [Cokely], in rare form, dug up and presented an intriguing array of articles, reports, even Jewish newspapers, which put in context every one of his statements which the media under the direction of the B'nai B'rith Anti-Defamation League (ADL) attempted to distort and label anti-Semitic or anti-Christian. Instead evidence revealed incontrovertible realities of vile plots being hatched against Black people by clandestine organizations dominated by Jewish interests, including the South Africa apartheid system, which was helped to be formed by Jewish doctors.

## KHALLID ABDUL MUHAMMAD

Aspiring to recognition as a mainstream black leader, Farrakhan has, in recent years, played the antisemitic tune an octave lower. Khallid Abdul Muhammad, a former protégée of Farrakhan, inherited the position as the country's most shrill black antisemite. Devoured by hate, Khallid saw white people as "the devil. I believe with all my heart that the government killed my heroes, and the government is representative of white folks and Jews. I have to hate all of them."[22] Born Harold Moore, Jr., in Houston around 1950—he did not reveal his year of birth—he was reared by a devoutly religious aunt, Carey Vann, who adopted him. Harold went to a segregated high school where he distinguished himself as a student and athlete. He attended Dillard University, where he was a student leader, for four years, but did not graduate. Influenced by the Black Power militancy, which was spreading in urban centers, and by *The Autobiography of Malcolm X*, Vann grew increasingly more radical. He wore a dashiki, cultivated an Afro, and wanted nothing to do with the "honkie." At times he wore the black beret and leather jacket, the insignia of the Black Panther party. But after hearing Farrakhan, then a chief aide to Elijah Muhammad, speak at Dillard, he was drawn to the Black Muslims, and by 1985, now called Khallid, which means "warrior," he had become part of Farrakhan's inner circle, serving as the leader's personal bodyguard and the Nation's minister of defense.

From 1988 to 1991 Khallid spent three years in a federal penitentiary for securing a home mortgage loan with a social security number that was not his own. At the time of sentencing, an angry Farrakhan declared that he would be barred from the ministry, but after his release, Khallid was made head of a mosque in Los Angeles.

On November 29, 1993, Khallid delivered a hate-filled speech before about 125 people at Kean College in New Jersey. The Anti-Defamation League, whose principal mandate is to monitor antisemitic outbursts and to enlighten the public as to their mythical character and danger, reproduced the tirade in a full-page ad in the *New York Times*. Suddenly Khallid had become a national figure, albeit a notorious one.

In his speech Khallid repeatedly vilified Jews, often feigning the accent of eastern European Jewish immigrants and reiterating ancient slurs: "Jesus was right: you're nothing but liars. The book of Revelations is right; you're from the Synagogue of Satan." And he quoted the gospel of John: "You are of your father, the Devil." In addition to controlling Hollywood and the media, the Jews "have our athletes in the palm of their hand. . . . And normally they will give you a white woman," evoking the taunt that Jews have always profited from prostitution and "white slavery." Khallid could not resist showing his cleverness: "Columbia Jew-niversity in Jew York City." Historians are indebted to Khallid for his insightful analysis of the Jewish contribution to German culture:

> You see, everybody always talk about Hitler exterminating six million Jews. But don't nobody ever ask, "What did they do to Hitler? What did they do to them folks?" They went in there to Germany, the way they do everywhere they go, and they supplanted, they usurped, they turned around and a German in his own country would almost have to go to a Jew to get money. They had undermined the very fabric of the society. Now he was an arrogant no-good devil bastard, Hitler, no question about it. He was wickedly great. Yes he was. He used his greatness for evil and wickedness. But they are wickedly great, too, brother, every where they go. And they always do it and hide their hand.

This was Khallid the wise; we also have Khallid the humane. After blacks obtain power in South Africa, he said the white man will be given

24 hours to get out of town by sundown. That's all. If he don't get out of town before sundown, we will kill everything white that ain't right that's in sight in South Africa. We kill the women. We kill the children. We kill the babies. (Applause throughout.) We kill the blind. We kill the cripples. We kill em all. We kill the faggot; we kill the lesbian. We kill em all. You say why kill the babies in South Africa? Because they're going to grow up one day to oppress our babies, so we kill the babies. Why kill the women? Because they lay on their back. They are the military or the army's manufacturing center. They lay on their back and reinforcements roll out from between their legs. So we kill the women too. You gonna kill the elders too? Kill the old ones too. Goddamnit, if they have a wheelchair, push em off a cliff in Cape Town. (Laughter and applause.) . . . Goddamnit and when you get through killing them all, go to the Goddamn graveyard and dig up the grave and kill em a-godadamn-gain, cause they didn't die hard enough. (Laughter and applause.)

Khallid's speech also attacked gays and the pope ("the old no-good Pope—you know that cracker, somebody need to raise that dress up and see what's really under there"), and created a furor. Farrakhan, who had repeatedly cautioned Khallid to tone down his rhetoric, was compelled to discipline his deputy. He suspended Khallid from his duties and condemned his rhetoric but not the "truths" that he spoke.

On February 23, 1994, Khallid spoke at Howard University, the "black Harvard"; Malik Shabazz, a law student at the university, prepared the audience for the main attraction with the following demagogic call and response.

"Who is it that caught and killed Nat Turner?" Mr. Shabazz asked.
"Jews!" responded the audience.
"Who is it that controls the Federal Reserve?"
"Jews!" . . .
"Who is it that controls the media and Hollywood?"
"Jews! Jews!"
"Who is it that has our entertainers in a vise grip and our athletes in a vise grip?
"Jews!"
"Who is it that have been spying on black leaders and spied on Martin Luther King and set up his death?"
"Jews!" Jews!" . . .
"I'm going to tell the truth to the world. . . . If you rejected Jesus, if you lied on him and you tried your best—and you did cause his assassination and his crucifixion—if you renounced Jesus Christ, how are we now to put any

weight on your condemnation of Minister Louis Farrakhan and Dr. [in fact, he had no doctorate] Khallid Muhammad?[23]

The following month Khallid went on another Jew-baiting rampage, this time belittling the Holocaust: "Tell us you lost 6 million. Historians, scholars, scientists, they went to the death camps. . . . It wasn't 6 million, it wasn't 5 million, it wasn't 4 million, it wasn't even 3 million. . . . Some of them say we'd be hard-pressed to get 1½ million. Reports on the six million Jews murdered by the Nazis were bloated, exaggerated, probably fabricated."

Aspiring for recognition by the principal black organizations, Farrakhan saw no political advantage to being linked to Khallid, whose obscene characterizations of Jews, women, gays, and the pope repelled many moderate blacks. Expelled from the Nation, Khallid, who died in 2001, became a leader in the New Black Panther party centered in Dallas and tried to court alienated ghetto youth: "My greatest appeal is among the grassroots, the hard core, the rough-necks, the gangsta-rap culture," he said.[24] Black college groups continued to invite him to speak at their campus. His address at San Francisco State University in May 1997, which earned him a long standing ovation, was another example of gutter antisemitism at its worst. Apparently Khallid, who drove a Rolls-Royce (estimated value $140,000), purchased a large house in Harlem's best neighborhood (estimated value after refurbishing, $1 million), and wore $2,000 custom-tailored suits and crocodile-skin shoes, did quite well for himself on the lecture circuit.

## THE SECRET RELATIONSHIP
## BETWEEN BLACKS AND JEWS

In 1991 *The Secret Relationship Between Blacks and Jews* was published under the Nation of Islam's imprint. The volume was prepared by the "Nation of Islam Historical Research Department," an unknown entity that has published nothing before or since. The authors of *Secret Relationship*—their names are not provided—intended to show: that Jews dominated the 400-year Atlantic slave trade and were its principal beneficiaries; Jews owned a disproportionate number of slaves; and the slave trade and chattel slavery constituted a holocaust far worse in numbers and suffering than the Shoah. The slave vessels were "holocaust ships" (p. 191); Jewish slave traders, slave owners, and militia members were the perpetrators, the equivalent of camp guards, "much like the Nazis at the concentration camps of Auschwitz, Treblinka or Buchenwald" (p. 207); and black slaves were "holocaust survivors" (p. 113). Not only is the Holocaust stolen from Jews but they were guilty of perpetrating a far worse human tragedy. Even with emancipation and the end of slavery, Jews were the chief exploiters of blacks: They were the store merchants and landlords who gouged blacks; the bankers who foreclosed on black farms and despoiled sharecroppers; the school teachers who stifled young black minds; the social workers who administered welfare programs with great insensitivity; and the chief opponents of affirmative action. Jews were "pioneers in this new brand of consumer exploitation" that was calculated "to maintain a psychological slavery" (p. 172). Readers acquainted with the writings of Holocaust deniers (see chapter 5) will find themselves on familiar territory when they turn to *Secret Relationship*. The format is that of seemingly serious scholarship, no less than 1,275 footnotes along with charts, lists, appendixes, and an extensive bibliography; it is described as "Volume One" of what promises to be a multivolume work. It cites numerous scholarly monographs, almost all of them authored by Jews, making the argument of Jewish "monumental culpability" (p. 128) appear all the more convincing. Yet like the Holocaust deniers, the authors of *Secret Relationship* violate every standard of historical inquiry. When one checks the quotations, a great many are inaccurate, emended to distort the original meaning, or taken out of context. Moreover, a large number of the works cited are obsolete or by authors who are neither historians nor authorities but publicists and ax-grinders. A work that promises to effect a fundamental shift in interpretation of an important historical topic must be based on an investigation of primary sources. But the authors of *Secret Relationship* do nothing of the sort; instead all their data are derived from secondary works. It is never indicated, much less explained, why standard works on slavery, whether by Jews or non-Jews, pay scant attention to Jewish involvement—the reason is, of course, that in comparison to Muslims, Catholics, Protestants, and black Africans, Jews were only marginally involved in slavery, either as traders or as owners. If no Jews had participated in the slave trade, the history of black slavery would have remained virtually the same.

The message of the authors of *Secret Relationship* to black people is clear: It was the Jews who oppressed us in the past and continue to oppress us today. Hence they seem to take a perverse delight in listing any Jew who was in some way linked to the Atlantic slave trade. Conversely, they simply ignore evidence that points to a different conclusion. The tactic of singling out the Jew as bearing a special guilt for the terrible iniquities inflicted on blacks is classic antisemitism, and like other accusations hurled at Jews by antisemites, this one is equally absurd. What would we think of a Jew-bating sociologist who, after researching prison records for the past fifty years, listed the names of Jewish convicts, described the offenses committed by some of them, and then, without comparing their criminal behavior with other definable groups, concluded that crime in America is dominated by Jews? The authors of *Secret Relationship* operate in the same reprehensible way.

Like the infamous *Protocols*, the authors of *Secret Relationship* are anonymous; most likely "the Historical Research Department" of the Nation of Islam that prepared it was a group of graduate students gathered in the Boston area. Readers of *Secret Relationship* who are acquainted with the *Protocols* will recognize the shared ideological landscape populated with the familiar stereotypes of the Jew as the embodiment of evil—cosmic conspirators who possess a demonic capacity to work in concert, secretly and across continents and centuries, to carry out their criminal enterprises: "Though scattered throughout the globe by political, economic and religious circumstances, they [the Jews] would reunite later in unholy alliance of kidnappers and slave makers" (pp. 12–13). The Jews are a criminal people armed with unnatural powers and driven by inhuman greed to acquire wealth and domination. Jewish law, which "very closely resembles business law," teaches its adherents that "money, not worship was the main objective" (p. 34). Slavery was "the greatest criminal endeavor ever undertaken" from which the Jews gained their "immense wealth"; now that their "complicity" is revealed, they are "accountable for many of those murders" over four centuries (pp. viii, 177). Jews abused and raped black women "with abandon" (p. 201) and forced them into prostitution to reap profits. Jews cleverly used liquor to maximize profits and to decimate their opponents: "Liquor, feverishly distilled in the American northeast, was used in Africa [by Jews] in much the same way as it was in the destruction of American Indian civilization" (p. 90), and apparently the stills in Newport, Rhode Island, for making rum for the notorious triangular trade belonged to Jews. Jews were engaged in a genocidal "pogrom" (p. 113) against Indians by supplying them with smallpox-infected blankets. Nor are Jews loyal Americans, but spies and foreign agents who "openly defied the Revolution" (p. 116) of 1776. During the Civil War, "the Jews served in disproportionately large numbers and with distinction to maintain the slavocracy from which they had grown so wealthy" (p. 157).

All this and more is "revealed" by *Secret Relationship*, just as the *Protocols* purports to expose clandestine Jewish designs for world domination. The *Protocols* regards secrecy as a powerful weapon of the Jews—"invisibility" makes the Jewish plotters "invincible"—but *Secret Relationship* proclaims proudly that the Jews have now been found out; now at last, from "deep within the recesses of the Jewish historical record" (p. vii), the truth is brought forth. In the past two hundred years Jews have been blamed for causing the French Revolution, the Russian Revolution, both world wars, and the disintegration of the Soviet Union. Depending on their politics, detractors have accused Jews of being the architects of liberalism, capitalism, and communism. To this long list of bizarre accusations directed at Jews, *Secret Relationship* has added a new one: the Jew as the mastermind behind slavery. And to compound the lie, the compilers of *Secret Relationship* argue that Jews have kept this fact from being known. In an interview with the *Amsterdam News* (January 8, 1994), Farrakhan stated that Jews "have never admitted until recently that they were involved in the slave trade. They put it on the Gentiles. They put it on the Arabs, but they never came out publicly until we published that book and said that they were involved." The authors of *Secret Relationship* represent themselves as enlightened researchers who have courageously lifted this veil of deception and exposed how their ancestors were cruelly victimized by Jewish people.

But the book has provided absolutely nothing new—neither new information nor new insights into the four-century Atlantic slave economy. That Jews were both slave traders and slave owners is well known. Since 1915 there has been a steady line of Jewish-authored monographs dealing with the Jews and African slavery. The issue also has been discussed in general histories of the Jews and in Jewish encyclopedias. The involvement in slavery is a distasteful part of Jewish history that Jewish scholars have unflinchingly explored. In their search for understanding, they have produced responsible works of scholarship. *Secret Relationship*, in contrast, is written by people whose only intent is to defame Jews. Consequently, it misuses and distorts the historical record to give the impression that Jews were the principal wheel in the slave trade and the principal exploiters of black slave labor, two conclusions that students of the subject simply dismiss as preposterous. The important scholarly works on slavery barely mention Jews, not because there is a conspiracy of silence imposed on scholars by Jews, as *Secret Relationship* implies, but for the simple reason that in the four centuries of Atlantic slave trading and slave labor, Jews were merely bit players.

*Secret Relationship* totally lacks a historical perspective. What is the purpose of relentlessly mentioning the names of Jews who participated in the slave trade, who owned slaves and the number each possessed, or who fought for the Confederacy without at the same time comparing this data with the activities of non-Jews? If one did this, the obvious conclusions are that Jews accounted for a small fraction of the slaves imported from Africa to the New World, owned a minute fraction of the slaves in the United States, and made up a miniscule portion of the Confederate army. Some three to four thousand

Jews served in the Confederate Army, but twice as many served in the Union Army, a fact *Secret Relationship* does not mention. Why does *Secret Relationship* not mention that freed blacks in the United States, Brazil, and the Caribbean were engaged in the slave trade and utilized slave labor? While black slave masters were not very significant numerically in the overall picture, they dwarfed the number of Jews who either traded in slaves or profited by their labor. According to the 1830 census, black slave owners in the South outnumbered Jewish slave owners by 15 to 1 and owned far more slaves than did Jews. By simply discussing the activities of Jews involved with slavery without employing a comparative approach, *Secret Relationship* leaves the reader with the impression that wicked Jews were primarily responsible for enslaving and abusing Africans and profiting from their labor.

Similarly, failure to provide the reader with the historical background needed for an understanding of slavery in general and African slavery in particular leads to the same erroneous conclusion—that slavery was largely a Jewish enterprise. Readers of *Secret Relationship* are not made aware that the institution of slavery was a worldwide practice since the time of recorded history. The peoples of the ancient Near East—Egyptians, Mesopotamians, Assyrians, and Persians—and the classical civilizations of Greece and Rome took slavery for granted. It was also practiced in Asia, Africa, and by Amerindians in both North and South America. The word *slave* derives from *Slav*, eastern European Caucasians who, from the seventh through the tenth centuries, were carried off by Viking marauders to the insatiable slave markets of the Byzantine Empire and of Muslim Arab societies. Beginning in the seventh century, seven hundred years before the Portuguese descended on the African continent in search of slaves, and well into the twentieth century—long after Westerners sought to stamp out the slave trade—Muslim Arabs were relentlessly dragooning Africa of its manpower,[25] an irony lost on the authors of *Secret Relationship*.* And Africans rulers themselves played a decisive part in the whole

---

* Both the slave trade and slavery itself, particularly plantation slavery, were indefensible atrocities. Slavery seems always to have had its defenders, but some thinkers, inspired by the Enlightenment or Christian teachings, denounced it as a great evil. What is unique about Western civilization is not that it practiced slavery—what civilization did not?—but that some enlightened people raised a voice against it and eventually it was abolished. The abolition of slavery was a momentous stage in world history that was made possible by the Industrial Revolution. A society can afford the moral luxury of abolition when it has machines to take the place of slaves. It was no accident that Britain, the pioneer of industrialization, initiated the end of the slave trade and slavery in 1807, 1811, 1815, and 1833. It was the British navy that enforced the prohibition more and more widely in the nineteenth century, although it never managed to shut

sordid business, another uncomfortable fact not discussed at all in *Secret Relationship.* African rulers ordered the hunts and roundups and launched the wars
to obtain captives. So brutal was the 500-mile march from the interior to the
coast that as many as half the captives died en route. The fact is that Africa was
from time immemorial a slave-holding society and African economies relied
heavily on both slavery and the slave trade. Thus in 1807, when Britain abolished the slave trade, there were more slaves in Africa than in the New World
and a much higher percentage of the population was enslaved; for example, as
many as three-quarters of the people in Senegambia (located between the
Senegal and Gambia rivers on the west coast of Africa that was divided between Britain and France in the late nineteenth century) were slaves. Hence
the complaints of African rulers when Britain shut down the slave trade. "We
think that this trade must go on," stated one king. "That is the verdict of our
oracle and the priests. They say that your country, however great, can never
stop a trade ordained by God himself."\*[26]

Judaism, Christianity, and Islam did not have any compunctions about the
Atlantic slave trade. Muslim *jihads* (holy wars), proclaimed by the *ulema* (religious and legal authorities), sanctified centuries of Arab slave hunts in Africa.
Popes and bishops blessed the Portuguese slave expeditions to West Africa
from the start in the 1440s. The Church of England had plantations in the
Caribbean with hundreds of slaves branded with SOCIETY or SPCK, the ini-
tials of the Society for the Propagation of Christian Knowledge. Quakers,
good people, dynamic capitalists, and later stalwarts in the abolition movement, were very active in exploiting slave labor, as were members of other
Protestant denominations. The ancient Hebrews, like other peoples of the
Near East, practiced slavery, imposing it on their kin, "brothers," as well as
strangers "from the nations round about you." Judaism, however, was the first

---

down the island of Zanzibar as a great slave port and mart on the east coast of Africa
that catered to the Arab world. In 1962 Zanzibar began its independence with a massacre of Arabs by blacks, who might be said to have understood the history of slavery
and the slave trade better than did the authors of *Secret Relationship.*

\* Slavery and the slave trade persisted in Africa well into the twentieth century:
Ethiopia could not enter the League of Nations until it abolished slavery in the 1920s;
Guinea abolished slavery in 1955, Cameroons and Nigeria in the 1960s, and Maurita-
nia in 1980; in Sudan, where slave hunting is a sport, it persists until this day. Kevin
Bales, in *Disposable People: New Slavery in the Global Economy* (Berkeley: University of
California Press, 1999), as well as UN reports indicate that at the end of the twentieth
century 27 million were enslaved in the world, mostly in Africa, and much of this traffic is in children.

religion to require humane treatment of slaves who were also seen as children of God. Enslaved Hebrews were to be freed—"proclaim liberation in the land for all its inhabitants"—in the jubilee year, a cycle of 50 years (Leviticus 25:10, 39–55). Jewish law also stipulated that slave owners had an ethical obligation to their non-Jewish slaves who were to be regarded as members of the household. Maimonides, the great medieval Jewish sage, condemned slavery: "He who increases the number of his slaves increases sin and iniquity in the world."[27] Nevertheless, few Jewish voices were raised against the enslavement of Africans; like Christians, Muslims, and Africans, Jews, if they gave slavery any thought, simply accepted it as a natural condition. Jews, like the Catholic minority, played a minor role in the abolitionist movement in the United States, and the views of southern Jews on race and slavery differed little from other white southerners who regarded slavery as the natural condition of blacks. An insecure minority eager to be accepted as equals by the society in which they dwelled, southern Jews, like other southerners, did not challenge the slave system.

American Jewish religious leaders may be faulted for not being in the forefront of the struggle against slavery*—a failure shared by many Christian clergy—but Jewish people bear little responsibility as traders, financiers, or owners, for the enslavement of Africans. Moreover, in that age of mercantile capitalism, slavery was viewed as a normal and legitimate business venture. Except for some enlightened thinkers and compassionate Christians, people either gave no consideration to the brutality of the enterprise or they hid their eyes. To this extent, the moral failing of Jews was no different from that of Christians and certainly no worse than that of Africans, who organized the slave hunts and sold their captives to Europeans. The Jews who did participate in the Atlantic slave trade—and, we shall see, the percentage was minute— were unexceptional; that is why historians of slavery have largely ignored them. Only a malicious intent leads the compilers of *Secret Relationship* to single them out and exaggerate their role.

---

* And yet as Saul S. Friedman observes: "It would be simple to marshal the names of a legion of Jews who actively opposed the institution of slavery." Then Friedman, relying on the work of Morris U. Schappes, the pioneer compiler of primary sources for the history of the Jews in the United States, lists numerous Jews who were members of abolitionist societies or vigorously denounced slavery. Saul S. Friedman, *Jews and the American Slave Trade* (New Brunswick, NJ: Transaction Publishers, 1998), 211–14. Over 10,000 Jews served in the Civil War armies, 6 to 7 percent of a population of about 150,000, two-thirds of whom were immigrants; over 6,000 Jews served in the Union army, many of them enlistees, and 7 received the Congressional Medal of Honor.

Starting in the 1440s, Portuguese Catholics pioneered in the African slave trade. The Portuguese procured slaves to toil on the new plantations they had established on islands off the African coast. (The mass enslavement of Native Americans was first carried out by Spanish Catholics.) So lucrative and economically necessary was slave labor that Portugal was soon followed by Spain, the Netherlands, France and Britain, and later Prussia, Sweden, and Denmark. In the early years of the slave trade, few Jews in Western Europe were able to participate in it. Jews had been expelled from England in 1290, from France in the fourteenth century, and substantial numbers from Italy and the Germanies in the fifteenth century. By the mid-fourteenth century, the Jews of the Netherlands had essentially disappeared, victims of the persecutions in the wake of the Black Plague; the few who remained were expelled by Philip II of Spain by 1570. Many displaced Jews found refuge in Poland, Lithuania, Ukraine, and the Ottoman territories in the Balkans, lands that had virtually nothing to do with the Atlantic slave trade. The surviving Jewish communities scattered about western and central Europe—ghettoized, threadbare, and subject to all types of restrictions—were in no position to get involved in the nefarious slave business.

This brings us to the "New Christians" (or *conversos* or Marranos)—descendants of Spanish and Portuguese Jews who were forced, frightened, or persuaded to convert to Catholicism in the century from 1391. The situation for Spanish Jews who had previously resisted the pressures to convert grew desperate in 1492, when they were presented with the choice of conversion or expulsion. In 1497, five years after the mass expulsion from Spain, some seventy thousand Jews—many of them refugees from Spain—were forcibly baptized in Portugal. Some of the Spanish and Portuguese Jews who converted remained secret Jews, although it is impossible to say what percentage; others, especially by the second and third generation, had become faithful Catholics. The Spanish and Portuguese Inquisitions closely scrutinized New Christians to make certain that they were not "secret Jews." Even those New Christians who had totally embraced Catholicism lived in fear of zealous inquisitors who were quick to submit suspected reprobates to hideous tortures to wrest confessions that led to the confiscation of property and death by burning. Moreover, "Old Christians"—those who were not "tainted by Jewish blood"—scorned the recent converts and the state imposed legal inferiority, segregation, and occupational restrictions on them, which lasted in Portugal until 1774, some twelve generations after their forebears' forced conversion. Seeking to distance themselves from the Inquisition and to find economic opportunities where the stain of their Jewish ancestry would be less of a hindrance, many

Portuguese New Christians fled to Portugal's colonies, where commercial enterprises, including the slave trade and slave plantation agriculture, beckoned.
Thus in the sixteenth to the eighteenth centuries, several hundred Portuguese
New Christians, like other merchants seeking profit, engaged in the slave
trade and were active in the development of sugar plantations in Brazil that
depended on slave labor.

In 1630 the Dutch West India Company seized parts of Brazil from Portugal. During the brief period of Dutch rule, from 1630 to 1654, New Christians were permitted to revert back to Judaism, and some did, and Jews from
other lands were permitted to settle in Brazil. (Neither Portugal nor Spain
permitted self-professing Jews to settle in their colonies.) After the Portuguese
regained control of the territory, the Jews, about 650 in number, fled, some
going to the Dutch colony at New Amsterdam, which became New York in
1664; others settled on Caribbean islands where they brought with them skills
in managing tropical plantations. The Portuguese Inquisition in Brazil hunted
down lapsed New Christians, some of whom were sent back to Lisbon to face
execution.

During the brief period of Dutch rule, when Jews were tolerated, some
30,000 slaves were imported from Africa; Jewish involvement in this traffic
consisted primarily of buying slaves at auctions and selling them to the owners
of sugar plantations. As middlemen, Jewish settlers were actively involved in
the slave trade for the brief time that they dwelled in Brazil. But the number of
slaves they bought and resold to planters constitutes only a pittance when
measured against the huge number of slaves imported into Brazil over three
centuries. The great bulk of Africans, over 3 million, were brought to Brazil in
the eighteenth and nineteenth centuries when there was virtually no Jewish
presence in either Portugal or Brazil. During this period the trade was controlled by Old Christians and descendants of New Christians. There is little
doubt that in the ten and more generations that had passed since the initial
conversions, virtually all of these people had become totally Catholic, with no
ties at all to Jewish rituals or laws, much less to Jewish communities. No one
considers them Jews except the authors of *Secret Relationship*, who, more stringent than the Nazis in reckoning Jewish descent, have adopted the peculiar
racist formula that if someone had a Jewish ancestor three hundred years ago,
that person was still Jewish, even though he or she identified fully with Christianity, neither maintained nor sought links to Jewish law or rituals, knew no
Jews—there were none in Portugal in the nineteenth century and only a handful of recent immigrants from eastern Europe in Brazil by the late nineteenth
century—and most likely shared a Catholic bias toward them.

Many of the Jews who were expelled by or fled from Spain and Portugal found refuge in the Netherlands, and some prospered. The Dutch West India Company, whose original board of directors consisted largely of Calvinists, was heavily involved in the Atlantic slave trade. Jews did invest in the company but had no role in policymaking, for they never served as directors. Jews constituted anywhere from 4 to 10 percent of the investors, depending on the year. The number of Jewish shareholders in a given year probably did not exceed eleven, less than 1 percent of the Jewish population of Amsterdam, and their total investment amounted to a mere 0.5 percent (one two-hundredth) of the company's capital.

Jews were actively involved in slavery on the Dutch-ruled island of Curaçao off the coast of Venezuela, but not nearly to the extent claimed by *Secret Relationship*. Jews, who may have constituted 50 percent of the island's population according to a government survey conducted in 1764, owned 15 percent of the island's 5,534 slaves; in the next few decades the percentage declined considerably. Moreover, the few thousand Jews on Curaçao, and in Suriname in Dutch Guiana where Jews also owned slave plantations, held only an infinitesimal amount of the 10 to 12, or possibly 15, million slaves imported into the New World.

At the zenith of the trade in the eighteenth century, when slavery was a big business dominated by England, France, and Holland, the Jewish presence was minimal. No Jews could be traced in Europe's leading slave trade centers—Liverpool and Bristol in Britain, Nantes in France, and Middelburg in the Netherlands.

The authors of *Secret Relationship* designate Jews as principal architects of black bondage in the United States. "In the North before 1800 and in the South all through the colonial period, slaves were stocked as commodities by Jewish merchants. Countless thousands of Africans were brought here in colonial times by Jewish merchant-shippers and in the South, Jews began to enter the planter class in substantial numbers" (pp. 89–90). In the nineteenth century, "Jews were masters of the slave trade" (p. 192). It is the compilers' malicious intent that produces such a grotesque mishandling of the data and such preposterous conclusions. In the United States, as in Britain, France, and Holland, the Jewish role in the slave trade was peripheral. The rise of slavery in the United States, the events leading up to the Civil War, and the conflict itself would have been quite unaffected had no Jews settled in the American colonies

Given the handful of Jews dwelling in America at the time, it is impossible for Jews to have been a major power in the American slave system, as *Secret Re-*

*lationship* declares.* According to the census of 1820, there were between 2,650 and 2,750 Jews in the United States, making up 0.03 percent of the total population, and most lived in the North. The overwhelming majority of slaves in the South toiled on large plantations, almost none of which were owned by Jews. *Secret Relationship* says that Jews entered the planter class "in substantial numbers," but the truth is that a Jewish plantation owner was a distinct oddity. In 1830, of the 59,000 Southerners who owned twenty or more slaves, a mere 23 were Jews. Jews, who lived predominately in urban areas in the South, employed slaves as domestic help. Since the number of southern Jews was extremely small—much less than 1 percent of the population—and the need for domestic help limited, Jews by necessity owned only a minute fraction of the enslaved blacks.

Nor were Jews prominent in the slave trade. Of the 400 slave merchants in South Carolina, only 1 minor trader was a Jew. In Richmond, Virginia, 3 of 70 slave brokers were Jews. No Jewish slave traders operated in Kentucky or Mississippi. Rabbi Bertram Korn, who was intimately familiar with the sources and remains a standard authority, concluded that "probably all of the Jewish slave traders in all of the Southern cities and towns combined did not buy and sell as many slaves as did the firm of Franklin and Armfield, the largest Negro traders in the South."[28]

In the North, Jewish participation in slavery was also minuscule. Jewish merchants were accountable for 113 of the 4,004 slaves who entered the port of New York between 1715 and 1765 (or 2.5 percent). The center of the American slave traffic was Newport, Rhode Island; between 1709 and 1807, Newport merchants brought back 106,594 African slaves. All the leading participants in the trade, with one exception, were Christians. Aaron Lopez, the principal Jewish slave trader—actually most of his wealth came from other cargoes—is described by *Secret Relationship* as a major player in the Atlantic slave trade. In actuality, he dispatched 14 vessels that returned with 1,165 slaves, a mere 1 percent of the total imported. The D'Wolf family (called De-Wolf in *Secret Relationship*), perhaps Rhode Island's most prominent slave dealers, is wrongly identified as Jewish in *Secret Relationship*. For several generations the family had belonged to an Episcopalian parish. Between 1709

---

* Much of the statistical data in this section come from Harold Brackman, *Ministry of Lies: The Truth Behind the Nation of Islam's* The Secret Relationship Between Blacks and Jews (New York: Four Walls Eight Windows, 1994), and two recent and well-researched books: Eli Faber, *Jews, Slaves, and the Slave Trade: Setting the Record Straight* (New York: New York University Press, 1998) and Friedman, *Jews and the American Slave Trade*.

and 1808, when the United States abolished the slave trade, Jewish merchants,
sometimes in partnership with Christians, participated in 34 slave trading ventures of the 929 known voyages organized from Newport, hardly a sign of
domination.

In *Jews and the American Slave Trade*, Saul S. Friedman tellingly explodes
the libel that Jews were a major factor in the slave trade:

> There were 697,681 slaves in America in 1790, 1,538,022 slaves in 1820. Ac-
> cording to official census records, Jews owned 209 slaves in 1790, 701 in
> 1820. During the formative years of the United States . . . when the import
> and sale of Africans was at its peak *Jews owned less than three-one hundredths of a*
> *percent, 0.03 percent of all the slaves in America.*
>
> Only a handful of Jews . . . figured prominently in the transport of slaves
> across the Atlantic and even their participation is relatively small. Actual
> British government shipping records show that Jewish owners accounted for
> less than 2 percent of all slaves imported into . . . North America in the eigh-
> teenth century. . . . [N]one of the 200 illegal slavers operating off the coast of
> Cuba after slavery was declared illegal in 1808 were Jews. . . . Jews played no
> role in the import of more than one million African slaves to Brazil in the
> nineteenth century. At no time were Jews among the major slave holders,
> planters, magnates, or traders in what was to become the United States. . . .
> According to public records, only one Jew . . . ever served as an overseer on a
> plantation.[29]

Over the four centuries of the Atlantic slave trade, Jews accounted for less
than 2 percent of the 600,000 Africans brought to the United States and considerably less than 1 percent of the about 10 million slaves who went to other
areas of the New World. In a review of Eli Faber's *Jews, Slaves, and the Slave
Trade* published in *The American Historical Review* (June 2000), David Eltis tells
us that a recently published database contains the "names of 31,260 individual
owners of transatlantic slave ventures. Eighty-four of these names are linked
to fifty or more voyages and only one of this 'elite group' has any possible Jewish connection." David Brion Davis, America's leading authority on the institution of slavery, comments on Jewish involvement: "It is easy enough to point
to a few Jewish slave traders in Amsterdam, Bordeaux, or Newport. But far
from indicating that Jews constituted a major force behind the exploitation of
Africa, inquiry shows that these merchants were highly exceptional, far outnumbered by Catholics and Protestants who flocked to share the great bo-
nanza. . . . [H]istory would have been the same with or without Jewish slave
traders and planters."[30]

In addition to accusing Jews of playing a major role in black bondage, *Secret Relationship* also pronounces them guilty for inventing the ideology that justified enslavement of blacks. The Talmud, says *Secret Relationship*, is responsible for "the misinterpretation of the Old Testament which offered the holy justification for oppression [i.e., enslavement] on purely racial grounds" (p. 203). In the Genesis account, Noah's son Ham sees his father, who had had too much wine, asleep naked in his tent. When Noah awoke and realized what his son had done, he pronounced a curse of slavery on Ham's son Canaan and his descendants. *Secret Relationship* makes the assertion that in the rabbinic interpretation of the story of Noah's curse, slavery is fused with blackness. Several people since the 1960s have stated that antiblack racism in Western civilization and the justification of black slavery have their origin in ancient rabbinical texts that are central to the Talmud. Since the accusers are unfamiliar with the languages, literature, and history essential to the study of Jewish antiquity, they depend on secondary works; they copy each other, each embellishing the argument with righteous anger, as we see in Tony Martin's caustic and sweeping rendition (to be discussed below).

The indictment relies on five references in the Talmud in which blackness is seen as divine punishment for disobedience. One text reads: "You prevented me [says Noah to Ham] from doing that which is done in the dark [the sexual act], therefore may your progeny be black and ugly."[31] Of the five texts cited, two are by later medieval travelers who speak for their individual selves. At least one and probably two of the texts may have been mistakenly interpreted to deal with blackness or slavery. The one or two texts that link blackness with slavery are paralleled by similar sentiments found in contemporary or earlier non-Jewish—Christian and Samaritan—sources. These lines are so fragmented that they cannot be said to express any rabbinic or talmudic view of blacks. They constitute .0006 percent of the 2.5 million words of the Talmud, and they are attributed to 2 persons among some 1,500 whose views are reported in the Talmud. Moreover, characteristically, the Talmud does not present an official position. Rather, it reads Rabbi A said . . . ; but then Rabbi B said; and Rabbi C said; although Rabbi D said. No decision is reached; it is left to readers to formulate their own conclusions.

According to one of these five texts in the Talmud, Ham, for disobeying God in the Ark, "was punished in his skin," which came to mean that he turned dark-skinned or black. This curse was not linked to race-based slavery and was never interpreted to mean God-given racial inferiority, for in the rabbis' tale black kings have white slaves. Seeking to justify Joshua's conquest of the land of Canaan, the rabbis assigned the status of slave to the Canaanites, who were light-skinned. No curse of slavery was placed on the innocent black descendants of Cush, Canaan's brother, said to be the forebears of Ethiopians and other blacks. For the rabbis there was no "curse of Ham" that linked slavery with black people.

It is true that in their few references to black or dark-skinned peoples, the rabbis expressed a preference for the light-skinned—their own coloring; this preference is consistent with what social scientists call the "somatic norm preference," meaning that we favor what is peculiar to ourselves. But the rabbis engaged in no systematic denigration of black people, and there are passages, such as the following, that stress a common humanity of all people: "In the messianic age, he who is light skinned will take hold of the hand of him who is dark and arm in arm they will walk together."[32]

How did the Genesis text become a justification for racism in Western civilization? Not from these scant and esoteric folk legends in the Talmud, which led nowhere: Neither the rabbis who compiled the Talmud nor latter-day Jewish thinkers constructed a systematic racial ideology that identified blackness with slavery. The "curse" of Ham or "Hamitic" myth—that is, the fusion of the curse of blackness with the curse of slavery—originated in an operational way in the seventh century, when it was fashioned by Muslims to justify Islam's practice of conducting slave raids in Africa. One oft-used word in Arabic for black is *ahd*, which means "slave." Once European Christians engaged in the slave trade starting in the fifteenth century, they adopted Islam's theological justification for slavery. "The curse of Ham is, indeed, an idea that has spawned devastating consequences in history," observes David M. Goldenberg. "It is not, however, found in Judaism."[33] And it will not do to pluck a few scattered quotations out of context from ancient Jewish sources—most of them fables and yarns, not philosophical-theological tracts—to blame modern racial prejudices on Jews. The reductio ad absurdum of this process is the declaration of Tony Martin, professor of African studies at Wellesley, that the Hamitic myth was the concoction of "talmudic scholars" that "provided the moral pretext upon which the entire [slave] trade grew and flourished; [it] killed many millions more [Africans] than all the anti-Jewish pogroms and holocausts in Europe."[34] This charge, responds David H. Aaron, is an example of one of those "nefarious formulations in the ideologically charged marketplace of ideas, a marketplace in which the loudest, most provocative voices often earn high dividends on the basis of their aggression rather than their accuracy."[*35]

---

* The same observation about "ideologically charged" ideas applies to versions of Afrocentrism that proclaim, among other things, that: Africa is the source of Western

Like the writings of Holocaust deniers, *The Secret Relationship Between Blacks and Jews* aims to foment hatred of Jews. It deliberately and maliciously repeats antisemitic slurs hurled against Jews over the centuries, leaving the uninitiated reader to conclude that these charges are true, that Jews indeed are predisposed to do evil. But also like the works of the deniers, *Secret Relationship* has been scorned and shunned by professional historians. The American Historical Association, whose membership consists of thousands of historians, including many with distinguished reputations, saw fit to condemn it. In January 1995 it enacted the following resolution: "The AHA deplores any misuse of history that distorts the historical record to demonize or demean a particular racial, ethnic, or cultural group. The association therefore condemns as false any statement that Jews played a disproportionate role in the exploitation of slave labor or in the Atlantic slave trade."[36] Perhaps the most insightful indictment of the book comes from Eugene D. Genovese, a recognized authority on the history of slavery in the United States: "*The Secret Relationship Between Blacks and Jews* rivals *The Protocols of the Learned Elders of Zion* in fantasy and gross distortion. The absurdity of its pretensions to scholarship are outweighed by its sheer viciousness. It must be taken with deadly seriousness as a transparent attempt to foment antisemitism, irrationality, and hatred, and to subvert intellectual discourse and common decency on our campuses."[37] Ultimately, the book's value is not to students of slavery and the slave trade but to scholars who study the history of antisemitism. As with other works of this genre, historians will analyze the motivation of the authors and try to explain why antisemitic beliefs that have no objective validity continue to appeal.

Nevertheless, the work continues to appeal to some black professors who view history through the prism of black militancy and to naive young black students who are receptive to Jewish conspiracy tales taught by their elders. No one now denies that the enslavement of Africans was a monstrous crime and an unforgettable tragedy; nor do students of the subject question that some Jews, who bought, traded, and exploited black Africans in the New

---

civilization; the ancient Egyptians were black as was Cleopatra; classical Greek culture derived from Egypt; Aristotle plagiarized from Egyptian thinkers; ancient Africans had invented the glider, the refracting telescope, the wet-cell battery, and semiconductors; and the Hebrews derived their monotheism from the Egyptian pharaoh Akhenaten. See Mary R. Lefkowitz and Guy Maclean Rogers, eds., *Black Athena Revisited* (Chapel Hill: University of North Carolina Press, 1996); Mary R. Lefkowitz, *Not Out of Africa: How Afrocentrism Became an Excuse to Teach Myth as History* (New York: Basic Books, 1996); and Stephen Howe, *Afrocentrism: Mythical Pasts and Imagined Homes* (New York: Verso, 1998).

World, contributed to the crime and the tragedy. But their pain should not lead blacks to engage in gutter antisemitism under the pretense of scholarship by singling out Jews as chief perpetrators of African bondage, that is, to distort the historical record and to create still another conspiratorial myth that demonizes Jews as a people. About one point the historical record is unambiguous: What has distinguished Jews from other white Americans is not their part in the dreadful business of slavery, which was both marginal and unexceptional, but their substantial overrepresentation in the civil rights movement. In any inquiry into black-Jewish relations, this is an appropriate beginning.

## SCAPEGOATING JEWS IS NOT THE ANSWER

In November 1998 the Anti-Defamation League published a study showing that antisemitism had declined significantly in America in recent years. Fewer Americans adhere to traditional stereotypes about Jews—that they wield too much power, control Wall Street, and are dishonest in business, and the like. In 1964, 29 percent of the adults surveyed fell into the category "most anti-Semitic"; in 1992, the figure had fallen to 20 percent. In 1999, only 12 percent of the adults surveyed, most of them poorly educated and comparatively older, could be classified as hardcore antisemites. While hatred of Jews among blacks had declined somewhat, they were nearly four times as likely as whites—34 percent to 9 percent—to fall into the group designated as "most anti-Semitic." Michael Meyers, executive director of the New York Civil Rights Coalition and himself African American, expressed his chagrin with the findings: "I myself find the level of anti-Semitism among blacks, both at the grass roots and among the professions, to be so pervasive as to be appalling, shocking, and deafening."[38] It is also self-defeating, as Hubert Locke remarked: "[T]he current battles being waged between the two communities are ideological luxuries neither can afford."[39]

Apparently the antisemitic ranting of the likes of Louis Farrakhan, Khallid Muhammad, Tony Martin, and Leonard Jeffries, Jr., cannot be dismissed as mere rhetoric; rather their endorsement and propagation of anti-Jewish myths have affected the thinking of a significant number of black people. Tony Martin came under attack at Wellesley for assigning *Secret Relationship* in class and defending it as legitimate history. In the preface to *The Jewish Onslaught Dispatches from the Wellesley Battlefield*, which vigorously defends the scholarship of *Secret Relationship*, Martin thanks numerous black intellectuals and many of his students, present and past, for supporting him in the "onslaught against me." No doubt many of his supporters are also spreading the same hateful message under the guise of scholarship and the quest for truth, for as Martin tells us, "his students who have studied *The Secret Relationship Between Blacks and Jews* for two semesters now have found nothing wrong with it."[40] In June 2002 Professor Martin spoke on "the Jewish role in the trans-Atlantic slave trade" at a conference organized by the Institute for Historical Review, the center for Holocaust denial, an entirely appropriate audience for his level of scholarship; he was joined by deniers and white supremacists that included Robert Countess, Robert Faurisson, and Mark Weber, all of whom, like Martin himself, had been rejected as unqualified and unreliable by the Human Rights Tribunal in Toronto. (See Appendix II.)

It is indeed tragic that African Americans, who have been the chief victims of racist hate and myths in the United States, should be noticeable participants, both as progenitors and receptive audiences, in a deliberate campaign to denigrate the Jewish people. And it is ironic that Louis Farrakhan, Muhammad Khallid, and other bigots who disparage European civilization have embraced one of the worst features of that civilization—Jew-hatred, particularly the myth of the evil conspiratorial Jew. Thus Nation of Islam bookstores sell *The Protocols of the Elders of Zion*, that infamous forgery about a cabal of Jews conspiring to take over the world. At Farrakhan appearances, vendors have sold this book and other antisemitic works, including *The Hoax of the Twentieth Century*, written by a leading Holocaust denier; *The International Jew* by Henry Ford; and *The Jews and Their Lies* by Martin Luther. Nation of Islam bookstores have also sold Steven Cokely's tapes about a world government controlled by Jews and Jewish doctors injecting black children with the AIDS virus. (Cokely is one of the people thanked by Martin.) Farrakhan, who defended Cokely in speeches, is very much attracted to conspiracy theories. He sees Monica Lewinsky as a Zionist agent trying to derail the Middle East peace process and spins a tale of secret meetings in Park Avenue mansions of rich and powerful Jews where evil plots are hatched. And, to the myth of the conspirator Jew, the Nation of Islam has added another: the Jew as the real power behind the slave trade. No doubt *The Secret Relationship Between Blacks and Jews* and lectures by bigoted black professors have led many blacks to believe and propagate this myth. "When I think about Jews," declared a City College student, "I'm constantly reminded of the fact that they funded a large amount of the slave trade. That's not anti-Semitism, it's just the historic truth."[41]

It is significant that *Secret Relationship*, which Henry Louis Gates, Jr., chairperson of the Afro-American Studies Department at Harvard University, calls "the Bible of the new anti-Semitism,"[42] is sold by the Institute of Historical Review, the leading Holocaust denial organization. The same neo-Nazi group offers for sale Tony Martin's companion piece, *The Jewish Onslaught*. Rightist antisemitic hate groups have employed the Nation of Islam's "research." Thus Matt Hale, head of the World Church of the Creator, which gained notoriety in 1999 when a member wounded six orthodox Jews near a synagogue in Chicago and killed a Philippine American postal worker, declares: "European Whites did not bring the slaves to America. On the contrary, it was the Asiatic Jews who brought them here (as Louis Fahrakhan [*sic*] has also pointed out)."[43]

And what should we think of black students who invited Khallid Muhammad to their campus to insult Jews and engage in rapturous chants every time he did so? Did they really believe that they would be enlightened by a bigot who refers to Jews as "so-called Jews," for, to him, contemporary Jews had no relationship to the people of ancient Israel who were really black Africans? Was Khallid saying that these "so-called Jews"—whose ancestors were murdered by the tens of thousands in mass burnings and by hate-filled mobs during the Middle Ages and early modern times; again by the tens of thousands at the hands of rampaging Cossacks in the seventeenth century and nationalist Ukrainians during the Russian civil war in the twentieth century; and by the millions in Hitler's gas chambers and execution pits—that these people, many of them still faithful to the Law of Moses, are not supposed to feel Jewish or identify with Jewish history? What insights into current social problems did these African American college students expect to derive from a hustler who venomously demeaned gays, feminists, and Pope John Paul II, saw Nazi persecution of Jews as a response to Jewish wrongdoing, and mocked Holocaust survivors? "There is no evidence, no proof that 6 million so-called Jews lost their lives in Nazi Germany," he told a cheering, applauding, and laughing audience at San Francisco State University on May 21, 1997. What perspective on their own tortured history did they anticipate learning at the feet of an intellectual buffoon and second-rate actor whose handling of facts was about as deft as a tone-deaf violinist playing Mozart? For example, to diminish the enormity of the 6 million Jews murdered in the Holocaust, Khallid, juxtaposing numbers for effect like a songwriter using June and moon, referred to the 600 million(!) African victims of the slave trade. Professional scholars who have studied all available records have concluded that some 10 to 12 million blacks crossed the Atlantic between the sixteenth and nineteenth centuries, about 600,000 of whom came to the Thirteen Colonies and later the United States. What the audience got from Khallid was vicious rhetoric, rehearsed posturing, lies, and half truths—the standard litany of demagogues seeking to captivate an audience. Khallid clearly exemplifies Gates' astute observation that "the newer black anti-Semitism is being whipped up by black demagogues in search of power."[44] It is a pity that the cheering black students did not recognize the obvious.

In recent years Farrakhan, to improve his image with mainstream black organizations, has shown signs of retreating from his antisemitism. In 1993 he performed Mendelssohn on the violin, which some saw as a deliberate act of reconciliation. And lately he has even praised Jews. He told Gates, who interviewed him for an article published in *The New Yorker* in the spring of 1996: "Jewish people are the world leaders, in my opinion. They are some of the most brilliant people on the planet. The Jews are some of the greatest scientists, the greatest thinkers, the greatest writers, the greatest theologians, the greatest in music, the greatest in business. And people hate them sometimes because of envy, and because the Jews succeed in spite of the hatred of their Gentile brethren, or anybody else's hatred. I admire that, as God is my witness."[45] It has been suggested that Farrakhan is in somewhat of a bind: He is reluctant to antagonize the growing number of young militants in his organization who favor a strong anti-Zionist and antisemitic stance. Moreover, such a position is endorsed by the Libyan dictator, who, in the past, has given the Nation of Islam considerable financial support.

At the end of 1999, after recovering from life-threatening prostate cancer, Louis Farrakhan, declaring that he was a changed man, apologized for his previous injurious remarks against others and pledged to "spend the rest of my days to uplift a fallen humanity, regardless of their color, their race, or their creed."[46] Several commentators hoped that Farrakhan was undergoing a sincere transformation, that he was abandoning his paranoid conspiracy theories and his bigotry and going mainstream. By advocating fasting during Ramadan and praying on Fridays, it also appeared that he was moving Nation of Islam members toward mainstream Islam. In support of this view was the attendance at the Nation's annual Saviors' Day convention in February 2000 of Wallace Deed Mohammed, Elijah Muhammad's son, and Sayyid Syeed, the head of the Islamic Society of North America, which has more than 4 million members.

At the convention, Farrakhan tried to dispel the charge of antisemitism, which is a principal obstacle to his acceptance as a mainstream leader. He had flown in from Brooklyn and Jerusalem several rabbis from the ultraorthodox Neturei Karta sect, who apologized for the "nerve of the Zionist leaders who attack the honorable Minister Farrakhan. All those who have called you an anti-Semite, let them be ashamed. . . . All those who say they are Jews who speak ill of Mr. Farrakhan are not Jews."[47] This was, of course, a transparent

ploy. The sect, which decries Zionism and denounces Israel as an "abomina-
tion of God," is totally unrepresentative of the Jewish people. If Farrakhan
sincerely wants to mend fences with the Jewish people, let him unequivocally
repudiate both his previous scurrilous antisemitic remarks and the *Secret Relationship*. Indeed, let the Nation invite serious scholars of slavery to comment
on the *Secret Relationship* and then publish their essays.

Years from now when scholars are assessing Louis Farrakhan's place in
American history, they may very well conclude that his principal significance
lay not in assuming the leadership of the Nation of Islam, whose membership
continues to remain minuscule; or in promoting black economic independence, for the performance of Nation enterprises has been dismal; or in spon-
soring the Million Man March, a spectacular event with no noticeable
long-term effects. Rather, future scholars might conclude that his enduring
legacy consists of raising the level of antisemitism among black people by circulating antique myths and creating new ones. And they might well point to
*The Secret Relationship Between Blacks and Jews* as one of the most influential antisemitic tracts of the twentieth century, sharing the pantheon of hate and
delusion with the *Protocols of the Learned Elders of Zion*, the *International Jew*,
*Mein Kampf, Der Stürmer, The Turner Diaries*, and "The Leuchter Report." To
this extent, Farrakhan will be linked to American Holocaust deniers, the Aryan
Nation, and other contemporary extremist groups that delight in inflicting
pain on Jews and deliberately propagate lies to do so. Minister Farrakhan, who
is very much concerned with his image, should ponder this possibility.

Nevertheless, we should conclude on a hopeful note. Despite the ugly
rhetoric and venomous myths circulated by the Nation of Islam and Khallid
Muhammad, its former national spokesman, we must not exaggerate the menace. Farrakhan and other vociferous antisemites gain much more attention in
the media than their reach or influence in black communities warrants. Black
Americans are not flocking en masse to either the Nation or the New Black
Panther party, and black and Jewish organizations across the country are
working in concert to reduce friction between the two groups and continue to
work harmoniously on issues of common concern. Mainstream black organizations do not share the Nation of Islam's views on Jews, and several prominent black spokespersons and national leaders, including Jesse Jackson, Julian
Bond, Coretta Scott King, and Cornel West and Henry Louis Gates, Jr., two
leading black academics, have forcefully condemned black antisemitism.[48] It is
a hopeful sign that Khallid's efforts to organize a "Million Youth March" in
Harlem for September 1999 were met with condemnations and calls for a boycott by several New York African American political leaders. Although some of

them had supported his march the previous year, they were now disgusted by Khallid's vicious attacks on white "devils" and Jewish "bloodsuckers," the threat of violence (the police had a confrontation with the marchers the previous year), and the "divisiveness" the march would produce in multiethnic New York City. "Enough is enough," declared Assemblyman Keith L. T. Wright of Harlem. "I cannot abide by Khallid Muhammad's evil message," stated State Comptroller H. Carl McCall. And Representative Charles B. Rangel, Harlem's most powerful political figure, urged his constituents to boycott the event. Councilman Bill Perkins, an outspoken critic of Khallid Muhammad, was harassed by his followers who pulled on his arm and screamed: "We are going to kill Uncle Toms like you." In a *New York Times* op-ed piece entitled "Endless Poison," columnist Bob Herbert vented his anger against Khallid Muhammad and

> his act—a low-budget street-corner version of the Farrakhan road show. . . .
>
> Are we tired of this yet? Have we had our fill? The reason this sort of thing continues to erupt in places like Harlem is that so many black leaders have refused for so long to unequivocally oppose the racists, anti-Semites, and the perpetrators of violence within the black community.
>
> Almost always there were excuses and rationalizations. Denunciations of anti-Semitic outbursts by Mr. Farrakhan and Mr. Muhammad, for example, were frequently accompanied by expressions of support for the "positive" aspects of their message.
>
> There is no positive aspect. . . . This should never have been a tough call. I don't remember too many black people looking for the constructive side of George Wallace or David Duke.[49]

The march turned out to be a nonevent, attracting about a thousand people, considerably fewer than the six thousand who had attended the previous year. In his speech, Khallid repeated his antisemitic rhetoric, but perhaps the most noteworthy development of the day was the frequent appeals for donations by the organizers of the event, who repeatedly passed buckets and bags throughout the crowd.

Despite the growing number of black Americans classified as "most antiSemitic," white Americans, often identified with extremist groups, are responsible for the overwhelming number of hate crimes committed against Jews, including in 1999 the torching of three Jewish synagogues in Sacramento, the shooting of Orthodox Jews in Chicago by a follower of Matt Hale, and the attack on a Jewish Community Center in Los Angeles by a neo-Nazi that left two adults and three children wounded. But as long as the Nation of Islam, whose head is now a nationally recognized "black leader," continues to circulate literature and tapes containing the same vile caricatures and myths employed historically by Jew-haters, black demagogues continue to vilify Jews before cheering audiences, particularly on college campuses, and black professors teach a libelous history that makes Jews a principal oppressor of blacks both in the past and the present, Jews at all levels will be reluctant to embrace causes endorsed by blacks. Although renewing the alliance between blacks and Jews that had contributed to the success of the civil rights movement is now largely a dead issue, Jews still provide more support than other groups for blacks running for office and for social programs that blacks favor.

Furthermore, more and more blacks will themselves become victims of these manufactured lies, for the hate aroused in the black community against Jews by self-aggrandizing demagogues and ill-informed and malicious instructors will benefit blacks in the same manner that it has proven a boon to the deluded souls who belong to American neo-Nazi movements. A peculiar street game is being played. Many enraged and frustrated black Americans delight in the anguished responses of Jews, who after all are white, to the inflammatory remarks made by militant blacks. And they admire the "brothers" for standing up to public pressure. But this form of catharsis is self-defeating: Maligning others is ultimately an immature avenue to self-respect, and recycling old myths about Jews and their conspiracies will, if the past is a model, only subvert rational thinking and inflame the worst elements of human nature, adding more impediments to the struggle against the poverty and social pathology that afflict many urban black communities. These problems have nothing to do with Jews, and bashing them, however emotionally gratifying it may feel to do so, solves nothing.

A principal lesson that the history of slavery and racism in America teaches is that myths are dangerous weapons—that people are prone to believe the most absurd theories about others who are different and to act on these beliefs in ways that are destructive to civilized values. The noblest lesson that black Americans might derive from their tragic past is that history has imposed on them a special responsibility to promote tolerance and goodwill by pointing out the terrible consequences stemming from myths that vilify and demonize whole groups of people. Crude antisemitism constitutes a sad betrayal of the high ideals and heroic efforts of the numerous black people who fought for a more just America. The best antidote for the antisemitic poison spewed by Farrakhan, Khallid, and others is simply for mainstream black organizations and responsible black spokespersons, faithful to their historic struggle and mission, to denounce unequivocally the message and to urge African Americans to shun the messengers. On their part, American Jews must continue to demonstrate that they are resolute supporters of social justice and equality, that the hurtful slurs hurled on them by a few black Jew-haters will not cause them to sever their commitment to these values. In this way they, too, will remain true to the best of their heritage.

# CONCLUSION

THE TWO-THOUSAND-YEAR HISTORY OF JEW-HATRED shows with agonizing clarity that the most dangerous myths are those that demonize and dehumanize a whole people, characterizing them as the evil and dangerous Other. Following are two examples of Nazi demonological myths. The first, written in 1936, is from Julius Streicher's *Der Stürmer;* the second is from a speech delivered by Joseph Goebbels at the Nuremberg party rally in 1937.

> The mobilization of the German people's will to destroy the bacillus lodged in its body is a declaration of war on all Jews throughout the world. . . . Those who vanquish the world-Jew will save the earth from the Devil.

> Look, there is the world's enemy, the destroyer of civilizations, the parasite among the peoples, the son of Chaos, the incarnation of evil, the ferment of decomposition, the demon who brings about the degeneration of mankind.[1]

These fabricated myths, which transformed the Jew into something less than human and the source of evil, proved to be more than malicious rhetoric: They were instrumental in creating an attitude of mind that fostered and justified every conceivable cruelty, including the starving, gassing, burning, shooting, and bludgeoning to death of little children. And just as medieval Christian crusaders massacred Jews, the enemies and killers of Christ, believing that they were honoring their Lord, so those Germans, and their collaborators from several lands, who rounded up, tortured, and murdered Jews also believed that they were serving a higher cause—the good of their nation and European civilization.

The demonization of the Jews did not originate with the Nazis but with Christian theology. In this book we have treated the archetypal myth of the Jews as Christ killers and a criminal people and some of its many offshoots and transformations: the Antichrist, the Wandering Jew, the Talmud Jew, ritual murderers, host desecrators, poisoners, cosmic conspirators in the service of

Satan plotting to destroy Christendom, and the Shylock monster of greed and economic exploitation. And we have dealt with two newly manufactured myths—the Holocaust is a Jewish invention and Jews dominated the slave trade—that drew their sustenance from centuries-old attempts to demonize the Jew. During the Middle Ages Christian myths about Jews shaped a mentality fraught with misconceptions and seething with hate that caused Jews to endure forcible ghettoization and impoverishment, forced conversion, persistent humiliation and persecution, and periodic massacres. It is true, of course, that Nazi racial theories were pseudoscientific, neopagan myths that emerged in a post-Christian age permeated by extreme nationalism. Although Nazism was fundamentally anti-Christian, Germans (and people in other countries) still affected by antique Christian myths that demonized the Jewish people were unlikely to recognize the dangers inherent in Nazi racial ideology at the time when Hitler was still struggling to gain power or in the early years of the Third Reich. And it is undeniable that the Jew-hatred expressed in these denigrating Christian myths prepared the mind to accept, if not embrace, Nazi myths about the Jews and to participate in or be indifferent to genocide. The Nazis' characterization of the Jews as evil subhumans found receptive listeners among people whose inherited folk memory viewed Jews as evil children of Satan and whose clergy often still propagated this myth.

Biological racism, rather than Christian anti-Judaism, determined the Nazis' extermination policy.* Yet the perpetrators often took special glee in destroying synagogues, burning holy books and scrolls, and singling out Orthodox Jews for humiliation; at times the local population in Nazi-occupied lands of eastern Europe, where Christian antisemitism fused with nationalist passions, participated in these assaults. During World War II a Polish physician recorded in his diary the murder of Jews by his fellow Poles and noted how the dehumanization of the Jews had affected his countrymen. In the entry dated November 26, 1942, he wrote that a "psychosis took hold of them and they emulate the Germans in that they don't see a human being in Jews, only some pernicious animal, which has to be destroyed by all means, like dogs sick with rabies, or rats."[2] Doubtless greed for Jewish possessions, a desire to ingratiate themselves with the German invaders who encouraged the murder of Jews by the local population, a grossly exaggerated identification of Jews with the recently departed and still-hated Soviet occupiers of eastern Poland, and nationalist sentiments that viewed Jews as inassimilable aliens prompted genocidal

---

* Modern racism, however, finds a precedent in the persecution of the Marranos of Spain and Portugal.

actions by some Poles.*³ Nevertheless, it is highly likely that the medieval
Christian myths of Christ killers, ritual murders, and sons of Satan, still very
alive in Catholic Poland, induced these Polish peasants and villagers to slaughter their Jewish neighbors. A survivor who observed the Poles in his village of

---

\* The story of Jewish-Polish relations during World War II is a very complex historical
issue. Both were victims of German oppression, for 3 million Polish Christians in addition to 3 million Polish Jews were murdered, a fifth of Poland's prewar population. In
1991 the bishops of Poland issued a pastoral letter, a historic milestone in Polish-Jewish
relations, that invokes a "commonality" of suffering at the hands of the Germans that
ought to bring Jews and Poles together. Yet Polish Christians also victimized Polish
Jews. They turned Jews over to the Germans for rewards, extorted money from them in
order not to inform on them, and murdered Jews, including Jewish partisans fighting
the Nazis and escapees from the ghettos and death camps. There are numerous accounts of Poles expressing agreement with the German extermination policy, which
they saw as a solution to their own Jewish problem and "a necessary evil" yet "the only
way to solve the problem." After the war, surviving Polish Jews surfaced from hiding,
made their way back home from the camps, and returned from Soviet Russia, where
they had fled or been deported. Fearing that these Jews would try to regain their property, then in the hands of Polish Christians, or opposed to the restoration of a Jewish
presence in Poland, Poles often made them unwelcome; they threatened and intimidated, murdered and set upon Jews in violent pogroms. It is estimated that in the first
year *after* the war, several hundred Jews were murdered by fellow Poles, most notoriously the pogrom inspired by ritual murder accusations at Kielce, and 100,000 fled.

But these sordid details are by no means the entire story. During the war, Polish
Christians organized *Zegota*, the underground Council for Aid to Jews, and at the risk
of their own lives Poles rescued Jews from the Nazis. It is estimated that 2 percent of
the Polish population helped Jews in one form or another, in the country where such
efforts were more difficult and more dangerous than anywhere else in German-occupied Europe. In Yad Vashem, the museum in Israel that is a memorial to the victims of
the Holocaust, trees have been planted along the Avenue of the Just to honor thousands
of righteous Polish gentiles.

*Neighbors: The Destruction of the Jewish Community in Jedwabne, Poland*, a book by
Jan T. Gross published in Poland in 2000 and in English a year later, has elicited
tremendous interest in Poland and is compelling Poles, as never before, to confront
their complicity in World War II atrocities committed against Jews. On July 11, 1941,
in the town of Jedwabne, the Polish Christian half of the population murdered the
Polish Jewish half. In an orgy of brutality, the Poles (whom the Germans did not permit to have guns) clubbed, stabbed, and drowned their Jewish neighbors and then
burned alive more than a thousand people, including children. After the war the Poles
built a monument that blamed the crime on the Germans, but *Neighbors*, on the basis
of survivors' and witnesses' accounts and trial records relates who actually did the
killing and how. The stir caused by the book has led to the (re)discovery of several
other incidents of the same murderous kind, although the extent to which Poles rather
than Germans initiated the atrocities at Jedwabne remains controversial since Gross
did not utilize the German archives. These revelations have induced some Polish
clergy and intellectuals to reexamine and reflect on their country's antisemitic past and

Radzilow forcing entire Jewish families out of their homes and beating them to death amid crowds of laughing Polish men, women, and children also speaks of the "propaganda . . . coming out from the upper echelons of Polish society which influenced the mob, stating that it was time to settle scores with those who had crucified Jesus Christ, with those who take Christian blood for matzoh and are a source of all evil in the world—the Jews. . . . It is time to cleanse Poland of these pests and bloodsuckers."[4]

The Holocaust, which left a permanent wound in the Jewish soul, also disturbed the Christian conscience. Increasingly Christian scholars and clergy have honestly confronted their churches' historical record with respect to the treatment of Jews and the connecting links between traditional Christian fulminations against Jews and Nazi antisemitism, and have labored to remove an anti-Jewish bias from Christian teachings. Jews and Christians engage in fruitful dialogues concerning the connecting strands between their faiths, including the Jewishness of Jesus and the ethical teachings and ceremonial practices that Christianity derived from Judaism. And in impressive displays of goodwill, Christian and Jewish clergy work together to combat intolerance. In particular, Christian schools have purged textbooks of passages distorting or denigrating Jews, and many other good works of a like kind.

Elites in Western lands have also learned from the Holocaust. Unlike before World War II, antisemitism is no longer respectable. Aware of the links between antisemitic demagoguery and extremist movements that threaten democratic society, influential people neither promulgate nor endorse antisemitism, and governments will not tolerate antisemitic violence. Admittedly, the antisemitic venom recently displayed by some of the European elite is an ominous sign, and there are, of course, far Right movements in every Western country that promote Jew-hatred.

In several eastern European countries, where historically antisemitism was vile and vicious, some political, intellectual, and religious leaders are making sincere efforts to come to terms with their nation's past and to resist a re-

---

to draw appropriate lessons that will strengthen young Polish democracy; others have reacted defensively, denouncing Gross for defaming his native Poland and lending himself to a New York–centered Jewish plot of "anti-Polonism." After an inquiry of nearly two years by Polish historians, however, Gross was vindicated: "[T]he role of Poles in this criminal act was decisive," according to their spokesman, Radoslaw Ignatiew; the German presence was important as a catalyst but the Polish role was "decisive"; at least 40 Poles participated in this "planned crime," but Gross' estimate of 1,600 dead is somewhat high. Steven Erlanger, "An Inquiry Confirms a Massacre of Jews by Poles in World War II," *New York Times*, July 10, 2002, A4.

birth of fascism, with which European antisemitism is strongly identified. In past generations, such figures had rarely attempted to rebut lethal antisemitic myths and often were in the forefront of those disseminating them or exploiting them as political weapons. The catastrophe inflicted on the Jews during the Nazi period has reversed this trend to a lesser or greater degree. Eastern European political and cultural elites are also aware that in the new Europe that is emerging with the decline of communism, the growth of neofascist parties with antisemitic agendas will arouse the ire of Western states whose friendship and support they need and are trying to cultivate.

Nevertheless, crude antisemitic myths and lies are still disseminated and believed, and desecration of Jewish cemeteries and vandalism of Jewish property still occur. A perennial problem stems from the ease with which the ordinary Christian believer can read or hear recited in church both the dramatic story of the crucifixion with its anti-Jewish bias and the anti-Jewish polemics that abound in the gospels. Taking these sacred texts literally, unaware of two centuries of scholarly qualification, reconstruction, emendation, and explanation, he or she comes away with a denigrating image of "the Jews." A recent example is that of two New York professional basketball players who participate with their teammates in a Bible-reading study group; for these young "theologians" nothing has changed: "[The Jews] spit in Jesus' face and hit him with their fists" and they "had his blood on their hands"; moreover, "[t]here are Christians getting persecuted by Jews every day." When queried, their explanation was that they only said "what happened biblically," the same response as a much more sophisticated public figure, who explained that in stating in his Easter message on the Web that Christ "was crucified by the Jews," he was "merely quoting Scripture."[5] Obviously the new theology and biblical interpretations formulated by Christian thinkers, which repudiate the deicide accusation as well as the intentions to convert Jews that had over the centuries inflicted so much suffering on the Jewish people, have not reached all the Bible readers or churchgoers in the pews.

There is also the problem of the Arab world aping Western antisemitic myths. Since the terrorist attacks of September 11, 2001, Islamist demagogic rhetoric has reproduced every element of historic Christian European antisemitism: The Jews constitute a secret conspiracy to conquer and dominate the world. Judaism is evil and requires Jews to harm non-Jews. The Talmud, among other nefarious commandments, requires them to commit ritual murder. By nature Jews are criminal and immoral. They are greedy for wealth and procure it by any means. They control the media and the economy—the banks, commerce, and they ruin their competitors, and are responsible for capitalism and/or communism. Jews are bent on subverting religion; they murdered Jesus and tried to poison Muhammad. They are inveterate traitors and cunning conspirators who destroyed the World Trade Center to stir up anti-Muslim sentiments. Not surprisingly, as the liberal Muslim theologian Khalid Durán deploringly remarked, "the 'Common Man' in the Muslim world is mostly fearful and suspicious of Jews."[6] These suspicions, fears, and hatreds are exacerbated by Islamist clerics, who see Muslims engaged in a "struggle for existence between Koran and Talmud" and teach "Jihadism" and martyrdom. Of late Arab/Muslim pronouncements on the Jews are increasingly genocidal, as when the Syrian defense minister said he kills any Jew he sees and that when all Arabs do the same, the "problem" will be "solved." In April 2002, a columnist for the Egyptian government daily, *Al-Akhbar,* wrote these chilling words: "Thus the Jews are accursed, the Jews of our time, those who preceded them and those who will come after them, if any Jews come after them. With regard to the fraud of the Holocaust . . . I, personally, complain to Hitler, from the bottom of my heart, 'If only you had done it, brother, if only it had really happened, so that the world could sigh in relief [without] the Jews' evil and sin.'"[7] In a bizarre twist, Islamist rhetoric has fused the United States, Europe, Christianity, and the Jews into one monstrous entity and calls for, in Osama bin Laden's words, a "Global Islamic Front to Fight Jews and Crusaders."[8]

Given the lethal history of the myth of deicide and the other myths we have examined, antisemitic delusions must not be dismissed as harmless residues of the past. Christians are particularly behooved to repudiate them and shun those deluded and wicked souls who propagate them and scholars are obliged to analyze them and to point out their logical absurdity and historical danger not only to Jews but to civilized values. It is with this conviction that we have written this book. Otherwise we shall never be free of the kind of irrational fixation reported by Victor Klemperer in his diary for June 11, 1940: "Today I heard: A [German] woman comes to see her wounded husband in the military hospital here [in Dresden]; on entering the room she sees a completely mutilated person, an ear, one half of the face, an arm have been torn off. She starts screaming and doesn't stop: 'It's the Jews' fault! It's the Jews' fault!' [To which Klemperer responded prophetically:] They really will put us [Jews] up against the wall yet."[9]

# JEWISH-MUSLIM
# RELATIONS IN HISTORY

JEWS PROSPERED IN THE ENORMOUS ARAB EMPIRE, participated in its "commercial revolution," and were transformed by the "bourgeois revolution," that socioeconomic transformation by which they ceased being what they always had been, a fundamentally rural people of farmers and craftsmen, and earned their livelihood as urbanites in commerce and finance as well as crafts. The huge Geniza collection of documents from 700 to 1100—found in Fustat, Old Cairo, Egypt at the end of the nineteenth century—shows that the mass of the Jewish population was involved in trade, the characteristic unit being small, the family firm or partnerships, and that they had plenty of competition from Greeks, Armenians, Syrians, and others, that these very small commercial fry operated on a shoestring of capital but with much support by coreligionists in the Diaspora. Jews were also artisans. No less than 265 crafts have been identified as being practiced by Jews, which is a suggestive index of how extensive Jewish participation in crafts and industry was and how advanced and specialized industry was in the Islamic world; the Geniza material indicates an astonishing total of about 450 professions and callings among Jews. That material also dispels the long-dominant "idea that banking during the Middle Ages consisted mainly of money lending and that the Jews were the Rothschilds of the Islamic world."[1] This myth owed much to the French scholar Louis Massignon, who unfortunately followed Werner Sombart in concluding that "the prohibition of usury caused the trade in money to be monopolized in the Muslim world, first by Christians, then by the Jews."[2] In contrast to medieval Christianity, Islam was very accepting of commerce and the merchant; after all, Muhammad was a merchant.

The heyday of the Jews in Islam was 800 to 1250, when a "near equality" prevailed in those spheres that were not specifically religious, notably economic activity, the area in which Jewish integration into host societies was always the most advanced. There followed many centuries of deterioration, economic decline, and military defeats, marked by the Mongols' destruction of the great Arab Empire and the capture of the caliph who was unceremoniously hanged in Baghdad in 1258. (The Mongols were the first on the list of external factors blamed for Arab-Islamic weakness and failure: Turks, Western imperialists, Jews/Israel, Americans, and so on.) The successor states were far less tolerant of the Jews than the caliphs in what had been an expanding economy and dynamic society for several centuries. The exception to prolonged decline was the rise of the Ottoman Empire, the greatest Muslim state in history, in which Jews flourished so long as the empire flourished, to about 1700; the Ottomans were more tolerant from the start and Jews enjoyed greater acceptance there until today, as was observed in the 1992 commemoration of the 500-year presence of Jews since their expulsion from Spain in 1492. The highly centralized Ottoman government promoted economic growth in the form of mercantilist policies. The economy was an example of state capitalism tempered by much local and provincial initiative on the part of governors and private entrepreneurs. In such an environment Jews could and did flourish. Some of them were great merchants, financiers, and government officials, but most were small traders and shopkeepers, peddlers, and artisans.

Jewish-Muslim relations are a complex story. While there is an antisemitic infrastructure extant in Islam, it is clear that Jews were much better off under Islam than in Christendom. There were polemics, intolerance, persecutions, and massacres, but far less than in Christendom. References to Jews in the Koran are mostly negative: "Wretchedness and baseness were stamped upon them, and they were visited with wrath from Allah. That was because they disbelieved in Allah's revelations and slew the prophets wrongfully"; "And for their taking usury which was prohibited for them, and because of their consuming people's wealth under false pretense, We have prepared for the unbelievers among them a painful punishment." The Koran requires their "abasement and poverty"; abasement took the form of the poll tax and the humiliating ceremony in which it was paid; in his "wrath" God has "cursed" the Jews and will turn them into apes/monkeys and swine and idol worshippers because they are "infidels."[3] The *Hadith* (tradition, law, legend) is even more scathing in attacking the Jews: They are debased, cursed, anathematized forever by God and so can never repent and be forgiven; they are cheats and traitors; defiant and stubborn; they killed the prophets; they are liars who falsify scripture and take bribes; as infidels they are ritually unclean, a foul odor emanating from them—such is the image of the Jew in classical Islam, degraded and malevolent. Yet, ordinarily, "the Jews" could not be said to have "killed" Muhammad, who was neither a Jew nor a god. There is no accusation of deicide (in fact, Sura 4:157 of the Koran, referring to the Jews and Jesus, says "they killed him not"), no appropriation of the Jewish Bible as an Islamic sacred text, and "virtuous Hebrews" is not translated into "virtuous Muslims" in contrast to the "stiff-necked, criminal Jews." Rather, Jews (and Christians) had the status of *dhimmis* (people of the covenant or protected minority). Developed in the later eighth century, the dhimmi code was intended to degrade and humiliate individuals as well as the religious community. Its laws specified that dhimmis had to pay heavier taxes; had to wear clothes and insignia distinguishing them from Muslims; were barred from holding public office, bearing arms, riding a horse or mule, intermarriage with Muslims; were disqualified as witnesses in litigation involving Muslims and had to swear a demeaning oath; could not erect new or repair old synagogues or proselytize. Later additions to the code included prohibitions on adopting Arab names, studying the Koran, selling alcoholic beverages, and so on. Thus Muslim antipathy for Jews has been a much more normal form of antagonism of one people, or one religion, for another than the Christian-Jewish encounter has been. The dhimmi system bestowed freedom of worship and protection of life and property in return for taxes, particularly the poll tax, or *jizya;* it followed Muhammad's formulation that infidels were to be fought "until they pay the *jizya* out of hand, and have been humbled." Dhimmi discrimination was often merely theory, and de facto toleration usually prevailed. Nevertheless, this battery of legislation was a perpetual potential menace to the dhimmis—a danger that materialized whenever a revolutionary or pious reactionary came to power. "Dhimmitude" was invoked very often down to our times, as by Egyptian president Anwar el-Sadat in 1972 before his journey to Jerusalem, when he urged the necessity of defeating Israel "so that they go back to be once again as our Book told us: 'Humiliation is destined for them, and poverty.'"[4]

The dhimmi system and Jewish status in Islamic society have been subjected to very varied judgments, from the more traditional "golden age" school to revisionists' "persecution and pogrom" interpretation. The traditional school follows the "pro-Islamic Jews," who were pioneering and empathetic historians of Islam, especially of the Arab and Ottoman periods, among whom were the German Moritz Steinschneider (1816–1917), the Hungarian Ignaz Goldziher (1850–1921), and several others. In response to Christian persecutions, from the Crusades on, which victimized Jews and Muslims alike, these scholars propounded the myth of a golden age or several great ages—notably Muslim Spain—when Jews prospered in economic freedom and presumably enjoyed equality and acceptance virtually undisturbed by persecution or discrimination; these pioneering scholars ignored the historical record of pervasive humiliation, discrimination, and periodic violence in a kind of solidarity with fellow "Semites" in the face of Christian hostility. The myth, says Bernard Lewis, was fashioned by Jews "as a reproach to Christians" and is now taken up by Muslims—invoking putative golden ages—"as a reproach to Jews."[5] According to Arab Muslim claims, frequently reiterated since 1948, Jews always enjoyed equality and social harmony under Islam: Muslims were "merciful brothers who regarded the Jews as fellow believers and did not allow religious differences to affect their treatment or attitude toward them." It was only with the twentieth century, in this view, that anti-Jewish feelings mounted in response to Zionism, ending the age-old idyllic pattern of fraternity and tolerance and prosperity. Such a romanticized interpretation serves as an Arab-Islamist weapon in what is primarily an ideological and political struggle against Israel. Fundamentalists also argue that under the yoke of the dhimmi system, Muslim-Jewish relations were good because Jews were held in check and Muslims were thus "protected" from them; the demise of the system under colonial rule and, worse, the coming of the state of Israel meant that Jews became "dangerous" to Muslims and Islam.

Such idealization of the past ignores a catalog of lesser-known hatred and massacres. Hostile attitudes manifested in the ninth century resulted in persecution and outbreaks of violence that took a heavy toll. Antisemitic propaganda of the tenth and eleventh centuries made Jews out to be untrustworthy, treacherous oppressors, and exploiters of Muslims, which inspired outbreaks of violence and caused many casualties in Egypt. Maimonides lamented that "a more hating nation [than Ishmael] has never risen against Israel, nor one which has come to degrade us and decimate us and make hating us their chief desire."[6] In Muslim Spain there were violent outbreaks in Cordoba in 1011 and Granada in 1066, because (some) Jews were wealthy and others, as viziers and the like, exercised authority over Muslims—that is, they "oppressed" Muslims. Muslim Spain exhibits as much ghetto as golden age. A Moorish poem of the eleventh century dubs the Jews a criminal people and complains that society is nearing collapse on account of Jewish wealth and domination, their exploitation and betrayal of Muslims; that Jews worship the devil, physicians poison their patients, and Jews poison food and water as required by Judaism, and so on; to Avraham Grossman, it is "one of the most poisonous poems ever penned against the Jews, and contains most of the antisemitic charges made against them in medieval and modern Christian Europe."[7] According to Menasseh ben Israel (1604–1657) a distinguished Dutch rabbi of Portuguese Marrano descent, "Our captivity under the Moslems is far more burdensome and grievous than under the Christians."[8] In every century there are travelers' reports like the observations of Edward William Lane, a British resident in Egypt in the 1820s to 1830s, that the Jews are "held in the utmost contempt and abhorrence by Muslims in general."[9] Arab antisemitic writings date from the decades following the 1840 Damascus blood libel, when antisemitism was introduced by Europeans and funneled into the Middle East by Arab Christians. It was "Islamized" by 1900 by reference to the Koran and early Muslim literature; the motif of the Jewish conspiracy stemmed from the *Protocols* and, equally important, August Rohling's *Talmud Jew*, which was translated into Arabic in 1899. Although there were periods when Jews enjoyed security, prosperity, and friendship with Muslims, their status was one of legal inequality and social inferiority, hedged about by humiliation and contempt, institutionalized, religiously ordained, and utterly routine. In the modern era the great majority of Jews in the Muslim world were abjectly poor.

On these themes, see the exchange between Mark R. Cohen, "The Neo-Lachrymose Conception of Jewish-Arab History" and Norman A. Stillman, "Myth, Countermyth, and Distortion" in *Tikkun* 6, 3 (1991): 55–64; Khalid Durán, with Abdelwahab Hechiche, *Children of Abraham* (New York: American Jewish Committee; Hoboken, NJ: KTAV, 2001); Bernard Lewis, *The Jews of Islam* (Princeton, NJ: Princeton University Press, 1984), idem, *What Went Wrong? Western Impact and Middle Eastern Response* (New York: Oxford University Press, 2002), and idem, "The Revolt of Islam," *The New Yorker* (Nov. 19, 2001): 51–63; S. D. Goitein, *Jews and Arabs: Their Contact Through the Ages* (New York: Schocken, 1955); Yehoshafat Harkabi, "On Arab Antisemitism Once More," *Antisemitism Through the Ages*, ed. Shmuel Almog (New York: Pergamon, 1988); Norman A. Stillman, *The Jews in Arab Lands: A History and Source Book* (Philadelphia: Jewish Publication Society, 1979) and *The Jews of Arab Lands in Modern Times* (Philadelphia: Jewish Publication Society, 1991). A work of great insight is Ronald L. Nettler, *Past Trials and Tribulations: A Muslim Fundamentalist's View of the Jews* (Oxford: Pergamon Press, 1987), a study of the Egyptian Sayyid Qutb (1906–1966), which includes a translation of his essay that greatly influenced Islamists, "Our Struggle with the Jews."

# CANADA'S ATTEMPTS TO CURB ERNST ZÜNDEL'S ANTISEMITIC ACTIONS AS A PUBLIC DANGER

WHILE WORKING ON THIS VOLUME, FREDERICK SCHWEITZER was asked to testify before the Canadian Human Rights Tribunal in Toronto in a case involving Ernst Zündel, a notorious neo-Nazi and Holocaust denier. In his testimony Dr. Schweitzer utilized ideas and data he and his coauthor, Marvin Perry, had assembled for this book. The following excerpts are from the decision of the Canadian Human Rights Tribunal, January 18, 2002, against Zündel, the respondent, which barred him from the Internet. The action was brought against him by the Canadian Human Rights Commission, the complainant, and other interested parties in "a hearing on the merits." The hearing—before a tribunal of three, then two members, with no jury—ran fifty-five contentious days but was spun out over the years 1996 to 2001, largely because Zündel's counsel sought to quash the proceedings by a medley of objections and motions to terminate the proceedings. Although he never spoke or took the witness stand, Zündel was invariably present at the sessions until February 2001, when he apparently gave up and left Canada—which had repeatedly denied him citizenship as a security risk—for the United States, where, married to an American citizen, he enjoys legal residence and freely disseminates hate literature. Nevertheless, the tribunal's decision, a judgment formulated by a public body following judicial procedures, places a stigma on him, as it does on those "experts," as notorious as he, summoned to testify on his behalf, all of whom were rejected by the tribunal: Robert Countess, Robert Faurisson, Tony Martin, and Mark Weber (who was the only one allowed to testify but solely for his knowledge of the way Holocaust deniers operate; he was rejected "as a historian"). We assisted counsel for the Human Rights Commission by preparing memoranda evaluating the credentials and "Anticipated Evidence" of the four deniers. Later, in June

2002, Tony Martin, who is black and a professor of African studies at Wellesley College, rejoined these deniers and white racists at a conference of the Institute for Historical Review, the main center of Holocaust denial in the United States, to accuse Jews of being the principal authors of the Atlantic slave trade.

One can only surmise why Zündel is so brutish an antisemite, for it is hard to imagine that he believes the fantasies he broadcasts; much more likely is that he relishes the notoriety, sadistic pleasure in inflicting pain and suffering on people, and making lots of money as a Holocaust entrepreneur and denial huckster. Reputedly Zündel the media mogul was/is the largest distributor of antisemitic and Holocaust denial propaganda in the world—books, pamphlets, newsletters, tapes, videos, his own and those of others. As a person, Zündel is repugnant and oafish; although not unintelligent he is at best half educated; he is of secular cast of mind rather than religious, certainly not Christian. Some find him to be "charismatic"; if so, none of it emerged in a court chamber.

Zündel was born in Germany in 1939, immigrated to Canada in 1958, and settled in Toronto in the 1960s, where he ran a successful photo-retouching business for magazines, a career for which he had been trained in Germany.[1] He emerged as the self-styled "führer" of the "Concerned Parents of German Descent" and cowrote *The Hitler We Loved and Why*. That book portrays Hitler as "this humble, totally dedicated savior" who had "the vision to create a happy and sound society," meaning *Judenrein* (no Jews, literally, Jew-clean or purified of Jews). Since Hitler "saved White civilization," Zündel's idolization of the führer closes with "WE LOVE YOU, ADOLPH [sic] HITLER." As he pursued his antisemitic course, Zündel held protests and demonstrations against the TV series "Holocaust," the film *The Boys from Brazil* that depicted Joseph Mengele and featured a clone of Hitler, and the life imprisonment of Hitler's one-time deputy Rudolf Hess. For a time this P. T. Barnum promoter took up UFO's, which he represents as Hitler's "secret weapon," saying that Nazi German research has been going on since the 1930s and is still being conducted underground. Zündel's proclamation of his belief in flying saucers is on a par with his proclamation of his disbelief in the mass murders of the Holocaust; he began in an appropriate business, retouching photographs, a kind of distortion and falsification that may have opened the door to Holocaust denial and, indeed, systematic falsification and deception.

As early as 1981 Zündel was subjected to a mail ban that lasted for a year. He founded the "German-Jewish Historical Commission," another instance of his posturing and fakery. The same applies to his choice of name for his publishing business, Samisdat. He was behind the prank—as nasty as it was juvenile—of Ernst Nielsen, a Zündel surrogate and unreconstructed Nazi, who first audited and the next term registered for the Holocaust course given by Michael Marrus and Jacques Kornberg at the University of Toronto; the intention, in addition to a sophomoric publicity stunt, was to disrupt the class and protest to the university administration that the course did not include "revisionist" works and was "nothing but hate literature." It ended with Nielsen's expulsion, twice, but not before Zündel's pseudonymous publications appeared in an attempt to make a national issue of the case.

By the early 1980s Zündel's violent antisemitism, Holocaust denial, and Nazi activities were out in the open and attempts to prosecute him began. The survivor Sabina Citron and the Holocaust Remembrance Association took the initiative in a private suit, but after some hesitation the case was taken up by public authority. In 1985 Zündel was tried in criminal court for knowingly spreading "false news" that was likely to do harm to a recognizable group of people, specifically for Zündel's dissemination of that denialist chestnut, *Did Six Million Really Die?* by Richard Harwood. Always the exhibitionist, Zündel showed up wearing a bulletproof vest and other outlandish garb (at a later proceeding he sported a yarmulke). Zündel himself testified and the prosecution showed, or attempted to show, that Zündel did not believe his own antisemitic propaganda but used it maliciously to justify his Nazi ideology and rehabilitation of Hitler. His counsel, Douglas Christie, is a veteran defender of Canada's antisemites, such as the teacher James Keegstra, and an unsuccessful politician. Christie is coarse and brutal in cross-examination, especially of Holocaust survivors. He ludicrously garbles witnesses' names, mocks them in every conceivable way, and tries to trap them in seeming inconsistencies or falsities. Christie used these devices on Raul Hilberg—who had to establish the truth of the Holocaust, since the court did not accept it as a given—with regard to casualty statistics, and Christie, in his sensationalism and caustic provocation, may have undermined the effectiveness of the historian's testimony, as he did that of some survivors. Nevertheless, the jury found Zündel guilty of spreading "false news" and he was sentenced to fifteen months in jail.

Pending appeal, Zündel was free on bail. In 1987 the Appeals Court found that the law making "false news" punishable was constitutional, but it granted a retrial on grounds of irregularities by the judge. The second trial in 1988 was a reprise of the first. This time, however, no survivors testified and Christopher Browning served as the leading historical expert for the prosecution. David Irving made his debut as a denier and witness for Zündel. Again Zündel was found guilty and sentenced to nine months imprisonment. In 1990 the Appeals Court upheld the decision, the sentence, and the constitutionality of the "false news" law. In 1992, however, the Canadian Supreme Court overturned Zündel's conviction on the grounds that the "false news" law was too vague and therefore unconstitutional.

Zündel was jubilant and celebrated his victory for "free speech." No doubt, his egomania and exhibitionism were, if possible, further inflated. On a trip to Germany his antics in Munich got him arrested for inciting race-hatred and other offences. Not surprisingly, he carried on more than ever putting forth his antisemitic hatred and fabricated denial trash, such as this on Kristallnacht: The Jews did it—"Mysterious people wearing SS uniforms suddenly appeared out of nowhere [in November 1938], set fire to the synagogues and just as suddenly and mysteriously vanished. The same tactics as the Zionists [a term he often employs to avoid the legal category of 'a recognizable group'] used against Germany as partisans, maquis and as members of the Jewish Brigade: false uniforms, false documents, etc." Mrs. Citron decided to try again.

The longest section of the decision addresses the constitutional issue of free speech. Under the rubric of "hate messages," the Canadian Human Rights Act specifies in Section 13(1) (cited herein as s. 13(1) of the act), that "It is a discriminatory practice for a person or a group of persons acting in concert to communicate telephonically or to cause to be so communicated, repeatedly, in whole or in part, . . . any matter that is likely to expose a person or persons to hatred or contempt by reason of the fact that that person or those persons are identifiable on the basis of a prohibited ground of discrimination." The tribunal had to reconcile its judgment that Zündel did so expose Jews to hatred and contempt with Canada's Charter of Rights and Freedoms, by which everyone enjoys "freedom of thought, belief, opinion and expression, including freedom of the press and other media of communication," subject only to "reasonable limits prescribed by law as can be demonstrably justified in a free and democratic society." Noting that hate mail does double damage, to the "listener" and to the party attacked, and that preventing "serious harms caused by hate propaganda remains a matter of pressing and substantial importance," the tribunal justified its infringement of Zündel's freedom as "minimal impairment." Canada's guarantees of freedom of speech are almost as fundamental as in the U.S. Constitution, but Canada is much more aware that, as the tribunal stated, "There are indeed limits to freedom of expression . . . that hate propaganda presents a serious threat to society," and requires preventive action. What impact the Canadian precedent may have here or there remains to be seen. The paragraph numbers in brackets are the same as in the original.

[120]   . . . The following examples of the commentary communicated via the Zundelsite were taken from a number of different messages authored by Mr. Zündel:

   a)    To claim that World War II was fought by the Germans, as the Holocaust Promotion Lobby incessantly claims, just to kill off the Jews as a group, is a deliberately planned, systematic deception amounting to financial, political, emotional and spiritual extortion. The "Holocaust." first propagandized as a tragedy, has over time deteriorated into a racket cloaked in the tenets of a new temporal religion. . . .

   d)    The fact is that the Jewish Lobby—or the Israeli Lobby, as some like to call it—have long had a deliberate policy of lying to non-Jewish Americans. They lied to us about Hitler and about National Socialist Germany, because they wanted America to go to war with Hitler to destroy this threat to their schemes. They have lied to us about their own role in setting up the Communist conspiracy, which spread out of London and New York to Russia and from there to other countries until it engulfed half the earth and consumed tens of millions of human lives. And they have lied to us about a great number of other things, too—including their most infamous lie and the most lucrative and crooked scheme: the so-called "Holocaust."

   e)    There is always that last straw that breaks the camel's back!

        I predict that once again the tribe's near-total victory will end in near-global disaster for them. In the affairs of men, and in nature, NOTHING LASTS FOREVER.

   f)    Until now, the "Holocaust" story and their stranglehold on the media in many parts of the world have made them immune, so far, from exposure—but now their defenses are crumbling, for every day brings to light more misdeeds, more con games, more insider trading, more lies and more cheating—and more crimes against the Germans, the Palestinians, the Lebanese, the Iraqis, and the hapless Russians during their Bolshevik reign of terror and destruction there.

        The day of global reckoning is dawning. The Jewish Century is drawing to a close. The Age of Truth is waiting to be ushered in, we will be its ushers. . . .

[121]   The Commission called two expert witnesses, Professors Prideaux and Schweitzer, to support their submission that this material was likely to expose Jews to hatred or contempt. In both cases the witnesses examined the documents found on the Zundelsite and analysed them from the perspective of their particular area of expertise. . . .

[122]    Professor Gary Prideaux [of Alberta University] testified as an expert in the field of discourse analysis, a sub set of linguistics. In this discipline, written and oral texts are examined in order to identify the methods employed by the initiator and the recipient of the communication for processing and comprehending language. A specific text is interpreted, or given meaning, through the use of established linguistic principles of general application, and specific strategies used to shade the meaning of otherwise neutral references. An understanding of these general principles and rhetorical strategies allows for the interpretation of text, and a determination of the likely impact of the communication.

[123]    Dr. Prideaux outlined a number of specific ways in which meaning permeates an intended message and allows the recipients to make sense of what they have heard or read:

a)    Specific techniques, such as generalization or the use of scare quotes, can inject an additional layer of content beyond the obvious;

b)    The choice of vocabulary can reflect the author's view of a particular group or event;

c)    The use of repetition may enhance the credibility of the author or persuade the audience of the veracity of a particular fact or assertion;

d)    A particular group may be singled out or targeted;

e)    Coding and the use of metaphor can establish a series of negative associations and interchangeable references or associations;

f)    Inversion strategies where commonly held views are inverted, so that for example the traditional victim becomes the aggressor and the aggressor the victim;

g)    Metonymy or extreme generalization ascribing negative characteristics to a broad range of behaviour or group of individuals based on an individual action or example.

[124]    Based on these and other established principles of discourse analysis, Dr. Prideaux analysed the structure, content and likely effect of the documents found on the Zundelsite, and concluded that, in his opinion, they were likely to expose Jews to hatred and contempt. The documents revealed a repeated pattern of singling out Jews, and ascribing extremely negative characteristics to them as a group and as individuals. This witness provided numerous examples where different rhetorical strategies were employed to characterize Jews in a distinctly derogatory manner.

[125]    A common strategy identified by this expert was the manner in which questions were raised regarding the existence or extent of the Holocaust. Three quasi scholarly articles included in the materials, "Jewish Soap," "66 Questions and Answers," and "Did Six Million Really Die," were treated by Dr. Prideaux as "framing documents" that provided a context and frame of reference for many of the other documents found on the site. In these texts, the authors led the reader to question all aspects of the Holocaust by raising doubts about some. The subtle message is that the "Holocaust" itself is questionable, and in Professor Prideaux's view, the impact of raising these doubts would, at a minimum, be to vastly diminish the horror of these events.

[126]    Dr. Prideaux described these texts as "unabashedly polemical," where the authors used lurid and inflammatory terms that would not typically appear in conventional scholarship. There were no specific citations or

references for factual, or historical references, and assertions were made that went beyond the logical extension of the material relied upon. Nonetheless, the academic tone of these documents lends an air of legitimacy to these documents and informs the context in which subsequent messages are communicated.

[127]   Dr. Prideaux further testified to other specific examples in the texts found on the Zundelsite that would expose Jews to hatred or contempt:

    a.   The use of epithets such as the "Jewish," "Holocaust," "Zionist" or "Marxist" Lobby;

    b.   The constant use of scare quotes to express doubts in regard to the "Holocaust" or "survivors";

    c.   Unsubstantiated assertions of Jewish control and influence;

    d.   Inversion strategies where those widely understood as the victims in Nazi Germany become the aggressors, and the aggressors become the victims;

    e.   Ascribing, or implying, negative attributes to all Jews upon reference to a single individual who it is asserted possesses those characteristics. . . .

[129]   Professor Frederick Schweitzer, an historian at Manhattan College in New York City, was called as an expert in the field of anti-Semitism and Jewish-Christian relations. Dr. Schweitzer provided an historical overview of the themes in classical anti-Semitism, and testified to the history of violence against Jews and the relationship of these violent episodes to specific periods of historical anti-Semitism.

[130]   Dr. Schweitzer discussed the many themes, and variations on themes, of anti-Semitism dating back to medieval times up to the modern period. Certain central motifs have appeared, and reappeared in more contemporary forms, which expressed very specific stereotypes:

    a)   the deicidal Jew, the murderer of Christ;

    b)   the Talmudic Jew, obligated by religion to harm, cheat, lie, and trick non Jews;

    c)   the criminal Jew;

    d)   the world domination Jew;

    e)   the Holocaust Jew.

[131]   When Dr. Schweitzer examined the documents found on the Zundelsite, he concluded that they were "virulently anti-Semitic," reflecting many of the classical anti-Semitic motifs found throughout history. Specifically, the Tribunal was referred to the following examples taken from the Zundelsite material:

    a)   Jews are denounced as criminals, thugs, gangsters and racketeers;

    b)   Jews are repeatedly described as liars who have fabricated the biggest lie of all, the "Holocaust," in order to extort reparations and promote their personal interests;

    c)   Jews have, and seek, a disproportionate degree of power and control in the media and government;

    d)   Jews are responsible for the humiliation of the Germans;

    e)   Jews are parasites and pose a menace to the civilised world.

[132]   Telephonic communication of hate messages is proscribed under the Act as a discriminatory practise if there is repeated communication of "any

matter that is likely to expose a person or persons to hatred or contempt by reason of the fact that that person or those persons are identifiable on the basis of a prohibited ground of discrimination."

[133]   We have already concluded that there has been repeated telephonic communication. The issue now under consideration is whether the material communicated is "likely to expose" a person or group to hatred or contempt. The cases in which this section has been considered, and the plain language used in s. 13(1), make it clear that it need not be established that hatred or contempt will be, or has been aroused by the communication at issue. It must only be established on a balance of probabilities that a person or a group is likely to be exposed to these extreme emotions of hostility.

[134]   For our purposes, it is sufficient if the communications at issue create conditions that allow hatred to flourish, leaving the identifiable group open or vulnerable to extreme ill will and hostility. We must determine whether members of a group are placed at risk of being hated, or being held in contempt by virtue of the messages communicated by the Respondent. . . .

[137]   We begin our analysis with a review of the material found on the Zundelsite, and the intertwining themes of its messages. The over arching theme found in these materials is an unrelenting questioning of the "truth" related to the extent of the persecution of Jews by Nazi Germany during the second World War. Virtually every aspect of the Holocaust is challenged: the numbers of those who died, how and why they died, and the reliability of the accounts of witnesses, survivors, confessors and the perished. Aspersions are cast on the legitimacy of post war legal and historical analysis, and doubts are raised regarding the veracity of a myriad of details related to the experience of Jews at this time.

[138]   A secondary theme, closely related to the first, is the assertion that the truth needs to be revealed, but that those who profit from the commonly held view of the Holocaust have thwarted this goal. There are repeated references to the individual and collective benefits that the Jewish peoples and Israel have realised from their continued promotion of the "Holocaust story."

[139]   In levelling these charges, Jews are branded as liars, swindlers, racketeers and extortionists. They are accused of wielding extraordinary power and control, all used only for their own advantage and to the great detriment of others. Jews are described as criminals and parasites, acting on a global level to elevate their own power and wealth. Jewish people are viciously targeted in the Zundelsite material on the basis of their religious and cultural associations.

[140]   The messages conveyed in these documents carry very specific assertions regarding the character and behaviour of Jews, none of it good. Jews are vilified in the most rabid and extreme manner, permitting, in our view, of "no redeeming qualities." Given our reading of the material communicated via the Zundelsite, we are satisfied that the test set out in [previous litigation] has been met. In our judgement, these messages create an environment in which it is likely that Jews will be exposed to extreme emotions of detestation and vilification. Based on our view that the Zundelsite materials characterize Jews as "liars, cheats, criminals and thugs" who have deliberately engaged in a monumental fraud designed to extort funds, we regard it as highly likely that readers of these materials will, at a minimum, hold Jews in very low regard,

viewing them either with contempt, scorn and disdain, or hatred, loathing and revulsion.

[141]   The expert evidence of Drs. Prideaux and Schweitzer reinforces our view that the material found on the Zundelsite is likely to expose Jews to hatred or contempt. The evidence of Dr. Prideaux and the use of specific rhetorical strategies to target and degrade Jews support our own interpretation of the Zundelsite documents. Professor Prideaux provided a number of detailed examples to support his own expert opinion that the material found on the Zundelsite was likely to expose Jews to hatred and contempt. We also note the striking similarities between the references found in the Zundelsite material and the classical motifs of anti-Semitism described by Dr. Schweitzer. Although we have found the expert evidence to be helpful, ultimately, it is the language used in the documents themselves that persuades us that this material offends s. 13(1) of the Act. The tone and expression of these messages is so malevolent in its depiction of Jews, that we find them to be hate messages within the meaning of the Act.

[142]   In arriving at our conclusion we have reviewed the Exhibits [downloaded from the Zundelsite] in their entirety. . . . The echoes of hatred that reverberate throughout the site infect and taint virtually all of the documents put before us. . . .

[295]   It was suggested during the course of the hearing that [since Zündel had left Canada for the United States], a cease and desist order issued against the Respondent would have virtually no effect in eliminating this material from the World Wide Web. As we have noted throughout this decision, Mr. Zündel did not participate in final argument on the merits of this complaint and so the Tribunal, in endeavouring to afford a fair hearing in the circumstances, raised this point during the Commission's submission.

[296]   One of the unique features of the Internet is the ease with which strangers to the creator of a particular site can access material and, if they choose, replicate the entire site at another web address. The evidence before us supports the contention that "mirror" sites already exist that duplicate in their totality the material currently found on the Zundelsite. We also accept that some individuals, in an attempt to rebuff efforts to limit speech or regulate the Internet, might be prompted to create mirror sites in direct response to an Order issued by this Tribunal. As there is no evidence that these sites are under the control of Mr. Zündel, it was submitted that even if we find that there has been a contravention of s. 13(1) of the Act, it would be totally ineffectual to issue a cease and desist order. Notwithstanding any Order that we might issue, the material found on the Zundelsite, which we have determined offends s. 13(1) of the Act, will remain accessible to anyone in Canada who can find a mirror site.

[297]   Counsel for the Commission and the interveners in aid of the Commission position maintained that the proposed remedy would serve both a symbolic and practical value. At a minimum, a cease and desist order would prevent the Respondent from continuing to update and promote this site.

[298]   We are extremely conscious of the limits of the remedial power available in this case. There always exists the possibility that an individual, wholly unrelated to a named respondent, will engage in a similar discriminatory practise. The technology involved in the posting of materials to the Internet, how-

ever, magnifies this problem and arguably makes it much easier to avoid the ultimate goal of eliminating the material from telephonic communication.

[299]   Nonetheless, as a Tribunal we are charged with the responsibility of determining the complaints referred to us, and then making an Order if we find that the Respondent has engaged in a discriminatory practise. We cannot be unduly influenced in this case by what others might do once we issue our Order. The Commission, or individual complainants, can elect to file other complaints, or respond in any other manner that they consider appropriate should they believe that there has been a further contravention of the Act.

[300]   Any remedy awarded by this, or any Tribunal, will inevitably serve a number of purposes: prevention and elimination of discriminatory practises is only one of the outcomes flowing from an Order issued as a consequence of these proceedings. There is also a significant symbolic value in the public denunciation of the actions that are the subject of this complaint. Similarly, there is the potential educative and ultimately larger preventative benefit that can be achieved by open discussion of the principles enunciated in this or any Tribunal decision.

[301]   Parliament, on behalf of all Canadians, has determined that the telephonic communication of hate messages is not to be tolerated in our society. In our view, the victims of hate are entitled to obtain the benefit of the full weight of our authority.

[302]   We have determined that the Respondent Ernst Zündel has engaged in a discriminatory practise by posting material to his website that is likely to expose Jews to hatred or contempt, and the granting of the remedy requested is warranted and appropriate.

[303]   We therefore order that the Respondent, Ernst Zündel, and any other individuals who act in the name of, or in concert with Ernst Zündel cease the discriminatory practise of communicating telephonically or causing to be communicated telephonically by means of the facilities of a telecommunication undertaking within the legislative authority of Parliament, matters of the type contained in Exhibit HR-2 and found on the Zundelsite, or any other messages of a substantially similar form or content that are likely to expose a person or persons to hatred or contempt by reason of the fact that that person or persons are identifiable on the basis of a prohibited ground of discrimination, contrary to s. 13(1) of the *Canadian Human Rights Act*.

> *Signed by:* Claude Pensa, Chairperson of the Tribunal,
> and Reva Devins, Member.

# NOTES

### INTRODUCTION, P. 1 TO P. 11

1. Nuremberg document NG-4589, letter, May 19, 1943, Himmler to Ernst Kaltenbrunner, in Léon Poliakov and Josef Wulf, *Das Dritte Reich und die Juden: Dokumente und Aufsätze* (Berlin: Arani Verlags, 1955), 359–60.
2. Quoted in James Shapiro, *Oberammergau: The Troubling Story of the World's Most Famous Passion Play* (New York: Pantheon, 2000), 76–77.
3. *Hitler's Secret Conversations 1941–1944*, introduction by H. R. Trevor-Roper, trans. N. Cameron and R. H. Stevens (New York: Signet Books of New American Library, 1961), evening of July 5, 1942, 526.
4. Christian Stückl quoted by Gordon Craig in review of Shapiro, *Oberammergau*, *New York Review of Books*, 47, no. 13 (Aug. 10, 2000): 46.
5. Walter Zwi Bacharach, *Anti-Jewish Prejudices in German-Catholic Sermons*, trans. Chaya Galai (Lewiston, NY: Edwin Mellen, 1993), 60; italics in the original.
6. Cited in David I. Kertzer, *The Popes against the Jews: The Vatican's Role in the Rise of Modern Anti-Semitism* (New York: Knopf, 2001), 147–48; a parallel accusation appears in Muslim propaganda, according to which Jews destroyed the World Trade Center to distract attention from their "crimes" and thus win sympathy in world public opinion.
7. James Carroll, *Constantine's Sword: The Church and the Jews, A History* (Boston: Houghton Mifflin, 2001), 22.
8. Kertzer, *Popes against the Jews*, 7.
9. Bernard Wasserstein, *Vanishing Diaspora: The Jews in Europe since 1945* (Cambridge, MA: Harvard University Press, 1996), 131.
10. For this and the preceding paragraph, see Gabriel Schoenfeld, "Israel and the Anti-Semites," *Commentary*, June, 2002.
11. Yehoshafat Harkabi, "On Arab Antisemitism Once More," *Antisemitism Through the Ages*, ed. Shmuel Almog (Oxford: Pergamon Press, 1988), 232; the mufti as quoted by Jonathan Rosen, "The Uncomfortable Question of Anti-Semitism," *New York Times*, magazine section, Nov. 4, 2001: www.nytimes.com/2001.
12. Ronald L. Nettler, *Past Trials and Present Tribulations: A Muslim Fundamentalist's View of the Jews* (New York: Pergamon Press, 1987), 6, 45, 51, 66, 83; Qutb's essay, "Our Struggle with the Jews," 72–87; although Qutb drew on the *Protocols* he did not cite it, but the Saudi editor of the 1970 version of the essay added four citations to the *Protocols* as proof texts.
13. Quoted from *Yedioth Ahronoth*, 14, on rbshulman@worldnet.att.net.

14. From the Muslim website, islamweb.net/english.

15. Eric J. Greenberg, "Protocols Surface for Islamic Audience," *The Jewish Week*, Oct. 26, 2001, www.thejewishweek.com/newscontent.phb3?artid=5274.

16. Quoted by Fiamma Nirenstein, "How Suicide Bombers are Made," *Commentary* 112 (Sept. 2001), 53.

17. Andrew Sullivan in the *Sunday Times* of London, Dec. 23, 2001.

18. From the Muslim website, islamweb.net/english.

19. Khalid Durán with Abdelwahab Hechiche, *Children of Abraham* (New York: American Jewish Committee; Hoboken, NJ: KTAV, 2001), 42, 262, 269.

20. Ibid., 51, 53, 62.

21. Bernard Lewis, "The Revolt of Islam," *The New Yorker*, Nov. 19, 2001, 56.

22. Sullivan in the *Sunday Times* of London, Dec. 23, 2001.

23. Jonathan Rosen, "The Uncomfortable Question of Anti-Semitism," *New York Times*, magazine section, Nov. 4, 2001: www.nytimes.com/2001.

24. Greenberg, "Protocols Surface for Islamic Audience."

25. Quoted by Durán, *Children of Abraham*, 75; see also "Osama bin Laden, An Interview," *Terrorism and 9/11, A Reader*, ed. Fredrik Logevall (Boston: Houghton Mifflin, 2002), 61–72.

CHAPTER 1

1. Quoted in Robert Chazan, *Medieval Stereotypes and Modern Antisemitism* (Los Angeles: University of California Press, 1997), 13–14; see Jonathan Riley-Smith, *The First Crusade and the Idea of Crusading* (Philadelphia: University of Pennsylvania Press, 1986), for the centrality of vengeance to crusading in general.

2. Quoted in H. H. Ben-Sasson, ed., *A History of the Jewish People* (London: Weidenfeld & Nicolson, 1976), 474.

3. Quoted in Paul Johnson, *A History of Christianity* (New York: Atheneum, 1977), 490.

4. Quoted by Irving Greenberg in *Auschwitz, Beginning of a New Era?*, ed. Eva Fleischner (New York: KTAV, 1976), 10–11.

5. The sources for this subject are enormous; we have relied mainly on the following: Raymond E. Brown, S. S., *The Death of the Messiah*, 2 vols. (New York: Doubleday, 1994), which seems to us greatly to exaggerate the historicity of the gospels as sources; we prefer John Dominic Crossan, who says that the gospels are 80 percent "prophecy historicized" and only 20 percent "history remembered" and that Brown reverses the proportions: *Who Killed Jesus? Exposing the Roots of Anti-Semitism in the Gospel Story of the Death of Jesus* (San Francisco: HarperSanFrancisco: 1995); idem, *The Cross that Spoke* (San Francisco: Harper & Row, 1988); John P. Meier, *A Marginal Jew*, vol. 1 (New York: Doubleday, 1991); Paul Winter, *On the Trial of Jesus*, 2nd ed., rev. T. A. Burkill and Geza Vermes (New York: Walter de Gruyter, 1974); Haim Cohn, *The Trial and Death of Jesus* (New York: KTAV, 1977); and the scintillating work by a nonprofessional inquirer, Weddig Fricke, *The Court-Martial of Jesus: A Christian Defends the Jews against the Charge of Deicide*, trans. Salvator Attansio (New York: Grove Weidenfeld, 1990). In revision of earlier drafts of this chapter, we have made much use of E. P. Sanders, *Jesus and Judaism* (Philadelphia: Fortress Press, 1985), masterful and up to date, and the series of articles on the historical Jesus

in *Theology Today* 51, 1 (April 1995): 1–97, especially the essays by Paula Fredriksen, Howard Kee, and Stephen Patterson. See also Sanders' review article, "In Quest of the Historical Jesus," *New York Review of Books* 48, 18 (Nov. 18, 2001): 33–36.

6. Crossan, *Who Killed Jesus?*, 32, 35.

7. Robert M. Grant, "The Trial of Jesus in the Light of History," *Judaism* 20 (1971): 42; Jeremy Cohen, ed., *Essential Papers on Judaism and Christianity in Conflict* (New York: New York University Press, 1991), 9–10; in Acts 2:23 and 3:15 Jews are said to have "killed the author of life"; cf. Paul, 1 Thessalonians 2:14.

8. "Even those Christian scholars who maintain that Jesus never existed concur that the Jews crucified him" is Simon Bernfeld's witticism expressing the emotional traps that litter the field of New Testament studies, quoted in Jacob Katz, "Was the Holocaust Predictable?" *Perspectives on the Holocaust*, vol. 1 of *The Nazi Holocaust: Historical Articles on the Destruction of European Jews*, ed. Michael Marrus (Westport, CT: Meckler, 1989), 133–34.

9. Sanders, *Jesus and Judaism*, 15; Fricke, *The Court-Martial of Jesus*, 12–13.

10. In a perceptive essay, "Marcion and the Jews" in *Separation and Polemic*, vol. 2 of *Anti-Judaism in Early Christianity*, ed. Stephen G. Wilson (Waterloo, Ontario: Wilfrid Laurier University Press, 1986), 58, Stephen G. Wilson argues that Marcion's radical disconnection of Christianity and Judaism, by which Judaism retained its God, scriptures, messiah, and law, might have preserved peace and tolerance, whereas Christianity's appropriation of these resulted in irreconcilable claims and conflicts. An example of the consequent antisemitism will be found in Marcion's near-contemporary "Melito of Sardis: The First Poet of Deicide," so called by E. Werner, *Hebrew Union College Annual* 37 (1966): 191–210.

11. James H. Charlesworth, *Jesus within Judaism* (New York: Doubleday, 1988), 26; we disagree with him that the new documents and scholarship have gone far to remedy the loss.

12. Crossan, *Who Killed Jesus?*, 78.

13. Sanders, *Jews and Judaism*, 110, thinks that Matthew 4:17 is a piece of church editorializing and notes that some manuscripts omit "Repent," that rather than national repentance and forgiveness, Jesus' call is for individual repentance and forgiveness.

14. 2 Corinthians 11:4; Galatians 1:7; 2 Corinthians 5:16 as cited in S. G. F. Brandon, "History or Theology? The Basic Problems of the Evidence of the Trial of Jesus," *Essential Papers on Judaism and Christianity in Conflict*, ed. Cohen, 118, 120; it is not clear whether Paul is so accusing his opponents, the "super-apostles," or they him.

15. *Apocrypha* is a Greek word meaning "hidden" or "secret" and originally referred to works so esoteric that only the initiated inner circle could grasp them; in time it came to mean works excluded because unimportant, questionable, or heretical, and then those works excluded from the Hebrew Bible; in general usage, it refers to pseudobiblical works written in the Second Temple period, 535 B.C.E. to 70 C.E. The term often is interchangeable with the term *pseudepigrapha*, which emphasizes the false claim of biblical authorship or origin. See James H. Charlesworth, ed., *The Old Testament Pseudepigrapha*, 2 vols. (Garden City, NY: Doubleday, 1983–85).

16. Charlesworth, *Jesus within Judaism*, 5.

17. Ibid., 13, 233, 11, 74; Sanders, *Jesus and Judaism*, 1–3, takes essentially the same view.

18. Sanders, *Jesus and Judaism*, 264–65; see also Michael J. Cook, "Jesus and the Pharisees—The Problem as It Stands Today," *Journal of Ecumenical Studies*, 15 (1978): 441–60.

19. Donald P. Gray, "Jesus Was a Jew," *Jewish-Christian Encounters over the Centuries*, ed. Marvin Perry and Frederick M. Schweitzer (New York: Peter Lang, 1994), 2.

20. Franklin Littell, *The Crucifixion of the Jews* (New York: Harper & Row, 1975), 2, 30.

21. "Notes for the Correct Way," *Catholic Jewish Relations: Documents from the Holy See*, intro. Eugene Fisher (London: Catholic Truth Society, 1999), VI, 25, pp.46–47.

22. See Charlesworth, *Jesus within Judaism*.

23. Sanders, *Jesus and Judaism*, 239–40, 318; John Meier, "Jesus" in *The New Jerome Biblical Commentary*, ed. Raymond E. Brown et al. (Englewood Cliffs, NJ: Prentice Hall, 1990), 1321–22.

24. Quoted in Fricke, *Court-Martial of Jesus*, 15; in an interview in *Christianity Today* (Jan. 1978): 518, Thielicke said that "the ultimate reason" for the Holocaust "is theological in nature," although he did not link it to Christian antisemitism and deicide.

25. Charlesworth, *Jesus within Judaism*, 103, 64–71; it is not definitive that the Teacher of Righteousness actually wrote these hymns (1QH), or that the community resided at Qumran, or that they were Essenes, but none of that affects the argument here, and certainly the Qumran community closely resembles the Essenes that we know of from other sources and Qumran could be called a variant of Essenism. For a stringent and authoritative assessment of Qumran, see Lawrence H. Schiffman, *Reclaiming the Dead Sea Scrolls: The History of Judaism, the Background of Christianity, the Lost Library of Qumran* (Philadelphia: Jewish Publication Society, 1994). To complicate further, Jesus could have been praising the piety of the *Anawim*, the poor ones, or the humble ones, a strand of Jewish observance that comes out of the prophets.

26. Sanders, *Jesus and Judaism*, 321; Stephen Patterson, "The End of Apocalypse," *Theology Today* 51, 1 (April 1995): 37.

27. Charlesworth, *Jesus within Judaism*, 32, 47; we would err badly if we did not acknowledge that several generations of scholars have sought to dispel these stereotypes, yet the last quarter century has been a watershed. The paradigmatic shift that has occurred in the study of Christian origins can be followed in Susannah Heschel's brilliant *Abraham Geiger and the Jewish Jesus* (Chicago: University of Chicago Press, 1998). Geiger (1810–1874) was a rabbi, theologian, historian, and leader of the Reform Judaism movement. He effected a Copernican revolution in the approach to our subject by insisting that: Jesus was and remained a Jew and a Pharisee; Christianity (and Islam) originated in and owe much to Judaism; Judaism was a vital and dynamic faith in the first century; Pharisaism manifested a rich ethical heritage and the exact opposite of the notorious stereotype; Christianity is not the religion of Jesus but a religion about Jesus founded by Paul; the execution of Jesus was a Roman matter; mastery of the Mishnah, Talmud, Midrashim, Targunim, and so on is as essential for an understanding of these questions as is the New and Old Testaments, Philo, Jose-

phus and classical sources; Judaism remained a vigorous and creative force at the heart of Western civilization—Geiger did not get much of a hearing from Christian scholars in his native Germany but has been thoroughly vindicated in this ecumenical age.

28. This assertion holds, even though some Jews, as Josephus relates, turned over Zealots and other rebels to the Romans in attempts to avoid danger and upheaval—to no avail obviously.

29. S. G. F. Brandon, *Jesus and the Zealots* (New York: Scribner's, 1967), 262.

30. Bruce Vawter, "Are the Gospels Anti-Semitic?" *Journal of Ecumenical Studies* 5 (Summer 1968): 483; Winter, *On the Trial of Jesus*, 33–34, in reference to Mark, although generally it applies to the other synoptic gospels, but not really to John.

31. Lawrence Schiffman, *Who Was a Jew? Rabbinic and Halakhic Perspectives on the Jewish-Christian Schism* (Hoboken, NJ: KTAV, 1985), 75–78, and not because of the claim to be a messiah.

32. Crossan, *Who Killed Jesus?*, 36, 219.

33. It is worth noting that as late as 62, according to the Jewish historian Josephus and the Christian bishop and historian Eusebius, as cited by Winter, *On the Trial of Jesus*, 171, 186, Pharisees sided with Jesus' later followers against a Sadducean high priest, suggesting that Jesus' affinities with Pharisaism were quite close.

34. "Notes for the Correct Way," *Catholic Jewish Relations: Documents from the Holy See*, IV, 21, A, p. 43. Vatican II's dogmatic constitution *Dei Verbum* anticipated the 1985 Notes in accepting the findings of modern biblical scholarship: It differentiates three phases and explains that the gospels were written after the authors gained a different and clearer understanding: "after they had been instructed by the events of Christ's risen life. . . . The sacred authors wrote the four gospels, selecting some things from the many which had been handed down by word of mouth or in writing, reducing some of them to a synthesis, explicating some things in view of the situation of their churches, and preserving the form of proclamation [kerygma]." For additional documents, Catholic and non-Catholic, see Helga Croner, compiler, *Stepping Stones to Further Jewish-Christian Relations* (New York: Stimulus Books, 1977), and idem, *More Stepping Stones to Jewish-Christian Relations* (New York: Paulist Press, 1983).

35. Stephen Patterson, "The End of Apocalypse: Rethinking the Eschatological Jesus," *Theology Today* 52 (April 1995): 43–46.

36. E. P. Sanders, "The Life of Jesus," in *Christianity and Rabbinic Judaism: A Parallel History of Their Origins and Early Development*, ed. Hershel Shanks (Washington, DC: Biblical Archaeology Society, 1992), 78–79.

37. On Josephus' father, Fricke, *Court-Martial of Jesus*, 49–50.

38. Haim Cohn, "Reflections on the Trial of Jesus," *Judaism* 20 (1971): 18f.

39. Winter, *On the Trial of Jesus*, 144–52; Robert Michael, "Antisemitism and the Church Fathers," *Jewish-Christian Encounters over the Centuries*, ed. Perry and Schweitzer, 113.

40. *Jewish Antiquities*, 18:63, as cited by Crossan, *Who Killed Jesus?*, 5, 117, 147–48, for whose interpretation the statement is crucial.

41. Winter, *On the Trial of Jesus*, 197–99; Fricke, *Court-Martial of Jesus*, 98–100, 192–93.

42. Sanders, *Jesus and Judaism*, 252, 270, 286, 302, 306–8; the quotation is from Sanders, "Life of Jesus," 55; three points to note: The priests later had St.

Stephen killed after he attacked the Temple; Jesus' claim that he would rebuild the Temple in three days is consistent with his "restoration eschatology"; on the cross Jesus is taunted about his boasts about the Temple.

43.  Quoted by Fricke, *Court-Martial of Jesus*, 204.

44.  Cohn, *The Trial and Death of Jesus*, 150.

45.  S. G. F. Brandon, "The Trial of Jesus," *Judaism* 20 (1971): 46, 48, finds that Mark's portrait of Pilate "astounds by its patent absurdity"; the efforts to explain away Jesus' execution by the Romans is "ludicrous," "illogical," a "nonsensical subterfuge," "ridiculous," and the like.

46.  Anatole France, *Mother of Pearl*, vol. 1 of *The Works of Anatole France*, trans. Frederic Chapman (New York: William H. Wise & Co., 1930), 27; France was by no means well disposed toward Jews or Judaism; John P. Meier, *A Marginal Jew* (New York: Doubleday, 1991), 1:57, 68; to be sure Tacitus, Dio Cassius, and Josephus speak of Jesus.

47.  The story is complicated by the personage of Joseph of Arimathaea, a member of the Sanhedrin (which made him, presumably, an enemy of Jesus), and one who "waited expectantly for the kingdom of God" (thus, presumably, a follower of Jesus); he was a Jewish official, possibly a member or the head of the burial society (perhaps that is why he is the owner of a tomb) responsible under Jewish law to bury the Jewish dead and do so by sundown. To Crossan, *Who Killed Jesus?*, 172–76, Joseph is "a total Markan creation in name, in place [no one can trace the place-name Arimathaea], and in function."

48.  See Cohn's exposition of this subject in *Trial and Death of Jesus*, 217–18, 227–28.

49.  Crossan, *Who Killed Jesus?*, 22–25, 222–27.

50.  Winter, *On the Trial of Jesus*, 138–39.

51.  Fricke, *Court-Martial of Jesus*, 215.

52.  For this series of queries, see Cohn, *Trial and Death of Jesus*, 165–68; possibly those who welcomed Jesus on Sunday were not the same people who turned against him on Friday; probably few rather than "multitudes" were involved.

53.  Crossan, *Who Killed Jesus?*, 69–70; that the gospels make no mention of the Zealot party may stem from a sensed need to keep affinities between insurrectionists and the Jesus movement secret.

54.  Quoted in Michael, "Antisemitism and the Church Fathers," *Jewish-Christian Encounters over the Centuries*, ed. Perry and. Schweitzer, 112.

55.  *Luther's Works*, ed. Jaroslav Pelikan (St. Louis: Concordia, 1955-), 14:257, 263; 22:86.

56.  Beda Rigaux, *L'Antéchrist et l'Opposition au Royaume Messianique dans l'Ancien et le Nouveau Testament* (Paris: Gabalda, 1932), 401–2.

57.  Quoted in Sanders, *Jesus and Judaism*, 44.

58.  Cohn, *Trial and Death of Jesus*, 261–75; the Matthean passage, says Cohn, 275, is "one more tragic touch to the disastrous and total misconception of the Jewish role in the trial of Jesus."

59.  A parallel exegetical problem is found in St. Paul's arrest as reported in Acts 21–27, where the author, Luke, struggles to put the Roman government in the best possible light and the Jews in the worst possible light—here again is a reflection of the missionary pitch and the desire to assuage Rome. Paul invoked his Roman citizenship, saying "I appeal to Caesar" (Acts 25:11) and should not be subjected to Jewish accusation.

60.  Winter, *On the Trial of Jesus*, 163.

61. Vawter, "Are the Gospels Anti-Semitic?," 486.

62. Ange de Chivasso, *Summa Angelica* as quoted by Léon Poliakov, *The History of Anti-Semitism*, vol. 3, *From Voltaire to Wagner*, trans. Miriam Kochan (New York: Vanguard, 1975), 6.

63. Quoted in Frederick M. Schweitzer, "Medieval Perceptions of Jews and Judaism," *Jewish-Christian Encounters over the Centuries*, ed. Perry and Schweitzer, 142–43.

64. For the last three paragraphs, see Jeremy Cohen, "The Jews as the Killers of Christ in the Latin Tradition, from Augustine to the Friars," *Traditio* 39 (1983): 3–27.

65. Quoted by Irving Greenberg in *Auschwitz: Beginning of a New Era?* 441–42, n. 7.

66. Quoted in Raul Hilberg, *The Destruction of the European Jews* (New York: Holmes & Meier, 1985), 3:1021.

67. Quoted by Meir Michaelis, "Italy," in *The World Reacts to the Holocaust*, ed. David Wyman (Baltimore: Johns Hopkins University Press, 1966), 533.

68. Eliezer Berkovits as cited by Geoffrey Wigoder, *Contemporary Jewish Religious Thought*, ed. Arthur A. Cohen and Paul Mendes-Flohr (New York: Free Press, 1988), 152.

### CHAPTER 2

1. Quoted in Saul S. Friedman, *The Incident at Massena* (New York: Stein & Day, 1978), 118.

2. Quoted in Ibid., 118.

3. Quoted in Ibid., 119.

4. Quoted in Frederick M. Schweitzer, "Medieval Perceptions of Jews and Judaism," *Jewish-Christian Encounters over the Centuries*, ed. Marvin Perry and Frederick M. Schweitzer (New York: Peter Lang, 1994), 149.

5. Hermann L. Strack, *The Jew and Human Sacrifice* (London: Cope and Fenwick, 1909), xi.

6. Ibid., 170.

7. Malcolm Hay, *Europe and the Jews* (Boston: Beacon Press, 1960), 120; Jonathan Frankel, *The Damascus Affair* (Cambridge: Cambridge University Press, 1997), 240.

8. Joseph Jacobs, "Little St. Hugh of Lincoln: Researches in History, Archeology, and Legend," *The Blood Libel Legend: A Casebook in Anti-Semitic Folklore*, ed. Alan Dundes (Madison: University of Wisconsin Press, 1991), 47.

9. John M. Efron, *Defenders of the Race: Jewish Doctors & Race Science in Fin-de-Siècle Europe* (New Haven, CT: Yale University Press, 1994), 70–71.

10. Hillel J. Kieval, "Masaryk and Czech Jewry: The Ambiguities of Friendship," *T. G. Masaryk (1850–1937)*, ed. Stanley B. Winters (New York: Macmillan, 1990), 311.

11. Quoted in Alan Dundes, "The Ritual Murder or Blood Libel Legend: A Study of Anti-Semitic Victimization through Protective Inversion," Dundes, ed., *The Blood Libel Legend*, 338.

12. Eusebius, *Ecclesiastical History, The Fathers of the Church: A New Translation*, trans. Roy J. Deferrari (New York: Fathers of the Church, 1953), vol. 19, book V, chap. 1, 278–79.

13. David Berger, ed., *The Jewish-Christian Debate in the High Middle Ages: A Critical Edition of the* Nizzahon Vetus (Northvale, NJ: Jason Aronson, 1996), 229.

14. *The Life and Miracles of St. William of Norwich by Thomas of Monmouth*, ed. Augustus Jessopp and Montague R. James (Cambridge: Cambridge University Press, 1896), 21.

15. Quoted in Joshua Trachtenberg, *The Devil and the Jews* (Philadelphia: Jewish Publication Society, 1943), 130.

16. Quoted in ibid., 131–32.

17. Excerpted in Solomon Grayzel, *The Church and the Jews in the XIIIth Century* (New York: Hermon Press, 1966), 263.

18. Excerpted in ibid., 271.

19. Excerpted in ibid., 275; see also Edward A. Synan, *The Popes and the Jews in the Middle Ages* (New York: Macmillan, 1965), 111–15.

20. Excerpted in Jacob R. Marcus, *The Jew in the Medieval World* (New York: World, 1960), 153–54.

21. Alina Cala, *The Image of the Jew in Polish Folk Culture* (Jerusalem: Magnes Press of Hebrew University, 1995), 227.

22. S. M. Dubnow, *History of the Jews in Russia and Poland*, trans. I. Friedlander (Philadelphia: Jewish Publication Society, 1918), I:100.

23. Ibid.,176–77.

24. Quoted in ibid., 179.

25. Reproduced in Cecil Roth, *The Ritual Murder Libel and the Jew: The Report by Cardinal Lorenzo Ganganelli* (London: Woburn Press, 1935), 68.

26. Quoted in ibid., 90.

27. Quoted in Dubnow, *History of the Jews in Russia and Poland*, I: 180.

28. Quoted in ibid., II: 74–75.

29. Quoted in ibid., II: 75.

30. Quoted in ibid., II: 83.

31. Quoted in Frankel, *The Damascus Affair*, 67.

32. Quoted in David I. Kertzer, *The Popes against the Jews: The Vatican's Role in the Rise of Modern Anti-Semitism* (New York: Knopf, 2001), 91.

33. Ibid., 84, 94–95.

34. Quoted in Frankel, 74.

35. Quoted in ibid., 117.

36. Quoted in ibid., 212.

37. Quoted in Strack, *The Jew and Human Sacrifice*, 221.

38. Quoted in Steven Beller, "The Hilsner Affair: Nationalism, Anti-Semitism and the Individual in the Hapsburg Monarchy at the Turn of the Century," *T. G. Masaryk (1850–1937)*, ed. Robert B. Pynsent (Basingstoke, Hampshire, UK: Macmillan, 1989), 2:53.

39. Quoted in Frantisek Cervinka, "The Hilsner Affair," Dundes, ed., *Blood Libel Legend*, 147.

40. Quoted in Beller, "The Hilsner Affair," 55.

41. Quoted in Cervinka, "The Hilsner Affair," 148–49.

42. Quoted in Maurice Samuel, *Blood Accusation: The Strange History of the Beilis Case* (Philadelphia: Jewish Publication Society, 1966), 17.

43. Quoted in Alexander B. Tager, *The Decay of Czarism: The Beilis Trial* (Philadelphia: Jewish Publication Society, 1935), 56.

44. Excerpted in Roth, *Ritual Murder Libel and the Jew*, 101.

45. Excerpted in Ezekiel Leikin, *The Beilis Transcripts* (Northvale, NJ: Jason Aronson, 1993), 184.

46. Excerpted in ibid., 217–18.
47. Mendel Beilis, *The Story of My Sufferings*, trans. Harrison Goldberg (New York: Mendel Beilis Publishing, 1926), 205.
48. Thos. H. Burgage, "Ritual Murder among the Jews," *Catholic Bulletin and Book Review* 3 (March 1911): 358.
49. Quoted in Kertzer, *Popes against the Jews*, 160.
50. Quoted in ibid., 221.
51. Quoted in Saul Friedländer, *The Years of Persecution, 1933–1939*, vol. 1 of *Nazi Germany and the Jews* (New York: HarperCollins, 1997), 124.
52. *Anti-Semitism Worldwide 1995/96*, 150, an annual report prepared by The Project for the Study of Anti-Semitism, Tel Aviv University, and distributed by the Anti-Defamation League and the World Jewish Congress.
53. Quoted by Efraim Karsh, "Intifada II: The Long Trail of Arab Anti-Semitism," *Commentary* 110 (Dec. 2000): 51.
54. These excerpts were provided to us by the Simon Wiesenthal Center. See also Dundes, "Ritual Murder or Blood Libel Legend," Dundes, ed., *Blood Libel Legend*, 350.
55. "Egyptian Press Update 'The Big Lie,'" *Response: The Wiesenthal Center World Report* 20 (Winter/Spring 1999): 9.
56. Special Dispatch—Saudi Arabia/Arab Antisemitism, 3/13/02, No. 354, cited from www.memri.org.
57. "The Long Shadow," *Newsweek* (May 7, 1990), 25; Cala, *Image of the Jew in Polish Folk Culture*, 130, notes "the popularity and vitality" of the idea of ritual murder in contemporary Poland.

CHAPTER 3

1. Quoted in Jacob Katz, *From Prejudice to Destruction: Antisemitism, 1700–1933* (Cambridge, MA: Harvard University Press, 1980), 252.
2. Quoted in Jerry Silverman, *The Undying Flame: Ballads and Songs of the Holocaust* (Syracuse: Syracuse University Press, 2002), xvi.
3. Origenis, *Commentariorum in Evangelium secundum Matthaeum* in *Patrologiae Cursus Completus*, Series Graeca Prior, ed. J.- P. Migne (Paris: Parisiorum, 1862), vol. 13, cols. 1494–95, pars. 775–76; trans. Joseph Castora for this volume.
4. Quoted in Mark R. Cohen, *Under Crescent & Cross: The Jews in the Middle Ages* (Princeton, NJ: Princeton University Press, 1994), 171.
5. Quoted in Edward H. Flannery, *The Anguish of the Jews* (London: Macmillan, 1965), 48.
6. See Randolph Braham, ed., *The Origins of the Holocaust: Christian Anti-Semitism* (Boulder, CO: Social Science Monographs and Institute for Holocaust Studies, City University of New York, distributed by Columbia University Press, 1986), 36.
7. Ibid., 37
8. Quoted in Bernard McGinn, *Antichrist: Two Thousand Years of Human Fascination with Evil* (San Francisco: HarperSanFrancisco, 1994), 100–103.
9. Quoted in Salo W. Baron, *A Social and Religious History of the Jews*, 2nd ed., 18 vols. (New York: Columbia University Press, 1952–83), 11:133.
10. Quoted in Robert C. Fuller, *Naming the Antichrist:: The History of an American Obsession* (New York: Oxford University Press, 1995), 138.
11. Ibid., 142–43.

12. Quoted in Robert Chazan, *Medieval Stereotypes and Modern Antisemitism* (Berkeley: University of California Press, 1997), 14.

13. Excerpted in Giles Constable, ed., *The Letters of Peter the Venerable* (Cambridge, MA: Harvard University Press, 1967), I: 328–29.

14. Léon Poliakov, *From the Time of Christ to the Court Jews*, vol. 1 of *The History of Anti-Semitism*, trans. Richard Howard (New York: Schocken, 1974), 106–7.

15. Quoted in ibid., 113.

16. Quoted in Eric W. Gritsch, "The Jews in Reformation Theology," *Jewish-Christian Encounters over the Centuries*, ed. Marvin Perry and Frederick M. Schweitzer (New York: Peter Lang, 1994), 197.

17. Quoted in Robert S. Wistrich, *Antisemitism: The Longest Hatred* (New York: Schocken, 1991), 39.

18. "That Jesus Christ was Born a Jew," ed. and trans. Walter I. Brandt, vol. 45 of *Luther's Works* (Philadelphia: Fortress Press, 1962), 299; excerpted from *On the Jews and their Lies*, ed. Franklin Sherman, trans. Martin H. Bertram, vol. 47 of *Luther's Works* (Philadelphia: Fortress Press, 1971), 268–74.

19. Quoted in Dennis Prager and Joseph Telushkin, *Why the Jews? The Reason for Antisemitism* (New York: Simon & Shuster, 1983), 107.

20. Quoted in Robert F. Byrnes, *Anti-Semitism in Modern France* (New York: Howard Fertig, 1969), 202.

21. Quoted in Friedrich Meinecke, *The German Catastrophe* (Boston: Beacon Press, 1963), 23–24. Paulsen also opposed antisemitism, but like many other Germans he believed that it was impossible to "remain a complete Jew and a complete German."

22. See the works of George L. Mosse, particularly, *The Crisis of German Ideology: Intellectual Origins of the Third Reich* (New York: Grosset & Dunlap, 1964).

23. Chaim Weizmann, *Trial and Error* (London: Hamish Hamilton, 1949), 143; Arnold Zweig, *Insulted and Exiled: The Truth about the German Jews* (London: John Miles, 1937), passim.

24. Quoted in Gilmer W. Blackburn, *Education in the Third Reich* (Albany: State University of New York Press, 1985), 144.

25. Quoted in Jacob Katz, *The Darker Side of Genius: Richard Wagner's Anti-Semitism* (Hanover, NH: Brandeis University Press and University Press of New England, 1986), 19.

26. Quoted in John Weiss, *Ideology of Death* (Chicago: Ivan R. Dee, 1996), 177.

27. Quoted in Katz, *Darker Side of Genius*, 19.

28. Quoted in Ernst Nolte, *Three Faces of Fascism*, trans. Leila Vennewitz (New York: Holt, Rinehart & Winston, 1966), 43.

29. Quoted in Geoffrey G. Field, *Evangelist of Race: The Germanic Vision of Houston Stewart Chamberlain* (New York: Columbia University Press, 1981), 90.

30. Quoted in ibid., 189.

31. Quoted in ibid., 225.

32. Quoted in ibid., 437, 441.

33. See Patrick Girard, "Historical Foundations of Anti-Semitism," Joel E. Dimsdale, ed., *Survivors, Victims, and Perpetrators* (Washington, DC: Hemisphere Publishing, 1980), 24; Shmuel Almog, *Nationalism and Antisemitism in Modern Europe, 1815–1945* (Oxford: Pergamon, 1990), 148.

34. Excerpted in Arthur Hertzberg, ed., *The Zionist Idea: An Historical Analysis and Reader* (New York: Meridian, 1960), 120–21.

35. Excerpted in Paul W. Massing, *Rehearsal for Destruction: A Study of Political Anti-Semitism* (New York: American Jewish Committee and Harper & Row, 1949), 147.

36. Adolf Hitler, *Mein Kampf*, trans. Ralph Mannheim (Boston: Houghton Mifflin, 1962), 289, 296, 688.

37. Ibid., 290, 295.

38. Ibid., 390, 305, 316, 328.

39. Paul Johnson, "Marxism Versus the Jews," *Antisemitism in the Contemporary World*, ed. Michael Curtis (London: Westview Press, 1986), 39.

40. *Protocols of the Meetings of the Learned Elders of Zion*, trans. Victor E. Marsden (Los Angeles: Christian Nationalist Crusade, n.d.), Protocol No. 1, para. 8.

41. Ibid., Protocol No. 14, para. 1.

42. Quoted in Binjamin W. Segel, *A Lie and a Libel: The History of the Protocols of the Elders of Zion*, trans. and ed. Richard S. Levy (Lincoln: University of Nebraska Press, 1995), 111.

43. Zosa Szajkowski, *Jews, War, and Communism* (New York: KTAV, 1972), 1:462.

44. Ibid., 1:4.

45. Isaac Deutscher, *The Non-Jewish Jew and Other Essays* (New York: Oxford University Press, 1968).

46. Quoted in Sharman Kadish, *Bolsheviks and British Jews* (London: Frank Cass, 1992), 71.

47. Quoted in Szajkowski, *Jews, War, and Communism*, 2:204.

48. Quotations from ibid., 2:151, 154, 185

49. Ibid., 2:176, 82.

50. Enzo Traverso, *The Marxists and the Jewish Question*, trans. Bernard Gibbons (Atlantic Highlands, NJ: Humanities Press, 1993), 153.

51. Derek J. Penslar, *Shylock's Children* (Berkeley: University of California Press, 2001), 246.

52. Quoted in Norman Cohn, *Warrant for Genocide* (New York: Harper Torchbooks, 1967), 186–87.

53. Quoted in ibid., 230; Stephen Eric Bronner, *A Rumor about the Jews* (New York: St. Martin's Press, 2000), 121.

54. Quoted in Cohn, *Warrant for Genocide*, 209.

55. Quoted in Daniel J. Goldhagen, *Hitler's Willing Executioners: Ordinary Germans and the Holocaust* (New York: Knopf, 1996), 71.

56. Quoted in Helmut Krausnick et al., eds., *Anatomy of the SS State* (London: Collins, 1968), 9.

57. Quoted in Richard S. Levy, *The Downfall of the Anti-Semitic Political Parties in Imperial Germany* (New Haven, CT: Yale University Press, 1975), 83.

58. Quoted in Peter G. J. Pulzer, *The Rise of Political Anti-Semitism in Germany and Austria* (New York: Wiley, 1969), 299.

59. Fritz Stern, *Dreams and Delusions* (New York: Knopf, 1987), 123.

60. Albert Speer, *Inside the Third Reich* (New York: Macmillan, 1970), 112.

61. Excerpted in George L. Mosse, ed., *Nazi Culture* (New York: Grosset & Dunlap, 1966), 206–7.

62. Quoted in Benno Müller-Hill, *Murderous Science* (Oxford: Oxford University Press, 1985), 46.

63. Quoted in Hermann Rauschning, *Voice of Destruction* (New York: Putnam's, 1940), 241.

64. Quoted in Saul Friedländer, *Nazi Germany and the Jews*, vol. 1 of *The Years of Persecution, 1933–1939* (New York: HarperCollins, 1997), 184.

65. Quoted in Cohn, *Warrant for Genocide*, 188.

66. Quoted in ibid., 180.

67. Quoted in Uriel Tal, "Consecration of Politics in the Nazi Era," *Judaism and Christianity under the Impact of National Socialism*, ed. Otto Dov Kulka and Paul R. Mendes-Flohr (Jerusalem: The Holocaust Society of Israel, 1987), 70.

68. Quoted in Marc Caplan, *Hitler's Apologists* (New York: Anti-Defamation League, 1993), 26.

69. Quoted in Bronner, *Rumor about the Jews*, 46.

70. Quoted in Steven Jacobs, *The Protocols Conspiracy: Answering the Lies of the Protocols of the Learned Elders of Zion* (Los Angeles: The Wiesenthal Center, forthcoming), chap. 2, "Historical Reflections."

71. Bernard Lewis, "The Arab World Discovers Anti-Semitism," *Anti-Semitism in Times of Crisis*, ed. Sander L. Gilman and Steven T. Katz (New York: New York University Press, 1991), 343–45.

72. Quoted in Wistrich, *Antisemitism*, 228–29.

73. Quoted by Andrew Sullivan in the *Sunday Times* of London, Dec. 23, 2001, excerpted from Naomi@naomiragen.com.

74. *Charter of Islamic Resistance Movement—Hamas, Gaza, August 1988, Selected Translations and Analysis* (Simon Wiesenthal Center, Fall 1988), 5, 8.

75. *New York Times* (October 16, 1997), A11.

76. Quoted in David G. Goodman and Masanori Miyazawa, *Jews in the Japanese Mind* (New York: Free Press, 1995), 245.

## CHAPTER 4

1. James Yaffe, *The American Jews* (New York: Random House, 1968), 227; emphasis added.

2. Mark Twain, "Concerning the Jews," *Collected Tales, Sketches, Speeches, & Essays, 1891–1910* (N.p.: Library of America, 1992), 362.

3. Herman Rauschning, *Voice of Destruction* (New York: Putnam's, 1940), 237–38.

4. For how false and unhistorical but deeply rooted is the age-old interpretation of Jesus and the money changers, see E. P. Sanders, *Jesus and Judaism* (Philadelphia: Fortress Press, 1985), 61–65.

5. Léon Poliakov, *The History of Anti-Semitism*, vol. 3, *From Voltaire to Wagner*, trans. Miriam Kochan (New York: Vanguard, 1975), 397.

6. Quoted by Julius Carlebach, *Karl Marx and the Radical Critique of Judaism* (London: Routledge & Kegan Paul, 1978), 192.

7. Jacob Neusner, *The Economics of the Mishnah* (Chicago: University of Chicago Press, 1990), ix–xiv, 1–5.

8. Heinrich Graetz, *The Structure of Jewish History and Other Essays*, trans. and ed. Ismar Schorsch (New York: Jewish Theological Seminary of America, 1975), 217.

9. Henri Pirenne, *Economic and Social History of the Middle Ages*, trans. I. E. Clegg (London: Kegan Paul, Trench, Trubner, 1936), 3.

10. Robert S. Lopez and Irving W. Raymond, eds., *Medieval Trade in the Mediterranean World* (New York: Norton, n.d.), 29–33.

11. Quoted in Salo W. Baron, *A Social and Religious History of the Jews*, 2nd ed., 18 vols. (New York: Columbia University Press, 1952–83), 4:151; hereafter cited as SWB.

12. Quoted in ibid., 12:177.

13.  Benjamin N. Nelson, "The Usurer and the Merchant Prince: Italian Business-men and the Ecclesiastical Law of Restitution, 1100–1550," *Journal of Economic History* 7, Supplement (1947): 120.

14.  Robert Chazan, *Medieval Jewry in Northern France: A Political and Social History* (Baltimore: Johns Hopkins University Press, 1973), 103; idem, *Medieval Stereotypes and Modern Antisemitism* (Berkeley: University of California Press, 1997), 122–23.

15.  James Parkes, *The Jew in the Medieval Community*, 2nd ed. (New York: Hermon Press, 1976), 337–38.

16.  Neusner, *Economics of the Mishnah*, 93.

17.  As paraphrased by Neusner, ibid., 102.

18.  Quoted in Parkes, *Medieval Community*, 341.

19.  SWB, 12:135.

20.  Sidney Painter, *The Reign of King John* (1949, reprint; Baltimore: John Hopkins University Press, 1968), 139.

21.  Quoted by SWB, 10:144.

22.  H. H. Ben-Sasson, ed., *A History of the Jewish People* (Cambridge, MA: Harvard University Press, 1976), 472.

23.  Charles de Secondat, Baron de Montesquieu, *The Spirit of Laws*, trans. Thomas Nugent, Rev. J. V. Prichard, vol. 38 of *The Great Books* (Chicago: Encyclopaedia Britannica, 1952), Book XXI, Chap. 20.

24.  Quoted in Salo W. Baron, *The Jewish Community* (Philadelphia: Jewish Publication Society, 1942), 1:211.

25.  SWB, 12:198–99.

26.  Baron, *Jewish Community*, 1:160.

27.  Quoted in SWB, 4:152.

28.  Parkes, *Medieval Community*, 149ff, 124.

29.  Petri Abaelardi, *Dialogus inter Philosophum, Judaeum et Christianum, Patrologiae Cursus Completus*, Series Latina, ed. J.-P. Migne (Paris: Parisiis, 1855), vol. 178, col. 1618.

30.  Norman Jones, *God and the Moneylenders: Usury and Law in Early Modern England* (Oxford: Blackwell, 1989), 20, 170, 199.

31.  Benzion Netanyahu, *The Origins of the Inquisition in Fifteenth Century Spain* (New York: Random House, 1995), 1042–43, 1049, 950.

32.  Quoted in Raphael Mahler, *A History of Modern Jewry, 1780–1815* (New York: Schocken, 1971), 282.

33.  Hillel Levine, *Economic Origins of Antisemitism: Poland and its Jews in the Early Modern Period* (New Haven, CT: Yale University Press, 1991), 151.

34.  Quoted in Magdalena Opalski, *The Jewish Tavern-Keeper and His Tavern in Nineteenth-Century Polish Literature* (Jerusalem: Zalman Center, 1986), 15, 48.

35.  Jonathan I. Israel, *European Jewry in the Age of Mercantilism, 1550–1750*, 3rd ed. (London: Vallentine Mitchell, 1998), 223.

36.  Francis L. Carsten, *Princes and Parliaments in Germany: From the Fourteenth to the Eighteenth Centuries* (Oxford: Clarendon Press, 1959), 123–32.

37.  Derek J. Penslar, *Shylock's Children: Economics and Jewish Identity in Modern Europe* (Berkeley: University of California Press, 2001), 21; see forthcoming review by F. Schweitzer in *The Historian*, Winter 2002 or Spring 2003.

38.  Quoted in Gedalia Yogev, *Diamonds and Coral: Anglo-Dutch Jews in Eighteenth-Century Trade* (New York: Holmes & Meier, 1978), 21.

39. Quoted in SWB, 15:108.
40. Israel, *European Jewry*, 92.
41. Quoted in ibid., 132.
42. Quoted in Zosa Szajkowski, *Jews and the French Revolutions of 1789, 1830 and 1848* (New York: KTAV, 1970), 502.
43. Israel, *European Jewry*, 216ff.
44. Szajkowski, *Jews and the French Revolutions*, 512.
45. Quoted in William Korey, *Russian Antisemitism, Pamyat, and the Demonology of Zionism* (Jerusalem: Vidal Sassoon Center, Harwood Academic Publishers, 1995), 6.
46. Bruce F. Pauley, *From Prejudice to Persecution: A History of Austrian Anti-Semitism* (Chapel Hill: University of North Carolina, 1992), 41, 42.
47. Statistics in Steven Beller, *Vienna and the Jews 1867–1938: A Cultural History* (Cambridge: Cambridge University Press, 1989), 33–37.
48. Pauley, *From Prejudice to Persecution*, 212; idem, *The Habsburg Legacy 1867–1939* (Malabar, FL: Krieger, 1972), 169.
49. Statistics for Hungary in R. J. Crampton, *Eastern Europe in the Twentieth Century and After,* 2nd ed. (London: Routledge, 1994), 173–74.
50. Koppel S. Pinson, *Modern Germany: Its History and Civilization*, 2nd ed. (New York: Macmillan, 1966), 219.
51. Fritz Stern, *Gold and Iron: Bismarck, Bleichröder, and the Building of the German Empire* (New York: Knopf, 1977), 498; we are aware that "the rise of the Jews" to unprecedented freedom, influence, and affluence in the West is an "objective factor" in the development of antisemitism since the end of the eighteenth century, which is the thesis of Albert S. Lindemann, *Esau's Tears: Modern Anti-Semitism and the Rise of the Jews* (Cambridge: Cambridge University Press, 1997); however, we find his emphasis excessive, the numbers of Jews too small to warrant such an interpretation (note how often Lindemann is compelled to use "paranoia" in explaining gentile reactions), that he understates the significance of the medieval heritage of chimerical antisemitism and myth, and that he applies his thesis too uniformly and abstractly to the West and especially to areas like Romania and Russia where it does not fit at all.
52. Werner E. Mosse, "Judaism, Jews and Capitalism: Weber, Sombart and Beyond" *Year Book XXIV of the Leo Baeck Institute* (London: Secker & Warburg, 1979), 7–8.
53. Peter Gay, Introduction to Ruth Gay, *The Jews of Germany* (New Haven, CT: Yale University Press, 1992), xi.
54. W. E. Mosse, *Jews in the German Economy: The German-Jewish Economic Élite 1820–1935* (Oxford: Clarendon Press, 1987), 108.
55. Quoted by Stern, *Gold and Iron*, 105, 113, 549.
56. Mosse, *Jews in the German Economy*, 108.
57. Ibid., 170.
58. Ibid., 372.
59. David S. Landes, "The Jewish Merchant: Typology and Stereotypology in Germany," *Year Book XIX of the Leo Baeck Institute* (London: Secker & Warburg, 1974), 23.
60. Quoted in Ernest K. Bramsted, *Aristocracy and the Middle Classes in Germany: Social Types in German Literature 1830–1900* (Chicago: University of Chicago Press, 1964), 55.

61. Miriam Beard, "Anti-Semitism—Product of Economic Myth," *Jews in a Gentile World: The Problem of Anti-Semitism*, ed. Isacque Graeber and Steuart H. Britt (New York: Macmillan, 1942), 400.

62. Quoted in Mosse, "Judaism, Jews and Capitalism," 11 n. 26.

63. Mosse, *Jews in the German Economy*, 16, 380.

64. Ibid., 28, 29.

65. Quoted in John Weiss, *Ideology of Death: Why the Holocaust Happened in Germany* (Chicago: Ivan R. Dee, 1996), 81.

66. Ibid., 160.

67. Quoted in Otto Pflanze, *Bismarck and the Development of Germany*, 3 vols. (Princeton, NJ: Princeton University Press, 1990), 2:316–17, 319.

68. Peter Gay, *Freud, Jews and Other Germans* (New York: Oxford University Press, 1978), 77.

69. Pauley, *From Prejudice to Persecution*, 318, 321, 133, 323; Weiss, *Ideology of Death*, 156–90.

70. William O. McCagg Jr., *A History of Habsburg Jews 1670–1918* (Bloomington: Indiana University Press, 1990), 196–97.

71. Quoted in Mosse, *Jews in the German Economy*, 402 n. 20, our translation.

72. Quoted in ibid., 405, our translation.

73. Stephen Birmingham, *"Our Crowd" The Great Jewish Families of New York* (New York: Harper & Row, 1967), 35.

74. *The International Jew* (N.p.: n.p., 1920), 2:85; Bernard Baruch was a self-made man who won a fortune in stock market speculation and had aided the Guggenheims in besting the Lewisohns.

75. Naomi W. Cohen, *Jacob H. Schiff: A Study in American Jewish Leadership* (Hanover, NH: Brandeis University Press, 1999), 34, 38.

76. Quotations in ibid., 134, 197.

77. Pat Robertson, *The New World Order* (Dallas: World Publishers, 1991), 65, 73, 123, 178.

78. Quoted in Howard M. Sachar, *A History of the Jews in America* (New York: Knopf, 1999), 94.

79. Cohen, *Jacob H. Schiff*, 6, summarizing the interpretation of the German Jewish business elite by Barry Supple.

80. Henry L. Feingold, *A Time for Searching: Entering the Mainstream, 1920–1945*, vol. 4 of *The Jewish People in America*, ed. Henry L. Feingold (Baltimore: Johns Hopkins University Press, 1992), 125.

81. Quoted in Carlebach, *Karl Marx*, 358.

82. Quoted in Poliakov, *History of Anti-Semitism*, 3:424.

83. For this paragraph and much of what follows on Marx, see Paul Lawrence Rose, *German Question/Jewish Question: Revolutionary Antisemitism from Kant to Wagner* (Princeton, NJ: Princeton University Press, 1990), 91–116, 251–63, passim.

84. All quotations from Marx are from the edition by Dagobert D. Runes, *Karl Marx: A World Without Jews* (New York: Philosophical Library, 1959), 36–45.

85. Rose, *German Question/Jewish Question*, 124, quoting Jacob Fries the disciple of Fichte; ibid., 144, quoting Ludwig Börne, a converted Jew.

86. Sander L. Gilman, *Jewish Self-Hatred* (Baltimore: Johns Hopkins University Press, 1986), 198, 202.

87. Quoted by Reinhard Rürup, "Jews," *Marxism, Communism and Western Society, A Comparative Encyclopedia*, ed. C. D. Kernig (New York: Herder and Herder, 1972), 4:425.

88.   Ibid.; Peter G. J. Pulzer, *The Rise of Political Anti-Semitism in Germany and Aus-tria* (New York: Wiley, 1964), 268; Lenin combated antisemitism but his regime inflicted enormous loss and suffering on many Jews as "bourgeois" and "capital-ists" who were categorized as *lishentsy* (deprived of citizenship rights).

89.   Rose, *German Question/Jewish Question*, 304, 301; "Antisemitism is really a ha-tred of capitalism," explained a German leftist terrorist in 1972, quoted in ibid., 304.

90.   Carlebach, *Karl Marx*, 352.

91.   Quoted in ibid., 302.

92.   In a scintillating polemical essay, "Marxism Versus the Jews," *Antisemitism in the Contemporary World*, ed. Michael Curtis (London: Westview Press, 1986), 39–50, Paul Johnson finds that Marx's "sinister achievement [was] to marry the economic antisemitism of the French Socialists [this is too broad a brush and should be limited to the Utopians Fourier, Proudhon, and possibly Toussenel] to the philosophical antisemitism of the German idealists and thereby to con-struct a new kind of conspiracy theory"; that "antisemitism is the father of all conspiracy theory."

93.   Landes, "Jewish Merchant," 21.

94.   Paul R. Mendes-Flohr, "Werner Sombart's *The Jews and Modern Capitalism:* An Analysis of its Ideological Premises," *Year Book XXI of the Leo Baeck Institute* (London: Secker & Warburg, 1976), 88, 91, 106.

95.   Werner Sombart, *The Jews and Modern Capitalism*, trans. M. Epstein (New York: Collier, 1911, 1962), 127; on the issue of Jewish brain power, Sander L. Gilman *Smart Jews: The Construction of the Image of Jewish Superior Intelligence* (Lincoln: University of Nebraska Press, 1996), who, however, says little about Jewish eco-nomic ability.

96.   Sombart, *Jews and Modern Capitalism*, 242–59.

97.   Ibid., 127, 200–202, 227, 276–77, 301–3.

98.   Salo W. Baron, *A Social and Religious History of the Jews*, 3 vols. (New York: Co-lumbia University Press, 1937), 2:177; Baron refers to capitalism's origins in the northern Italian city-states of the thirteenth and fourteenth centuries, when Jews were completely excluded.

99.   Sombart, *Jews and Modern Capitalism*, 77–123.

100.  Ibid., 199.

101.  For Sombart on sexuality, see ibid., 221–27, 236.

102.  Ibid., 209–10.

103.  Ellis Rivkin, *The Shaping of Jewish History: A Radical New Interpretation* (New York: Scribner's, 1971), 141.

104.  Quoted in SWB, 4:220.

105.  Max Weber, *The Sociology of Religion*, trans. Ephraim Fischoff (Boston: Beacon Press, 1963), 251, 255, 258.

106.  Gilman, *Jewish Self-Hatred*, 68–86.

107.  Sombart, *Jews and Modern Capitalism*, 176.

108.  Fernand Braudel, *The Mediterranean and the Mediterranean World in the Age of Philip II*, trans. Sian Reynolds (New York: Harper & Row, 1973), 2:804.

109.  Quoted in Beryl Smalley, *The Study of the Bible in the Middle Ages*, 2nd ed. (Notre Dame, IN: Notre Dame University Press, 1964), 78.

110.  Gentz, quoted by Weiss, *Ideology of Death*, 157; Mark Twain, "Concerning the Jews," 361; Gilman, *Smart Jews*, 93–94; Gay, *Freud, Jews and Other Germans*, 99,

dismisses all this: "There is a historical and sociological study that desperately needs to be undertaken: stupid Jews. The material would be abundant, and the results would correct the widespread and untenable notion that Jews are by endowment more intelligent than other people."

111. See Carlebach, *Karl Marx*, 63, for Ber Borochov's interpretation of Jewish economic evolution in Poland and Russia.

112. Thorstein Veblen, *Essays in Our Changing Order*, ed. Leon Ardzrooni (New York: Augustus Kelley, 1964), 222, 224, 226–27; Veblen's subject is "The Intellectual Pre-eminence of Jews in Modern Europe," but his analysis is more broadly applicable; Sombart, *Jews and Modern Capitalism*, 229, 267–68, 322, refers to the prohibition on mixed marriages and "inbreeding" as preserving "Jewish racial purity," and so on.

113. Weber, *Sociology of Religion*, 248.

114. In chapter 5 of *Jews and Modern Capitalism*, Sombart offered an exaggerated account of the court Jew and the German prince marching shoulder to shoulder—like "Faust and Mephistopheles," "arm in arm"—to build the modern German state; quote from 67.

115. Quoted in Norman Cohn, *Warrant for Genocide: The Myth of the Jewish World-Conspiracy and the Protocols of the Elders of Zion* (London: Eyre & Spottiswoode, 1961), 164.

116. Neil Baldwin, *Henry Ford and the Jews: The Mass Production of Hate* (New York: Public Affairs, 2001), 3–7; in later life Ford vehemently resisted attempts to remove *The Merchant of Venice* from the public school curriculum.

117. Lloyd Gartner, "The Two Continuities of Antisemitism in the United States," *Antisemitism through the Ages*, ed. Shmuel Almog (Oxford: Pergamon, 1988), 317.

118. Quoted in Albert Lee, *Henry Ford and the Jews* (New York: Stein & Day, 1980), 13–14.

119. Quoted in Morton Rosenstock, *Louis Marshall, Defender of Jewish Rights* (Detroit: Wayne State University Press, 1965), 138.

120. Quoted in Lee, *Henry Ford*, 63.

121. Quoted in Rosenstock, *Louis Marshall*, 142.

122. Quoted in Lee, *Henry Ford*, 26–27.

123. Quoted in ibid., 139, 140.

124. Cited by Baldwin, *Henry Ford*, 97; Lee, *Henry Ford*, 33.

125. Baldwin, *Henry Ford*, 160, 164–65, 213.

126. Quoted in Cohn, *Warrant for Genocide*, 162; Lee, *Henry Ford*, 46.

127. Lee, *Henry Ford*, 59.

128. Baldwin, *Henry Ford*, 177–79, citing trans. of Eckart in *Nationalist Socialist World* 2 (Fall 1966): 13ff.; Ernst Nolte, *Three Faces of Fascism*, trans. Leila Venniwitz (New York: Holt, Rinehart & Winston, 1966), 331–32, 523 n. 132.

129. Adolf Hitler, *Mein Kampf: Complete and Unabridged, Fully Annotated*, editorial sponsors, John Chamberlain et al. (New York: Reynal & Hitchcock, 1939), 930.

130. Quoted in Baldwin, *Henry Ford*, 271.

131. Quoted in Rosenstock, *Louis Marshall*, 138.

132. Ron Rosenbaum, *Explaining Hitler* (New York: Random House, 1998), xxxviii-xxxix; Carey McWilliams, in reference to Ford, wrote in 1948, "one of the cruel ironies of history [is] that the savage anti-Semitism which developed in Germany . . . should have been stimulated in part by an American industrialist"; quoted in Baldwin, *Henry Ford*, 172.

133. Quoted in Gustavus Myers, *History of Bigotry in the United States* (New York: Random House, 1943), 359.

134. Baldwin, *Henry Ford*, 271.

135. Quoted in Lee, *Henry Ford*, 106, 110.

136. Quoted in Rosenstock, *Louis Marshall*, 178.

137. Quotations in Sachar, *History of the Jews in America*, 319; Lee, *Henry Ford*, 122.

138. Cohn, *Warrant for Genocide*, 159.


CHAPTER 5

1. Quoted in Marc Caplan, *Liberty Lobby: Hate Central* (New York: Anti-Defamation League, 1995), 10.

2. Quoted in Deborah E. Lipstadt, *Denying the Holocaust: The Growing Assault on Truth and Memory* (New York: Free Press, 1993), 64.

3. Quoted in Kenneth B. Stern, *Holocaust Denial* (New York: American Jewish Committee, 1993), 33.

4. Quoted in Pierre Vidal-Naquet, *Assassins of Memory: Essays on the Denial of the Holocaust* (New York: Columbia University Press, 1992), xiii. The quotation is from the foreword by Jeffrey Méhlman who translated the essays.

5. Austin J. App, *A Straight Look at the Third Reich* (Takoma Park, MD: Boniface Press, 1974), 5, 18.

6. Austin J. App, *The Six Million Swindle* (Takoma Park, MD: Boniface Press, 1973), 12–13, 15.

7. Quoted in Marc Caplan, *Hitler's Apologists* (New York: Anti-Defamation League, 1993), 27.

8. Quoted in Gill Seidel, *The Holocaust Denial: Antisemitism, Racism and the New Right* (Leeds, UK: Beyond the Pale Collective, 1986), 117–18.

9. Quoted in Caplan, *Hitler's Apologists*, 21.

10. Quoted in Richard Evans, *Lying about Hitler: History, Holocaust and the David Irving Trial* (New York: Basic Books, 2001), 45.

11. Quoted in ibid., 46

12. Quoted in ibid., 125.

13. Ibid., 137.

14. Quoted in ibid., 148.

15. Quoted in Lipstadt, *Denying the Holocaust*, 178.

16. Quoted in Stern, *Holocaust Denial*, 48.

17. Quoted in Marc Caplan, *Holocaust Denial: A Pocket Guide* (New York: Anti-Defamation League, 1997), 21. See also Caplan, *Hitler's Apologists*, 22.

18. Quoted in Ron Rosenbaum, *Explaining Hitler* (New York: Random House, 1998), 222.

19. Ibid., 234.

20. John Lukacs, *The Hitler of History* (New York: Alfred A. Knopf, 1997), 26.

21. Evans, *Lying about Hitler*, xi.

22. Ibid., 70.

23. Ibid., 103.

24. Quoted in Stern, *Holocaust Denial*, 17.

25. Quoted in Lipstadt, *Denying the Holocaust*, 198.

26. Quoted in ibid.

27. Quoted in Stern, *Holocaust Denial*, 106.

28. Quoted in Caplan, *Holocaust Denial: A Pocket Guide*, 8–9.

29. Quoted in ibid., 9.

30. Arthur R. Butz, "The International 'Holocaust Controversy,'" *Journal of Historical Review* 1 (Spring 1980): 20.

31. Gavin I. Langmuir, *History, Religion, and Anti-Semitism* (Berkeley: University of California Press, 1990), 350.

32. Nuremberg Military Tribunals, Case 6: I. G. Farben, *Nuremberg War Crimes Trials Online:* CD-Rom (Seattle: Aristarchus, 1995), 6:6,487.

33. Arno Mayer, *Why Did the Heavens Not Darken? The "Final Solution" in History* (New York: Pantheon, 1988), 362; Mayer's distinction between "normal" or "natural" deaths and murder by shooting, gassing, starvation, and so on, 365, is exploited by deniers in the same way; Mayer's shortcomings as a historian of the Holocaust have been pointed out by specialists like Richard Breitman and Saul Friedländer.

34. International Military Tribunal, *Trial of the Major War Criminals*, 42 vols. (Washington, DC: US Government Printing Office, 1947-49), 29:115-16, document 1919-PS.

35. A. R. Butz, *The Hoax of the Twentieth Century* (Richmond, Surrey, UK: Historical Review Press, 1976), 195.

36. Quoted in Leni Yahil, *The Holocaust* (New York: Oxford University Press, 1990), 269.

37. Helmut Krausnick et al., *Anatomy of the SS State* (London: Collins, 1968), 64.

38. Excerpted in Raul Hilberg, ed., *Documents of Destruction* (Chicago: Quadrangle, 1971), 56–57.

39. *Nazi Conspiracy and Aggression*, 8 vols. (Washington, DC: U.S. Government Printing Office, 1946), 5:696–98.

40. Butz, *Hoax*, 197; see also 198–202.

41. Quoted in Caplan, *Liberty Lobby*, 21.

42. Christopher Browning, "Evidence for the Implementation of the Final Solution," Category V: Jewish escapees, 5.4.5.3 Downloaded from www.fpp.co.uk/Legal/Penguin/experts/Browning/report/part1.html.

43. Rudolf Höss, *Death Dealer: The Memoirs of the SS Kommandant at Auschwitz*, ed. Steven Paskuly, trans. Andrew Pollinger (Buffalo, NY: Prometheus Books, 1992), 27.

44. *Nazi Conspiracy and Aggression*, 6:787–89.

45. Quoted in Franciszek Piper, "Gas Chambers and Crematoria," *Anatomy of the Auschwitz Death Camp*, ed. Yisrael Gutman and Michael Berenbaum (Bloomington: Indiana University Press, 1994), 163.

46. Quoted in Franciszek Piper, "The Number of Victims," ibid., 64.

47. Quoted in Piper, "Gas Chambers and Crematoria," ibid., 160.

48. Anna Pawelczynska, *Values and Violence in Auschwitz*, trans. Catherine S. Leach (Berkeley: University of California Press, 1979), 54, 78.

49. Quoted in Joseph Borkin, *The Crime and Punishment of I. G. Farben* (New York: Free Press, 1978), 143.

50. Quoted in Vidal-Naquet, *Assassins of Memory*, 112–13.

51. Quoted in ibid., 113.

52. Jean-Claude Pressac, "The Deficiencies and Inconsistencies of 'The Leuchter Report,'" *Truth Prevails*, ed. Shelley Shapiro (New York: Beate Klarsfeld Foundation, 1990), 36–37; italics in the original.

53. Ibid., 38–39.

54. Ibid., 45.
55. Ibid., 36, 40, 46, 55.
56. Butz, *Hoax*, 239.
57. Ibid., 243.
58. Quoted in Caplan, *Hitler's Apologists*, 23.
59. Quoted in Evans, *Lying about Hitler*, 179.
60. Quoted in Stern, *Holocaust Denial*, 3.
61. "We Remember: A Reflection on the Shoah," *Catholic Jewish Relations: Documents from the Holy See*, ed. Eugene Fisher (London: Catholic Truth Society, 1999), 59–60.
62. See Lipstadt, *Denying the Holocaust*, 58–59.
63. Richard Harwood, *Did Six Million Really Die?* (Sussex, UK: Historical Review Press Reprint, n.d.), 20.
64. Vidal-Naquet, *Assassins of Memory*, 22.
65. Harwood, *Did Six Million Really Die?*, 19.
66. Quoted in Stem, *Holocaust Denial*, 52.
67. Quoted in Martin E. Lee, *The Beast Reawakens* (New York: Little, Brown, 1997), 225.
68. Ibid., 229.
69. Ibid., 259.

CHAPTER 6

1. *New York Times*, Jan. 14, 1994, 24; the name also appears as Khalid.
2. *A Testament of Hope: The Essential Writings of Martin Luther King, Jr.*, ed. James Melvin Washington (San Francisco: Harper & Row, 1986), 370.
3. Quoted in Murray Friedman, *What Went Wrong? The Creation & Collapse of the Black-Jewish Alliance* (New York: Free Press, 1995), 146.
4. Hubert Locke, *Learning from History: A Black Christian's Perspective on the Holocaust* (Westport, CT: Greenwood Press, 2000), 13.
5. See Tamar Jacoby, *Someone Else's House: America's Unfinished Struggle for Integration* (New York: Free Press, 1998), chap. 6; Friedman, *What Went Wrong?*, 257–63; Jonathan Kaufman, *Broken Alliance: The Turbulent Times Between Blacks and Jews in America* (New York: Simon & Schuster, 1995), chap. 4.
6. James Traub, "The Hearts and Minds of City College," *The New Yorker* (June 7, 1993): 43.
7. Quoted in Leonard Dinnerstein, *Antisemitism in America* (New York: Oxford University Press, 1994), 219.
8. Quoted in Robert Alan Goldberg, *Enemies Within: The Culture of Conspiracy in Modern America* (New Haven, CT: Yale University Press, 2001), 163; "Jews were willing to share decency, but not power" with blacks, he said in the 1970s, ibid.
9. Malcolm X, *The Autobiography of Malcolm X* (New York: Grove Press, 1966), 164–66.
10. Henry Louis Gates, Jr., "A Reporter at Large: The Charmer," *The New Yorker* (Apr. 29–May 6, 1996): 124.
11. Robert Singh, *The Farrakhan Phenomenon* (Washington, DC: Georgetown University Press, 1997), 56.
12. *Testament of Hope*, 296–97.
13. Quoted in Arthur J. Magida, *Prophet of Rage: A Life of Louis Farrakhan and His Nation* (New York: Basic Books, 1996), 146, 148–49.

14. Singh, *The Farrakhan Phenomenon*, 46.

15. Julius Lester, "Farrakhan in the Flesh: The Time Has Come," *The New Republic* (Oct. 28, 1985): 12.

16. Michael Kramer, "Loud and Clear: Farrakhan's Anti-Semitism," *New York* (Oct. 21, 1985): 23.

17. Ibid., 22.

18. Julius Lester, "Farrakhan in the Flesh," 11.

19. *Washington Post*, Mar. 1, 1990, A16.

20. Ibid., March 3, 1990, A24.

21. Jonathan Brent, "Political Perversity in Chicago," *The New Republic* (Aug. 8, 1988): 17.

22. Peter Noel, "Blood Brother," *New York* (Sept. 7, 1998): 24.

23. Quoted in *Forward* (Jan. 20, 1995): 5.

24. Peter Noel, "One-Man March," *New York* (Sept. 7, 1998): 25.

25. Bernard Lewis, *Race and Slavery in the Middle East: An Historical Inquiry* (New York: Oxford University Press, 1990), vi. Lewis notes that the documentation available for the study of Islamic slavery "in law, in doctrine, in practice" is enormous but virtually unexplored owing to "the extreme sensitivity of the subject"; thus the "myth" of the absence of racism and practice of slavery in Muslim societies persists; ibid., 99–102.

26. Quoted in Hugh Thomas, *The Slave Trade: The Story of the Atlantic Slave Trade 1440–1870* (New York: Simon & Schuster, 1997), 556.

27. Quoted in *Essays on Maimonides: Octocentennial Volume*, ed. Salo W. Baron (New York: Columbia University Press, 1941), 248.

28. Quoted in Saul S. Friedman, *Jews and the American Slave Trade* (New Brunswick, NJ: Transaction Publishers, 1998), 13.

29. Ibid., 217–18.

30. David Brion Davis, "The Slave Trade and the Jews," *New York Review of Books* (Dec. 22, 1994): 15–16.

31. Quoted in David M. Goldenberg, "The Curse of Ham: A Case of Rabbinic Racism?" in *Struggles in the Promised Land*, ed. Jack Salzman and Cornel West (New York: Oxford University Press, 1997), 24. We rely on this excellent article for much of the material dealing with the Hamitic myth.

32. Ibid., 38.

33. Ibid., 33.

34. Tony Martin, *The Jewish Onslaught Dispatches from the Wellesley Battlefront* (Dover, MA: Majority Press, 1993), 33, 35.

35. David H. Aaron, "The Early Rabbinic Exegesis on Noah's Son Ham and the So-Called Hamitic Myth," *Journal of the American Academy of Religion* 63 (1995): 73.

36. Karen J. Winkler, "Historical Group Issues Statement on Role of Jews in Slave Trade," *Chronicle of Higher Education* (Feb. 17, 1995): A15.

37. Excerpted in Marc Caplan, *Jew-Hatred as History* (New York: Anti-Defamation League, 1993), ii.

38. Quoted in Clyde Haberman, "Bias Recedes, Letting Jews Look Inward," *New York Times*, Nov. 24, 1998, B1.

39. Locke, *Learning from History*, 104.

40. Martin, *Jewish Onslaught*, vii, ix.

41. Quoted in Eli Faber, *Jews, Slaves, and the Slave Trade: Setting the Record Straight* (New York: New York University Press, 1998), 7.

42. Henry Louis Gates, Jr., "Black Demagogues and Pseudo-Scholars," *New York Times*, op-ed page, July 20, 1992, A15.

43. Rev. Matt Hale, *Facts That the Government and the Media Don't Want You to Know* (East Peoria, IL: Creativity Movement, n.d.), 9–10.

44. Henry Louis Gates, Jr., "Memoirs of an Anti-Anti-Semite," *Blacks and Jews Alliances and Arguments*, ed. Paul Berman (New York: Delacorte Press, 1994), 227.

45. Henry Louis Gates, Jr., "A Reporter At Large: The Charmer," *New Yorker* (Apr. 29-May 6, 1996): 125.

46. Quoted in Neal Pollack, "Chicago Dispatch: Karta Before the Horse," *The New Republic* (Mar. 13, 2000): 20.

47. Ibid., 21.

48. Locke, *Learning from History*, 10; more generally, Hubert Locke, *The Black Antisemitism Controversy: Protestant Views and Perspectives* (Selinsgrove, PA: Susquehanna University Press, 1994).

49. Bob Herbert, "Endless Poison," *New York Times*, Aug. 26, 1999, A1, B6

## CONCLUSION

1. Both quoted in Norman Cohn, *Warrant for Genocide* (New York: Harper & Row, 1967), 204.

2. Quoted by Jan T. Gross, *Neighbors: The Destruction of the Jewish Community in Jedwabne, Poland* (Princeton, NJ: Princeton University Press, 2001), 162.

3. In the view of Abraham Brumberg, "The Treatment of the Holocaust in Poland," *Anti-Semitism and the Treatment of the Holocaust in Postcommunist Eastern Europe*, ed. Randolph L. Braham (Boulder, CO: Social Science Monographs, 1994), 156, during the war antisemitism actually declined in Poland and aside from the Germans, the Lithuanians and Ukrainians have a worse record than the Poles: "the reputation of Poles as the principal offenders against the Jews is based on misperceptions."

4. Quoted in Gross, *Neighbors*, 65.

5. Chris Broussard, "Comments by 2 Knicks Called Anti-Semitic," *New York Times*, April 21, 2001, D4; Jonathan S. Tobin, "Civility and Deicide," *Jewish Sentinel*, Mar. 11–17, 2001, 2.

6. Khalid Durán with Abdelwahab Hechiche, *Children of Abraham* (New York: American Jewish Committee; Hoboken, NJ: KTAV, 2001), 135.

7. Translation from www.memri.org.

8. Quoted in Durán, *Children of Abraham*, 75.

9. Victor Klemperer, *I Will Bear Witness: A Diary of the Nazi Years 1933–1941*, trans. Martin Chalmers (New York: Random House, 1998), 343.

## APPENDIX I

1. S. D. Goitein, *A Mediterranean Society* (Berkeley: University of California Press, 1967), 1:229.

2. Maxime Rodinson, *Islam and Capitalism*, trans. Brian Pearce (Austin, University of Texas Press, 1978), 37.

3. Norman A. Stillman, *The Jews in Arab Lands: A History and Source Book* (Philadelphia: Jewish Publication Society, 1979), 149–51.

4. Quoted by Yehoshafat Harkabi, "On Arab Antisemitism Once More," *Antisemitism Through the Ages*, ed. Shmuel Almog (New York: Pergamon Press, 1988), 236.

5. Bernard Lewis, *Islam in History* (New York: Library Press, 1973), 130, 134–35.

6. Quoted by Avraham Grossman, "The Economic and Social Background of Hostile Attitudes Toward the Jews in the Ninth and Tenth Century Caliphate," *Antisemitism Through the Ages*, ed. Shmuel Almog (New York: Pergamon Press, 1988), 184 n. 3.

7. Ibid., 179.

8. Menasseh ben Israel, *"Vindicae Judaeorum"* (A Vindication of the Jews), *Menasseh ben Israel's Mission to Oliver Cromwell: Being a Reprint of the Pamphlets Published by Menasseh ben Israel to promote the Re-admission of the Jews to England*, ed. Lucien Wolf (London: Macmillan, 1901), 108–15, par. 11.

9. Quoted by Norman A. Stillman, "Myth, Countermyth, and Distortion," *Tikkun* 6, 3 (1991): 62.

### APPENDIX II

1. For background on Zündel, see Marilyn F. Nefsky, "Current State of Three Canadian Hate Mongers," *From Prejudice to Destruction: Western Civilization in the Shadow of Auschwitz*, ed. G. Jan Colijn and Marcia Sachs Littell (Münster, Germany: Lit Verlag, 1995), 199–221; Jean-François Moisan, "Fighting Antisemitism in Canada's Unique Context: The Example of the League for Human Rights [of B'nai B'rith]," *Parcours Judaïques IV*, ed. Danièle Frison (Paris: Centre de Recherches sur les Juifs dans les Pays Anglophone, 1998), 113–32; and Manuel Prutschi, "The Zündel Affair," *Antisemitism in Canada: History and Interpretation*, ed. Alan Davies (Waterloo, Ontario, Canada: Wilfrid Laurier University Press, 1992), 249–77.

# INDEX